LECTURES

ON

THE TRUE, THE BEAUTIFUL AND THE GOOD.

BY M. V. COUSIN.
INCREASED BY
An Appendix on French Art.
TRANSLATED, WITH THE APPROBATION OF M. COUSIN, BY

O. W. WIGHT,
TRANSLATOR OF COUSIN'S "COURSE OF THE HISTORY OF MODERN PHILOSOPHY," AMERICAN EDITOR OF THE PHILOSOPHY OF SIR WILLIAM HAMILTON, BART., AUTHOR OF "THE ROMANCE OF ABELARD AND HELOISE," ETC., ETC.

****

"God is the life of the soul, as the soul is the life of the body."

-- The Platonists and the Fathers.

TO

SIR WILLIAM HAMILTON, BART.,

Professor of Logic and Metaphysics in the University of Edinburgh:

WHO HAS CLEARLY ELUCIDATED, AND, WITH GREAT ERUDITION,
SKETCHED THE HISTORY OF THE DOCTRINE OF

COMMON SENSE;

WHO, FOLLOWING IN THE FOOTSTEPS OF HIS ILLUSTRIOUS
COUNTRYMAN, REID

HAS ESTABLISHED THE DOCTRINE OF THE

IMMEDIATENESS OF PERCEPTION,

THEREBY FORTIFYING PHILOSOPHY AGAINST THE ASSAULTS OF
SKEPTICISM;

WHO, TAKING A STEP IN ADVANCE OF ALL OTHERS,
HAS GIVEN TO THE WORLD A DOCTRINE OF THE

CONDITIONED,

THE ORIGINALITY AND IMPORTANCE OF WHICH ARE
ACKNOWLEDGED BY THE

FEW QUALIFIED TO JUDGE IN SUCH MATTERS; WHOSE
NEW ANALYTIC OF LOGICAL FORMS
COMPLETES THE HITHERTO UNFINISHED WORKS OF ARISTOTLE;

THIS TRANSLATION OF M. COUSIN'S
Lectures on the True, the Beautiful, and the Good,
IS RESPECTFULLY DEDICATED,

IN ADMIRATION OF A PROFOUND AND INDEPENDENT THINKER,
OF AN INCOMPARABLE MASTER OF PHILOSOPHIC CRITICISM;
AS A TOKEN OF ESTEEM FOR A MAN IN WHOM GENIUS
AND ALMOST UNEQUALLED LEARNING
HAVE BEEN ADORNED BY
TRUTH, BEAUTY, AND GOODNESS OF LIFE.

AUTHOR'S PREFACE.

For some time past we have been asked, on various sides, to collect in a body of doctrine the theories scattered in our different works, and to sum up, in just proportions, what men are pleased to call our philosophy.

This *résumé* was wholly made. We had only to take again the lectures already quite old, but little known, because they belonged to a time when the courses of the Faculté des Lettres had scarcely any influence beyond the Quartier Latin, and, also, because they could be found only in a considerable collection, comprising all our first instruction, from 1815 to 1821.[1] These lectures were there, as it were, lost in the crowd. We have drawn them hence, and give them apart, severely corrected, in the hope that they will thus be accessible to a greater number of readers, and that their true character will the better appear.

The eighteen lectures that compose this volume have in fact the particular trait that, if the history of philosophy furnishes their frame-work, philosophy itself occupies in them the first place, and that, instead of researches of erudition and criticism, they present a regular exposition of the doctrine which was at first fixed in our mind, which has not ceased to preside over our labors.

This book, then, contains the abridged but exact expression of our convictions on the fundamental points of philosophic science. In it will be openly seen the method that is the soul of our enterprise, our principles, our processes, our results.

Under these three heads, the True, the Beautiful, the Good, we embrace psychology, placed by us at the head of all philosophy, æsthetics, ethics, natural right, even public right to a certain extent, finally theodicea, that perilous *rendez-vous* of all systems, where different principles are condemned or justified by their consequences.

---

[1] 1st Series of our work, Cours de l'Histoire de la Philosophie Moderne, five volumes.

It is the affair of our book to plead its own cause. We only desire that it may be appreciated and judged according to what it really is, and not according to an opinion too much accredited.

Eclecticism is persistently represented as the doctrine to which men deign to attach our name. We declare that eclecticism is very dear to us, for it is in our eyes the light of the history of philosophy; but the source of that light is elsewhere. Eclecticism is one of the most important and most useful applications of the philosophy which we teach, but it is not its principle.

Our true doctrine, our true flag is spiritualism, that philosophy as solid as generous, which began with Socrates and Plato, which the Gospel has spread abroad in the world, which Descartes put under the severe forms of modern genius, which in the seventeenth century was one of the glories and forces of our country, which perished with the national grandeur in the eighteenth century, which at the commencement of the present century M. Royer-Collard came to re-establish in public instruction, whilst M. de Chateaubriand, Madame de Staël, and M. Quatremère de Quincy transferred it into literature and the arts. To it is rightly given the name of spiritualism, because its character in fact is that of subordinating the senses to the spirit, and tending, by all the means that reason acknowledges, to elevate and ennoble man. It teaches the spirituality of the soul, the liberty and responsibility of human actions, moral obligation, disinterested virtue, the dignity of justice, the beauty of charity; and beyond the limits of this world it shows a God, author and type of humanity, who, after having evidently made man for an excellent end, will not abandon him in the mysterious development of his destiny. This philosophy is the natural ally of all good causes. It sustains religious sentiment; it seconds true art, poesy worthy of the name, and a great literature; it is the support of right; it equally repels the craft of the demagogue and tyranny; it teaches all men to respect and value themselves, and, little by little, it conducts human societies to the true republic, that dream of all generous souls which in our times can be realized in Europe only by constitutional monarchy.

To aid, with all our power, in setting up, defending, and propagating this noble philosophy, such is the object that early inspired us, that has sustained during a career already lengthy, in which difficulties have not been wanting. Thank God, time has rather strengthened than weakened our convictions, and we end as we began: this new edition of one of our first works is a last effort in favor of the holy cause for which we have combated nearly forty years.

May our voice be heard by new generations as it was by the serious youth of the Restoration! Yes, it is particularly to you that we address this work, young men whom we no longer know, but whom we bear in our heart, because you are the seed and the hope of the future. We have shown you the principle of our evils and their remedy. If you love liberty and your country, shun what has destroyed them. Far from you be that sad philosophy which preaches to you materialism and atheism as new doctrines destined to regenerate the world: they kill, it is true, but they do not regenerate. Do not listen to those superficial spirits who give themselves out as profound thinkers, because after Voltaire they have discovered difficulties in Christianity: measure your progress in philosophy by your progress in tender veneration for the religion of the Gospel. Be well persuaded that, in France, democracy will always traverse liberty, that it brings all right into disorder, and through disorder into dictatorship. Ask, then, only a moderated liberty, and attach yourself to that with all the powers of your soul. Do not bend the knee to fortune, but accustom yourselves to bow to law. Entertain the noble sentiment of respect. Know how to admire,—possess the worship of great men and great things. Reject that enervating literature, by turns gross and refined, which delights in painting the miseries of human nature, which caresses all our weaknesses, which pays court to the senses and the imagination, instead of speaking to the soul and awakening thought. Guard yourselves against the malady of our century, that fatal taste of an accommodating life, incompatible with all generous ambition. Whatever career you embrace, propose to yourselves an elevated aim, and put in its service an unalterable constancy. *Sursum corda*, value highly your heart, wherein is seen all philosophy, that which we have retained from all our studies, which we have taught to your predecessors, which we leave to you as our last word, our final lecture.

V. COUSIN.
June 15, 1853.

A too indulgent public having promptly rendered necessary a new edition of this book, we are forced to render it less unworthy of the suffrages which it has obtained, by reviewing it with severe attention, by introducing a mass of corrections in detail, and a considerable number of additions, among which the only ones that need be indicated here are some pages on Christianity at the end of Lecture XVI., and the notes placed as an Appendix[2] at the end of the volume, on various works of French masters which we have quite recently seen in England, which have confirmed and increased our old admiration for our national art of the seventeenth century.

November 1, 1853.

---

[2] The Appendix has been translated by Mr. N. E. S. A. Hamilton of the British Museum, who is alone entitled to credit and alone responsible.—Tr.

TRANSLATOR'S PREFACE.

The nature of this publication is sufficiently explained in the preface of M. Cousin.

We have attempted to render his book, without comment, faithfully into English. Not only have we endeavored to give his thought without increase or diminution, but have also tried to preserve the main characteristics of his style. On the one hand, we have carefully shunned idioms peculiar to the French; on the other, when permitted by the laws of structure common to both languages, we have followed the general order of sentences, even the succession of words. It has been our aim to make this work wholly Cousin's in substance, and in form as nearly his as possible, with a total change of dress. That, however, we may have nowhere missed a shade of meaning, nowhere introduced a gallicism, is too much to be hoped for, too much to be demanded.

M. Cousin, in his Philosophical Discussions, defines the terms that he uses. In the translation of these we have maintained uniformity, so that in this regard no farther explanation is necessary.

This is, perhaps, in a philosophical point of view, the most important of all M. Cousin's works, for it contains a complete summary and lucid exposition of the various parts of his system. It is now the last word of European philosophy, and merits serious and thoughtful attention.

This and many more like it, are needed in these times, when noisy and pretentious demagogues are speaking of metaphysics with idiotic laughter, when utilitarian statesmen are sneering at philosophy, when undisciplined sectarians of every kind are decrying it; when, too, earnest men, in state and church, men on whose shoulders the social world really rests, are invoking philosophy, not only as the best instrument of the highest culture and the severest mental discipline, but also as the best human means of guiding politics towards the eternally true and the eternally just, of preserving theology from the aberrations of a zeal without knowledge, and from the perversion of the interested and the cunning; when many an artist, who feels the nobility of his calling, who would address the mind of man rather than his senses, is asking a generous philosophy to explain to him that ravishing and torturing Ideal which is ever eluding his grasp, which often discourages unless understood; when, above all, devout and tender souls are learning to prize philosophy, since, in harmony with Revelation, it strengthens their belief in God, freedom, immortality.

Grateful to an indulgent public, on both sides of the ocean, for a kindly and very favorable reception of our version of M. Cousin's "Course of the History of Modern Philosophy," we add this translation of his "Lectures on the True, the Beautiful, and the Good," hoping that his explanation of human nature will aid some in solving the grave problem of life,—for there are always those, and the most gifted, too, who feel the need of understanding themselves,—believing that his eloquence, his elevated sentiment, and elevated thought, will afford gratification to a refined taste, a chaste imagination, and a disciplined mind.

O. W. WIGHT.
London, Dec. 21, 1853

LECTURES

ON

THE TRUE, THE BEAUTIFUL, AND THE GOOD.

DISCOURSE

PRONOUNCED AT THE OPENING OF THE COURSE,

December 4, 1817.

PHILOSOPHY IN THE NINETEENTH CENTURY.

Spirit and general principles of the Course.—Object of the Lectures of this year:—application of the principles of which an exposition is given, to the three Problems of the True, the Beautiful, and the Good.

It seems natural that a century, in its beginning, should borrow its philosophy from the century that preceded it. But, as free and intelligent beings, we are not born merely to continue our predecessors, but to increase their work, and also to do our own. We cannot accept from them an inheritance except under the condition of improving it. Our first duty is, then, to render to ourselves an account of the philosophy of the eighteenth century; to recognize its character and its principles, the problems which it agitated, and the solutions which it gave of them; to discern, in fine, what it transmits to us of the true and the productive, and what it also leaves of the sterile and the false, in order that, with reflective choice, we may embrace the former and reject the latter.[3] Placed at the entrance of the new times, let us know, first of all, with what views we would occupy ourselves. Moreover,—why should I not say it?—after two years of instruction, in which the professor, in some sort, has been investigating himself, one has a right to demand of him what he is; what are his most general principles on all the essential parts of philosophic science; what flag, in fine, in the midst of parties which contend with each other so violently, he proposes for you, young men, who frequent this auditory, and who are called upon to participate in a destiny still so uncertain and so obscure in the nineteenth century, to follow.

****

It is not patriotism, it is a profound sentiment of truth and justice, which makes us place the whole philosophy now expanded in the world under the invocation of the name of Descartes. Yes, the whole of modern philosophy is the work of this great man, for it owes to him the spirit that animates it, and the method that constitutes its power.

After the downfall of scholasticism and the mournful disruptures of the sixteenth century, the first object which the bold good sense of Descartes proposed to itself was to make philosophy a human science, like astronomy, physiology,

---

[3] We have so much felt the necessity of understanding well the philosophy of the century that ours succeeds, that three times we have undertaken the history of philosophy in the eighteenth century, here first, in 1818, then in 1819 and 1820, and that is the subject of the last three volumes of the 1st Series of our works; finally, we resumed it in 1829, vol. ii. and iii. of the 2d Series.

medicine, subject to the same uncertainties and to the same aberrations, but capable also of the same progress.

Descartes encountered the skepticism spread on every side in the train of so many revolutions, ambitious hypotheses, born out of the first use of an ill-regulated liberty, and the old formulas surviving the ruins of scholasticism. In his courageous passion for truth, he resolved to reject, provisorily at least, all the ideas that hitherto he had received without controlling them, firmly decided not to admit any but those which, after a serious examination, might appear to him evident. But he perceived that there was one thing which he could not reject, even provisorily, in his universal doubt,—that thing was the existence itself of his doubt, that is to say, of his thought; for although all the rest might be only an illusion, this fact, that he thought, could not be an illusion. Descartes, therefore, stopped at this fact, of an irresistible evidence, as at the first truth which he could accept without fear. Recognizing at the same time that thought is the necessary instrument of all the investigations which he might propose to himself, as well as the instrument of the human race in the acquisition of its natural knowledges,[4] he devoted himself to a regular study of it, to the analysis of thought as the condition of all legitimate philosophy, and upon this solid foundation he reared a doctrine of a character at once certain and living, capable of resisting skepticism, exempt from hypotheses, and affranchised from the formulas of the schools.

Thus the analysis of thought, and of the mind which is the subject of it, that is to say, psychology, has become the point of departure, the most general principle, the important method of modern philosophy.[5]

---

[4] This word was used by the old English writers, and there is no reason why it should not be retained.

[5] On the method of Descartes, see 1st Series, vol. iv., lecture 20; 2d Series, vol. i., lecture 2; vol. ii., lecture 11; 3d Series, vol. iii., Philosophie Moderne, as well as Fragments de Philosophie Cartésienne; 5th Series, Instruction Publique, vol. ii., Défense de l'Université et de la Philosophie, p. 112, etc.

Nevertheless, it must indeed be owned, philosophy has not entirely lost, and sometimes still retains, since Descartes and in Descartes himself, its old habits. It rarely belongs to the same man to open and run a career, and usually the inventor succumbs under the weight of his own invention. So Descartes, after having so well placed the point of departure for all philosophical investigation, more than once forgets analysis, and returns, at least in form, to the ancient philosophy.[6] The true method, again, is more than once effaced in the hands of his first successors, under the always increasing influence of the mathematical method.

Two periods may be distinguished in the Cartesian era,—one in which the method, in its newness, is often misconceived; the other, in which one is forced, at least, to re-enter the salutary way opened by Descartes. To the first belong Malebranche, Spinoza, Leibnitz himself; to the second, the philosophers of the eighteenth century.

Without doubt Malebranche, upon some points, descended very far into interior investigation; but most of the time he gave himself up to wander in an imaginary world, and lost sight of the real world. It is not a method that is wanting to Spinoza, but a good method; his error consists in having applied to philosophy the geometrical method, which proceeds by axioms, definitions, theorems, corollaries; no one has made less use of the psychological method; that is the principle and the condemnation of his system. The *Nouveaux Essais sur l'Entendement Humain* exhibit Leibnitz opposing observation to observation, analysis to analysis; but his genius usually hovers over science, instead of advancing in it step by step; hence the results at which he arrives are often only brilliant hypotheses, for example, the pre-established harmony, now relegated among the analogous hypotheses of occasional causes and a plastic mediator. In general,

---

[6] On this return to the scholastic form in Descartes, see 1st Series, vol iv., lecture 12, especially three articles of the Journal des Savants, August, September, and October, 1850, in which we have examined anew the principles of Cartesianism, à propos the Leibnitii Animadversiones ad Cartesii Principia Philosophiæ.

the philosophy of the seventeenth century, by not employing with sufficient rigor and firmness the method with which Descartes had armed it, produced little else than systems, ingenious without doubt, bold and profound, but often also rash,—systems that have failed to keep their place in science.[7] In fact, nothing is durable except that which is founded upon a sound method; time destroys all the rest; time, which re-collects, fecundates, aggrandizes the least germs of truth deposited in the humblest analyses, strikes without pity, engulfs hypotheses, even those of genius. Time takes a step, and arbitrary systems are overturned; the statues of their authors alone remain standing over their ruins. The task of the friend of truth is to search for the useful remains of them, that survive and can serve for new and more solid constructions.

The philosophy of the eighteenth century opens the second period of the Cartesian era; it proposed to itself to apply the method already discovered and too much neglected,—it applied itself to the analysis of thought. Disabused of ambitious and sterile attempts, and, like Descartes, disdainful of the past, the eighteenth century dared to think that every thing in philosophy was to be done over again, and that, in order not to wander anew, it was necessary to set out with the modest study of man. Instead, therefore, of building up all at once systems risked upon the universality of things, it undertook to examine what man knows, what he can know; it brought back entire philosophy to the study of our faculties, as physics had just been brought back to the study of the properties of bodies,—which was giving to philosophy, if not its end, at least its true beginning.

The great schools which divide the eighteenth century are the English and French school, the Scotch school, and the German school, that is to say, the school of Locke and Condillac, that of Reid, that of Kant. It is impossible to misconceive the

---

[7] See on Malebranche, Spinoza, and Leibnitz, 2d Series, vol. ii., lectures 11 and 12; 3d Series, vol. iv., Introduction aux Œuvres Philosophiques de M. de Biran, p. 288; and the Fragments de Philosophie Cartésienne, passim.

common principle which animates them, the unity of their method. When one examines with impartiality the method of Locke, he sees that it consists in the analysis of thought; and it is thereby that Locke is a disciple, not of Bacon and Hobbes, but of our great countryman, Descartes.[8] To study the human understanding as it is in each one of us, to recognize its powers, and also its limits, is the problem which the English philosopher proposed to himself, and which he attempted to solve. I do not wish to judge here of the solution which he gave of this problem; I limit myself to indicating clearly what was for him the fundamental problem. Condillac, the French disciple of Locke, made himself everywhere the apostle of analysis; and analysis was also in him, or at least should have been, the study of thought. No philosopher, not even Spinoza, has wandered farther than Condillac[9] from the true experimental method, and has strayed farther on the route of abstractions, even verbal abstractions; but, strange enough, no one is severer than he against hypotheses, save that of the statue-man. The author of the *Traité des Sensations* has very unfaithfully practised analysis; but he speaks of it without cessation. The Scotch school combats Locke and Condillac; it combats them, but with their own arms, with the same method which it pretends to apply better.[10] In Germany, Kant wishes to replace in light and honor the superior element of human consciousness, left in the shade, and decried by the philosophy of his times; and for that end, what does he do? He undertakes a profound examination of the faculty of knowing; the title of his principal work is, *Critique of Pure Reason*;[11] it is a critique, that is to say again, an analysis; the method of Kant is then no other than that of Locke and Reid. Follow it until it

---

[8] On Locke, see 1st Series, vol. iii., lecture 1, especially 2d Series, vol. iii., Examen du Système de Locke.

[9] 1st Series, vol. iii., lectures 2 and 3.

[10] 1st Series, vol. iv., lectures on the Scotch School.

[11] See on Kant and the Critique of Pure Reason, vol. v. of the 1st Series, where that great work is examined with as much extent as that of Reid in vol. iv., and the Essay of Locke in vol. iii. of the 2d Series.

reaches the hands of Fichte,[12] the successor of Kant, who died but a few years since; there, again, the analysis of thought is given as the foundation of philosophy. Kant was so firmly established in the subject of knowledge, that he could scarcely go out of it—that, in fact, he never did legitimately go out of it. Fichte plunged into the subject of knowledge so deeply that he buried himself in it, and absorbed in the human *me* all existences, as well as all sciences—sad shipwreck of analysis, which signalizes at once its greatest effort and its rock!

The same spirit, therefore, governs all the schools of the eighteenth century; this century disdains arbitrary formulas; it has a horror for hypotheses, and attaches itself, or pretends to attach itself, to the observation of facts, and particularly to the analysis of thought.

Let us acknowledge with freedom and with grief, that the eighteenth century applied analysis to all things without pity and without measure. It cited before its tribunal all doctrines, all sciences; neither the metaphysics of the preceding age, with their imposing systems, nor the arts with their prestige, nor the governments with their ancient authority, nor the religions with their majesty,—nothing found favor before it. Although it spied abysses at the bottom of what it called philosophy, it threw itself into them with a courage which is not without grandeur; for the grandeur of man is to prefer what he believes to be truth to himself. The eighteenth century let loose tempests. Humanity no more progressed, except over ruins. The world was again agitated in that state of disorder in which it had already been once seen, at the decline of the ancient beliefs, and before the triumphs of Christianity, when men wandered through all contraries, without power to rest anywhere, given up to every disquietude of spirit, to every misery of heart, fanatical and atheistical, mystical and incredulous, voluptuous and sanguinary.[13] But if the philosophy

---

[12] On Fichte, 2d Series, vol. i., lecture 12; 3d Series, vol. iv., Introduction aux Œuvres de M. de Biran, p. 324.

[13] We expressed ourselves thus in December, 1817, when, following the great wars of the Revolution, and after the downfall of the empire, the constitutional

of the eighteenth century has left us a vacuity for an inheritance, it has also left us an energetic and fecund love of truth. The eighteenth century was the age of criticism and destructions; the nineteenth should be that of intelligent rehabilitations. It belongs to it to find in a profounder analysis of thought the principles of the future, and with so many remains to raise, in fine, an edifice that reason may be able to acknowledge.

A feeble but zealous workman, I come to bring my stone; I come to do my work; I come to extract from the midst of the ruins what has not perished, what cannot perish. This course is at once a return to the past, an effort towards the future. I propose neither to attack nor to defend any of the three great schools that divide the eighteenth century. I will not attempt to perpetuate and envenom the warfare which divides them, complacently designating the differences which separate them, without taking an account of the community of method which unites them. I come, on the contrary, a devoted soldier of philosophy, a common friend of all the schools which it has produced, to offer to all the words of peace.

The unity of modern philosophy, as we have said, resides in its method, that is to say, in the analysis of thought—a method superior to its own results, for it contains in itself the means of repairing the errors that escape it, of indefinitely adding new riches to riches already acquired. The physical sciences themselves have no other unity. The great physicians who have appeared within two centuries, although united amongst themselves by the same point of departure and by the same end, generally accepted, have nevertheless proceeded with independence and in ways often opposite. Time has re-collected in their different theories the part of truth that produced them and sustained them; it has neglected their errors from which they were unable to extricate themselves, and uniting all the discoveries worthy of the name, it has little by little formed of them a vast and harmonious whole. Modern

---

monarchy, still poorly established, left the future of France and of the world obscure. It is sad to be obliged to hold the same language in 1835, over the ruins accumulated around us.

philosophy has also been enriched during the two centuries with a multitude of exact observations, of solid and profound theories, for which it is indebted to the common method. What has hindered her from progressing at an equal pace with the physical sciences whose sister she is? She has been hindered by not understanding better her own interests, by not tolerating diversities that are inevitable, that are even useful, and by not profiting by the truths which all the particular doctrines contain, in order to deduce from them a general doctrine, which is successively and perpetually purified and aggrandized.

Not, indeed, that I would recommend that blind syncretism which destroyed the school of Alexandria, which attempted to bring contrary systems together by force; what I recommend is an enlightened eclecticism, which, judging with equity, and even with benevolence, all schools, borrows from them what they possess of the true, and neglects what in them is false. Since the spirit of party has hitherto succeeded so ill with us, let us try the spirit of conciliation. Human thought is immense. Each school has looked at it only from its own point of view. This point of view is not false, but it is incomplete, and moreover, it is exclusive. It expresses but one side of truth, and rejects all the others. The question is not to decry and recommence the work of our predecessors, but to perfect it in reuniting, and in fortifying by that reunion, all the truths scattered in the different systems which the eighteenth century has transmitted to us.

Such is the principle to which we have been conducted by two years of study upon modern philosophy, from Descartes to our times. This principle, badly disengaged at first, we applied for the first time within the narrowest limits, and only to theories relative to the question of personal existence.[14] We then extended it to a greater number of questions and theories; we touched the principal points of the intellectual and moral order,[15] and at the same time that we were continuing the investigations of our illustrious predecessor, M. Royer-Collard, upon the schools of

---

[14] 1st Series, vol. i., Course of 1816.
[15] Ibid., Course of 1817.

France, England, and Scotland, we commenced the study new among us, the difficult but interesting and fecund study, of the philosophy of Kœnigsberg. We can at the present time, therefore, embrace all the schools of the eighteenth century, and all the problems which they agitated.

Philosophy, in all times, turns upon the fundamental ideas of the true, the beautiful, and the good. The idea of the true, philosophically developed, is psychology, logic, metaphysic; the idea of the good is private and public morals; the idea of the beautiful is that science which, in Germany, is called æsthetics, the details of which pertain to the criticism of literature, the criticism of arts, but whose general principles have always occupied a more or less considerable place in the researches, and even in the teaching of philosophers, from Plato and Aristotle to Hutcheson and Kant.

Upon these essential points which constitute the entire domain of philosophy, we will successively interrogate the principal schools of the eighteenth century.

When we examine them all with attention, we can easily reduce them to two,—one of which, in the analysis of thought, the common subject of all their works, gives to sensation an excessive part; the other of which, in this same analysis, going to the opposite extreme, deduces consciousness almost wholly from a faculty different from that of sensation—reason. The first of these schools is the empirical school, of which the father, or rather the wisest representative, is Locke, and Condillac the extreme representative; the second is the spiritualistic or rationalistic school, as it is called, which reckons among its illustrious interpreters Reid, who is the most irreproachable, and Kant, who is the most systematic. Surely there is truth in these two schools, and truth is a good which must be taken wherever one finds it. We willingly admit, with the empirical school, that the senses have not been given us in vain; that this admirable organization which elevates us above all other animate beings, is a rich and varied instrument, which it would be folly to neglect. We are convinced that the spectacle of the world is a permanent source of sound and sublime instruction. Upon this point neither Aristotle, nor Bacon, nor Locke, has in us an adversary, but a disciple. We acknowledge, or rather we proclaim, that in the analysis of human knowledge, it is necessary to assign to the senses an important part. But when the empirical school pretends that all that passes beyond the reach of the senses is a chimera, then we abandon it, and go over to the opposite school. We profess to believe, for example, that, without an agreeable impression, never should we have conceived the beautiful, and that, notwithstanding, the beautiful is not merely the agreeable; that, thank heaven, happiness is usually added to virtue, but that the idea itself of virtue is essentially different from that of happiness. On this point we are openly of the opinion of Reid and Kant. We have also established, and will again establish, that the reason of man is in possession of principles which sensation precedes but does not explain, and which are directly suggested to us by the power of reason alone. We will follow Kant thus far, but not farther. Far from following him, we will combat him, when, after having victoriously defended the great principles of every kind against empiricism, he strikes them with sterility, in pretending that they have no value beyond the inclosure of the reason which possesses them, condemning also to impotence that same reason which he has just elevated so high, and opening the way to a refined and learned skepticism which, after all, ends at the same abyss with ordinary skepticism.

You perceive that we shall be by turns with Locke, with Reid, and with Kant, in that just and strong measure which is called eclecticism.

Eclecticism is in our eyes the true historical method, and it has for us all the importance of the history of philosophy; but there is something which we place above the history of philosophy, and, consequently, above eclecticism,—philosophy itself.

The history of philosophy does not carry its own light with it, it is not its own end. How could eclecticism, which has no other field than history, be our only, our primary, object?

It is, doubtless, just, it is of the highest utility, to discriminate in each system what there is true in it from what there is false in it; first, in order to appreciate this system rightly; then, in order to render the false of no account, to disengage and re-collect the true, and thus to enrich and aggrandize philosophy by history. But you conceive that we must already know what truth is, in order to recognize it, and to distinguish it from the error with which it is mixed; so that the criticism of systems almost demands a system, so that the history of philosophy is constrained to first borrow from philosophy the light which it must one day return to it with usury.

In fine, the history of philosophy is only a branch, or rather an instrument, of philosophical science. Surely it is the interest which we feel for philosophy that alone attaches us to its history; it is the love of truth which makes us everywhere pursue its vestiges, and interrogate with a passionate curiosity those who before us have also loved and sought truth.

Thus philosophy is at once the supreme object and the torch of the history of philosophy. By this double title it has a right to preside over our instruction.

In regard to this, one word of explanation, I beg you.

He who is speaking before you to-day is, it is true, officially charged only with the course of the history of philosophy; in that is our task, and in that, once more, our guide shall be eclecticism.[16] But, we confess, if philosophy has not the right to present itself here in some sort on the first plan; if it should appear only behind its history, it in reality holds dominion; and to it all our wishes, as well as all our efforts, are related. We hold, doubtless, in great esteem, both Brucker and Tennemann,[17] so wise, so judicious; nevertheless our models, our veritable masters,

---

[16] On the legitimate employment and the imperative conditions of eclecticism, see 3d Series, Fragments Philosophiques, vol. iv., preface of the first edition, p. 41, &c., especially the article entitled De la Philosophie en Belgique, pp. 228 and 229.

[17] We have translated his excellent Manual of the History of Philosophy. See the second edition, vol. ii., 8vo., 1839.

always present to our thought, are, in antiquity, Plato and Socrates, among the moderns, Descartes, and, why should I hesitate to say it, among us, and in our times, the illustrious man who has been pleased to call us to this chair. M. Royer-Collard was also only a professor of the history of philosophy; but he rightly pretended to have an opinion in philosophy; he served a cause which he has transmitted to us, and we will serve it in our turn.

This great cause is known to you; it is that of a sound and generous philosophy, worthy of our century by the severity of its methods, and answering to the immortal wants of humanity, setting out modestly from psychology, from the humble study of the human mind, in order to elevate itself to the highest regions, and to traverse metaphysics, æsthetics, theodicea, morals, and politics.

Our enterprise is not then simply to renew the history of philosophy by eclecticism; we also wish, we especially wish, and history well understood, thanks to eclecticism, will therein powerfully assist us, to deduce from the study of systems, their strifes, and even their ruins, a system which may be proof against criticism, and which can be accepted by your reason, and also by your heart, noble youth of the nineteenth century!

In order to fulfil this great object, which is our veritable mission to you, we shall dare this year, for the first and for the last time, to go beyond the narrow limits which are imposed upon us. In the history of the philosophy of the eighteenth century, we have resolved to leave a little in the shade the history of philosophy, in order to make philosophy itself appear, and while exhibiting to you the distinctive traits of the principal doctrines of the last century, to expose to you the doctrine which seems to us adapted to the wants and to the spirit of our times, and still, to explain it to you briefly, but in its full extent, instead of dwelling upon some one of its parts, as hitherto we have done. With years we will correct, we will task ourselves to aggrandize and elevate our work. To-day we present it you very imperfect still, but established upon foundations which we believe solid, and already stamped with a character that will not change.

You will here see, then, brought together in a short space, our principles, our processes, our results. We ardently desire to recommend them to you, young men, who are the hope of science as well as of your country. May we at least be able, in the vast career which we have to run, to meet in you the same kindness which hitherto has sustained us.

PART FIRST.
THE TRUE.

LECTURE I.

THE EXISTENCE OF UNIVERSAL AND NECESSARY PRINCIPLES.

Two great wants, that of absolute truths, and that of absolute truths that may not be chimeras. To satisfy these two wants is the problem of the philosophy of our time.—Universal and necessary principles.—Examples of different kinds of such principles.—Distinction between universal and necessary principles and general principles.—Experience alone is incapable of explaining universal and necessary principles, and also incapable of dispensing with them in order to arrive at the knowledge of the sensible world.—Reason as being that faculty of ours which discovers to us these principles.—The study of universal and necessary principles introduces us to the highest parts of philosophy.

To-day, as in all time, two great wants are felt by man. The first, the most imperious, is that of fixed, immutable principles, which depend upon neither times nor places nor circumstances, and on which the mind reposes with an unbounded confidence. In all investigations, as long as we have seized only isolated, disconnected facts, as long as we have not referred them to a general law, we possess the materials of science, but there is yet no science. Even physics commence only when universal truths appear, to which all the facts of the same order that observation discovers to us in nature may be referred. Plato has said, that there is no science of the transitory.

This is our first need. But there is another, not less legitimate, the need of not being the dupe of chimerical principles, of barren abstractions, of combinations more or less ingenious, but artificial, the need of resting upon reality and life, the need of experience. The physical and natural sciences, whose regular and rapid conquests strike and dazzle the most ignorant, owe their progress to the experimental method. Hence the immense popularity of this method, which is carried to such an extent that one would not now condescend to lend the least attention to a science over which this method should not seem to preside.

To unite observation and reason, not to lose sight of the ideal of science to which man aspires, and to search for it and find it by the route of experience,—such is the problem of philosophy.

Now we address ourselves to your recollections of the last two years:—have we not established, by the severest experimental method, by reflection applied to the study of the human mind, with the deliberation and the rigor which such demonstrations exact,—have we not established that there are in all men, without distinction, in the wise and the ignorant, ideas, notions, beliefs, principles which the most determined skeptic cannot in the slightest degree deny, by which he is unconsciously, and in spite of himself, governed both in his words and actions, and which, by a striking contrast with our other knowledges, are marked with the at once marvellous and incontestable character, that they are encountered in the most common experience, and that, at the same time, instead of being circumscribed within the limits of this experience, they surpass and govern it, universal in the midst of particular phenomena to which they are applied; necessary, although mingled with things contingent; to our eyes infinite and absolute, even while appearing within us in that relative and finite being which we are? It is not an unpremeditated paradox that we present to you; we are only expressing here the result of numerous lectures.[18]

It was not difficult for us to show that there are universal and necessary principles at the head of all sciences.

---

[18] 1st Series of our Course, vol. i.

It is very evident that there are no mathematics without axioms and definitions, that is to say, without absolute principles.

What would logic become, those mathematics of thought, if you should take away from it a certain number of principles, which are a little barbarous, perhaps, in their scholastic form, but must be universal and necessary in order to preside over all reasoning and every demonstration?

Are physics possible, if every phenomenon which begins to appear does not suppose a cause and a law?

Without the principle of final causes, could physiology proceed a single step, render to itself an account of a single organ, or determine a single function?

Is not the principle on which the whole of morals rests, the principle which obligates man to good and lays the foundation of virtue, of the same nature? Does it not extend to all moral beings, without distinction of time and place? Can you conceive of a moral being who does not recognize in the depth of his conscience that reason ought to govern passion, that it is necessary to preserve sworn faith, and, against the most pressing interest, to restore the treasure that has been confided to us?

And these are not mere metaphysical prejudices and formulas of the schools: I appeal to the most vulgar common sense.

If I should say to you that a murder has just been committed, could you not ask me when, where, by whom, wherefore? That is to say, your mind is directed by the universal and necessary principles of time, of space, of cause, and even of final cause.

If I should say to you that love or ambition caused the murder, would you not at the same instant conceive a lover, an ambitious person? This means, again, that there is for you no act without an agent, no quality and phenomenon without a substance, without a real subject.

If I should say to you that the accused pretends that he is not the same person who conceived, willed, and executed this murder, and that, at intervals, his personality has more than once been changed, would you not say he is a fool if he is sincere, and that, although the acts and the incidents have varied, the person and the being have remained the same?

Suppose that the accused should defend himself on this ground, that the murder must serve his interest; that, moreover, the person killed was so unhappy that life was a burden to him; that the state loses nothing, since in place of two worthless citizens it acquires one who becomes useful to it; that, in fine, mankind will not perish by the loss of an individual, &c.; to all these reasonings would you not oppose the very simple response, that this murder, useful perhaps to its author, is not the less unjust, and that, therefore, under no pretext was it permitted?

The same good sense which admits universal and necessary truths, easily distinguishes them from those that are not universal and necessary, and are only general, that is to say, are applied only to a greater or less number of cases.

For example, the following is a very general truth: the day succeeds the night; but is it a universal and necessary truth? Does it extend to all lands? Yes, to all known lands. But does it extend to all possible lands? No; for it is possible to conceive of lands plunged in eternal night, another system of the world being given. The laws of the material world are what they are; they are not necessary. Their Author might have chosen others. With another system of the world one conceives other physics, but we cannot conceive other mathematics and other morals. Thus it is possible to conceive that day and night may not be in the same relation to each as that in which we see them; therefore the truth that day succeeds night is a very general truth, perhaps even a universal truth, but by no means a necessary truth.

Montesquieu has said that liberty is not a fruit of warm climates. I acknowledge, if it is desired, that heat enervates the spirit, and that warm countries maintain free governments with difficulty; but it does not follow that there may be no possible exception to this principle: moreover, there have been exceptions; hence it is not an absolutely universal principle, much less is it a necessary principle. Could you say as much of the principle of cause? Could you in any way conceive, in any time and in any place, a phenomenon which begins to appear without a cause, physical or moral?

And were it possible to reduce universal and necessary principles to general principles, in order to employ and apply these principles thus abased, and to found upon them any reasoning whatever, it would be necessary to admit what is called in logic the principle of contradiction, viz., that a thing cannot at the same time be and not be, in order to maintain the integrity of each part of the reasoning; as well as the principle of sufficient reason, which alone establishes their connection and the legitimacy of the conclusion. Now, these two principles, without which there is no reasoning, are themselves universal and necessary principles; so that the circle is manifest.

Even were we to destroy in thought all existences, save that of a single mind, we should be compelled to place in that mind, in order that it might exercise itself at all—and the mind is such only on the condition that it thinks—several necessary principles; it would be beyond the power of thought to conceive it deprived of the principle of contradiction and the principle of sufficient reason.

How many times have we demonstrated the vanity of the efforts of the empirical school to disturb the existence or weaken the bearing of universal and necessary principles! Listen to this school: it will say to you that the principle of cause, given by us as universal and necessary, is, after all, only a habit of the mind, which, seeing in nature a fact succeeding another fact, puts between these that connection which we have called the relation of effect to cause. This explanation is nothing but the destruction, not only of the principle of causality, but even of the notion of cause. The senses show me two balls, one of which begins to move, the other of which moves after it. Suppose that this succession is renewed and continues; it will be constancy added to succession; it will by no means be the connection of a causative power with its effect; for example, that which consciousness attests to us is the least effort of volition. Thus a consequent empiricist, like Hume,[19] easily proves that no sensible experience legitimately gives the idea of cause.

What we say of the notion of cause we might say of all notions of the same kind. Let us at least instance those of substance and unity.

The senses perceive only qualities, phenomena. I touch the extension, I see the color, I am sensible of the odor; but do our senses attain the substance that is extended, colored, or odorous? On this point Hume[20] indulges in pleasantries. He asks which one of our senses takes cognizance of substance. What, then, according to him and in the system of empiricism, is the notion of substance? An illusion like the notion of cause.

Neither do the senses give us unity; for unity is identity, is simplicity, and the senses show us every thing in succession and composition. The works of art possess unity only because Art, that is to say, the mind of man puts it there. If we perceive unity in the works of nature, it is not the senses that discover it to us. The arrangement of the different parts of an object may contain unity, but it is a unity of organization, an ideal and moral unity which the mind alone conceives, and which escapes the senses.

If the senses are not able to explain simple notions, much less still are they able to explain the principles in which these notions are met, which are universal and necessary. In fact, the senses clearly perceive such and such facts, but it is impossible for them to embrace what is universal; experience attests what is, it does not reach what cannot but be.

We go farther. Not only is empiricism unable to explain universal and necessary principles; but we maintain that, without these principles, empiricism cannot even account for the knowledge of the sensible world.

Take away the principle of causality, and the human mind is condemned never to go out of itself and its own modifications. All the sensations of hearing, of smell, of taste, of touch, of feeling even, cannot inform you what their cause is, nor whether

---

[19] 1st Series, vol. i.
[20] Ibid.

they have a cause. But give to the human mind the principle of causality, admit that every sensation, as well as every phenomenon, every change, every event, has a cause, as evidently we are not the cause of certain sensations, and that especially these sensations must have a cause, and we are naturally led to recognize for those sensations causes different from ourselves, and that is the first notion of an exterior world. The universal and necessary principle of causality alone gives it and justifies it. Other principles of the same order increase and develop it.

As soon as you know that there are external objects, I ask you whether you do not conceive them in a place that contains them. In order to deny it, it would be necessary to deny that every body is in a place, that is to say, to reject a truth of physics, which is at the same time a principle of metaphysics, as well as an axiom of common sense. But the place that contains a body is often itself a body, which is only more capacious than the first. This new body is in its turn in a place. Is this new place also a body? Then it is contained in another place more extended, and so on; so that it is impossible for you to conceive a body which is not in a place; and you arrive at the conception of a boundless and infinite place, that contains all limited places and all possible bodies: that boundless and infinite place is space.

And I tell you in this nothing that is not very simple. Look. Do you deny that this water is in a vase? Do you deny that this vase is in this hall? Do you deny that this hall is in a larger place, which is in its turn in another larger still? I can thus carry you on to infinite space. If you deny a single one of these propositions, you deny all, the first as well as the last; and if you admit the first, you are forced to admit the last.

It cannot be supposed that sensibility, which is not able to give us even the idea of body, alone elevates us to the idea of space. The intervention of a superior principle is, therefore, here necessary.

As we believe that every body is contained in a place, so we believe that every event happens in time. Can you conceive an event happening, except in some point of duration? This duration is extended and successively increased to your mind's eye, and you end by conceiving it unlimited like space. Deny duration, and you deny all the sciences that measure it, you destroy all the natural beliefs upon which human life reposes. It is hardly necessary to add that sensibility alone no more explains the notion of time than that of space, both of which are nevertheless inherent in the knowledge of the external world.

Empiricism is, therefore, convicted of being unable to dispense with universal and necessary principles, and of being unable to explain them.

Let us pause: either all our preceding works have terminated in nothing but chimeras, or they permit us to consider as a point definitely acquired for science, that there are in the human mind, for whomsoever interrogates it sincerely, principles really stamped with the character of universality and necessity.

After having established and defended the existence of universal and necessary principles, we might investigate and pursue this kind of principles in all the departments of human knowledge, and attempt an exact and rigorous classification; but illustrious examples have taught us to fear to compromise truths of the greatest price by mixing with them conjectures which, in giving brilliancy, perhaps, to the spirit of philosophy, diminish its authority in the eyes of the wise. We, also, following the example of Kant, attempted before you, last year,[21] a classification, even a reduction of universal and necessary principles, and of all the notions that are connected with them. This work has not lost for us its importance, but we will not reproduce it. In the interest of the great cause which we serve, and taking thought here only to establish upon solid foundations the doctrine which is adapted to the French genius in the nineteenth century, we will carefully shun every thing that might seem personal and hazardous; and, instead of examining, criticising,[22] and reconstituting the classification which the philosophy of Kœnigsberg has given of universal and necessary principles, we prefer, we find it much more useful, to

---

[21] 1st Series, vol. i., Fragments of the Course of 1817.

[22] See that criticism, 1st Series, vol. v., Kant, lecture 8.

enable you to penetrate deeper into the nature of these principles, by showing you what faculty of ours it is that discovers them to us, and to which they are related and correspond.

The peculiarity of these principles is, that each one of us in reflection recognizes that he possesses them, but that he is not their author. We conceive them and apply them, we do not constitute them. Let us interrogate our consciousness. Do we refer to ourselves, for example, the definitions of geometry, as we do certain movements of which we feel ourselves to be the cause? If it is I who make these definitions, they are therefore mine, I can unmake them, modify them, change them, even annihilate them. It is certain that I cannot do it. I am not, then, the author of them. It has also been demonstrated that the principles of which we have spoken cannot be derived from sensation, which is variable, limited, incapable of producing and authorizing any thing universal and necessary. I arrive, then, at the following consequence, also necessary:—truth is in me and not by me. As sensibility puts me in relation with the physical world, so another faculty puts me in communication with the truths that depend upon neither the world nor me, and that faculty is reason.

There are in men three general faculties which are always mingled together, and are rarely exercised except simultaneously, but which analysis divides in order to study them better, without misconceiving their reciprocal play, their intimate connection, their indivisible unity. The first of these faculties is activity, voluntary and free activity, in which human personality especially appears, and without which the other faculties would be as if they were not, since we should not exist for ourselves. Let us examine ourselves at the moment when a sensation is produced in us; we shall recognize that there is perception only so far as there is some degree of attention, and that perception ends at the moment when our activity ends. One does not recollect what he did in perfect sleep or in a swoon; because then he had lost voluntary activity, consequently consciousness; consequently, again, memory. Passion often, in depriving us of liberty, deprives us, at the same time, of the consciousness of our actions and of ourselves; then, to use a just and common expression, one knows not what he does. It is by liberty that man is truly man, that he possesses himself and governs himself; without it, he falls again under the yoke of nature; he is, without it, only a more admirable and more beautiful part of nature. But while I am endowed with activity and liberty, I am also passive in other respects; I am subject to the laws of the external world; I suffer and I enjoy without being myself the author of my joys and my sufferings; I feel rising within me needs, desires, passions, which I have not made, which by turns fill my life with happiness and misery. Finally, besides volition and sensibility, man has the faculty of knowing, has understanding, intelligence, reason, the name matters little, by means of which he is elevated to truths of different orders, and among others, to universal and necessary truths, which suppose in reason, attached to its exercise, principles entirely distinct from the impressions of the senses and the resolutions of the will.[23]

Voluntary activity, sensibility, reason, are all equally certain. Consciousness verifies the existence of necessary principles, which direct the reason quite as well as that of sensations and volitions. I call every thing real that falls under observation. I suffer; my suffering is real, inasmuch as I am conscious of it: it is the same with liberty: it is the same with reason and the principles that govern it. We can affirm, then, that the existence of universal and necessary principles rests upon the testimony of observation, and even of the most immediate and surest observation, that of consciousness.

But consciousness is only a witness,—it makes what is appear; it creates nothing. It is not because consciousness announces it to you, that you have produced such or such a

---

[23] This classification of the human faculties, save some differences more nominal than real, is now generally adopted, and makes the foundation of the psychology of our times. See our writings, among others, 1st Series, Course of 1816, lectures 23 and 24: Histoire du moi; ibid., Des faits de Conscience; vol. iii., lecture 3, Examen de la Théorie des Facultés dans Condillac; vol. iv., lecture 21, des Facultés selon Reid; vol. v., lecture 8, Examen de la Théorie de Kant; 3d Series, vol iv., Preface de la Première Edition, Examen des Leçons de M. Laromiguière, Introduction aux Œuvres de M. de Biran, etc.

movement, that you have experienced such or such an impression. Neither is it because consciousness says to us that reason is constrained to admit such or such a truth, that this truth exists; it is because it exists that it is impossible for reason not to admit it. The truths that reason attains by the aid of universal and necessary principles with which it is provided, are absolute truths; reason does not create them, it discovers them. Reason is not the judge of its own principles, and cannot account for them, for it only judges by them, and they are to it its own laws. Much less does consciousness make these principles, or the truths which they reveal to us; for consciousness has no other office, no other power than in some sort to serve as a mirror for reason. Absolute truths are, therefore, independent of experience and consciousness, and at the same time, they are attested by experience and consciousness. On the one hand, these truths declare themselves in experience; on the other, no experience explains them. Behold how experience and reason differ and agree, and how, by means of experience, we come to find something which surpasses it.

So the philosophy which we teach rests neither upon hypothetical principles, nor upon empirical principles. It is observation itself, but observation applied to the higher portion of our knowledge, which furnishes us with the principles that we seek, with a point of departure at once solid and elevated.[24]

This point of departure we have found, and we do not abandon it. We remain immovably attached to it. The study of

---

[24] This lecture on the existence of universal and necessary principles, which was easily comprehended, in 1818, by an auditory to which long discussions had already been presented during the two previous years, appearing here without the support of these preliminaries, will not perhaps be entirely satisfactory to the reader. We beseech him to consult carefully the first volume of the 1st Series of our Course, which contains an abridgment, at least, of the numerous lectures of 1816 and 1817, of which this is a résumé; especially to read in the third, fourth, and fifth volumes of the 1st Series, the developed analyses, in which, under different forms, universal and necessary principles are demonstrated as far as may be, and in the third volume of the 2d Series the lectures devoted to establish against Locke the same principles.

universal and necessary principles, considered under their different aspects, and in the great problems which they solve, is almost the whole of philosophy; it fills it, measures it, divides it. If psychology is the regular study of the human mind and its laws, it is evident that that of universal and necessary principles which preside over the exercise of reason, is the especial domain of psychology, which in Germany is called rational psychology, and is very different from empirical psychology. Since logic is the examination of the value and the legitimacy of our different means of knowing, its most important employment must be to estimate the value and the legitimacy of the principles which are the foundations of our most important cognitions. In fine, the meditation of these same principles conducts us to theodicea, and opens to us the sanctuary of philosophy, if we would ascend to their true source, to that sovereign reason which is the first and last explanation of our own.

LECTURE II.

ORIGIN OF UNIVERSAL AND NECESSARY PRINCIPLES.

Résumé of the preceding Lecture. A new question, that of the origin of universal and necessary principles.—Danger of this question, and its necessity.—Different forms under which truth presents itself to us, and the successive order of these forms: theory of spontaneity and reflection.—The primitive form of principles; abstraction that disengages them from that form, and gives them their actual form.—Examination and refutation of the theory that attempts to explain the origin of principles by an induction founded on particular notions.

We may regard as a certain conquest of the experimental method and of true psychological analysis, the establishment of principles which at the same time that they are given to us by the surest of all experiences, that of consciousness, have a bearing superior to experience, and open to us regions inaccessible to empiricism. We have recognized such principles at the head of nearly all the sciences; then, searching among our different faculties for that which may have given them to us, we have ascertained that it is impossible to refer them to any other faculty than to that general faculty of knowing which we call reason, very different from reasoning, to which it furnishes its laws.

That is the point at which we have arrived. But is it possible to stop there?

In human intelligence, as it is now developed, universal and necessary principles are offered to us under forms in some sort consecrated. The principle of causality, for example, is thus enounced to us:—Every thing that begins to appear necessarily has a cause. Other principles have this same axiomatic form. But have they always had it, and did they spring from the human mind with this logical and scholastic apparel, as Minerva sprang all armed from the head of Jupiter? With what characters did they show themselves at first, before taking those in which they are now clothed, and which can scarcely be their primitive characters? In a word, is it possible to find the origin of universal and necessary principles, and the route which they must have followed in order to arrive at what they are to-day? A new problem, the importance of which it is easy to feel; for, if it can be resolved, what light will be shed upon these principles! On the other hand, what difficulties must be encountered! How can we penetrate to the sources of human knowledge, which are concealed, like those of the Nile? Is it not to be feared that, in plunging into the obscure past, instead of truth, one may encounter an hypothesis; that, attaching himself, then, to this hypothesis, he may transport it from the past to the present, and that, being deceived in regard to the origin of principles, he may be led to misconceive their actual and certain characters, or, at least, to mutilate and enfeeble those which the adopted origin would not easily explain? This danger is so great, this rock is so celebrated in shipwrecks, that before braving it one should know how to take many precautions against the seductions of the spirit of the system. It is even conceived that great philosophers, who were timid in no place, have suppressed the perilous problem. In fact, by undertaking to grapple with this problem at first, Locke and Condillac went far astray,[25] and it must be said, corrupted all philosophy at its source. The empirical school, which lauds the experimental method so much, turns its back upon it, thus to speak, when, instead of commencing by the study of the actual characters of our cognitions, as they are attested to us by consciousness and reflection, it plunges, without light and without guidance, into the pursuit of their origin. Reid[26] and Kant[27] showed themselves much more observing by confining themselves within the limits of the present, through fear of losing themselves in the darkness of the past. Both freely treat of universal and necessary principles in the form which they now have, without asking what was their

---

[25] First Series, vol. iv., lectures 1, 2, and 3.
[26] Ibid., vol. iv., etc.
[27] Ibid., vol. v., lecture 8.

primitive form. We much prefer this wise circumspection to the adventurous spirit of the empirical school. Nevertheless, when a problem is given out, so long as it is not solved, it troubles and besets the human mind. Philosophy ought not to shun it then, but its duty is to approach it only with extreme prudence and a severe method.

We cannot recollect too well, for the sake of others and ourselves, that the primitive state of human cognitions is remote from us; we can scarcely bring it within the reach of our vision and submit it to observation; the actual state, on the contrary, is always at our disposal: it is sufficient for us to enter into ourselves, to fathom consciousness by reflection, and make it give up what it contains. Setting out from certain facts, we shall not be liable to wander subsequently into hypotheses, or if, in ascending to the primitive state, we fall into any error, we shall be able to perceive it and repair it by the aid of the truth which an impartial observation shall have given us; every origin which shall not legitimately end at the point where we are, is by that alone convicted of being false, and will deserve to be discarded.[28]

You know that a large portion of the last year was spent upon this question. We took, one by one, universal and necessary questions submitted to our examination, in order to determine the origin of each one of them, its primitive form, and the different forms which have successively clothed it; only after having operated thus upon a sufficiently large number of principles, did

---

[28] We have everywhere called to mind, maintained, and confirmed by the errors of those who have dared to break it, this rule of true psychological analysis, that, before passing to the question of the origin of an idea, a notion, a belief, any principle whatever, the actual characters of this idea, this notion, this belief, this principle, must have been a long time studied and well established, with the firm resolution of not altering them under any pretext whatever in wishing to explain them. We believe that we have, as Leibnitz says, settled this point. See 1st Series, vol. i., Programme of the Course of 1817, and the Opening Discourse; vol. iii., lecture 1, Locke; lecture 2, Condillac; lecture 3, almost entire, and lecture 8, p. 260; 2d Series, vol. iii., Examen du Système de Locke, lecture 16, p. 77-87; 3d Series, vol. iv., Examination of the Lectures of M. Loremquière, p. 268.

we come slowly to a general conclusion, and that conclusion we believe ourselves entitled to express here briefly as the solid result of a most circumspect analysis, and, at least, a most methodical labor. We must either renew before you this labor, this analysis, and thereby run the risk of not being able to complete the long course that we have marked out for ourselves, or we must limit ourselves to reminding you of the essential traits of the theory at which we arrived.

This theory, moreover, is in itself so simple, that, without the dress of regular demonstrations upon which it is founded, its own evidence will sufficiently establish it. It wholly rests upon the distinction between the different forms under which truth is presented to us. It is, in its somewhat arid generality, as follows:

1st. One can perceive truth in two different ways. Sometimes one perceives it in such or such a particular circumstance. For example, in presence of two apples or two stones, and of two other similar objects placed by the side of the first, I perceive this truth with absolute certainty, viz., that these two stones and these two other stones make four stones,—which is in some sort a concrete apperception of the truth, because the truth is given to us in regard to real and determinate objects. Sometimes I also affirm in a general manner that two and two equal four, abstracting every determinate object,—which is the abstract conception of truth.

Now, of these two ways of knowing truth, which precedes in the chronological order of human knowledge? Is it not certain, may it not be avowed by every one, that the particular precedes the general, that the concrete precedes the abstract, that we begin by perceiving such or such a determinate truth, in such or such a case, at such or such a moment, in such or such a place, before conceiving a general truth, independently of every application and different circumstances of place and time?

2d. We can perceive the same truth without asking ourselves this question: Have we the ability not to admit this truth? We perceive it, then, by virtue alone of the intelligence which has been given us, and which enters spontaneously into exercise; or rather, we try to doubt the truth which we perceive, we attempt to deny it; we are not able to do it, and then it is presented to reflection as superior to all possible negation; it appears to us no longer only as a truth, but as a necessary truth.

Is it not also evident, that we do not begin by reflection, that reflection supposes an anterior operation, and that this operation, in order not to be one of reflection, and not to suppose another before it, must be entirely spontaneous; that thus the spontaneous and instinctive intuition of truth precedes its reflection and necessary conception?

Reflection is a progress more or less tardy in the individual and in the race. It is, *par excellence*, the philosophic faculty; it sometimes engenders doubt and skepticism, sometimes convictions that, for being rational, are only the more profound. It constructs systems, it creates artificial logic, and all those formulas which we now use by the force of habit as if they were natural to us. But spontaneous intuition is the true logic of nature. It presides over the acquisition of nearly all our cognitions. Children, the people, three-fourths of the human race never pass beyond it, and rest there with boundless security.

The question of the origin of human cognitions is thus resolved for us in the simplest manner: it is enough for us to determine that operation of the mind which precedes all others, without which no other would take place, and which is the first exercise, and the first form of our faculty of knowing.[29]

Since every thing that bears the character of reflection cannot be primitive, and supposes an anterior state, it follows, that the

---

[29] This theory of spontaneity and of reflection, which in our view is the key to so many difficulties, continually recurs in our works. One may see, vol. i. of the 1st Series, in a programme of the Course of 1817, and in a fragment entitled De la Spontanéité et de la Réflexion; vol. iv. of the same Series, Examination of Reid's Philosophy, passim; vol. v., Examination of Kant's System, lecture 8; 2d Series, vol. i., passim; vol. iii., Lectures on Judgment; 3d Series, Fragments Philosophiques, vol. iv., preface of the first edition, p. 37, etc.; it will be found in different lectures of this volume, among others, in the third, On the value of Universal and Necessary Principles; in the fifth, On Mysticism; and in the eleventh, Primary Data of Common Sense.

principles which are the subject of our study could not have possessed at first the reflective and abstract character with which they are now marked, that they must have shown themselves at their origin in some particular circumstance, under a concrete and determinate form, and that in time they were disengaged from this form, in order to be invested with their actual, abstract, and universal form. These are the two ends of the chain; it remains for us to seek how the human mind has been from one to the other, from the primitive state to the actual state, from the concrete state to the abstract state.

How can we go from the concrete to the abstract? Evidently by that well-known operation which is called abstraction. Thus far, nothing is more simple. But it is necessary to discriminate between two sorts of abstractions.

In presence of several particular objects, you omit the characters which distinguish them, and separately consider a character which is common to them all—you abstract this character. Examine the nature and conditions of this abstraction; it proceeds by means of comparison, and it is founded on a certain number of particular and different cases. Take an example: examine how we form the abstract and general idea of color. Place before my eyes for the first time a white object. Can I here at the first step immediately arrive at a general idea of color? Can I at first place on one side the whiteness, and on the other side the color? Analyze what passes within you. You experience a sensation of whiteness. Omit the individuality of this sensation, and you wholly destroy it; you cannot neglect the whiteness, and preserve or abstract the color; for, a single color being given, which is a white color, if you take away that, there remains to you absolutely nothing in regard to color. Let a blue object succeed this white object, then a red object, etc.; having sensations differing from each other, you can neglect their differences, and only consider what they have in common, that they are sensations of sight, that is to say, colors, and you thus obtain the abstract and general idea of color. Take another example: if you had never smelled but a single flower, the violet, for instance, would you have had the idea of odor in general? No. The odor of the violet would be for you the only odor, beyond which you would not seek, you could not even imagine another. But if to the odor of the violet is added that of the rose, and other different odors, in a greater or less number, provided there be several, and a comparison be possible, and consequently, knowledge of their differences and their resemblances, then you will be able to form the general idea of odor. What is there in common between the odor of one flower and that of another flower, except that they have been smelled by aid of the same organ, and by the same person? What here renders generalization possible, is the unity of the sentient subject which remembers having been modified, while remaining the same, by different sensations; now, this subject can feel itself identical under different modifications, and it can conceive in the qualities of the object felt some resemblance and some dissimilarity, only on the condition of a certain number of sensations experienced, of odors smelled. In that case, but in that case alone, there can be comparison, abstraction, and generalization, because there are different and similar elements.

In order to arrive at the abstract form of universal and necessary principles, we have no need of all this labor. Let us take again, for example, the principle of cause. If you suppose six particular cases from which you have abstracted this principle, it will contain neither more nor less ideas than if you had deduced it from a single one. To be able to say that the event which I see must have a cause, it is not indispensable to have seen several events succeed each other. The principle which compels me to pronounce this judgment, is already complete in the first as in the last event; it can change in respect to its object, it cannot change in itself; it neither increases nor decreases with the greater or less number of its applications. The only difference that it is subject to in regard to us, is, that we apply it whether we remark it or not, whether we disengage it or not from its particular application. The question is not to eliminate the particularity of the phenomenon, wherein it appears to us, whether it be the fall of a leaf or the murder of a man, in order immediately to conceive, in a general and abstract manner, the necessity of a cause for every thing that begins to exist. Here, it is not because I have been the same, or have been affected in the same manner in several different cases, that I have come to this general and abstract conception. A leaf falls: at the same instant I think, I believe, I declare that this falling of the leaf must have a cause. A man has been killed: at the same instant I believe, I proclaim that this death must have a cause. Each one of these facts contains particular and variable circumstances, and something universal and necessary, to wit, both of them cannot but have a cause. Now, I am perfectly able to disengage the universal from the particular, in regard to the first fact as well as in regard to the second fact, for the universal is in the first quite as well as in the second. In fact, if the principle of causality is not universal in the first fact, neither will it be in the second, nor in the third, nor in a thousandth; for a thousand are not nearer than one to the infinite, to absolute universality. It is the same, and still more evidently, with necessity. Pay particular attention to this point: if necessity is not in the first fact, it cannot be in any; for necessity cannot be formed little by little, and by successive increment. If, at the first murder that I see, I do not exclaim that this murder necessarily has a cause, at the thousandth murder, although it shall have been proved that all the others have had causes, I shall have the right to think that this new murder has, very probably, also its cause; but I shall never have the right to declare that it necessarily has a cause. But when necessity and universality are already in a single case, that case alone is sufficient to entitle us to deduce them from it.[30]

We have established the existence of universal and necessary principles: we have marked their origin; we have shown that they appear to us at first from a particular fact, and we have shown by what process, by what sort of abstraction the mind disengages them from the determinate and concrete form which envelops them, but does not constitute them. Our task, then, seems accomplished. But it is not,—we must defend the solution which

---

[30] On immediate abstraction and comparative abstraction, see 1st Series, vol. i., Programme of the Course of 1817, and everywhere in our other Courses.

we have just presented to you of the problem of the origin of principles against the theory of an eminent metaphysician, whose just authority might seduce you. M. Maine de Biran[31] is, like us, the declared adversary of the philosophy of sensation,—he admits universal and necessary principles; but the origin which he assigns to them, puts them, according to us, in peril, and would lead back by a *detour* to the empirical school.

Universal and necessary principles, if expressed in propositions, embrace several terms. For example, in the principle that every phenomenon supposes a cause; and in this, that every quality supposes a substance, by the side of the ideas of quality and phenomenon are met the ideas of cause and substance, which seem the foundation of these two principles. M. de Biran pretends that the two ideas are anterior to the two principles which contain them, and that we at first find these ideas in ourselves in the consciousness that we are cause and substance, and that, these ideas once being thus acquired, induction transports them out of ourselves, makes us conceive causes and substances wherever there are phenomena and qualities, and that the principles of cause and substance are thus explained. I beg pardon of my illustrious friend; but it is impossible to admit in the least degree this explanation.

The possession of the origin of the idea of cause is by no means sufficient for the possession of the origin of the principle of causality; for the idea and the principle are things essentially different. You have established, I would say to M. de Biran, that the idea of cause is found in that of productive volition:—you will to produce certain effects, and you produce them; hence the idea of a cause, of a particular cause, which is yourself; but between this fact and the axiom that all phenomena which appear necessarily have a cause, there is a gulf.

You believe that you can bridge it over by induction. The idea of cause once found in ourselves, induction applies it, you say, wherever a new phenomenon appears. But let us not be

---

[31] On M. de Biran, on his merits and defects, see our Introduction at the head of his Works.

deceived by words, and let us account for this extraordinary induction. The following dilemma I submit with confidence to the loyal dialectics of M. de Biran:

Is the induction of which you speak universal and necessary? Then it is a different name for the same thing. An induction which forces us universally and necessarily to associate the idea of cause with that of every phenomenon that begins to appear is precisely what is called the principle of causality. On the contrary, is this induction neither universal nor necessary? It cannot supply the place of the principle of cause, and the explanation destroys the thing to be explained.

It follows from this that the only true result of these various psychological investigations is, that the idea of personal and free cause precedes all exercise of the principle of causality, but without explaining it.

The theory which we combat is much more powerless in regard to other principles which, far from being exercised before the ideas from which it is pretended to deduce them, precede them, and even give birth to them. How have we acquired the idea of time and that of space, except by aid of the principle that the bodies and events, which we see are in time and in space? We have seen[32] that, without this principle, and confined to the data of the senses and consciousness, neither time nor space would exist for us. Whence have we deduced the idea of the infinite, except from the principle that the finite supposes the infinite, that all finite and defective things, which we perceive by our senses and feel within us, are not sufficient for themselves, and suppose something infinite and perfect? Omit the principle, and the idea of the infinite is destroyed. Evidently this idea is derived from the application of the principle, and it is not the principle which is derived from the idea.

Let us dwell a little longer on the principle of substances. The question is to know whether the idea of subject, of substance, precedes or follows the exercise of the principle. Upon what

---

[32] See lecture I.

ground could the idea of substance be anterior to the principle that every quality supposes a substance? Upon the ground alone that substance be the object of self-observation, as cause is said to be. When I produce a certain effect, I may perceive myself in action and as cause; in that case, there would be no need of the intervention of any principle; but it is not, it cannot be, the same, when the question is concerning the substance which is the basis of the phenomena of consciousness, of our qualities, our acts, our faculties even; for this substance is not directly observable; it does not perceive itself, it conceives itself. Consciousness perceives sensation, volition, thought, it does not perceive their subject. Who has ever perceived the soul? Has it not been necessary, in order to attain this invisible essence, to set out from a principle which has the power to bind the visible to the invisible, phenomenon to being, to wit, the principle of substances?[33] The idea of substance is necessarily posterior to the application of the principle, and, consequently, it cannot explain its formation.

Let us be well understood. We do not mean to say that we have in the mind the principle of substances before perceiving a phenomenon, quite ready to apply the principle to the phenomenon, when it shall present itself; we only say that it is impossible for us to perceive a phenomenon without conceiving at the same instant a substance, that is to say, to the power of perceiving a phenomenon, either by the senses or by consciousness, is joined that of conceiving the substance in which it inheres. The facts thus take place:—the perception of phenomena and the conception of the substance which is their basis are not successive, they are simultaneous. Before this impartial analysis fall at once two equal and opposite errors—one, that experience, exterior or interior, can beget principles; the other, that principles precede experience.[34]

---

[33] See vol. i. of the 1st Series, course of 1816, and 2d Series, vol. iii., lecture 18, p. 140-146.
[34] We have developed this analysis, and elucidated these results in the 17th lecture of vol. ii. of the 2d Series.

To sum up, the pretension of explaining principles by the ideas which they contain, is a chimerical one. In supposing that all the ideas which enter into principles are anterior to them, it is necessary to show how principles are deduced from these ideas,— which is the first and radical difficulty. Moreover, it is not true that in all cases ideas precede principles, for often principles precede ideas,—a second difficulty equally insurmountable. But whether ideas are anterior or posterior to principles, principles are always independent of them; they surpass them by all the superiority of universal and necessary principles over simple ideas.[35]

We should, perhaps, beg your pardon for the austerity of this lecture. But philosophical questions must be treated philosophically: it does not belong to us to change their character. On other subjects, another language. Psychology has its own language, the entire merit of which is a severe precision, as the highest law of psychology itself is the shunning of every hypothesis, and an inviolable respect for facts. This law we have religiously followed. While investigating the origin of universal and necessary principles, we have especially endeavored not to destroy the thing to be explained by a systematic explanation. Universal and necessary principles have come forth in their integrity from our analysis. We have given the history of the different forms which they successively assume, and we have shown, that in all these changes they remain the same, and of the same authority, whether they enter spontaneously and

---

[35] We have already twice recurred, and more in detail, to the impossibility of legitimately explaining universal and necessary principles by any association or induction whatever, founded upon any particular idea, 2d Series, vol. iii., Examen du Système de Locke, lecture 19, p. 166; and 3d Series, vol. iv., Introduction aux Œuvres de M. de Biran, p. 319. We have also made known the opinion of Reid, 1st Series, vol. iv., lecture 22, p. 489. Finally, the profoundest of Reid's disciples, the most enlightened judge that we know of things philosophical, Sir W. Hamilton, professor of logic in the University of Edinburgh, has not hesitated to adopt the conclusions of our discussion, to which he is pleased to refer his readers:—Discussions on Philosophy and Literature, etc., by Sir William Hamilton, London, 1852. Appendix I, p. 588.

involuntarily into exercise, and apply themselves to particular and determinate objects, or reflection turns them back upon themselves in order to interrogate them in regard to their nature, or abstraction makes them appear under the form in which their universality and their necessity are manifest. Their certainty is the same under all their forms, in all their applications; it has neither generation nor origin; it is not born such or such a day, and it does not increase with time, for it knows no degrees. We have not commenced by believing a little in the principle of causality, of substances, of time, of space, of the infinite, etc., then believing a little more, then believing wholly. These principles have been, from the beginning, what they will be in the end, all-powerful, necessary, irresistible. The conviction which they give is always absolute, only it is not always accompanied by a clear consciousness. Leibnitz himself has no more confidence in the principle of causality, and even in his favorite principle of sufficient reason, than the most ignorant of men; but the latter applies these principles without reflecting on their power, by which he is unconsciously governed, whilst Leibnitz is astonished at their power, studies it, and for all explanation, refers it to the human mind, and to the nature of things, that is to say, he elevates, to borrow the fine expression of M. Royer-Collard,[36] the ignorance of the mass of men to its highest source. Such is, thank heaven, the only difference that separates the peasant from the philosopher, in regard to those great principles of every kind which, in one way or another, discover to men the same truths indispensable to their physical, intellectual, and moral existence, and, in their ephemeral life, on the circumscribed point of space

---

[36] Œuvres de Reid, vol. iv., p. 435. "When we revolt against primitive facts, we equally misconceive the constitution of our intelligence and the end of philosophy. Is explaining a fact any thing else than deriving it from another fact, and if this kind of explanation is to terminate at all, does it not suppose facts inexplicable? The science of the human mind will have been carried to the highest degree of perfection it can attain, it will be complete, when it shall know how to derive ignorance from the most elevated source."

and time where fortune has thrown them, reveal to them something of the universal, the necessary, and the infinite.

LECTURE III.

ON THE VALUE OF UNIVERSAL AND NECESSARY PRINCIPLES.

Examination and refutation of Kant's skepticism.—Recurrence to the theory of spontaneity and reflection.

After having recognized the existence of universal and necessary principles, their actual characters, and their primitive characters, we have to examine their value, and the legitimacy of the conclusions which may be drawn from them,—we pass from psychology to logic.

We have defended against Locke and his school the necessity and universality of certain principles. We now come to Kant, who recognizes with us these principles, but confines their power within the limits of the subject that conceives them, and, so far as subjective, declares them to be without legitimate application to any object, that is to say, without objectivity, to use the language of the philosopher of Kœnigsberg, which, right or wrong, begins to pass into the philosophic language of Europe.

Let us comprehend well the import of this new discussion. The principles that govern our judgments, that preside over most sciences, that rule our actions,—have they in themselves an absolute truth, or are they only regulating laws of our thought? The question is, to know whether it is true in itself, that every phenomenon has a cause, and every quality a subject, whether every thing extended is really in space, and every succession in time, etc. If it is not absolutely true that every quality has its subject of inherence, it is not, then, certain, that we have a soul, a real substance of all the qualities which consciousness attests. If the principle of causality is only a law of our mind, the external world, which this principle discovers to us, loses its reality, it is only a succession of phenomena, without any effective action over each other, as Hume would have it, and even the impressions of our senses are destitute of causes. Matter exists no more than the soul. Nothing exists; every thing is reduced to mobile appearances, given up to a perpetual becoming, which again is accomplished we know not where, since in reality there is neither time nor space. Since the principle of sufficient reason only serves to put in motion human curiosity, once in possession of the fatal secret that it can attain nothing real, this curiosity would be very good to weary itself in searching for reasons which inevitably escape it, and in discovering relations which correspond only to the wants of our mind, and do not in the least correspond to the nature of things. In fine, if the principle of causality, of substances, of final causes, of sufficient reason, are only our modes of conception, God, whom all these principles reveal to us, will no more be any thing but the last of chimeras, which vanishes with all the others in the breath of the Critique.

Kant has established, as well as Reid and ourself, the existence of universal and necessary principles; but an involuntary disciple of his century, an unconscious servant of the empirical school, to which he places himself in the attitude of an adversary, he makes to it the immense concession that these principles are applied only to the impressions of sensibility, that their part is to put these impressions in a certain order, but that beyond these impressions, beyond experience, their power expires. This concession has ruined the whole enterprise of the German philosopher.

This enterprise was at once honest and great. Kant, grieved at the skepticism of his times, proposed to arrest it by fairly meeting it. He thought to disarm Hume by conceding to him that our highest conceptions do not extend themselves beyond the inclosure of the human mind; and at the same time, he supposed that he had sufficiently vindicated the human mind by restoring to it the universal and necessary principles which direct it. But, according to the strong expression of M. Royer-Collard, "one does not encounter skepticism,—as soon as he has penetrated into the human understanding he has completely taken it by storm." A severe circumspection is one thing, skepticism is another. Doubt is not only permitted, it is commanded by reason itself in the employment and legitimate applications of our different faculties; but when it is applied to the legitimacy itself of our faculties, it no longer elucidates reason, it overwhelms it. In fact, with what would you have reason defend herself, when she has called herself in question? Kant himself, then, overturned the dogmatism which he proposed at once to restrain and save, at least in morals, and he put German philosophy upon a route, at the end of which was an abyss. In vain has this great man—for his intentions and his character, without speaking of his genius, merit for him this name—undertaken with Hume an ingenious and learned controversy; he has been vanquished in this controversy, and Hume remains master of the field of battle.

What matters it, in fact, whether there may or may not be in the human mind universal and necessary principles, if these principles only serve to classify our sensations, and to make us ascend, step by step, to ideas that are most sublime, but have for ourselves no reality? The human mind is, then, as Kant himself well expressed it, like a banker who should take bills ranged in order on his desk for real values;—he possesses nothing but papers. We have thus returned, then, to that conceptualism of the middle age, which, concentrating truth within the human intelligence, makes the nature of things a phantom of intelligence projecting itself everywhere out of itself, at once triumphant and impotent, since it produces every thing, and produces only chimeras.[37]

---

[37] On conceptualism, as well as on nominalism and realism, see the Introduction to the inedited works of Abelard, and also 1st Series, vol. iv., lecture 21, p. 457; 2d Series, vol. iii., lecture 20, p. 215, and the work already cited on the Metaphysics of Aristotle, p. 49: "Nothing exists in this world which has not its law more general than itself. There is no individual that is not related to a species; there are no phenomena bound together that are not united to a plan. And it is necessary there should really be in nature species and a plan, if every thing has been made with weight and measure, cum pondere et mensura, without which our very ideas of species and a plan would only be chimeras, and human science a systematic illusion. If it is pretended that there are individuals and no species, things in juxtaposition and no plan; for example, human individuals more or less different, and no human type, and a thousand

The reproach which a sound philosophy will content itself with making to Kant, is, that his system is not in accordance with facts. Philosophy can and must separate itself from the crowd for the explanation of facts; but, it cannot be too often repeated, it must not in the explanation destroy what it pretends to explain; otherwise it does not explain, it imagines. Here, the important fact which it is the question to explain is the belief of the human mind, and the system of Kant annihilates it.

In fact, when we are speaking of the truth of universal and necessary principles, we do not believe they are true only for us:— we believe them to be true in themselves, and still true, were there no minds of ours to conceive them. We regard them as independent of us; they seem to us to impose themselves upon our intelligence by the force of the truth that is in them. So, in order to express faithfully what passes within us, it would be necessary to reverse the proposition of Kant, and instead of saying with him, that these principles are the necessary laws of our mind, therefore they have no absolute value out of mind; we should much rather say, that these principles have an absolute value in themselves, therefore we cannot but believe them.

And even this necessity of belief with which the new skepticism arms itself, is not the indispensable condition of the application of principles. We have established[38] that the necessity of believing supposes reflection, examination, an effort to deny and the want of power to do it; but before all reflection, intelligence spontaneously seizes the truth, and, in the spontaneous apperception, is not the sentiment of necessity, nor consequently that character of subjectivity of which the German school speaks so much.

---

other things of the same sort, well and good; but in that case there is nothing general in the world, except in the human understanding, that is to say, in other terms, the world and nature are destitute of order and reason except in the head of man."

[38] See preceding lecture.

Let us, then, here recur to that spontaneous intuition of truth, which Kant knew not, in the circle where his profoundly reflective and somewhat scholastic habits held him captive.

Is it true that there is no judgment, even affirmative in form, which is not mixed with negation?

It seems indeed that every affirmative judgment is at the same time negative; in fact, to affirm that a thing exists, is to deny its non-existence; as every negative judgment is at the same time affirmative; for to deny the existence of a thing, is to affirm its non-existence. If it is so, then every judgment, whatever may be its form, affirmative or negative, since these two forms come back to each other, supposes a pre-established doubt in regard to the existence of the thing in question, supposes some exercise of reflection, in the course of which the mind feels itself constrained to bear such or such a judgment, so that at this point of view the foundation of the judgment seems to be in its necessity; and then recurs the celebrated objection:—if you judge thus only because it is impossible for you not to do it, you have for a guaranty of the truth nothing but yourself and your own ways of conceiving; it is the human mind that transports its laws out of itself; it is the subject that makes the object out of its own image, without ever going beyond the inclosure of subjectivity.

We respond, going directly to the root of the difficulty:—it is not true that all our judgments are negative. We admit that in the reflective state every affirmative judgment supposes a negative judgment, and reciprocally. But is reason exercised only on the condition of reflection? Is there not a primitive affirmation which implies no negation? As we often act without deliberating on our action, without premeditating it, and as we manifest in this case an activity that is free still, but free with a liberty that is not reflective; so reason often perceives the truth without traversing doubt or error. Reflection is a return to consciousness, or to an operation wholly different from it. We do not find, then, in any primitive fact, that every judgment which contains it presupposes another in which it is not. We thus arrive at a judgment free from all reflection, to an affirmation without any mixture of negation, to an immediate intuition, the legitimate child of the natural energy of thought, like the inspiration of the poet, the instinct of the hero, the enthusiasm of the prophet. Such is the first act of the faculty of knowing. If one contradicts this primitive affirmation, the faculty of knowing falls back up upon itself, examines itself, attempts to call in doubt the truth it has perceived; it cannot; it affirms anew what it had affirmed at first; it adheres to the truth already recognized, but with a new sentiment, the sentiment that it is not in its power to divest itself of the evidence of this same truth; then, but only then, appears that character of necessity and subjectivity that some would turn against the truth, as though truth could lose its own value, while penetrating deeper into the mind and there triumphing over doubt; as though reflective evidence of it were the less evidence; as though, moreover, the necessary conception of it were the only form, the primary form of the perception of truth. The skepticism of Kant, to which good sense so easily does justice, is driven to the extreme and forced within its intrenchment by the distinction between spontaneous reason and reflective reason. Reflection is the theatre of the combats which reason engages in with itself, with doubt, sophism, and error. But above reflection is a sphere of light and peace, where reason perceives truth without returning on itself, for the sole reason that truth is truth, and because God has made the reason to perceive it, as he has made the eye to see and the ear to hear.

Analyze, in fact, with impartiality, the fact of spontaneous apperception, and you will be sure that it has nothing subjective in it except what it is impossible it should not have, to wit, the *me* which is mingled with the fact without constituting it. The *me* inevitably enters into all knowledge, since it is the subject of it. Reason directly perceives truth; but it is in some sort augmented, in consciousness, and then we have knowledge. Consciousness is there its witness, and not its judge; its only judge is reason, a faculty subjective and objective together, according to the language of Germany, which immediately attains absolute truth, almost without personal intervention on our part, although it might not enter into exercise if personality did not precede or were not added to it.[39]

Spontaneous apperception constitutes natural logic. Reflective conception is the foundation of logic properly so called. One is based upon itself, *verum index sui*; the other is based upon the impossibility of the reason, in spite of all its efforts, not betaking itself to truth and believing in it. The form of the first is an affirmation accompanied with an absolute security, and without the least suspicion of a possible negation; the form of the second is reflective affirmation, that is to say, the impossibility of denying and the necessity of affirming. The idea of negation governs ordinary logic, whose affirmations are only the laborious product of two negations. Natural logic proceeds by affirmations stamped with a simple faith, which instinct alone produces and sustains.

Now, will Kant reply that this reason, which is much purer than that which he has known and described, which is wholly pure, which is conceived as something disengaged from reflection, from volition, from every thing that constitutes personality, is nevertheless personal, since we have a consciousness of it, and since it is thus marked with subjectivity? To this argument we have nothing to respond, except that it is destroyed in the excess of its pretension. In fact, if, that reason may not be subjective, we must in no way participate in it, and must not have even a consciousness of its exercise, then there is no means of ever escaping this reproach of subjectivity, and the ideal of objectivity which Kant pursued is a chimerical, extravagant ideal, above, or rather beneath, all true intelligence, all reason worthy the name; for it is demanding that this intelligence and this reason should cease to have consciousness of themselves, whilst this is precisely what characterizes intelligence and reason.[40] Does Kant mean,

---

[39] On the just limits of the personality and the impersonality of reason, see the following lecture, near the close.
[40] We have everywhere maintained, that consciousness is the condition, or rather the necessary form of intelligence. Not to go beyond this volume, see farther on, lecture 5.

then, that reason, in order to possess a really objective power, cannot make its appearance in a particular subject, that it must be, for example, wholly outside of the subject which I am? Then it is nothing for me; a reason that is not mine, that, under the pretext of being universal, infinite, and absolute in its essence, does not fall under the perception of my consciousness, is for me as if it were not. To wish that reason should wholly cease to be subjective, is to demand something impossible to God himself. No, God himself can understand nothing except in knowing it, with his intelligence and with the consciousness of this intelligence. There is subjectivity, then, in divine knowledge itself; if this subjectivity involves skepticism, God is also condemned to skepticism, and he can no more escape from it than men; or indeed, if this is too ridiculous, if the knowledge which God has of the exercise of his own intelligence does not involve skepticism for him, neither do the knowledge which we have of the exercise of our intelligence, and the subjectivity attached to this knowledge, involve it for us.

In truth, when we see the father of German philosophy thus losing himself in the labyrinth of the problem of the subjectivity and the objectivity of first principles, we are tempted to pardon Reid for having disdained this problem, for limiting himself to repeating that the absolute truth of universal and necessary principles rests upon the veracity of our faculties, and that upon the veracity of our faculties we are compelled to accept their testimony. "To explain," says he, "why we are convinced by our senses, by consciousness, by our faculties, is an impossible thing; we say—this is so, it cannot be otherwise, and we can go no farther. Is not this the expression of an irresistible belief, of a belief which is the voice of nature, and against which we contend in vain? Do we wish to penetrate farther, to demand of our faculties, one by one, what are their titles to our confidence, and to refuse them confidence until they have produced their claims? Then, I fear that this extreme wisdom would conduct us to folly, and that, not having been willing to submit to the common lot of humanity, we should be deprived of the light of common sense."[41]

Let us support ourselves also by the following admirable passage of him who is, for so many reasons, the venerated master of the French philosophy of the nineteenth century. "Intellectual life," says M. Royer-Collard, "is an uninterrupted succession, not only of ideas, but of explicit or implicit beliefs. The beliefs of the mind are the powers of the soul and the motives of the will. That which determines us to belief we call evidence. Reason renders no account of evidence; to condemn reason to account for evidence, is to annihilate it, for it needs itself an evidence which is fitted for it. These are fundamental laws of belief which constitute intelligence, and as they flow from the same source they have the same authority; they judge by the same right; there is no appeal from the tribunal of one to that of another. He who revolts against a single one revolts against all, and abdicates his whole nature."[42]

Let us deduce the consequences of the facts of which we have just given an exposition.

1st. The argument of Kant, which is based upon the character of necessity in principles in order to weaken their objective authority, applies only to the form imposed by reflection on these principles, and does not reach their spontaneous application, wherein the character of necessity no longer appears.

2d. After all, to conclude with the human race from the necessity of believing in the truth of what we believe, is not to conclude badly; for it is reasoning from effect to cause, from the sign to the thing signified.

3d. Moreover, the value of principles is above all demonstration. Psychological analysis seizes, takes, as it were, by surprise, in the fact of intuition, an affirmation that is absolute, that is inaccessible to doubt; it establishes it; and this is equivalent

---

[41] 1st Series, vol. iv., lecture 22, p. 494.
[42] Œuvres de Reid, vol. iii., p. 450.

to demonstration. To demand any other demonstration than this, is to demand of reason an impossibility, since absolute principles, being necessary to all demonstration, could only be demonstrated by themselves.[43]

---

[43] We have not thought it best to make this lecture lengthy by an exposition and detailed refutation of the Critique of Pure Reason and its sad conclusion; the little that we say of it is sufficient for our purpose, which is much less historical than dogmatical. We refer the reader to a volume that we have devoted to the father of German philosophy, 1st Series, vol. v., in which we have again taken up and developed some of the arguments that are here used, in which we believe that we have irresistibly exposed the capital defect of the transcendental logic of Kant, and of the whole German school, that it leads to skepticism, inasmuch as it raises superhuman, chimerical, extravagant problems, and, when well understood, cannot solve them. See especially lectures 6 and 8.

LECTURE IV.

GOD THE PRINCIPLE OF PRINCIPLES.

Object of the lecture: What is the ultimate basis of absolute truth?—Four hypotheses: Absolute truth may reside either in us, in particular beings and the world, in itself, or in God. 1. We perceive absolute truth, we do not constitute it. 2. Particular beings participate in absolute truth, but do not explain it; refutation of Aristotle. 3. Truth does not exist in itself; defence of Plato. 4. Truth resides in God.—Plato; St. Augustine; Descartes; Malebranche; Fénelon; Bossuet; Leibnitz.—Truth the mediator between God and man.—Essential distinctions.

We have justified the principles that govern our intelligence; we have become confident that there is truth outside of us, that there are verities worthy of that name, which we can perceive, which we do not make, which are not solely conceptions of our mind, which would still exist although our mind should not perceive them. Now this other problem naturally presents itself: What, then, in themselves, are these universal and necessary truths? where do they reside? whence do they come? We do not raise this problem, and the problems that it embraces; the human mind itself proposes them, and it is fully satisfied only when it has resolved them, and when it has reached the extreme limit of knowledge that it is within its power to attain.

It is certain that the principles which, in all the orders of knowledge, discover to us absolute and necessary truths, constitute part of our reason, which surely makes its dwelling in us, and is intimately connected with personality in the depths of intellectual life. It follows that the truth, which reason reveals to us, falls thereby into close relation with the subject that perceives it, and seems only a conception of our mind. Nevertheless, as we have proved, we perceive truth, we are not the authors of it. If the person that I am, if the individual *me* does not, perhaps, explain the whole of reason, how could it explain truth, and absolute truth? Man, limited and passing away, perceives necessary, eternal, infinite truth; that is for him a privilege sufficiently high; but he is neither the principle that sustains truth, nor the principle that gives it being. Man may say, My reason; but give him credit for never having dared to say, My truth.

If absolute truths are beyond man who perceives them, once more, where are they, then? A peripatetic would respond—In nature. Is it, in fact, necessary to seek for them any other subject than the beings themselves which they govern? What are the laws of nature, except certain properties which our mind disengages from the beings and phenomena in which they are met, in order to consider them apart? Mathematical principles are nothing more. For example, the axiom thus expressed—The whole is greater than any of its parts, is true of any whole and part whatever. The principle of contradiction, considered in its logical title, as the condition of all our judgments, of all our reasonings, constitutes a part of the essence of all being, and no being can exist without containing it. The universal exists, says Aristotle, but it does not exist apart from particular beings.[44]

This theory which considers universals as having their basis in things, is a progress towards the pure conceptualism which we have in the beginning indicated and shunned. Aristotle is much more of a realist than Abelard and Kant. He is quite right in maintaining that universals are in particular things, for particular things could not be without universals; universals give to them their fixity, even for a day, and their unity. But from the fact that universals are in particular beings, is it necessary to conclude that they, wholly and exclusively, reside there, and that they have no other reality than that of the objects to which they are applied? It is the same with principles of which universals are the constitutive elements. It is, it is true, in the particular fact, of a particular cause producing a particular event, that is given us the universal principle of causality; but this principle is much more extensive

---

[44] See our work entitled, Metaphysics of Aristotle, 2d edition, passim. In Aristotle himself, see especially Metaphysics, book vii., chap. xii., and book xiii., chap. ix.

than the facts, for it is applied, not only to this fact, but to a thousand others. The particular fact contains the principle, but it does not wholly contain it, and, far from giving the basis of the principle, it is based upon it. As much may be said of other principles.

Perhaps it will be replied that, if a principle is certainly more extensive than such a fact, or such a being, it is not more extensive than all facts and all beings, and that nature, considered as a whole, can explain that which each particular being does not explain. But nature, in its totality, is still only a finite and contingent thing, whilst the principles to be explained have a necessary and infinite bearing. The idea of the infinite can come neither from any particular being, nor from the whole of beings. Entire nature will not furnish us the idea of perfection, for all the beings of nature are imperfect. Absolute principles govern, then, all facts and all beings, they do not spring from them.

Will it be necessary to come to the opinion, then, that absolute truths, being explicable neither by humanity nor by nature, subsist by themselves, and are to themselves their own foundation and their own subject?

But this opinion contains still more absurdities than the preceding; for, I ask, what are truths, absolute or contingent, that exist by themselves, out of things in which they are found, and out of the intelligence that conceives them? Truth is, then, only a realized abstraction. There are no quintessential metaphysics which can prevail against good sense; and if such is the Platonic theory of ideas, Aristotle is right in his opposition to it. But such a theory is only a chimera that Aristotle created for the pleasure of combating it.

Let us hasten to remove absolute truths from this ambiguous and equivocal state. And how? By applying to them a principle which should now be familiar to you. Yes, truth necessarily appeals to something beyond itself. As every phenomenon has its subject of inherence, as our faculties, our thoughts, our volitions, our sensations, exist only in a being which is ourselves, so truth supposes a being in which it resides, and absolute truths suppose a being absolute as themselves, wherein they have their final foundation. We come thus to something absolute, which is no longer suspended in the vagueness of abstraction, but is a being substantially existing. This being, absolute and necessary, since it is the subject of necessary and absolute truths, this being which is at the foundation of truth as its very essence, in a single word, is called *God*.[45]

This theory, which conducts from absolute truth to absolute being, is not new in the history of philosophy: it goes back to Plato.

Plato,[46] in searching for the principles of knowledge clearly saw, with Socrates his master, that the least definition, without which there can be no precise knowledge, supposes something universal and one, which does not come within the reach of the senses, which reason alone can discover; this something universal and one he called *Idea*.

Ideas, which possess universality and unity, do not come from material, changing, and mobile things, to which they are applied, and which render them intelligible. On the other hand, it is not the human mind that constitutes ideas; for man is not the measure of truth.

Plato calls Ideas veritable beings, τὰ οντως ὄντα, since they alone communicate to sensible things and to human cognitions their truth and their unity. But does it follow that Plato gives to Ideas a substantial existence, that he makes of them beings

---

[45] There are doubtless many other ways of arriving at God, as we shall successively see; but this is the way of metaphysics. We do not exclude any of the known and accredited proofs of the existence of God; but we begin with that which gives all the others. See further on, part ii., God, the Principle of Beauty, and part iii., God, the Principle of the Good, and the last lecture, which sums up the whole course.

[46] We have said a word on the Platonic theory of ideas, 1st Series, vol. iv., p. 461 and 522. See also, vol. ii. of the 2d Series, lecture 7, on Plato and Aristotle, especially 3d Series, vol. i., a few words on the Language of the Theory of Ideas, p. 121; our work on the Metaphysics of Aristotle, p. 48 and 149, and our translation of Plato, passim.

properly so called? It is important that no cloud should be left on this fundamental point of the Platonic theory.

At first, if any one should pretend that in Plato Ideas are beings subsisting by themselves, without interconnection and without relation to a common centre, numerous passages of the *Timaeus* might be objected to him,[47] in which Plato speaks of Ideas as forming in their whole an ideal unity, which is the reason of the unity of the visible world.[48]

Will it be said that this ideal world forms a distinct unity, a unity separate from God? But, in order to sustain this assertion, it is necessary to forget so many passages of the *Republic*, in which the relations of truth and science with the Good, that is to say, with God, are marked in brilliant characters.

Let not that magnificent comparison be forgotten, in which, after having said that the sun produces in the physical world light and life, Socrates adds: "So thou art able to say, intelligible beings not only hold from the *Good* that which renders them intelligible, but also their being and their essence."[49] So, intelligible beings, that is to say, Ideas, are not beings that exist by themselves.

Men go on repeating with assurance that the Good, in Plato, is only the idea of the good, and that an idea is not God. I reply, that the Good is in fact an idea, according to Plato, but that the idea here is not a pure conception of the mind, an object of thought, as the peripatetic school understood it; I add, that the Idea of the Good is in Plato the first of Ideas, and that, for this reason, while remaining for us an object of thought, it is confounded as to existence with God. If the Idea of the Good is not God himself, how will the following passage, also taken from the *Republic*, be explained? "At the extreme limits of the

---

[47] Aristotle first stated this; modern peripatetics have repeated it; and after them, all who have wished to decry the ancient philosophy, and philosophy in general, by giving the appearance of absurdity to its most illustrious representative.

[48] See particularly p. 121 of the Timaeus, vol. xii. of our translation.

[49] Republic, book vi., vol. x. of our translation, p. 57.

intellectual world is the Idea of the Good, which is perceived with difficulty, but, in fine, cannot be perceived without concluding that it is the source of all that is beautiful and good; that in the visible world it produces light, and the star whence the light directly comes, that in the invisible world it directly produces truth and intelligence."[50] Who can produce, on the one hand, the sun and light, on the other, truth and intelligence, except a real being?

But all doubt disappears before the following passages from the *Phædrus*, neglected, as it would seem designedly, by the detractors of Plato: "In this transition, (the soul) contemplates justice, contemplates wisdom, contemplates science, not that wherein enters change, nor that which shows itself different in the different objects which we are pleased to call beings, but science as it exists in that which is called being, *par excellence*...."[51]—"It belongs to the soul to conceive the universal, that is to say, that which, in the diversity of sensations, can be comprehended under a rational unity. This is the remembrance of what the soul has seen during its journey *in the train of Deity*, when, disdaining what we improperly call beings, it looked upwards to the only true being. So it is just that the thought of the philosopher should alone have wings; for its remembrance is always as much as possible with *the things which make God a true God, inasmuch as he is with them.*"[52]

So the objects of the philosopher's contemplation, that is to say, Ideas, are in God, and it is by these, by his essential union with these, that God is the true God, the God who, as Plato admirably says in the *Sophist*, participates in *august and holy intelligence*.[53]

It is therefore certain, that, in the true Platonic theory, Ideas are not beings in the vulgar sense of the word, beings which would be neither in the mind of man, nor in nature, nor in God,

---

[50] Republic, book vii., p. 20.
[51] Phædrus, vol. vi., p. 51.
[52] Phædrus, vol. vi., p. 55.
[53] Vol. xi., p. 261.

and would subsist only by themselves. No, Plato considers Ideas as being at once the principles of sensible things, of which they are the laws, and the principles also of human knowledge, which owes to them its light, its rule, and its end, and the essential attributes of God, that is to say, God himself.

Plato is truly the father of the doctrine which we have explained, and the great philosophers who have attached themselves to his school have always professed this same doctrine.

The founder of Christian metaphysics, St. Augustine, is a declared disciple of Plato: everywhere he speaks, like Plato, of the relation of human reason to the divine reason, and of truth to God. In the *City of God*, book x., chap. ii., and in chap. ix. of book vii. of the *Confessions*, he goes to the extent of comparing the Platonic doctrine with that of St. John.

He adopts, without reserve, the theory of Ideas. *Book of Eighty-three Questions*, question 46: "Ideas are the primordial forms, and, as it were, the immutable reasons of things; they are not created, they are eternal, and always the same: they are contained in the divine intelligence; and without being subject to birth and death, they are the types according to which is formed every thing that is born and dies."[54]

"What man, pious, and penetrated with true religion, would dare to deny that all things that exist, that is to say, all things that, each of its kind, possess a determinate nature, have been created by God? This point being once conceded, can it be said that God has created things without reason? If it is impossible to say or think this, it follows that all things have been created with reason. But the reason of the existence of a man cannot be the same as the reason of the existence of a horse; that is absurd; each thing has therefore been created by virtue of a reason that is peculiar to it. Now, where can these reasons be, except in the mind of the Creator? For he saw nothing out of himself, which he could use as

---

[54] Edit. Bened., vol. vi., p. 17: Idex sunt formæ quædam principales et rationes rerum stabiles atque incommutabiles, quæ ipsæ formatæ non sunt ac per hoc æternæ ac semper eodem modo sese habentes, quæ in divina intelligentia continentur....

a model for creating what he created: such an opinion would be sacrilege.[55]

"If the reasons of things to be created and things created are contained in the divine intelligence, and if there is nothing in the divine intelligence but the eternal and immutable, the reasons of things which Plato calls Ideas, are the eternal and immutable truths, by the participation in which every thing that is is such as it is."[56]

St. Thomas himself, who scarcely knew Plato, and who was often enough held by Aristotle in a kind of empiricism, carried away by Christianity and St. Augustine, let the sentiment escape him, "that our natural reason is a sort of participation in the divine reason, that to this we owe our knowledge and our judgments, that this is the reason why it is said, that we see every thing in God."[57] There are in St. Thomas many other similar passages, of perhaps an expressive Platonism, which is not the Platonism of Plato, but of the Alexandrians.

The Cartesian philosophy, in spite of its profound originality, and its wholly French character, is full of the Platonic spirit. Descartes has no thought of Plato, whom apparently he has never read; in nothing does he imitate or resemble him: nevertheless, from the first, he is met in the same regions with Plato, whither he goes by a different route.

The notion of the infinite and the perfect is for Descartes what the universal, the Idea, is for Plato. No sooner has Descartes found by consciousness that he thinks, than he concludes from

---

[55] Edit. Bened., vol. vi., p. 18. Singula igitur propriis creata sunt rationibus. Has autem rationes ubi arbitrandum est esse nisi in mente Creatoris? non enim extra se quidquam intuebatur, ut secundum id constitueret quod constituebat: nam hoc opinari sacrilegum est.

[56] Ibid. See also, book of the Confessions, book ii. of the Free Will, book xii. of the Trinity, book vii. of the City of God, &c.

[57] Summa totius theologiæ. Primæ partis quæst. xii. art. II. Ad tertium dicendum, quod omnia dicimus in Deo videre, et secundum ipsum de omnibus judicare, in quantum per participationem sui luminis omnia cognoscimus et dijudicamus. Nam et ipsum lumen naturale rationis participatio quædam est divini luminis.

this that he exists, then, in course, by consciousness still, he recognizes himself as imperfect, full of defects, limitations, miseries, and, at the same time, conceives something infinite and perfect. He possesses the idea of the infinite and the perfect; but this idea is not his own work, for he is imperfect; it must then have been put into him by another being endowed with perfection, whom he conceives, whom he does not possess:—that being is God. Such is the process by which Descartes, setting out from his own thought, and his own being, elevated himself to God. This process, so simple, which he so simply exposes in the *Discours de la Méthode*, he will put successively, in the *Méditations*, in the *Réponses aux Objections*, in the *Principes*, under the most diverse forms, he will accommodate it, if it is necessary, to the language of the schools, in order that it may penetrate into them. After all, this process is compelled to conclude, from the idea of the infinite and the perfect, in the existence of a cause of this idea, adequate, at least, to the idea itself, that is to say, infinite and perfect. One sees that the first difference between Plato and Descartes is, that the ideas which in Plato are at once conceptions of our mind, and the principles of things, are for Descartes, as well as for all modern philosophy, only our conceptions, amongst which that of the infinite and perfect occupies the first place; the second difference is, that Plato goes from ideas to God by the principle of substances, if we may be allowed to use this technical language of modern philosophy; whilst Descartes employs rather the principle of causality, and concludes—well understood without syllogism—from the idea of the infinite and the perfect in a cause also perfect and infinite.[58] But under these differences, and in spite of many more, is a common basis, a genius the same, which at first elevates us above the senses, and, by the intermediary of marvellous ideas that are

---

[58] On the doctrine of Descartes, and on the proof of the existence of God and the true process that he employs, see 1st Series, vol. iv., lecture 12, p. 64, lecture 22, p. 509-518; vol. v., lecture 6, p. 205; 2d Series, vol. xi., lecture 11; especially the three articles, already cited, of the Journal des Savants for the year 1850.

incontestably in us, bears us towards him who alone can be their substance, who is the infinite and perfect author of our idea of infinity and perfection. For this reason, Descartes belongs to the family of Plato and Socrates.

The idea of the perfect and the finite being once introduced into the philosophy of the seventeenth century, it becomes there for the successors of Descartes what the theory of ideas became for the successors of Plato.

Among the French writers, Malebranche, perhaps, reminds us with the least disadvantage, although very imperfectly still, of the manner of Plato: he sometimes expresses its elevation and grace; but he is far from possessing the Socratic good sense, and, it must be confessed, no one has clouded more the theory of ideas by exaggerations of every kind which he has mingled with them.[59] Instead of establishing that there is in the human reason, wholly personal as it is by its intimate relation with our other faculties, something also which is not personal, something universal which permits it to elevate itself to universal truths, Malebranche does not hesitate to absolutely confound the reason that is in us with the divine reason itself. Moreover, according to Malebranche, we do not directly know particular things, sensible objects; we know them only by ideas; it is the intelligible extension and not the material extension that we immediately perceive; in vision the proper object of the mind is the universal, the idea; and as the idea is in God, it is in God that we see all things. We can understand how well-formed minds must have been shocked by such a theory; but it is not just to confound Plato with his brilliant and unfaithful disciple. In Plato, sensibility directly attains sensible things; it makes them known to us as they are,

---

[59] See on Malebranche, 2d Series, lecture 2, and 3d Series, vol. iii., Modern Philosophy, as well as the Fragments of Cartesian Philosophy; preface of the 1st edition of our Pascal:—"On this basis, so pure, Malebranche is not steady; is excessive and rash, I know; narrow and extreme, I do not fear to say; but always sublime, expressing only one side of Plato, but expressing it in a wholly Christian spirit and in angelic language. Malebranche is a Descartes who strays, having found divine wings, and lost all connection with the earth."

that is to say, as very imperfect and undergoing perpetual change, which renders the knowledge that we have of them almost unworthy of the name of knowledge. It is reason, different in us from sensibility, which, above sensible objects, discovers to us the universal, the idea, and gives a knowledge solid and durable. Having once attained ideas, we have reached God himself, in whom they have their foundation, who finishes and consummates true knowledge. But we have no need of God, nor of ideas, in order to perceive sensible objects, which are defective and changing; for this our senses are sufficient. Reason is distinct from the senses; it transcends the imperfect knowledge of what they are capable; it attains the universal, because it possesses something universal itself; it participates in the divine reason, but it is not the divine reason; it is enlightened by it, it comes from it,—it is not it.

Fenelon is inspired at once by Malebranche and Descartes in the treatise, *de l'Existence de Dieu*. The second part is entirely Cartesian in method, in the order and sequence of the proofs. Nevertheless, Malebranche also appears there, especially in the fourth chapter, on the nature of ideas, and he predominates in all the metaphysical portions of the first part. After the explanations which we have given, it will not be difficult for you to discern what is true and what is at times excessive in the passages which follow:[60]

Part i., chap. lii. "Oh! how great is the mind of man! It bears in itself what astonishes itself and infinitely surpasses itself. Its ideas are universal, eternal, and immutable.... The idea of the infinite is in me as well as that of lines, numbers, and circles....— Chap. liv. Besides this idea of the infinite, I have also universal and immutable notions, which are the rule of all my judgments. I can judge of nothing except by consulting them, and it is not in my power to judge against what they represent to me. My thoughts, far from being able to correct this rule, are themselves

---

[60] We use the only good edition of the treatise on the Existence of God, that which the Abbé Gosselin has given in the collection of the Works of Fenelon. Versailles, 1820. See vol. i., p. 80.

corrected in spite of me by this superior rule, and they are irresistibly adjusted to its decision. Whatever effort of mind I may make, I can never succeed in doubting that two and two are four; that the whole is not greater than any of its parts; that the centre of a perfect circle is not equidistant from all points of the circumference. I am not at liberty to deny these propositions; and if I deny these truths, or others similar to them, I have in me something that is above me, that forces me to the conclusion. This fixed and immutable rule is so internal and so intimate that I am inclined to take it for myself; but it is above me since it corrects me, redresses me, and puts me in defiance against myself, and reminds me of my impotence. It is something that suddenly inspires me, provided I listen to it, and I am never deceived except in not listening to it.... This internal rule is what I call my reason....—Chap. lv. In truth my reason is in me; for I must continually enter into myself in order to find it. But the higher reason which corrects me when necessary, which I consult, exists not by me, and makes no part of me. This rule is perfect and immutable; I am changing and imperfect. When I am deceived, it does not lose its integrity. When I am undeceived, it is not this that returns to its end: it is this which, without ever having deviated, has the authority over me to remind me of my error, and to make me return. It is a master within, which makes me keep silent, which makes me speak, which makes me believe, which makes me doubt, which makes me acknowledge my errors or confirm my judgments. Listening to it, I am instructed; listening to myself, I err. This master is everywhere, and its voice makes itself heard, from end to end of the universe, in all men as well as in me....—Chap. lvi.... That which appears the most in us and seems to be the foundation of ourselves, I mean our reason, is that which is least of all our own, which we are constrained to believe to be especially borrowed. We receive without cessation, and at all moments, a reason superior to us, as we breathe without cessation the air, which is a foreign body....—Chap. lvii. The internal and universal master always and everywhere speaks the same truths. We are not this master. It is true that we often speak without it, and more loftily than it. But we are then deceived, we are stammering, we do not understand ourselves. We even fear to see that we are deceived, and we close the ear through fear of being humiliated by its corrections. Without doubt, man, who fears being corrected by this incorruptible reason, who always wanders in not following it, is not that perfect, universal, immutable reason which corrects him in spite of himself. In all things we find, as it were, two principles within us. One gives, the other receives; one wants, the other supplies; one is deceived, the other corrects; one goes wrong by its own inclination, the other rectifies it.... Each one feels within himself a limited and subaltern reason, which wanders when it escapes a complete subordination, which is corrected only by returning to the yoke of another superior, universal, and immutable power. So every thing in us bears the mark of a subaltern, limited, partial, borrowed reason, which needs another to correct it at every moment. All men are rational, because they possess the same reason which is communicated to them in different degrees. There is a certain number of wise men; but the wisdom which they receive, as it were, from the fountain-head, which makes them what they are, is one and the same....—Chap. lviii. Where is this wisdom? Where is this reason, which is both common and superior to all the limited and imperfect reasons of the human race? Where, then, is this oracle which is never silent, against which the vain prejudices of peoples are always impotent? Where is this reason which we ever need to consult, which comes to us to inspire us with the desire of listening to its voice? Where is this light *that lighteneth every man that cometh into the world*.... The substance of the human eye is not light; on the contrary, the eye borrows at each moment the light of the sun's rays. So my mind is not the primitive reason, the universal and immutable truth, it is only the medium that conducts this original light, that is illuminated by it....—Chap. lx. I find two reasons in myself,—one is myself, the other is above me. That which is in me is very imperfect, faulty, uncertain, preoccupied, precipitate, subject to aberration, changing, conceited, ignorant, and limited; in fine, it possesses nothing but what it borrows. The other is common to all men, and is superior to all; it is perfect, eternal, immutable, always ready to communicate itself in all places, and to rectify all minds that are deceived, in fine, incapable of ever being exhausted or divided, although it gives itself to those who desire it. Where is this perfect reason, that is so near me and so different from me? Where is it? It must be something real.... Where is this supreme reason? Is it not God that I am seeking?"

Part ii., chap. i., sect. 28.[61] "I have in me the idea of the infinite and of infinite perfection.... Give me a finite thing as great as you please—let it quite transcend the reach of my senses, so that it becomes, as it were, infinite to my imagination; it always remains finite in my mind; I conceive a limit to it, even when I cannot imagine it. I am not able to mark the limit; but I know that it exists; and far from confounding it with the infinite, I conceive it as infinitely distant from the idea that I have of the veritable infinite. If one speaks to me of the indefinite as a mean between the two extremes of the infinite and the limited, I reply, that it signifies nothing, that, at least, it only signifies something truly finite, whose boundaries escape the imagination without escaping the mind.... Sect. 29. Where have I obtained this idea, which is so much above me, which infinitely surpasses me, which astonishes me, which makes me disappear in my own eyes, which renders the infinite present to me? Whence does it come? Where have I obtained it?... Once more, whence comes this marvellous representation of the infinite, which pertains to the infinite itself, which resembles nothing finite? It is in me, it is more than myself; it seems to me every thing, and myself nothing. I can neither efface, obscure, diminish, nor contradict it. It is in me; I have not put it there, I have found it there; and I have found it there only because it was already there before I sought it. It remains there invariable, even when I do not think of it, when I think of something else. I find it whenever I seek it, and it often presents itself when I am not seeking it. It does not depend upon me; I

---

[61] Edit. de Versailles, p. 145.

depend upon it.... Moreover, who has made this infinite representation of the infinite, so as to give it to me? Has it made itself? Has the infinite image[62] of the infinite had no original, according to which it has been made, no real cause that has produced it? Where are we in relation to it? And what a mass of extravagances! It is, therefore, absolutely necessary to conclude that it is the infinitely perfect being that renders himself immediately present to me, when I conceive him, and that he himself is the idea which I have of him...."

Chap. iv., sect. 49. "... My ideas are myself; for they are my reason.... My ideas, and the basis of myself, or of my mind, appear but the same thing. On the other hand, my mind is changing, uncertain, ignorant, subject to error, precipitate in its judgments, accustomed to believe what it does not clearly understand, and to judge without having sufficiently consulted its ideas, which are by themselves certain and immutable. My ideas, then, are not myself, and I am not my ideas. What shall I believe, then, they can be?... What then! are my ideas God? They are superior to my mind, since they rectify and correct it; they have the character of the Divinity, for they are universal and immutable like God; they really subsist, according to a principle that we have already established: nothing exists so really as that which is universal and immutable. If that which is changing, transitory, and derived, truly exists, much more does that which cannot change, and is necessary. It is then necessary to find in nature something existing and real, that is, my ideas, something that is within me, and is not myself, that is superior to me, that is in me even when I am not thinking of it, with which I believe myself to be alone, as though I were only with myself, in fine, that is more present to me, and more intimate than my own foundation. I know not what this

---

[62] It is not necessary to remark how incorrect are the expressions, representation of the infinite, image of the infinite, especially infinite image of the infinite. We cannot represent to ourselves, we cannot imagine to ourselves the infinite. We conceive the infinite; the infinite is not an object of the imagination, but of the understanding, of reason. See 1st Series, vol. v., lecture 6, p. 223, 224.

something, so admirable, so familiar, so unknown, can be, except God."

Let us now hear the most solid, the most authoritative of the Christian doctors of the seventeenth century—let us hear Bossuet in his *Logic*, and in the *Treatise on the Knowledge of God and Self*.[63]

Bossuet may be said to have had three masters in philosophy—St. Augustine, St. Thomas, and Descartes. He had been taught at the college of Navarre the doctrine of St. Thomas, that is to say, a modified peripateticism; at the same time he was nourished by the reading of St. Augustine, and out of the schools he found spread abroad the philosophy of Descartes. He adopted it, and had no difficulty in reconciling it with that of St. Augustine, while, upon more than one point, it corroborated the doctrine of St. Thomas. Bossuet invented nothing in philosophy; he received every thing, but every thing united and purified, thanks to that supreme good sense which in him is a quality predominating over force, grandeur, and eloquence.[64] In the

---

[63] By a trifling anachronism, for which we shall be pardoned, we have here joined to the Traité de la Connaissance de Dieu et de Soi-même, so long known, the Logique, which was only published in 1828.

[64] 4th Series, vol. i., preface of the 1st edition of Pascal: "Bossuet, with more moderation, and supported by a good sense which nothing can shake, is, in his way, a disciple of the same doctrine, only the extremes of which according to his custom, he shunned. This great mind, which may have superiors in invention, but has no equal for force in common sense, was very careful not to place revelation and philosophy in opposition to each other: he found it the safer and truer way to give to each its due, to borrow from philosophy whatever natural light it can give, in order to increase it in turn with the supernatural light, of which the Church has been made the depository. It is in this sovereign good sense, capable of comprehending every thing, and uniting every thing, that resides the supreme originality of Bossuet. He shunned particular opinions as small minds seek them for the triumph of self-love. He did not think of himself; he only searched for truth, and wherever he found it he listened to it, well assured that if the connection between truths of different orders sometimes escapes us, it is no reason for closing the eyes to any truth. If

passages which I am about to exhibit to you, which I hope you will impress upon your memories, you will not find the grace of Malebranche, the exhaustless abundance of Fenelon; you will find what is better than either, to wit, clearness and precision—all the rest in him is in some sort an addition to these.

Fenelon disengages badly enough the process which conducts from ideas, from universal and necessary truths, to God. Bossuet renders to himself a strict account of this process, and marks it with force; it is the principle that we have invoked, that which concludes from attributes in a subject, from qualities in a being, from laws in a legislator, from eternal verities in an eternal mind that comprehends them and eternally possesses them. Bossuet cites St. Augustine, cites Plato himself, interprets him and defends him in advance against those who would make Platonic ideas beings subsisting by themselves, whilst they really exist only in the mind of God.

Logic, book i., chap. xxxvi. "When I consider a rectilineal triangle as a figure bounded by three straight lines, and having three angles equal to two right angles, neither more nor less; and when I pass from this to an equilateral triangle with its three sides and its three angles equal, whence it follows, that I consider each angle of this triangle as less than a right angle; and when I come again to consider a right-angled triangle, and what I clearly see in this idea, in connection with the preceding ideas, that the two angles of this triangle are necessarily acute, and that these two acute angles are exactly equal to one right angle, neither more nor less—I see nothing contingent and mutable, and consequently, the ideas that represent to me these truths are eternal. Were there not in nature a single equilateral or right-angled triangle, or any triangle whatever, every thing that I have just considered would

---

we wished to give a scholastic name to Bossuet, according to the custom of the Middle Age, we would have to call him the infallible doctor. He is not only one of the highest, he is also one of the best and solidest intelligences that ever existed; and this great conciliator has easily reconciled religion and philosophy, St. Augustine and Descartes, tradition and reason."

remain always true and indubitable. In fact, I am not sure of having ever seen an equilateral or rectilineal triangle. Neither the rule nor the dividers could assure me that any human hand, however skilful, could ever make a line exactly straight, or sides and angles perfectly equal to each other. In strictness, we should only need a microscope, in order, not to understand, but to see at a glance, that the lines which we trace deviate from straightness, and differ in length. We have never seen, then, any but imperfect images of equilateral, rectilineal, or isosceles triangles, since they neither exist in nature, nor can be constructed by art. Nevertheless, what we see of the nature and the properties of a triangle, independently of every existing triangle, is certain and indubitable. Place an understanding in any given time, or at any point in eternity, thus to speak, and it will see these truths equally manifest; they are, therefore, eternal. Since the understanding does not give being to truth, but is only employed in perceiving truth, it follows, that were every created understanding destroyed, these truths would immutably subsist...."

Chap. xxxvii. "Since there is nothing eternal, immutable, independent, but God alone, we must conclude that these truths do not subsist in themselves, but in God alone, and in his eternal ideas, which are nothing else than himself.

"There are those who, in order to verify these eternal truths which we have proposed, and others of the same nature, have figured to themselves eternal essences aside from deity—a pure illusion, which comes from not understanding that in God, as in the source of being, and in his understanding, where resides the art of making and ordering all things, are found primitive ideas, or as St. Augustine says, the eternally subsisting reasons of things. Thus, in the thought of the architect is the primitive idea of a house which he perceives in himself; this intellectual house would not be destroyed by any ruin of houses built according to this interior model; and if the architect were eternal, the idea and the reason of the house would also be eternal. But, without recurring to the mortal architect, there is an immortal architect, or rather a primitive eternally subsisting art in the immutable thought of

God, where all order, all measure, all rule, all proportion, all reason, in a word, all truth are found in their origin.

"These eternal verities which our ideas represent, are the true object of science; and this is the reason why Plato, in order to render us truly wise, continually reminds us of these ideas, wherein is seen, not what is formed, but what is, not what is begotten and is corrupt, what appears and vanishes, what is made and defective, but what eternally subsists. It is this intellectual world which that divine philosopher has put in the mind of God before the world was constructed, which is the immutable model of that great work. These are the simple, eternal, immutable, unbegotten, incorruptible ideas to which he refers us, in order to understand truth. This is what has made him say that our ideas, images of the divine ideas, were also immediately derived from the divine ideas, and did not come by the senses, which serve very well, said he, to awaken them, but not to form them in our mind. For if, without having ever seen any thing eternal, we have so clear an idea of eternity, that is to say, of being that is always the same; if, without having perceived a perfect triangle, we understand it distinctly, and demonstrate so many incontestable truths concerning it, it is a mark that these ideas do not come from our senses."

Treatise on the Knowledge of God and Self.[65] Chap. iv., sect. 5. *Intelligence has for its object eternal truths, which are nothing else than God himself, in whom they are always subsisting and perfectly understood.*

"... We have already remarked that the understanding has eternal verities for its object. The standards by which we measure all things are eternal and invariable. We know clearly that every thing in the universe is made according to proportion, from the greatest to the least, from the strongest to the weakest, and we know it well enough to understand that these proportions are related to the principles of eternal truth. All that is demonstrated in mathematics, and in any other science whatever, is eternal and

---

[65] The best, or, rather, only good edition is that which was published from an authentic copy, in 1846, by Lecoffre.

immutable, since the effect of the demonstration is to show that the thing cannot be otherwise than as it is demonstrated to be. So, in order to understand the nature and the properties of things which I know, for example, a triangle, a square, a circle, or the relations of these figures, and all other figures, to each other, it is not necessary that I should find such in nature, and I may be sure that I have never traced, never seen, any that are perfect. Neither is it necessary that I should think that there is motion in the world in order to understand the nature of motion itself, or that of the lines which every motion describes, and the hidden proportions according to which it is developed. When the idea of these things is once awakened in my mind, I know that, whether they have an actual existence or not, so they must be, that it is impossible for them to be of another nature, or to be made in a different way. To come to something that concerns us more nearly, I mean by these principles of eternal truth, that they do not depend on human existence, that, so far as he is capable of reasoning, it is the essential duty of man to live according to reason, and to search for his maker, through fear of lacking the recognition of his maker, if in fault of searching for him, he should be ignorant of him. All these truths, and all those which I deduce from them by sure reasoning, subsist independently of all time. In whatever time I place a human understanding, it will know them, but in knowing them it will find them truths, it will not make them such, for our cognitions do not make their objects, but suppose them. So these truths subsist before all time, before the existence of a human understanding: and were every thing that is made according to the laws of proportion, that is to say, every thing that I see in nature, destroyed except myself, these laws would be preserved in my thought, and I should clearly see that they would always be good and always true, were I also destroyed with the rest.

"If I seek how, where, and in what subject they subsist eternal and immutable, as they are, I am obliged to avow the existence of a being in whom truth is eternally subsisting, in whom it is always understood; and this being must be truth itself, and must be all truth, and from him it is that truth is derived in every thing that exists and has understanding out of him.

"It is, then, in him, in a certain manner, who is incomprehensible[66] to me, it is in him, I say, that I see these eternal truths; and to see them is to turn to him who is immutably all truth, and to receive his light.

"This eternal object is God eternally subsisting, eternally true, eternally truth itself.... It is in this eternal that these eternal truths subsist. It is also by this that I see them. All other men see them as well as myself, and we see them always the same, and as having existed before us. For we know that we have commenced, and we know that these truths have always been. Thus we see them in a light superior to ourselves, and it is in this superior light that we see whether we act well or ill, that is to say, whether we act according to these constitutive principles of our being or not. In that, then, we see, with all other truths, the invariable rules of our conduct, and we see that there are things in regard to which duty is indispensable, and that in things which are naturally indifferent, the true duty is to accommodate ourselves to the greatest good of society. A well-disposed man conforms to the civil laws, as he conforms to custom. But he listens to an inviolable law in himself, which says to him that he must do wrong to no one, that it is better to be injured than to injure.... The man who sees these truths, by these truths judges himself, and condemns himself when he errs. Or, rather, these truths judge him, since they do not accommodate themselves to human judgments, but human judgments are accommodated to them. And the man judges rightly when, feeling these judgments to be variable in their nature, he gives them for a rule these eternal verities.

"These eternal verities which every understanding always perceives the same, by which every understanding is governed, are something of God, or rather, are God himself....

---

[66] These words, d'une certaine manière qui m'est incompréhensible, c'est en lui, dis-je, are not in the first edition of 1722.

"Truth must somewhere be very perfectly understood, and man is to himself an indubitable proof of this. For, whether he considers himself or extends his vision to the beings that surround him, he sees every thing subjected to certain laws, and to immutable rules of truth. He sees that he understands these laws, at least in part,—he who has neither made himself, nor any part of the universe, however small, and he sees that nothing could have been made had not these laws been elsewhere perfectly understood; and he sees that it is necessary to recognize an eternal wisdom wherein all law, all order, all proportion, have their primitive reason. For it is absurd to suppose that there is so much sequence in truths, so much proportion in things, so much economy in their arrangement, that is to say, in the world, and that this sequence, this proportion, this economy, should nowhere be understood:—and man, who has made nothing, veritably knowing these things, although not fully knowing them, must judge that there is some one who knows them in their perfection, and that this is he who has made all things...."

Sect. 6 is wholly Cartesian. Bossuet there demonstrates that the soul knows by the imperfection of its own intelligence that there is elsewhere a perfect intelligence.

In sect. 9, Bossuet elucidates anew the relation of truth to God.

"Whence comes to my intelligence this impression, so pure, of truth? Whence come to it those immutable rules that govern reasoning, that form manners, by which it discovers the secret proportions of figures and of movements? Whence come to it, in a word, those eternal truths which I have considered so much? Do the triangles, the squares, the circles, that I rudely trace on paper, impress upon my mind their proportions and their relations? Or are there others whose perfect trueness produces this effect? Where have I seen these circles and these triangles so true,—I who am not sure of ever having seen a perfectly regular figure, and, nevertheless, understand this regularity so perfectly? Are there somewhere, either in the world or out of the world, triangles or circles existing with this perfect regularity, whereby it could be impressed upon my mind? And do these rules of reasoning and conduct also exist in some place, whence they communicate to me their immutable truth? Or, indeed, is it not rather he who has everywhere extended measure, proportion, truth itself, that impresses on my mind the certain idea of them?... It is, then, necessary to understand that the soul, made in the image of God, capable of understanding truth, which is God himself, actually turns towards its original, that is to say, towards God, where the truth appears to it as soon as God wills to make the truth appear to it.... It is an astonishing thing that man understands so many truths, without understanding at the same time that all truth comes from God, that it is in God, that it is God himself.... It is certain that God is the primitive reason of all that exists and has understanding in the universe; that he is the true original, and that every thing is true by relation to his eternal idea, that seeking truth is seeking him, and that finding truth is finding him...."

Chap. v., sect. 14. "The senses do not convey to the soul knowledge of truth. They excite it, awaken it, and apprize it of certain effects: it is solicited to search for causes, but it discovers them, it sees their connections, the principles which put them in motion, only in a superior light that comes from God, or is God himself. God is, then, truth, which is always the same to all minds, and the true source of intelligence. For this reason intelligence beholds the light, breathes, and lives."

At the close of the seventeenth century, Leibnitz comes to crown these great testimonies, and to complete their unanimity.

Here is a passage from an important treatise entitled, *Meditationes de Cognitione, Veritate et Idæis*, in which Leibnitz declares that primary notions are the attributes of God. "I know not," he says, "whether man can perfectly account to himself for his ideas, except by ascending to primary ideas for which he can no more account, that is to say, to the absolute attributes of God."[67]

---

[67] Leibnitzii Opera, edit. Deutens, vol. ii., p. 17.

The same doctrine is in the *Principia Philosophiæ seu Theses in Gratiam Principis Eugenii.* "The intelligence of God is the region of eternal truths, and the ideas that depend upon them."[68]

Theodicea, part ii., sect. 189.[69] "It must not be said with the Scotists that eternal truths would subsist if there were no understanding, not even that of God. For, in my opinion, it is the divine understanding that makes the reality of eternal truths."

Nouveaux Essais sur l'Entendement Humain, book ii., chap. xvii. "The idea of the absolute is in us internally like that of being. *These absolutes are nothing else than the attributes of God*, and it may be said they are just as much the source of ideas as God is in himself the principle of beings."

Ibid., book iv., chap. xi. "But it will be demanded where those ideas would be if no mind existed, and what would then become of the real foundation of this certainty of eternal truths? That brings us in fine to the last foundation of truths, to wit, to that supreme and universal mind which cannot be destitute of existence, whose understanding, to speak truly, is the region of eternal truths, as St. Augustine saw and clearly enough expressed it. And that it may not be thought necessary to recur to it, we must consider that these necessary truths contain the determinating reason and the regulative principle of existences themselves, and, in a word, the laws of the universe. So these unnecessary truths, being anterior to the existences of contingent beings, must have their foundation in the existence of a necessary substance. It is there that I find the original of truths which are stamped upon our souls, not in the form of propositions, but as sources, the application and occasions of which will produce actual enunciations."

So, from Plato to Leibnitz, the greatest metaphysicians have thought that absolute truth is an attribute of absolute being. Truth is incomprehensible without God, as God is

---

[68] Ibid., p. 24.

[69] 1st edition, Amsterdam, 1710, p. 354, edit. of M. de Jaucourt, Amsterdam, 1747, vol. ii., p. 93.

incomprehensible without truth. Truth is placed between human intelligence and the supreme intelligence, as a kind of mediator. In the lowest degree, as well as at the height of being, God is everywhere met, for truth is everywhere. Study nature, elevate yourselves to the laws that govern it and make of it as it were a living truth:—the more profoundly you understand its laws, the nearer you approach to God. Study, above all, humanity; humanity is much greater than nature, for it comes from God as well as nature, and knows him, while nature is ignorant of him. Especially seek and love truth, and refer it to the immortal being who is its source. The more you know of the truth, the more you know of God. The sciences, so far from turning us away from religion, conduct us to it. Physics, with their laws, mathematics, with their sublime ideas, especially philosophy, which cannot take a single step without encountering universal and necessary principles, are so many stages on the way to Deity, and, thus to speak, so many temples in which homage is perpetually paid to him.

But in the midst of these high considerations, let us carefully guard ourselves against two opposite errors, from which men of fine genius have not always known how to preserve themselves, —against the error of making the reason of man purely individual, and against the error of confounding it with truth and the divine reason.[70] If the reason of man is purely individual

---

[70] We have many times designated these two rocks, for example, 2d Series, vol. i., lecture 5, p. 92:—"One cannot help smiling when, in our times, he hears individual reason spoken against. In truth it is a great waste of declamation, for the reason is not individual; if it were, we should govern it as we govern our resolutions and our volitions, we could at any moment change its acts, that is to say, our conceptions. If these conceptions were merely individual, we should not think of imposing them upon another individual, for to impose our own individual and personal conceptions on another individual, on another person, would be the most extravagant despotism.... We call those mad who do not admit the relations of numbers, the difference between the beautiful and the ugly, the just and the unjust. Why? Because we know that it is not the individual that constitutes these conceptions, or, in other terms, we know that the reason has something universal and absolute, that upon this ground it obligates all individuals; and an individual, at the same time that he knows that

because it is in the individual, it can comprehend nothing that is not individual, nothing that transcends the limits wherein it is confined. Not only is it unable to elevate itself to any universal and necessary truth, not only is it unable to have any idea of it, even any suspicion of it, as one blind from his birth can have no suspicion that a sun exists; but there is no power, not even that of God, that by any means could make penetrate the reason of man any truth of that order absolutely repugnant to its nature; since, for this end, it would not be sufficient for God to lighten our mind; it would be necessary to change it, to add to it another faculty. Neither, on the other hand, must we, with Malebranche, make the reason of man to such a degree impersonal that it takes the place of truth which is its object, and of God who is its principle. It is truth that to us is absolutely impersonal, and not reason. Reason is in man, yet it comes from God. Hence it is individual and finite, whilst its root is in the infinite; it is personal by its relation to the person in which it resides, and must also possess I know not what character of universality, of necessity even, in order to be capable of conceiving universal and necessary truths; hence it seems, by turns, according to the point of view from which it is regarded, pitiable and sublime. Truth is in some sort lent to human reason, but it belongs to a totally different reason, to wit, that supreme, eternal, uncreated reason, which is God himself. The truth in us is nothing else than our object; in God, it is one of his attributes, as well as justice, holiness, mercy, as we shall subsequently see. God exists; and so far as he exists, he thinks, and his thoughts are truths, eternal as himself, which are reflected in the laws of the universe, which the reason of man has received the power to attain. Truth is the offspring, the utterance, I was about to say, the eternal word of God, if it is permitted philosophy to borrow this divine language from that holy religion

---

he himself is obligated by it, knows that all others are obligated by it on the same ground."—Ibid., p. 93: "Truth misconceived is thereby neither altered nor destroyed; it subsists independently of the reason that perceives it or perceives it ill. Truth in itself is independent of our reason. Its true subject is the universal and absolute reason."

which teaches us to worship God in spirit and in truth. Of old, the theory of Ideas, which manifest God to men, and remind them of him, had given to Plato the surname of the precursor; on account of that theory of Ideas he was dear to St. Augustine, and is invoked by Bossuet. It is by this same theory, wisely interpreted, and purified by the light of our age, that the new philosophy is attached to the tradition of great philosophies, and to that of Christianity.

The last problem that the science of the true presented is resolved:—we are in possession of the basis of absolute truths. God is substance, reason, supreme cause, and the unity of all these truths; God, and God alone, is to us the boundary beyond which we have nothing more to seek.

LECTURE V.

ON MYSTICISM.

Distinction between the philosophy that we profess and mysticism. Mysticism consists in pretending to know God without an intermediary.—Two sorts of mysticism.—Mysticism of sentiment. Theory of sensibility. Two sensibilities—the one external, the other internal, and corresponding to the soul as external sensibility corresponds to nature.—Legitimate part of sentiment.—Its aberrations.—Philosophical mysticism. Plotinus: God, or absolute unity, perceived without an intermediary by pure thought.—Ecstasy.—Mixture of superstition and abstraction in mysticism.—Conclusion of the first part of the course.

Whether we turn our attention to the forces and the laws that animate and govern matter without belonging to it, or as the order of our labors calls us to do, reflect upon the universal and necessary truths which our mind discovers but does not constitute, the least systematic use of reason makes us naturally conclude from the forces and laws of the universe that there is a first intelligent mover, and from necessary truths that there is a necessary being who alone is their substance. We do not perceive God, but we conceive him, upon the faith of this admirable world exposed to our view, and upon that of this other world, more admirable still, which we bear in ourselves. By this double road we succeed in going to God. This natural course is that of all men: it must be sufficient for a sound philosophy. But there are feeble and presumptuous minds that do not know how to go thus far, or do not know how to stop there. Confined to experience, they do not dare to conclude from what they see in what they do not see, as if at all times, at the sight of the first phenomenon that appears to their eyes, they did not admit that this phenomenon has a cause, even when this cause does not come within the reach of their senses. They do not perceive it, yet they believe in it, for the simple reason that they necessarily conceive it. Man and the universe are also facts that cannot but have a cause, although this cause may neither be seen by our eyes nor touched by our hands. Reason has been given us for the very purpose of going, and without any circuit of reasoning, from the visible to the invisible, from the finite to the infinite, from the imperfect to the perfect, and also, from necessary and universal truths, which surround us on every side, to their eternal and necessary principle. Such is the natural and legitimate bearing of reason. It possesses an evidence of which it renders no account, and is not thereby less irresistible to whomsoever does not undertake to contest with God the veracity of the faculties which he has received. But one does not revolt against reason with impunity. It punishes our false wisdom by giving us up to extravagance. When one has confined himself to the narrow limits of what he directly perceives, he is smothered by these limits, wishes to go out of them at any price, and invokes some other means of knowing; he did not dare to admit the existence of an invisible God, and now behold him aspiring to enter into immediate communication with him, as with sensible objects, and the objects of consciousness. It is an extreme feebleness for a rational being thus to doubt reason, and it is an incredible rashness, in this despair of intelligence, to dream of direct communication with God. This desperate and ambitious dream is mysticism.

It behooves us to separate with care this chimera, that is not without danger, from the cause that we defend. It behooves us so much the more to openly break with mysticism, as it seems to touch us more nearly, as it pretends to be the last word of philosophy, and as by an appearance of greatness it is able to seduce many a noble soul, especially at one of those epochs of lassitude, when, after the cruel disappointment of excessive hopes, human reason, having lost faith in its own power without having lost the need of God, in order to satisfy this immortal need, addresses itself to every thing except itself, and in fault of knowing how to go to God by the way that is open to it, throws itself out of common sense, and tries the new, the chimerical, even the absurd, in order to attain the impossible.

Mysticism contains a pusillanimous skepticism in the place of reason, and, at the same time, a faith blind and carried even to the oblivion of all the conditions imposed upon human nature. To conceive God under the transparent veil of the universe and above the highest truths, is at once too much and too little for mysticism. It does not believe that it knows God, if it knows him only in his manifestations and by the signs of his existence: it wishes to perceive him directly, it wishes to be united to him, sometimes by sentiment, sometimes by some other extraordinary process.

Sentiment plays so important a part in mysticism, that our first care must be to investigate the nature and proper function of this interesting and hitherto ill-studied part of human nature.

It is necessary to distinguish sentiment well from sensation. There are, in some sort, two sensibilities: one is directed to the external world, and is charged with transmitting to the soul the impressions that it sees; the other is wholly interior, and is related to the soul as the other is to nature,—its function is to receive the impression, and, as it were, the rebound of what passes in the soul. Have we discovered any truth? there is something in us which feels joy on account of it. Have we performed a good action? we receive our reward in a feeling of satisfaction less vivid, but more delicate and more durable than all the agreeable sensations that come from the body. It seems as if intelligence also had its intimate organ, which suffers or enjoys, according to the state of the intelligence. We bear in ourselves a profound source of emotion, at once physical and moral, which expresses the union of our two natures. The animal does not go beyond sensation, and pure thought belongs only to the angelic nature. The sentiment that partakes of sensation and thought is the portion of humanity. Sentiment is, it is true, only an echo of reason; but this echo is sometimes better understood than reason itself, because it resounds in the most intimate, the most delicate portions of the soul, and moves the entire man.

It is a singular, but incontestable fact, that as soon as reason has conceived truth, the soul attaches itself to it, and loves it. Yes, the soul loves truth. It is a wonderful thing that a being strayed into one corner of the universe, alone charged with sustaining himself against so many obstacles, who, it would seem, has enough to do to think of himself, to preserve and somewhat embellish his life, is capable of loving what is not related to him, and exists only in an invisible world! This disinterested love of truth gives evidence of the greatness of him who feels it.

Reason takes one step more:—it is not contented with truth, even absolute truth, when convinced that it possesses it ill, that it does not possess it as it really is; as long as it has not placed it upon its eternal basis; having arrived there, it stops as before its impassable barrier, having nothing more to seek, nothing more to find. Sentiment follows reason, to which it is attached; it stops, it rests, only in the love of the infinite being.

In fact, it is the infinite that we love, while we believe that we are loving finite things, even while loving truth, beauty, virtue. And so surely is it the infinite itself that attracts and charms us, that its highest manifestations do not satisfy us until we have referred them to their immortal source. The heart is insatiable, because it aspires after the infinite. This sentiment, this need of the infinite, is at the foundation of the greatest passions, and the most trifling desires. A sigh of the soul in the presence of the starry heavens, the melancholy attached to the passion of glory, to ambition, to all the great emotions of the soul, express it better without doubt, but they do not express it more than the caprice and mobility of those vulgar loves, wandering from object to object in a perpetual circle of ardent desires, of poignant disquietudes, and mournful disenchantments.

Let us designate another relation between reason and sentiment.

The mind at first precipitates itself towards its object without rendering to itself an account of what it does, of what it perceives, of what it feels. But, with the faculty of thinking, of feeling, it has also that of willing; it possesses the liberty of returning to itself, of reflecting on its own thought and sentiment, of consenting to this, or of resisting it, of abstaining from it, or of reproducing its thought and sentiment, while stamping them with a new character. Spontaneity, reflection,—these are the two great forms of intelligence.[71] One is not the other; but, after all, the latter does little more than develop the former; they contain at bottom the same things:—the point of view alone is different. Every thing that is spontaneous is obscure and confused; reflection carries with it a clear and distinct view.

Reason does not begin by reflection; it does not at first perceive the truth as universal and necessary; consequently, when it passes from idea to being, when it refers truth to the real being that is its subject, it has not sounded, it even has no suspicion of the depth of the chasm it passes; it passes it by means of the power which is in it, but it is not astonished at what it has done. It is subsequently astonished, and undertakes by the aid of the liberty with which it is endowed, to do the opposite of what it has done, to deny what it has affirmed. Here commences the strife between sophism and common sense, between false science and natural truth, between good and bad philosophy, both of which come from free reflection. The sad and sublime privilege of reflection is error; but reflection is the remedy for the evil it produces. If it can deny natural truth, usually it confirms it, returns to common sense by a longer or shorter circuit; it opposes in vain all the tendencies of human nature, by which it is almost always overcome, and brought back submissive to the first inspirations of reason, fortified by this trial. But there is nothing more in the end than there was at the beginning; only in primitive inspiration there was a power which was ignorant of itself, and in the legitimate results of reflection there is a power which knows itself:—one is the triumph of instinct, the other, that of true science.

Sentiment which accompanies intelligence in all its proceedings presents the same phenomena.

The heart, like reason, pursues the infinite, and the only difference there is in these pursuits is, that sometimes the heart

---

[71] See the preceding lectures.

seeks the infinite without knowing that it seeks it, and sometimes it renders to itself an account of the final end of the need of loving what disturbs it. When reflection is added to love, if it finds that the object loved is in fact worthy of being loved, far from enfeebling love, it strengthens it; far from clipping its divine wings, it develops them, and nourishes them, as Plato[72] says. But if the object of love is only a symbol of the true beauty, only capable of exciting the desire of the soul without satisfying it, reflection breaks the charm which held the heart, dissipates the chimera that enchained it. It must be very sure in regard to its attachments, in order to dare to put them to the proof of reflection. O Psyche! Psyche! preserve thy good fortune; do not sound the mystery too deeply. Take care not to bring the fearful light near the invisible lover with whom thy soul is enamored. At the first ray of the fatal lamp love is awakened, and flies away. Charming image of what takes place in the soul, when to the serene and unsuspecting confidence of sentiment succeeds reflection with its bitter train. This is perhaps also the meaning of the biblical account of the tree of knowledge.[73] Before science and reflection are innocence and faith. Science and reflection at first engender doubt, disquietude, distaste for what one possesses, the disturbed pursuit of what one knows not, troubles of mind and soul, sore travail of thought, and, in life, many faults, until innocence, forever lost, is replaced by virtue, simple faith by true science, until love, through so many vanishing illusions, finally succeeds in reaching its true object.

Spontaneous love has the native grace of ignorance and happiness. Reflective love is very different; it is serious, it is great, even in its faults, with the greatness of liberty. Let us not be in haste to condemn reflection: if it often produces egotism, it also produces devotion. What, in fact, is self-devotion? It is giving ourselves freely, with full knowledge of what we are doing.

---

[72] See the Phædrus and the Banquet, vol. vii. of our translation.

[73] We shall not be accused of perverting the holy Scriptures by these analogies, for we give them only as analogies, and St. Augustine and Bossuet are full of such.

Therein consists the sublimity of love, love worthy of a noble and generous creature, not an ignorant and blind love. When affection has conquered selfishness, instead of loving its object for its own sake, the soul gives itself to its object, and miracle of love, the more it gives the more it possesses, nourishing itself by its own sacrifices, and finding its strength and its joy in its entire self-abandonment. But there is only one being who is worthy of being thus loved, and who can be thus loved without illusions, and without mistakes, at once without limits, and without regret, to wit, the perfect being who alone does not fear reflection, who alone can fill the entire capacity of our heart.

Mysticism corrupts sentiment by exaggerating its power.

Mysticism begins by suppressing in man reason, or, at least, it subordinates and sacrifices reason to sentiment.

Listen to mysticism: it says that by the heart alone is man in relation with God. All that is great, beautiful, infinite, eternal, love alone reveals to us. Reason is only a lying faculty. Because it may err, and does err, it is said that it always errs. Reason is confounded with every thing that it is not. The errors of the senses, and of reasoning, the illusions of the imagination, even the extravagances of passion, which sometimes give rise to those of mind, every thing is laid to the charge of reason. Its imperfections are triumphed over, its miseries are complacently exhibited; the most audacious dogmatical system—since it aspires to put man and God in immediate communication—borrows against reason all the arms of skepticism.

Mysticism goes farther: it attacks liberty itself; it orders liberty to renounce itself, in order to identify itself by love with him from whom the infinite separates us. The ideal of virtue is no longer the courageous perseverance of the good man, who, in struggling against temptation and suffering, makes life holy; it is no longer the free and enlightened devotion of a loving soul; it is the entire and blind abandonment of ourselves, of our will, of our being, in a barren contemplation of thought, in a prayer without utterance, and almost without consciousness.

The source of mysticism is in that incomplete view of human nature, which knows not how to discern in it what therein is most profound, which betakes itself to what is therein most striking, most seizing, and, consequently, also most seizable. We have already said that reason is not noisy, and often is not heard, whilst its echo of sentiment loudly resounds. In this compound phenomenon, it is natural that the most apparent element should cover and dim the most obscure.

Moreover, what relations, what deceptive resemblances between these two faculties! Without doubt, in their development, they manifestly differ; when reason becomes reasoning, one easily distinguishes its heavy movement from the flight of sentiment; but spontaneous reason is almost confounded with sentiment,—there is the same rapidity, the same obscurity. Add that they pursue the same object, and almost always go together. It is not, then, astonishing that they should be confounded.

A wise philosophy distinguishes[74] them without separating them. Analysis demonstrates that reason precedes, and that sentiment follows. How can we love what we are ignorant of? In order to enjoy the truth, is it not necessary to know it more or less? In order to be moved by certain ideas, is it not necessary to have possessed them in some degree? To absorb reason in sentiment is to stifle the cause in the effect. When one speaks of the light of the heart, he designates, without knowing it, that light of the spontaneous reason which discovers to us truth by a pure and immediate intuition entirely opposite to the slow and laborious processes of the reflective reason and reasoning.

Sentiment by itself is a source of emotion, not of knowledge. The sole faculty of knowledge is reason. At bottom, if sentiment is different from sensation, it nevertheless pertains on all sides to general sensibility, and it is, like it, variable; it has, like it, its interruptions, its vivacity, and its lassitude, its exaltation and its

---

[74] See part ii., The Beautiful, lecture 6, and part iii., lecture 13, on the Morals of Sentiment. See also our Pascal, preface of the last edition, p. 8, etc., vol. i. of the 4th Series.

short-comings. The inspirations of sentiment, then, which are essentially mobile and individual, cannot be raised to a universal and absolute rule. It is not so with reason; it is constantly the same in each one of us, the same in all men. The laws that govern its exercise constitute the common legislation of all intelligent beings. There is no intelligence that does not conceive some universal and necessary truth, and, consequently, the infinite being who is its principle. These grand objects being once known excite in the souls of all men the emotions that we have endeavored to describe. These emotions partake of the dignity of reason and the mobility of imagination and sensibility. Sentiment is the harmonious and living relation between reason and sensibility. Suppress one of the two terms, and what becomes of the relation? Mysticism pretends to elevate man directly to God, and does not see that in depriving reason of its power, it really deprives him of that which makes him know God, and puts him in a just communication with God by the intermediary of eternal and infinite truth.

The fundamental error of mysticism is, that it discards this intermediary, as if it were a barrier and not a tie: it makes the infinite being the direct object of love. But such a love can be sustained only by superhuman efforts that end in folly. Love tends to unite itself with its object: mysticism absorbs love in its object. Hence the extravagances of that mysticism so severely and so justly condemned by Bossuet and the Church in quietism.[75] Quietism lulls to sleep the activity of man, extinguishes his intelligence, substitutes indolent and irregular contemplation for the seeking of truth and the fulfilment of duty. The true union of the soul with God is made by truth and virtue. Every other union is a chimera, a peril, sometimes a crime. It is not permitted man to reject, under any pretext, that which makes him man, that which renders him capable of comprehending God, and expressing in himself an imperfect image of God, that is to say, reason, liberty, conscience. Without doubt, virtue has its prudence, and if we

---

[75] See the admirable work of Bossuet, Instruction sur les états d'Oraison.

must never yield to passion, there are diverse ways of combating it in order to conquer it. One can let it subside, and resignation and silence may have their legitimate employment. There is a portion of truth, of utility even, in the *Spiritual Letters,* even in the *Maxims of the Saints.* But, in general, it is unsafe to anticipate in this world the prerogatives of death, and to dream of sanctity when virtue alone is required of us, when virtue is so difficult to attain, even imperfectly. The best quietism can, at most, be only a halt in the course, a truce in the strife, or rather another manner of combating. It is not by flight that battles are gained; in order to gain them it is necessary to come to an engagement, so much the more as duty consists in combating still more than in conquering. Of the two opposite extremes—stoicism and quietism—the first, taken all in all, is preferable to the second; for if it does not always elevate man to God, it maintains, at least, human personality, liberty, conscience, whilst quietism, in abolishing these, abolishes the entire man. Oblivion of life and its duties, inertness, sloth, death of soul,—such are the fruits of that love of God, which is lost in the sterile contemplation of its object, provided it does not cause still sadder aberrations! There comes a moment when the soul that believes itself united with God, puffed up with this imaginary possession, despises both the body and human personality to such an extent that all its actions become indifferent to it, and good and evil are in its eyes the same. Thus it is that fanatical sects have been seen mingling crime and devotion, finding in one the excuse, often even the motive, of the other, and prefacing infamous irregularities or abominable cruelties with mystic transports,—deplorable consequences of the chimera of pure love, of the pretension of sentiment to rule over reason, to serve alone as a guide to the human soul, and to put itself in direct communication with God, without the intermediary of the visible world, and without the still surer intermediary of intelligence and truth.

But it is time to pass to another kind of mysticism, more singular, more learned, more refined, and quite as unreasonable, although it presents itself in the very name of reason.

We have seen[76] that reason, if one of the principles which govern it be destroyed, cannot lay hold of truth, not even absolute truths of the intellectual and moral order; it refers all universal, necessary, absolute truths, to the being that alone can explain them, because in him alone are necessary and absolute existence, immutability, and infinity. God is the substance of uncreated truths, as he is the cause of created existences. Necessary truths find in God their natural subject. If God has not arbitrarily made them,—which is not in accordance with their essence and his,— he constitutes them, inasmuch as they are himself. His intelligence possesses them as the manifestations of itself. As long as our intelligence has not referred them to the divine intelligence, they are to it an effect without cause, a phenomenon without substance. It refers them, then, to their cause and their substance. And in that it obeys an imperative need, a fixed principle of reason.

Mysticism breaks in some sort the ladder that elevates us to infinite substance: it regards this substance alone, independently[77]

---

[76] Lecture 4.

[77] See especially in our writings the regular and detailed refutation of the double extravagance of considering substance apart from its determinations and its qualities, or of considering its qualities and its facilities apart from the being that possesses them. 1st Series, vol. iii., lecture 3, On Condillac, and vol. v., lectures 5 and 6, On Kant. We say, the same Series, vol. iv., p. 56: "There are philosophers beyond the Rhine, who, to appear very profound, are not contented with qualities and phenomena, and aspire to pure substance, to being in itself. The problem stated as follows, is quite insoluble: the knowledge of such a substance is impossible, for this very simple reason, that such a substance does not exist. Being in itself, das Ding in sich, which Kant seeks, escapes him, and this does not humiliate Kant and philosophy; for there is no being in itself. The human mind may form to itself an abstract and general idea of being, but this idea has no real object in nature. All being is determinate, if it is real; and to be determinate is to possess certain modes of being, transitory and accidental, or constant and essential. Knowledge of being in itself is then not merely interdicted to the human mind; it is contrary to the nature of things. At the other extreme of metaphysics is a powerless psychology, which,

of the truth that manifests it, and it imagines itself to possess also the pure absolute, pure unity, being in itself. The advantage which mysticism here seeks, is to give to thought an object wherein there is no mixture, no division, no multiplicity, wherein every sensible and human element has entirely disappeared. But in order to obtain this advantage, it must pay the cost of it. It is a very simple means of freeing theodicea from every shade of anthropomorphism; it is reducing God to an abstraction, to the abstraction of being in itself. Being in itself, it is true, is free from all division, but upon the condition that it have no attribute, no quality, and even that it be deprived of knowledge and intelligence; for intelligence, if elevated as it might be, always supposes the distinction between the intelligent subject and the intelligible object. A God from whom absolute unity excludes intelligence, is the God of the mystic philosophy.

How could the school of Alexandria, how could Plotinus, its founder,[78] in the midst of the lights of the Greek and Latin civilization, have arrived at such a strange notion of the Divinity? By the abuse of Platonism, by the corruption of the best and severest method, that of Socrates and Plato.

The Platonic method, the dialectic process, as its author calls it, searches in particular, variable, contingent things, for what they also have general, durable, one, that is to say, their Idea, and is

---

by fear of a hollow ontology, is condemned to voluntary ignorance. We are not able, say these philosophers, Mr. Dugald Stewart, for example, to attain being in itself; it is permitted us to know only phenomena and qualities: so that, in order not to wander in search of the substance of the soul, they do not dare affirm its spirituality, and devote themselves to the study of its different faculties. Equal error, equal chimera! There are no more qualities without being, than being without qualities. No being is without its determinations, and reciprocally its determinations are not without it. To consider the determinations of being independently of the being which possesses them, is no longer to observe; it is to abstract, to make an abstraction quite as extravagant as that of being considered independently of its qualities."

[78] On the school of Alexandria, see 2d Series, vol. ii., Sketch of a General History of Philosophy, lecture 8, p. 211, and 3d Series, vol. i., passim.

thus elevated to Ideas, as to the only true objects of intelligence, in order to be elevated still from these Ideas, which are arranged in an admirable hierarchy, to the first of all, beyond which intelligence has nothing more to conceive, nothing more to seek. By rejecting in finite things their limit, their individuality, we attain genera, Ideas, and, by them, their sovereign principle. But this principle is not the last of genera, nor the last of abstractions; it is a real and substantial principle.[79] The God of Plato is not called merely unity, he is called the Good; he is not the lifeless substance of the Eleatics;[80] he is endowed with *life and movement*;[81] strong expressions that show how much the God of the Platonic metaphysics differs from that of mysticism. This God is the *father of the world*.[82] He is also the father of truth, that light of spirits.[83] He dwells in the midst of Ideas *which make him a true God inasmuch as he is with them*.[84] He possesses *august and holy intelligence*.[85] He has made the world without any external necessity, and for the sole reason that he is good.[86] In

---

[79] See the previous lecture.

[80] 3d Series, vol. i., Ancient Philosophy, article Xenophanes, and article Zeno.

[81] The Sophist, vol. xi. of our translation, p. 261.

[82] Timæus, vol. xii., p. 117.

[83] Republic, book vii., p. 70 of vol. x.

[84] Phædrus, vol. vi., p. 55.

[85] The Sophist, p. 261, 262. The following little-known and decisive passage, which we have translated for the first time, must be cited:—"Stranger. But what, by Zeus! shall we be so easily persuaded that in reality, motion, life, soul, intelligence, do not belong to absolute being? that this being neither lives nor thinks, that this being remains immobile, immutable, without having part in august and holy intelligence?—Theatetus. That would be consenting, dear Eleatus, to a very strange assertion.—Stranger. Or, indeed, shall we accord to this being intelligence while we refuse him life?—Theatetus. That cannot be.—Stranger. Or, again, shall we say that there is in him intelligence and life, but that it is not in a soul that he possesses them?—Theatetus. And how could he possess them otherwise?—Stranger. In fine, that, endowed with intelligence, soul, and life, all animated as he is, he remains incomplete immobility.—Theatetus. All that seems to me unreasonable."

[86] Timæus, p. 119: "Let us say that the cause which led the supreme ordainer to produce and compose this universe was, that he was good."

fine, he is beauty without mixture, unalterable, immortal, that makes him who has caught a glimpse of it disdain all earthly beauties.[87] The beautiful, the absolute good, is too dazzling to be looked on directly by the eye of mortal; it must at first be contemplated in the images that reveal it to us, in truth, in beauty, in justice, as they are met here below, and among men, as the eye of one who has been a chained captive from infancy, must be gradually habituated to the light of the sun.[88] Our reason, enlightened by true science, can perceive this light of spirits; reason rightly led can go to God, and there is no need, in order to reach him, of a particular and mysterious faculty.

Plotinus erred by pushing to excess the Platonic dialectics, and by extending them beyond the boundary where they should stop. In Plato they terminate at ideas, at the idea of the good, and produce an intelligent and good God; Plotinus applies them without limit, and they lead him into an abyss of mysticism. If all truth is in the general, and if all individuality is imperfection, it follows, that as long as we are able to generalize, as long as it is possible for us to overlook any difference, to exclude any determination, we shall not be at the limit of dialectics. Its last object, then, will be a principle without any determination. It will not spare in God being itself. In fact, if we say that God is a being, by the side of and above being, we place unity, of which being partakes, and which it cannot disengage, in order to consider it alone. Being is not here simple, since it is at once being and unity; unity alone is simple, for one cannot go beyond that. And still when we say unity, we determine it. True absolute unity must, then, be something absolutely indeterminate, which is not, which, properly speaking, cannot be named, the *unnamable*, as Plotinus says. This principle, which exists not, for a still stronger reason, cannot think, for all thought is still a determination, a manner of being. So being and thought are excluded from absolute unity. If Alexandrianism admits them, it is only as a

---

[87] Bouquet, discourse of Diotimus, vol. vi., and the 2d part of this vol., The Beautiful, lecture 7.
[88] Republic. Ibid.

forfeiture, a degradation of unity. Considered in thought, and in being, the supreme principle is inferior to itself; only in the pure simplicity of its indefinable essence is it the last object of science, and the last term of perfection.

In order to enter into communication with such a God, the ordinary faculties are not sufficient, and the theodicea of the school of Alexandria imposes upon it a quite peculiar psychology.

In the truth of things, reason conceives absolute unity as an attribute of absolute being, but not as something in itself, or, if it considers it apart, it knows that it considers only an abstraction. Does one wish to make absolute unity something else than an attribute of an absolute being, or an abstraction, a conception of human intelligence? Reason could accept nothing more on any condition. Will this barren unity be the object of love? But love, much more than reason, aspires after a real object. One does not love substance in general, but a substance that possesses such or such a character. In human friendships, suppress all the qualities of a person, or modify them, and you modify or suppress the love. This does not prove that you do not love this person; it only proves that the person is not for you without his qualities.

So neither reason nor love can attain the absolute unity of mysticism. In order to correspond to such an object, there must be in us something analogous to it, there must be a mode of knowing that implies the abolition of consciousness. In fact, consciousness is the sign of the *me*, that is to say, of that which is most determinate: the being who says, *me*, distinguishes himself essentially from every other; that is for us the type itself of individuality. Consciousness should degrade the ideal of dialectic knowledge, or every division, every determination must be wanting, in order to respond to the absolute unity of its object. This mode of pure and direct communication with God, which is not reason, which is not love, which excludes consciousness, is ecstasy (ἔκστασις). This word, which Plotinus first applied to this singular state of the soul, expresses this separation from ourselves which mysticism exacts, and of which it believes man capable. Man, in order to communicate with absolute being, must go out of himself. It is necessary that thought should reject all determinate thought, and, in falling back within its own depths, should arrive at such an oblivion of itself, that consciousness should vanish or seem to vanish. But that is only an image of ecstasy; what it is in itself, no one knows; as it escapes all consciousness, it escapes memory, escapes reflection, and consequently all expression, all human speech.

This philosophical mysticism rests upon a radically false notion of absolute being. By dint of wishing to free God from all the conditions of finite existence, one comes to deprive him of all the conditions of existence itself; one has such a fear that the infinite may have something in common with the finite, that he does not dare to recognize that being is common to both, save difference of degree, as if all that is not were not nothingness itself! Absolute being possesses absolute unity without any doubt, as it possesses absolute intelligence; but, once more, absolute unity without a real subject of inherence is destitute of all reality. Real and determinate are synonyms. What constitutes a being is its special nature, its essence. A being is itself only on the condition of not being another; it cannot but have characteristic traits. All that is, is such or such. Difference is an element as essential to being as unity itself. If, then, reality is in determination, it follows that God is the most determinate of beings. Aristotle is much more Platonic than Plotinus, when he says that God is the thought of thought,[89] that he is not a simple power, but a power effectively acting, meaning thereby that God to be perfect, ought to have nothing in himself that is not completed. To finite nature it belongs to be, in a certain sense, indeterminate, since being finite, it has always in itself powers that are not realized; this indetermination diminishes as these powers are realized. So true divine unity is not abstract unity, it is the precise unity of perfect being in which every thing is accomplished. At the summit of existence, still more than at its low degree, every thing is determinate, every thing is developed,

---

[89] Book xii. of the Metaphysics. De la Métaphysique d'Aristotle, 2d edition, p. 200, etc.

every thing is distinct, every thing is one. The richness of determinations is a certain sign of the plenitude of being. Reflection distinguishes these determinations from each other, but it is not necessary that it should in these distinctions see the limits. In us, for example, does the diversity of our faculties and their richest development divide the *me* and alter the identity and the unity of the person? Does each one of us believe himself less than himself, because he possesses sensibility, reason, and will? No, surely. It is the same with God. Not having employed a sufficient psychology, Alexandrian mysticism imagined that diversity of attributes is incompatible with simplicity of essence, and through fear of corrupting simple and pure essence, it made of it an abstraction. By a senseless scruple, it feared that God would not be sufficiently perfect, if it left him all his perfections; it regards them as imperfections, being as a degradation, creation as a fall; and, in order to explain man and the universe, it is forced to put in God what it calls failings, not having seen that these pretended failings are the very signs of his infinite perfection.

The theory of ecstasy is at once the necessary condition and the condemnation of the theory of absolute unity. Without absolute unity as the direct object of knowledge, of what use is ecstasy in the subject of knowledge? Ecstasy, far from elevating man to God, abases him below man; for it effaces in him thought, by taking away its condition, which is consciousness. To suppress consciousness, is to render all knowledge impossible; it is not to comprehend the perfection of this mode of knowing, wherein the limitation of subject and object gives at once the simplest, most immediate, and most determinate knowledge.[90]

---

[90] On this fundamental point, see lecture 3, in this vol.—2d Series, vol. i., lecture 5, p. 97. "The peculiarity of intelligence is not the power of knowing, but knowing in fact. On what condition is there intelligence for us? It is not enough that there should be in us a principle of intelligence; this principle must be developed and exercised, and take itself as the object of its intelligence. The necessary condition of intelligence is consciousness—that is to say, difference. There can be consciousness only where there are several terms, one of which perceives the other, and at the same time perceives itself. That is knowing, and knowing self; that is intelligence. Intelligence without consciousness is the

The Alexandrian mysticism is the most learned and the profoundest of all known mysticisms. In the heights of abstraction where it loses itself, it seems very far from popular superstitions; and yet the school of Alexandria unites ecstatic contemplation and theurgy. These are two things, in appearance, incompatible, but they pertain to the same principle, to the pretension of directly perceiving what inevitably escapes all our efforts. On the one hand, a refined mysticism aspires to God by ecstasy; on the other, a gross mysticism thinks to seize him by the senses. The processes, the faculties employed, differ, but the foundation is the same, and from this common foundation necessarily spring the most opposite extravagances. Apollonius of Tyanus is a popular Alexandrianist, and Jamblicus is Plotinus become a priest, mystagogue, and hierophant. A new worship shone forth by miracles; the ancient worship would have its own miracles, and philosophers boasted that they could make the divinity appear before other men. They had demons for themselves, and, in some sort, for their own orders; the gods were not only invoked, but evoked. Ecstasy for the initiates, theurgy for the crowd.

At all times and in all places, these two mysticisms have given each other the hand. In India and in China, the schools where the most subtle idealism is taught, are not far from pagodas of the most abject idolatry. One day the Bhagavad-Gita or Lao-tseu[91] is read, an indefinable God is taught, without essential and determinate attributes; the next day there is shown to the people such or such a form, such or such a manifestation of this God, who, not having a form that belongs to him, can receive all forms, and being only substance in itself, is necessarily the

---

abstract possibility of intelligence, it is not real intelligence. Transfer this from human intelligence to divine intelligence, that is to say, refer ideas, I mean ideas in the sense of Plato, of St. Augustine, of Bossuet, of Leibnitz, to the only intelligence to which they can belong, and you will have, if I may thus express myself, the life of the divine intelligence ..., etc."

[91] Vol. ii. of the 2d Series, Sketch of a General History of Philosophy, lectures 5 and 6, On the Indian Philosophy.

substance of every thing, of a stone and a drop of water, of a dog, a hero, and a sage. So, in the ancient world under Julien, for example, the same man was at once professor in the school of Athens and guardian of the temple of Minerva or Cybele, by turns obscuring the *Timæus* and the *Republic* by subtile commentaries, and exhibiting to the eyes of the multitude sometimes the sacred vale,[92] sometimes the shrine of the good goddess,[93] and in either function, as priest or philosopher, imposing on others and himself, undertaking to ascend above the human mind and falling miserably below it, paying in some sort the penalty of an unintelligible metaphysics, in lending himself to the most shameless superstitions.

When the Christian religion triumphed, it brought humanity under a discipline that puts a rein upon this deplorable mysticism. But how many times has it brought back, under the reign of spiritual religion, all the extravagances of the religions of nature! It was to appear especially at the *renaissance* of the schools and of the genius of Paganism in the sixteenth century, when the human mind had broken with the philosophy of the Middle Age, without yet having arrived at modern philosophy.[94] The Paracelsuses and the Von Helmonts renewed the Apolloniuses and the Jamblicuses, abusing some chemical and medical knowledge, as the former had abused the Socratic and Platonic method, altered in its character, and turned from its true object. And so, in the midst of the eighteenth century, has not Swedenborg united in his own person an exalted mysticism and a sort of magic, opening thus the way to those senseless[95] persons

---

[92] See the Euthyphron, vol. i. of our translation.
[93] Lucien, Apuleius, Lucius of Patras.
[94] 2d Series, vol. ii., Sketch of a General History of Philosophy, lecture 10, On the Philosophy of the Renaissance.
[95] One was then ardently occupied with magnetism, and more than a magnetizer, half a materialist, half a visionary, pretended to convert us to a system of perfect clairvoyance of soul, obtained by means of artificial sleep. Alas! the same follies are now renewed. Conjunctions are the fashion. Spirits are interrogated, and they respond! Only let there be consciousness that one does not interrogate, and superstition alone counterpoises skepticism.

who contest with me in the morning the solidest and best-established proofs of the existence of the soul and God, and propose to me in the evening to make me see otherwise than with my eyes, and to make me hear otherwise than with my ears, to make me use all my faculties otherwise than by their natural organs, promising me a superhuman science, on the condition of first losing consciousness, thought, liberty, memory, all that constitutes me an intelligent and moral being. I should know all, then, but at the cost of knowing nothing that I should know. I should elevate myself to a marvellous world, which, awakened and in a natural state, I am not even able to suspect, of which no remembrance will remain to me:—a mysticism at once gross and chimerical, which perverts both psychology and physiology; an imbecile ecstasy, renewed without genius from the Alexandrine ecstasy; an extravagance which has not even the merit of a little novelty, and which history has seen reappearing at all epochs of ambition and impotence.

This is what we come to when we wish to go beyond the conditions imposed upon human nature. Charron first said, and after him Pascal repeated it, that whoever would become an angel becomes a beast. The remedy for all these follies is a severe theory of reason, of what it can and what it cannot do; of reason enveloped first in the exercise of the senses, than elevating itself to universal and necessary ideas, referring them to their principle, to a being infinite and at the same time real and substantial, whose existence it conceives, but whose nature it is always interdicted to penetrate and comprehend. Sentiment accompanies and vivifies the sublime intuitions of reason, but we must not confound these two orders of facts, much less smother reason in sentiment. Between a finite being like man and God, absolute and infinite substance, there is the double intermediary of that magnificent universe open to our gaze, and of those marvellous truths which reason conceives, but has not made more than the eye makes the beauties it perceives. The only means that is given us of elevating ourselves to the Being of beings, without being dazzled and bewildered, is to approach him by the aid of a divine intermediary; that is to say, to consecrate ourselves to the study and the love of truth, and, as we shall soon see, to the contemplation and reproduction of the beautiful, especially to the practice of the good.

PART SECOND
THE BEAUTIFUL.

LECTURE VI.

THE BEAUTIFUL IN THE MIND OF MAN.

The method that must govern researches on the beautiful and art is, as in the investigation of the true, to commence by psychology.—Faculties of the soul that unite in the perception of the beautiful.—The senses give only the agreeable; reason alone gives the idea of the beautiful.—Refutation of empiricism, that confounds the agreeable and the beautiful.—Pre-eminence of reason.—Sentiment of the beautiful; different from sensation and desire.—Distinction between the sentiment of the beautiful and that of the sublime.—Imagination.—Influence of sentiment on imagination.—Influence of imagination on sentiment.—Theory of taste.

Let us recall in a few words the results at which we have arrived.

Two exclusive schools are opposed to each other in the eighteenth century; we have combated both, and each by the other. To empiricism we have opposed the insufficiency of sensation, and its own inevitable necessity to idealism. We have admitted, with Locke and Condillac, in regard to the origin of knowledge, particular and contingent ideas, which we owe to the senses and consciousness; and above the senses and consciousness, the direct sources of all particular ideas, we have recognized, with Reid and Kant, a special faculty, different from sensation and consciousness, but developed with them,—reason, the lofty source of universal and necessary truths. We have established, against Kant, the absolute authority of reason, and the truths which it discovers. Then, the truths that reason revealed to us have themselves revealed to us their eternal principle,—God.

Finally, this rational spiritualism, which is both the faith of the human race and the doctrine of the greatest minds of antiquity and modern times, we have carefully distinguished from a chimerical and dangerous mysticism. Thus the necessity of experience and the necessity of reason, the necessity of a real and infinite being which is the first and last foundation of truth, a severe distinction between spiritualism and mysticism, are the great principles which we have been able to gather from the first part of this course.

The second part, the study of the beautiful, will give us the same results elucidated and aggrandized by a new application.

It was the eighteenth century that introduced, or rather brought back into philosophy, investigations on the beautiful and art, so familiar to Plato and Aristotle, but which scholasticism had not entertained, to which our great philosophy of the seventeenth century had remained almost a stranger.[96] One comprehends that it did not belong to the empirical school to revive this noble part of philosophic science. Locke and Condillac did not leave a chapter, not even a single page, on the beautiful. Their followers treated beauty with the same disdain; not knowing very well how to explain it in their system, they found it more convenient not to perceive it at all. Diderot, it is true, had an enthusiasm for beauty and art, but enthusiasm was never so ill placed. Diderot had genius; but, as Voltaire said of him, his was a head in which every thing fermented without coming to maturity. He scattered here and there a mass of ingenious and often contradictory perceptions; he has no principles; he abandons himself to the impression of the moment; he knows not what the ideal is; he delights in a kind of nature, at once common and mannered, such as one might expect from the author of the *Interprétation de la Nature*, the *Père de Famille*, the *Neveu de*

---

[96] Except the estimable Essay on the Beautiful, by P. André, a disciple of Malebranche, whose life was considerably prolonged into the eighteenth century. On P. André, see 3d Series, vol. iii., Modern Philosophy, p. 207, 516.

Rameau, and *Jacques le Fataliste*. Diderot is a fatalist in art as well as in philosophy; he belongs to his times and his school, with a grain of poetry, sensibility, and imagination.[97] It was worthy of the Scotch[98] school and Kant[99] to give a place to the beautiful in their doctrine. They considered it in the soul and in nature; but they did not even touch the difficult question of the reproduction of the beautiful by the genius of man. We will try to embrace this great subject in its whole extent, and we are about to offer at least a sketch of a regular and complete theory of beauty and art.

Let us begin by establishing well the method that must preside over these investigations.

One can study the beautiful in two ways:—either out of us, in itself and in the objects, whatever they may be, that bear its impress; or in the mind of man, in the faculties that attain it, in the ideas or sentiments that it excites in us. Now, the true method, which must now be familiar to you, makes setting out from man to arrive at things a law for us. Therefore psychological analysis will here again be our point of departure, and the study of the state of the soul in presence of the beautiful will prepare us for that of the beautiful considered in itself and its objects.

Let us interrogate the soul in the presence of beauty.

Is it not an incontestable fact that before certain objects, under very different circumstances, we pronounce the following judgment:—This object is beautiful? This affirmation is not always explicit. Sometimes it manifests itself only by a cry of admiration; sometimes it silently rises in the mind that scarcely has a consciousness of it. The forms of this phenomenon vary, but the phenomenon is attested by the most common and most certain observation, and all languages bear witness of it.

---

[97] See in the works of Diderot, Pensées sur la Sculpture, les Salons, etc.

[98] See 1st Series, vol. iv., explained and estimated, the theories of Hutcheson and Reid.

[99] The theory of Kant is found in the Critique of Judgment, and in the Observations on the Sentiment of the Beautiful and the Sublime. See the excellent translation made by M. Barny, 2 vols., 1846.

Although sensible objects, with most men, oftenest provoke the judgment of the beautiful, they do not alone possess this advantage; the domain of beauty is more extensive than the domain of the physical world exposed to our view; it has no bounds but those of entire nature, and of the soul and genius of man. Before an heroic action, by the remembrance of a great sacrifice; even by the thought of the most abstract truths firmly united with each other in a system admirable at once for its simplicity and its productiveness; finally, before objects of another order, before the works of art, this same phenomenon is produced in us. We recognize in all these objects, however different, a common quality in regard to which our judgment is pronounced, and this quality we call beauty.

The philosophy of sensation, in faithfulness to itself, should have attempted to reduce the beautiful to the agreeable.

Without doubt, beauty is almost always agreeable to the senses, or at least it must not wound them. Most of our ideas of the beautiful come to us by sight and hearing, and all the arts, without exception, are addressed to the soul through the body. An object which makes us suffer, were it the most beautiful in the world, very rarely appears to us such. Beauty has little influence over a soul occupied with grief.

But if an agreeable sensation often accompanies the idea of the beautiful, we must not conclude that one is the other.

Experience testifies that all agreeable things do not appear beautiful, and that, among agreeable things, those which are most so are not the most beautiful,—a sure sign that the agreeable is not the beautiful; for if one is identical with the other, they should never be separated, but should always be commensurate with each other.

Far from this, whilst all our senses give us agreeable sensations, only two have the privilege of awakening in us the idea of beauty. Does one ever say: This is a beautiful taste, this is a beautiful smell? Nevertheless, one should say it, if the beautiful is the agreeable. On the other hand, there are certain pleasures of odor and taste that move sensibility more than the greatest beauties of nature and art; and even among the perceptions of hearing and sight, those are not always the most vivid that most excite in us the idea of beauty. Do not pictures, ordinary in coloring, often move us more deeply than many dazzling productions, more seductive to the eye, less touching to the soul? I say farther; sensation not only does not produce the idea of the beautiful, but sometimes stifles it. Let an artist occupy himself with the reproduction of voluptuous forms; while pleasing the senses, he disturbs, he repels in us the chaste and pure idea of beauty. The agreeable is not, then, the measure of the beautiful, since in certain cases it effaces it and makes us forget it; it is not, then, the beautiful, since it is found, and in the highest degree, where the beautiful is not.

This conducts us to the essential foundation of the distinction between the idea of the beautiful and the sensation of the agreeable, to wit, the difference already explained between sensibility and reason.

When an object makes you experience an agreeable sensation, if one asks you why this object is agreeable to you, you can answer nothing, except that such is your impression; and if one informs you that this same object produces upon others a different impression and displeases them, you are not much astonished, because you know that sensibility is diverse, and that sensations must not be disputed. Is it the same when an object is not only agreeable to you, but when you judge that it is beautiful? You pronounce, for example, that this figure is noble and beautiful, that this sunrise or sunset is beautiful, that disinterestedness and devotion are beautiful, that virtue is beautiful; if one contests with you the truth of these judgments, then you are not as accommodating as you were just now; you do not accept the dissent as an inevitable effect of different sensibilities, you no longer appeal to your sensibility which naturally terminates in you, you appeal to an authority which is made for others as well as you, that of reason; you believe that you have the right of accusing him with error who contradicts your judgment, for here your judgment rests no longer on something variable and individual, like an agreeable or painful sensation. The agreeable is confined for us within the inclosure of our own organization, where it changes every moment, according to the perpetual revolutions of this organization, according to health and sickness, the state of the atmosphere, that of our nerves, etc. But it is not so with beauty; beauty, like truth, belongs to none of us; no one has the right to dispose of it arbitrarily, and when we say: this is true, this is beautiful, it is no longer the particular and variable impression of our sensibility that we express, it is the absolute judgment that reason imposes on all men.

Confound reason and sensibility, reduce the idea of the beautiful to the sensation of the agreeable, and taste no longer has a law. If a person says to me, in the presence of the Apollo Belvidere, that he feels nothing more agreeable than in presence of any other statue, that it does not please him at all, that he does not feel its beauty, I cannot dispute his impression; but if this person thence concludes that the Apollo is not beautiful, I proudly contradict him, and declare that he is deceived. Good taste is distinguished from bad taste; but what does this distinction signify, if the judgment of the beautiful is resolved into a sensation? You say to me that I have no taste. What does that mean? Have I not senses like you? Does not the object which you admire act upon me as well as upon you? Is not the impression which I feel as real as that which you feel? Whence comes it, then, that you are right,—you who only give expression to the impression which you feel, and that I am wrong,—I who do precisely the same thing? Is it because those who feel like you are more numerous than those who feel like me? But here the number of voices means nothing? The beautiful being defined as that which produces on the senses an agreeable impression, a thing that pleases a single man, though it were frightfully ugly in the eyes of all the rest of the human race, must, nevertheless, and very legitimately, be called beautiful by him who receives from it an agreeable impression, for, so far as he is concerned, it satisfies the definition. There is, then, no true beauty; there are only relative and changing beauties, beauties of circumstance, custom, fashion, and all these beauties, however different, will have a right to the same respect, provided they meet sensibilities to which they are agreeable. And as there is nothing in this world, in the infinite diversity of our dispositions, which may not please some one, there will be nothing that is not beautiful; or, to speak more truly, there will be nothing either beautiful or ugly, and the Hottentot Venus will equal the Venus de Medici. The absurdity of the consequences demonstrates the absurdity of the principle. But there is only one means of escaping these consequences, which is to repudiate the principle, and recognize the judgment of the beautiful as an absolute judgment, and, as such, entirely different from sensation.

Finally, and this is the last rock of empiricism, is there in us only the idea of an imperfect and finite beauty, and while we are admiring the real beauties that nature furnishes, are we not elevating ourselves to the idea of a superior beauty, which Plato, with great excellence of expression, calls the Idea of the beautiful, which, after him, all men of delicate taste, all true artists call the Ideal? If we establish decrees in the beauty of things, is it not because we compare them, often without noticing it, with this ideal, which is to us the measure and rule of all our judgments in regard to particular beauties? How could this idea of absolute beauty enveloped in all our judgments on the beautiful,—how could this ideal beauty, which it is impossible for us not to conceive, be revealed to us by sensation, by a faculty variable and relative like the objects that it perceives?

The philosophy which deduces all our ideas from the senses falls to the ground, then, before the idea of the beautiful. It remains to see whether this idea can be better explained by means of sentiment, which is different from sensation, which so nearly resembles reason that good judges have often taken it for reason, and have made it the principle of the idea of the beautiful as well as that of the good. It is already a progress, without doubt, to go from sensation to sentiment, and Hutcheson and Smith[100] are in our eyes very different philosophers from Condillac and Helvetius;[101] but we believe that we have sufficiently established [102] that, in confounding sentiment with reason, we deprive it of its foundation and rule, that sentiment, particular and variable in its nature, different to different men, and in each man continually changing, cannot be sufficient for itself. Nevertheless, if sentiment is not a principle, it is a true and important fact, and, after having distinguished it well from reason, we ourselves proceed to elevate it far above sensation, and elucidate the important part it plays in the perception of beauty.

Place yourself before an object of nature, wherein men recognize beauty, and observe what takes place within you at the sight of this object. Is it not certain that, at the same time that you judge that it is beautiful, you also feel its beauty, that is to say, that you experience at the sight of it a delightful emotion, and that you are attracted towards this object by a sentiment of sympathy and love? In other cases you judge otherwise, and feel an opposite sentiment. Aversion accompanies the judgment of the ugly, as love accompanies the judgment of the beautiful. And this sentiment is awakened not only in presence of the objects of nature: all objects, whatever they may be, that we judge to be ugly or beautiful, have the power to excite in us this sentiment. Vary the circumstances as much as you please, place me before an admirable edifice or before a beautiful landscape; represent to my mind the great discoveries of Descartes and Newton, the exploits of the great Condé, the virtue of St. Vincent de Paul; elevate me still higher; awaken in me the obscure and too much forgotten idea of the infinite being; whatever you do, as often as you give birth within me to the idea of the beautiful, you give me an

---

[100] On Hutcheson and Smith, their merits and defects, the part of truth and the part of error, which their philosophy contains, see the detailed lectures which we have devoted to them, 1st Series, vol. iv.

[101] See the exposition and refutation of the doctrine of Condillac and Helvetius, Ibid., vol. iii.

[102] See lecture 5, in this vol.

internal and exquisite joy, always followed by a sentiment of love for the object that caused it.

The more beautiful the object is, the more lively is the joy which it gives the soul, and the more profound is the love without being passionate. In admiration judgment rules, but animated by sentiment. Is admiration increased to the degree of impressing upon the soul an emotion, an ardor that seems to exceed the limits of human nature? this state of the soul is called enthusiasm:

"Est Deus in nobis, agitante calescimus illo."

The philosophy of sensation explains sentiment, as well as the idea of the beautiful, only by changing its nature. It confounds it with agreeable sensation, and, consequently, for it the love of beauty can be nothing but desire. There is no theory more contradicted by facts.

What is desire? It is an emotion of the soul which has, for its avowed or secret end, possession. Admiration is in its nature respectful, whilst desire tends to profane its object.

Desire is the offspring of need. It supposes, then, in him who experiences it, a want, a defect, and, to a certain point, suffering. The sentiment of the beautiful is to itself its own satisfaction.

Desire is burning, impetuous, sad. The sentiment of the beautiful, free from all desire, and always without fear, elevates and warms the soul, and may transport it even to enthusiasm, without making it know the troubles of passion. The artist sees only the beautiful where the sensual man sees only the alluring and the frightful. On a vessel tossed by a tempest, while the passengers tremble at the sight of the threatening waves, and at the sound of the thunder that breaks over their heads, the artist remains absorbed in the contemplation of the sublime spectacle. Vernet has himself lashed to the mast in order to contemplate for a longer time the storm in its majestic and terrible beauty. When he knows fear, when he participates in the common feeling, the artist vanishes, there no more remains any thing but the man.

The sentiment of the beautiful is so far from being desire, that each excludes the other. Let me take a common example. Before a table loaded with meats and delicious wines, the desire of enjoyment is awakened, but not the sentiment of the beautiful. Suppose that if, instead of thinking of the pleasures which all these things spread before my eyes promise me, I only take notice of the manner in which they are arranged and set upon the table, and the order of the feast, the sentiment of the beautiful might in some degree be produced; but surely this will be neither the need nor the desire of appropriating this symmetry, this order.

It is the property of beauty not to irritate and inflame desire, but to purify and ennoble it. The more beautiful a woman is,—I do not mean that common and gross beauty which Reubens in vain animates with his brilliant coloring, but that ideal beauty which antiquity and Raphael understood so well,—the more, at the sight of this noble creature is desire tempered by an exquisite and delicate sentiment, and is sometimes even replaced by a disinterested worship. If the Venus of the Capitol, or the Saint Cecilia, excites in you sensual desires, you are not made to feel the beautiful. So the true artist addresses himself less to the senses than to the soul; in painting beauty he only seeks to awaken in us sentiment; and when he has carried this sentiment as far as enthusiasm, he has obtained the last triumph of art.

The sentiment of the beautiful is, therefore, a special sentiment, as the idea of the beautiful is a simple idea. But is this sentiment, one in itself, manifested only in a single way, and applied only to a single kind of beauty? Here again—here, as always—let us interrogate experience.

When we have before our eyes an object whose forms are perfectly determined, and the whole easy to embrace,—a beautiful flower, a beautiful statue, an antique temple of moderate size,—each of our faculties attaches itself to this object, and rests upon it with an unalloyed satisfaction. Our senses easily perceive its details; our reason seizes the happy harmony of all its parts. Should this object disappear, we can distinctly represent it to ourselves, so precise and fixed are its forms. The soul in this contemplation feels again a sweet and tranquil joy, a sort of efflorescence.

Let us consider, on the other hand, an object with vague and indefinite forms, which may nevertheless be very beautiful: the impression which we experience is without doubt a pleasure still, but it is a pleasure of a different order. This object does not call forth all our powers like the first. Reason conceives it, but the senses do not perceive the whole of it, and imagination does not distinctly represent it to itself. The senses and the imagination try in vain to attain its last limits; our faculties are enlarged, are inflated, thus to speak, in order to embrace it, but it escapes and surpasses them. The pleasure that we feel comes from the very magnitude of the object; but, at the same time, this magnitude produces in us I know not what melancholy sentiment, because it is disproportionate to us. At the sight of the starry heavens, of the vast sea, of gigantic mountains, admiration is mingled with sadness. These objects, in reality finite, like the world itself, seem to us infinite, in our want of power to comprehend their immensity, and, resembling what is truly without bounds, they awaken in us the idea of the infinite, that idea which at once elevates and confounds our intelligence. The corresponding sentiment which the soul experiences is an austere pleasure.

In order to render the difference which we wish to mark more perceptible, examples may be multiplied. Are you affected in the same way at the sight of a meadow, variegated in its rather limited dimensions, whose extent the eye can easily take in, and at the aspect of an inaccessible mountain, at the foot of which the ocean breaks? Do the sweet light of day and a melodious voice produce upon you the same effect as darkness and silence? In the intellectual and moral order, are you moved in the same way when a rich and good man opens his purse to the indigent, and when a magnanimous man gives hospitality to his enemy, and saves him at the peril of his own life? Take some light poetry in which measure, spirit, and grace, everywhere predominate; take an ode, and especially an epistle of Horace, or some small verses of Voltaire, and compare them with the Iliad, or those immense Indian poems that are filled with marvellous events, wherein the highest metaphysics are united to recitals by turns graceful or pathetic, those poems that have more than two hundred thousand verses, whose personages are gods or symbolic beings; and see whether the impressions that you experience will be the same. As a last example, suppose, on the one hand, a writer who, with two or three strokes of the pen, sketches an analysis of intelligence, agreeable and simple, but without depth, and, on the other, a philosopher who engages in a long labor in order to arrive at the most rigorous decomposition of the faculty of knowing, and unfolds to you a long chain of principles and consequences,—read the *Traité des Sensations* and *the Critique of Pure Reason*, and, even leaving out of the account the truth and the falsehood they may contain, with reference solely to the beautiful, compare your impressions.

These are, then, two very different sentiments; different names have also been given them: one has been more particularly called the sentiment of the beautiful, the other that of the sublime.

In order to complete the study of the different faculties that enter into the perception of beauty, after reason and sentiment, it remains to us to speak of a faculty not less necessary, which animates them and vivifies them,—imagination.

When sensation, judgment, and sentiment have been produced by the occasion of an external object, they are reproduced even in the absence of this object; this is memory.

Memory is double:—not only do I remember that I have been in the presence of a certain object, but I represent to myself this absent object as it was, as I have seen, felt, and judged it:—the remembrance is then an image. In this last case, memory has been called by some philosophers imaginative memory. Such is the foundation of imagination; but imagination is something more still.

The mind, applying itself to the images furnished by memory, decomposes them, chooses between their different traits, and forms of them new images. Without this new power, imagination would be captive in the circle of memory.

The gift of being strongly affected by objects and reproducing their absent or vanished images, and the power of modifying these images so as to compose of them new ones,—do they fully constitute what men call imagination? No, or at least, if these are indeed the proper elements of imagination, there must be something else added, to wit, the sentiment of the beautiful in all its degrees. By this means is a great imagination preserved and kindled. Did the careful reading of Titus Livius enable the author of the *Horaces* to vividly represent to himself some of the scenes described, to seize their principal traits and combine them happily? From the outset, sentiment, love of the beautiful, especially of the morally beautiful, were requisite; there was required that great heart whence sprang the word of the ancient Horace.

Let us be well understood. We do not say that sentiment is imagination, we say that it is the source whence imagination derives its inspirations and becomes productive. If men are so different in regard to imagination, it is because some are cold in presence of objects, cold in the representations which they preserve of them, cold also in the combinations which they form of them, whilst others, endowed with a particular sensibility, are vividly moved by the first impressions of objects, preserve strong recollections of them, and carry into the exercise of all their faculties this same force of emotion. Take away sentiment and all else is inanimate; let it manifest itself, and every thing receives warmth, color, and life.

It is then impossible to limit imagination, as the word seems to demand, to images properly so called, and to ideas that are related to physical objects. To remember sounds, to choose between them, to combine them in order to draw from them new effects,—does not this belong to imagination, although sound is not an image? The true musician does not possess less imagination than the painter. Imagination is conceded to the poet when he retraces the images of nature; will this same faculty be refused him when he retraces sentiments? But, besides images and sentiments, does not the poet employ the high thoughts of justice, liberty, virtue, in a word, moral ideas? Will it be said that in moral paintings, in pictures of the intimate life of the soul, either graceful or energetic, there is no imagination?

You see what is the extent of imagination: it has no limits, it is applied to all things. Its distinctive character is that of deeply moving the soul in the presence of a beautiful object, or by its remembrance alone, or even by the idea alone of an imaginary object. It is recognized by the sign that it produces, by the aid of its representations, the same impression as, and even an impression more vivid than, nature by the aid of real objects. If beauty, absent and dreamed of, does not affect you as much as, and more than, present beauty, you may have a thousand other gifts,—that of imagination has been refused you.

In the eyes of imagination, the real world languishes in comparison with its own fictions. One may feel that imagination is his master by the *ennui* that real and present things give him. The phantoms of imagination have a vagueness, an indefiniteness of form, which moves a thousand times more than the clearness and distinctness of actual perceptions. And then, unless we are wholly mad,—and passion does not always render this service,— it is very difficult to see reality otherwise than as it is not, that is to say, very imperfectly. On the other hand, one makes of an image what he wishes, unconsciously metamorphoses it, embellishes it to his own liking. There is at the bottom of the human soul an infinite power of feeling and loving to which the entire world does not answer, still less a single one of its creatures, however charming. All mortal beauty, viewed near by, does not suffice for this insatiable power which it excites and cannot satisfy. But from afar, its effects disappear or are diminished, shades are mingled and confounded in the clear-obscure of memory and dream, and the objects please more because they are less determinate. The peculiarity of men of imagination is, that they represent men and things otherwise than as they are, and that they have a passion for such fantastic images. Those that are called positive men, are men without imagination, who perceive only what they see, and deal with reality as it is instead of transforming it. They have, in general, more reason than sentiment; they may be seriously, profoundly honest; they will never be either poets or artists. What makes the poet or artist is, with a foundation of good sense and reason—without which all the rest is useless—a sensitive, even a passionate heart; above all, a vivid, a powerful imagination.

If sentiment acts upon imagination, we see that imagination returns with usury to sentiment what it gives.

This pure and ardent passion, this worship of beauty that makes the great artist, can be found only in a man of imagination. In fact, the sentiment of the beautiful may be awakened in each one of us before any beautiful object; but, when this object has disappeared, if its image does not subsist vivaciously retraced, the sentiment which it for a moment excited is little by little effaced; it may be revived at the sight of another object, but only to be extinguished again,—always dying to be born again at hazard; not being nourished, increased, exalted by the vivacious and continuous reproduction of its object in the imagination, it wants that inspiring power, without which there is no artist, no poet.

A word more on another faculty, which is not a simple faculty, but a happy combination of those which have just been mentioned,—taste, so ill treated, so arbitrarily limited in all theories.

If, after having heard a beautiful poetical or musical work, admired a statue or a picture, you are able to recall what your senses have perceived, to see again the absent picture, to hear again the sounds that no longer exist; in a word, if you have imagination, you possess one of the conditions without which there is no true taste. In fact, in order to relish the works of imagination, is it not necessary to have taste? Do we not need, in order to feel an author, not to equal him, without doubt, but to resemble him in some degree? Will not a man of sensible, but dry and austere mind, like Le Batteux or Condillac, be insensible to the happy darings of genius, and will he not carry into criticism a narrow severity, a reason very little reasonable—since he does not comprehend all the parts of human nature,—an intolerance that mutilates and blemishes art while thinking to purify it?

On the other hand, imagination does not suffice for the appreciation of beauty. Moreover, that vivacity of imagination so precious to taste, when it is somewhat restrained, produces, when it rules, only a very imperfect taste, which, not having reason for a basis, carelessly judges, runs the risk of misunderstanding the greatest beauty,—beauty that is regulated. Unity in composition, harmony of all the parts, just proportion of details, skilful combination of effects, discrimination, sobriety, measure, are so many merits it will little feel, and will not put in their place. Imagination has doubtless much to do with works of art; but, in fine, it is not every thing. Is it only imagination that makes the *Polyeucte* and the *Misanthrope*, two incomparable marvels? Is there not, also, in the profound simplicity of plan, in the measured development of action, in the sustained truth of characters, a superior reason, different from imagination which furnishes the superior colors, and from sensibility that gives the passion?

Besides imagination and reason, the man of taste ought to possess an enlightened but ardent love of beauty; he must take delight in meeting it, must search for it, must summon it. To comprehend and demonstrate that a thing is not beautiful, is an ordinary pleasure, an ungrateful task; but to discern a beautiful thing, to be penetrated with its beauty, to make it evident, and make others participate in our sentiment, is an exquisite joy, a generous task. Admiration is, for him who feels it, at once a happiness and an honor. It is a happiness to feel deeply what is beautiful; it is an honor to know how to recognize it. Admiration is the sign of an elevated reason served by a noble heart. It is above a small criticism, that is skeptical and powerless; but it is the soul of a large criticism, a criticism that is productive: it is, thus to speak, the divine part of taste.

After having spoken of taste which appreciates beauty, shall we say nothing of genius which makes it live again? Genius is nothing else than taste in action, that is to say, the three powers of taste carried to their culmination, and armed with a new and mysterious power, the power of execution. But we are already entering upon the domain of art. Let us wait, we shall soon find art again and the genius that accompanies it.

LECTURE VII.

THE BEAUTIFUL IN OBJECTS.

Refutation of different theories on the nature of the beautiful: the beautiful cannot be reduced to what is useful.—Nor to convenience.—Nor to proportion.—Essential characters of the beautiful.—Different kinds of beauties. The beautiful and the sublime. Physical beauty. Intellectual beauty. Moral beauty.—Ideal beauty: it is especially moral beauty.—God, the first principle of the beautiful.—Theory of Plato.

We have made known the beautiful in ourselves, in the faculties that perceive it and appreciate it, in reason, sentiment, imagination, taste; we come, according to the order determined by the method, to other questions: What is the beautiful in objects? What is the beautiful taken in itself? What are its characters and different species? What, in fine, is its first and last principle? All these questions must be treated, and, if possible, solved. Philosophy has its point of departure in psychology; but, in order to attain also its legitimate termination, it must set out from man, and reach things themselves.

The history of philosophy offers many theories on the nature of the beautiful: we do not wish to enumerate nor discuss them all; we will designate the most important.[103]

There is one very gross, which defines the beautiful as that which pleases the senses, that which procures an agreeable impression. We will not stop at this opinion. We have

---

[103] If one would make himself acquainted with a simple and piquant refutation, written two thousand years ago, of false theories of beauty, he may read the Hippias of Plato, vol. iv. of our translation. The Phædrus, vol. vi., contains the veiled exposition of Plato's own theory; but it is in the Banquet (Ibid.), and particularly in the discourse of Diotimus, that we must look for the thought of Plato carried to its highest degree of development, and clothed with all the beauty of human language.

sufficiently refuted it in showing that it is impossible to reduce the beautiful to the agreeable.

A sensualism a little more wise puts the useful in the place of the agreeable, that is to say, changes the form of the same principle. Neither is the beautiful the object which procures for us in the present moment an agreeable but fugitive sensation, it is the object which can often procure for us this same sensation or others similar. No great effort of observation or reasoning is necessary to convince us that utility has nothing to do with beauty. What is useful is not always beautiful. What is beautiful is not always useful, and what is at once useful and beautiful is beautiful for some other reason than its utility. Observe a lever or a pulley: surely nothing is more useful. Nevertheless, you are not tempted to say that this is beautiful. Have you discovered an antique vase admirably worked? You exclaim that this vase is beautiful, without thinking to seek of what use it may be to you. Finally, symmetry and order are beautiful things, and at the same time, are useful things, because they economize space, because objects symmetrically disposed are easier to find when one wants them; but that is not what makes for us the beauty of symmetry, for we immediately seize this kind of beauty, and it is often late enough before we recognize the utility that is found in it. It even sometimes happens, that after having admired the beauty of an object, we are not able to divine its use, although it may have one. The useful is, then, entirely different from the beautiful, far from being its foundation.

A celebrated and very ancient[104] theory makes the beautiful consist in the perfect suitableness of means to their end. Here the beautiful is no longer the useful, it is the suitable; these two ideas must be distinguished. A machine produces excellent effects, economy of time, work, etc.; it is therefore useful. If, moreover, examining its construction, I find that each piece is in its place, and that all are skilfully disposed for the result which they should produce; even without regarding the utility of this result, as the

---

[104] See the Hippias.

means are well adapted to their end, I judge that there is suitableness in it. We are already approaching the idea of the beautiful; for we are no longer considering what is useful, but what is proper. Now, we have not yet attained the true character of beauty; there are, in fact, objects very well adapted to their end, which we do not call beautiful. A bench without ornament and without elegance, provided it be solid, provided all the parts are firmly connected, provided one may sit down on it with safety, provided it may be for this purpose suitable, agreeable even, may give an example of the most perfect adaptation of means to an end; it will not, therefore, be said that this bench is beautiful. There is here always this difference between suitableness and utility, that an object to be beautiful has no need of being useful, but that it is not beautiful if it does not possess suitableness, if there is in it a disagreement between the end and the means.

Some have thought to find the beautiful in proportion, and this is, in fact, one of the conditions of beauty, but it is not the only one. It is very certain, that an object ill-proportioned cannot be beautiful. There is in all beautiful objects, however far they may be from geometric form, a sort of living geometry. But, I ask, is it proportion that is dominant in this slender tree, with flexible and graceful branches, with rich and shady foliage? What makes the terrible beauty of a storm, what makes that of a great picture, of an isolated verse, or a sublime ode? It is not, I know, wanting in law and rule, neither is it law and rule: often, even what at first strikes us is an apparent irregularity. It is absurd to pretend that what makes us admire all these things and many more, is the same quality that makes us admire a geometric figure, that is to say, the exact correspondence of parts.

What we say of proportion may be said of order, which is something less mathematical than proportion, but scarcely explains better what is free, varied, and negligent in certain beauties.

All these theories which refer beauty to order, harmony, and proportion, are at foundation only one and the same theory which in the beautiful sees unity before all. And surely unity is beautiful; it is an important part of beauty, but it is not the whole of beauty.

The most probable theory of the beautiful is that which composes it of two contrary and equally necessary elements, unity and variety. Behold a beautiful flower. Without doubt, unity, order, proportion, symmetry even, are in it; for, without these qualities, reason would be absent from it, and all things are made with a marvellous reason. But, at the same time, what a diversity! How many shades in the color, what richness in the least details! Even in mathematics, what is beautiful is not an abstract principle, it is a principle carrying with itself a long chain of consequences. There is no beauty without life, and life is movement, is diversity.

Unity and variety are applied to all orders of beauty. Let us rapidly run over these different orders.

In the first place, there are beautiful objects, to speak properly, and sublime objects. A beautiful object, we have seen, is something completed, circumscribed, limited, which all our faculties easily embrace, because the different parts are on a somewhat narrow scale. A sublime object is that which, by forms not in themselves disproportionate, but less definite and more difficult to seize, awakens in us the sentiment of the infinite.

There are two very distinct species of beauty. But reality is inexhaustible, and in all the degrees of reality there is beauty.

Among sensible objects, colors, sounds, figures, movements, are capable of producing the idea and the sentiment of the beautiful. All these beauties are arranged under that species of beauty which, right or wrong, is called physical beauty.

If from the world of sense we elevate ourselves to that of mind, truth, and science, we shall find there beauties more severe, but not less real. The universal laws that govern bodies, those that govern intelligences, the great principles that contain and produce long deductions, the genius that creates, in the artist, poet, or philosopher,—all these are beautiful, as well as nature herself: this is what is called intellectual beauty.

Finally, if we consider the moral world and its laws, the idea of liberty, virtue, and devotedness, here the austere justice of an Aristides, there the heroism of a Leonidas, the prodigies of charity or patriotism, we shall certainly find a third order of beauty that still surpasses the other two, to wit, moral beauty.

Neither let us forget to apply to all these beauties the distinction between the beautiful and the sublime. There are, then, the beautiful and the sublime at once in nature, in ideas, in sentiments, in actions. What an almost infinite variety in beauty!

After having enumerated all these differences, could we not reduce them? They are incontestable; but, in this diversity is there not unity? Is there not a single beauty of which all particular beauties are only reflections, shades, degrees, or degradations?

Plotinus, in his treatise *On the Beautiful*,[105] proposed to himself this question. He asks—What is the beautiful in itself? I see clearly that such or such a form is beautiful, that such or such an action is also beautiful; but why and how are these two objects, so dissimilar, beautiful? What is the common quality which, being found in these two objects, ranges them under the general idea of the beautiful?

It is necessary to answer this question, or the theory of beauty is a maze without issue; one applies the same name to the most diverse things, without understanding the real unity that authorizes this unity of name.

Either the diversities which we have designated in beauty are such that it is impossible to discover their relation, or these diversities are especially apparent, and have their harmony, their concealed unity.

Is it pretended that this unity is a chimera? Then physical beauty, moral beauty, and intellectual beauty, are strangers to each other. What, then, will the artist do? He is surrounded by different beauties, and he must make a work; for such is the recognized law of art. But if this unity that is imposed upon him is a factitious unity, if there are in nature only essentially

---

[105] First Ennead, book vi., in the work of M. B. Saint-Hillaire, on the School of Alexandria, the translation of this morsel of Plotinus, p. 197.

dissimilar beauties, art deceives and lies to us. Let it be explained, then, how falsehood is the law of art. That cannot be; the unity that art expresses, it must have somewhere caught a glimpse of, in order to transport it into its works.

We neither retract the distinction between the beautiful and the sublime, nor the other distinctions just now indicated; but it is necessary to re-unite after having distinguished them. These distinctions and these re-unions are not contradictory: the great law of beauty, like that of truth, is unity as well as variety. All is one, and all is diverse. We have divided beauty into three great classes—physical beauty, intellectual beauty, and moral beauty. We must now seek the unity of these three sorts of beauty. Now, we think that they resolve themselves into one and the same beauty, moral beauty, meaning by that, with moral beauty properly so called, all spiritual beauty.

Let us put this opinion to the proof of facts.

Place yourself before that statue of Apollo which is called Apollo Belvidere, and observe attentively what strikes you in that master-piece. Winkelmann, who was not a metaphysician, but a learned antiquarian, a man of taste without system, made a celebrated analysis of the Apollo.[106] It is curious to study it. What

---

[106] Winkelmann has twice described the Apollo, History of Art among the Ancients, Paris, 1802, 3 vols., in 4to. Vol. i., book iv., chap. iii., Art among the Greeks:—"The Apollo of the Vatican offers us that God in a movement of indignation against the serpent Python, which he has just killed with arrow-shots, and in a sentiment of contempt for a victory so little worthy of a divinity. The wise artist, who proposed to represent the most beautiful of the gods, placed the anger in the nose, which, according to the ancients, was its seat; and the disdain on the lips. He expressed the anger by the inflation of the nostrils, and the disdain by the elevation of the under lip, which causes the same movement in the chin."—Ibid., vol. ii., book iv., chap. vi., Art under the Emperors:—"Of all the antique statues that have escaped the fury of barbarians and the destructive hand of time, the statue of Apollo is, without contradiction, the most sublime. One would say that the artist composed a figure purely ideal, and employed matter only because it was necessary for him to execute and represent his idea. As much as Homer's description of Apollo

surpasses the descriptions which other poets have undertaken after him, so much this statue excels all the figures of this god. Its height is above that of man, and its attitude proclaims the divine grandeur with which it is filled. A perennial spring-time, like that which reigns in the happy fields of Elysium, clothes with lovable youth the beautiful body, and shines with sweetness over the noble structure of the limbs. In order to feel the merit of this chef-d'œuvre of art, we must be penetrated with intellectual beauty, and become, if possible, the creatures of a celestial nature; for there is nothing mortal in it, nothing subject to the wants of humanity. That body, whose forms are not interrupted by a vein, which is not agitated by a nerve, seems animated with a celestial spirit, which circulates like a sweet vapor in all the parts of that admirable figure. The god has just been pursuing Python, against which he has bent, for the first time, his formidable bow; in his rapid course, he has overtaken him, and given him a mortal wound. Penetrated with the conviction of his power, and lost in a concentrated joy, his august look penetrates far into the infinite, and is extended far beyond his victory. Disdain sits upon his lips; the indignation that he breathes distends his nostrils, and ascends to his eyebrows; but an unchangeable serenity is painted on his brow, and his eye is full of sweetness, as though the Muses were caressing him. Among all the figures that remain to us of Jupiter, there is none in which the father of the gods approaches the grandeur with which he manifested himself to the intelligence of Homer; but in the traits of the Apollo Belvidere, we find the individual beauties of all the other divinities united, as in that of Pandora. The forehead is the forehead of Jupiter, inclosing the goddess of wisdom; the eyebrows, by their movement, announce his supreme will; the large eyes are those of the queen of the gods, orbed with dignity, and the mouth is an image of that of Bacchus, where breathed voluptuousness. Like the tender branches of the vine, his beautiful locks flow around his head, as if they were lightly agitated by the zephyr's breath. They seem perfumed with the essence of the gods, and are charmingly arranged over his head by the hand of the Graces. At the sight of this marvel of art, I forget every thing else, and my mind takes a supernatural disposition, fitted to judge of it with dignity; from admiration I pass to ecstasy; I feel my breast dilating and rising, like those who are filled with the spirit of prophecy; I am transported to Delos, and the sacred groves of Syria,—places which Apollo honored with his presence:—the statue seems to be animated as it were with the beauty that sprung of old from the hands of Pygmalion. How can I describe thee, O inimitable master-piece? For this it would be necessary

Winkelmann extols before all, is the character of divinity stamped upon the immortal youth that invests that beautiful body, upon the height, a little above that of man, upon the majestic altitude, upon the imperious movement, upon the *ensemble*, and all the details of the person. The forehead is indeed that of a god,—an unalterable placidity dwells upon it. Lower down, humanity reappears somewhat; and that is very necessary, in order to interest humanity in the works of art. In that satisfied look, in the distension of the nostrils, in the elevation of the under lip, are at once felt anger mingled with disdain, pride of victory, and the little fatigue which it has cost. Weigh well each word of Winkelmann: you will find there a moral impression. The tone of the learned antiquary is elevated, little by little, to enthusiasm, and his analysis becomes a hymn to spiritual beauty.

Instead of a statue, observe a real and living man. Regard that man who, solicited by the strongest motives to sacrifice duty to fortune, triumphs over interest, after an heroic struggle, and sacrifices fortune to virtue. Regard him at the moment when he is about to take this magnanimous resolution; his face will appear to you beautiful, because it expresses the beauty of his soul. Perhaps, under all other circumstances, the face of the man is common, even trivial; here, illuminated by the soul which it manifests, it is ennobled, and takes an imposing character of beauty. So, the natural face of Socrates[107] contrasts strongly with the type of Grecian beauty; but look at him on his death-bed, at the moment of drinking the hemlock, convening with his disciples on the immortality of the soul, and his face will appear to you sublime.[108]

---

that art itself should deign to inspire my pen. The traits that I have just sketched, I lay before thee, as those who came to crown the gods, put their crowns at their feet, not being able to reach their heads."

[107] See the last part of the Banquet, the discourse of Alcibiades, p. 326 of vol. vi. of our translation.

[108] We here have in mind, and we avow it, the Socrates of David, which appears to us, the theatrical character being admitted, above its reputation. Besides Socrates, it is impossible not to admire Plato listening to his master, as it were from the bottom of his soul, without looking at him, with his back

At the highest point of moral grandeur, Socrates expires: — you have before your eyes no longer any thing but his dead body; the dead face preserves its beauty, as long as it preserves traces of the mind that animated it; but little by little the expression is extinguished or disappears; the face then becomes vulgar and ugly. The expression of death is hideous or sublime,—hideous at the aspect of the decomposition of the matter that no longer retains the spirit,—sublime when it awakens in us the idea of eternity.

Consider the figure of man in repose: it is more beautiful than that of an animal, the figure of an animal is more beautiful than the form of any inanimate object. It is because the human figure, even in the absence of virtue and genius, always reflects an intelligent and moral nature, it is because the figure of an animal reflects sentiment at least, and something of soul, if not the soul entire. If from man and the animal we descend to purely physical nature, we shall still find beauty there, as long as we find there some shade of intelligence, I know not what, that awakens in us some thought, some sentiment. Do we arrive at some piece of matter that expresses nothing, that signifies nothing, neither is the idea of beauty applied to it. But every thing that exists is animated. Matter is shaped and penetrated by forces that are not material, and it obeys laws that attest an intelligence everywhere present. The most subtle chemical analysis does not reach a dead and inert nature, but a nature that is organized in its own way, that is neither deprived of forces nor laws. In the depths of the earth, as in the heights of the heavens, in a grain of sand as in a gigantic mountain, an immortal spirit shines through the thickest coverings. Let us contemplate nature with the eye of the soul as well as with the eye of the body:—everywhere a moral expression will strike us, and the forms of things will impress us as symbols of thought. We have said that with man, and with the animal even, the figure is beautiful on account of the expression. But, when you are on the summit of the Alps, or before the immense Ocean, when you behold the rising or setting of the sun, at the

---

turned upon the scene that is passing, and lost in the contemplation of the intelligible world.

beginning or the close of the day, do not these imposing pictures produce on you a moral effect? Do all these grand spectacles appear only for the sake of appearing? Do we not regard them as manifestations of an admirable power, intelligence, and wisdom? And, thus to speak, is not the face of nature expressive like that of man?

Form cannot be simply a form, it must be the form of something. Physical beauty is, then, the sign of an internal beauty, which is spiritual and moral beauty; and this is the foundation, the principle, the unity of the beautiful.[109]

All the beauties that we have just enumerated and reduced compose what is called the really beautiful. But, above real beauty, is a beauty of another order—ideal beauty. The ideal resides neither in an individual, nor in a collection of individuals. Nature or experience furnishes us the occasion of conceiving it, but it is essentially distinct. Let it once be conceived, and all natural figures, though never so beautiful, are only images of a superior beauty which they do not realize. Give me a beautiful action, and I will imagine one still more beautiful. The Apollo itself is open to criticism in more than one respect. The ideal continually recedes as we approach it. Its last termination is in the infinite, that is to say, in God; or, to speak more correctly, the true and absolute ideal is nothing else than God himself.

God, being the principle of all things, must for this reason be that of perfect beauty, and, consequently, of all natural beauties that express it more or less imperfectly; he is the principle of

---

[109] We are fortunate in finding this theory, which is so dear to us, confirmed by the authority of one of the severest and most circumspect minds:—it may be seen in Reid, 1st Series, vol. iv., lecture 23. The Scotch philosopher terminates his Essay on Taste with these words, which happily remind us of the thought and manner of Plato himself:—"Whether the reasons that I have given to prove that sensible beauty is only the image of moral beauty appear sufficient or not, I hope that my doctrine, in attempting to unite the terrestrial Venus more closely to the celestial Venus, will not seem to have for its object to abase the first, and render her less worthy of the homage that mankind has always paid her."

beauty, both as author of the physical world and as father of the intellectual and moral world.

Is it not necessary to be a slave of the senses and of appearances in order to stop at movements, at forms, at sounds, at colors, whose harmonious combinations produce the beauty of this visible world, and not to conceive behind this scene so magnificent and well regulated, the orderer, the geometer, the supreme artist?

Physical beauty serves as an envelope to intellectual and moral beauty.

What can be the principle of intellectual beauty, that splendor of the true, except the principle of all truth?

Moral beauty comprises, as we shall subsequently see,[110] two distinct elements, equally but diversely beautiful, justice and charity, respect and love of men. He who expresses in his conduct justice and charity, accomplishes the most beautiful of all works; the good man is, in his way, the greatest of all artists. But what shall we say of him who is the very substance of justice and the exhaustless source of love? If our moral nature is beautiful, what must be the beauty of its author! His justice and goodness are everywhere, both in us and out of us. His justice is the moral order that no human law makes, that all human laws are forced to express, that is preserved and perpetuated in the world by its own force. Let us descend into ourselves, and consciousness will attest the divine justice in the peace and contentment that accompany virtue, in the troubles and tortures that are the invariable punishments of vice and crime. How many times, and with what eloquence, have men celebrated the indefatigable solicitude of Providence, its benefits everywhere manifest in the smallest as well as in the greatest phenomena of nature, which we forget so easily because they have become so familiar to us, but which, on reflection, call forth our mingled admiration and gratitude, and proclaim a good God, full of love for his creatures!

---

[110] Part iii., lecture 15.

Thus, God is the principle of the three orders of beauty that we have distinguished, physical beauty, intellectual beauty, moral beauty.

In him also are reunited the two great forms of the beautiful distributed in each of these three orders, to wit, the beautiful and the sublime. God is, *par excellence*, the beautiful—for what object satisfies more all our faculties, our reason, our imagination, our heart! He offers to reason the highest idea, beyond which it has nothing more to seek; to imagination the most ravishing contemplation; to the heart a sovereign object of love. He is, then, perfectly beautiful; but is he not sublime also in other ways? If he extends the horizon of thought, it is to confound it in the abyss of his greatness. If the soul blooms at the spectacle of his goodness, has it not also reason to be affrighted at the idea of his justice, which is not less present to it? God is at once mild and terrible. At the same time that he is the life, the light, the movement, the ineffable grace of visible and finite nature, he is also called the Eternal, the Invisible, the Infinite, the Absolute Unity, and the Being of beings. Do not these awful attributes, as certain as the first, produce in the highest degree in the imagination and the soul that melancholy emotion excited by the sublime? Yes, God is for us the type and source of the two great forms of beauty, because he is to us at once an impenetrable enigma and still the clearest word that we are able to find for all enigmas. Limited beings as we are, we comprehend nothing in comparison with that which is without limits, and we are able to explain nothing without that same thing which is without limits. By the being that we possess, we have some idea of the infinite being of God; by the nothingness that is in us, we lose ourselves in the being of God; and thus always forced to recur to him in order to explain any thing, and always thrown back within ourselves under the weight of his infinitude, we experience by turns, or rather at the same time, for this God who raises and casts us down, a sentiment of irresistible attraction and astonishment, not to say insurmountable terror, which he alone can cause and allay, because he alone is the unity of the sublime and the beautiful.

Thus absolute being, which is both absolute unity and infinite variety,—God, is necessarily the last reason, the ultimate foundation, the completed ideal of all beauty. This is the marvellous beauty that Diotimus had caught a glimpse of, and thus paints to Socrates in the *Banquet*:

"Eternal beauty, unbegotten and imperishable, exempt from decay as well as increase, which is not beautiful in such a part and ugly in such another, beautiful only, at such a time, in such a place, in such a relation, beautiful for some, ugly for others, beauty that has no sensible form, no visage, no hands, nothing corporeal, which is not such a thought or such a particular science, which resides not in any being different from itself, as an animal, the earth, or the heavens, or any other thing, which is absolutely identical and invariable by itself, in which all other beauties participate, in such a way, nevertheless, that their birth or their destruction neither diminishes nor increases, nor in the least changes it!... In order to arrive at this perfect beauty, it is necessary to commence with the beauties of this lower world, and, the eyes being fixed upon the supreme beauty, to elevate ourselves unceasingly towards it, by passing, thus to speak, through all the degrees of the scale, from a single beautiful body to two, from two to all others, from beautiful bodies to beautiful sentiments, from beautiful sentiments to beautiful thoughts, until from thought to thought we arrive at the highest thought, which has no other object than the beautiful itself, until we end by knowing it as it is in itself.

"O my dear Socrates," continued the stranger of Mantinea, "that which can give value to this life is the spectacle of the eternal beauty.... What would be the destiny of a mortal to whom it should be granted to contemplate the beautiful without alloy, in its purity and simplicity, no longer clothed with the flesh and hues of humanity, and with all those vain charms that are condemned to perish, to whom it should be given to see face to face, under its sole form, the divine beauty!"[111]

---

[111] Vol. vi. of our translation, p. 816-818

LECTURE VIII

ON ART.

Genius:—its attribute is creative power.—Refutation of the opinion that art is the imitation of nature.—M. Emeric David, and M. Quatremère de Quincy.—Refutation of the theory of illusion. That dramatic art has not solely for its end to excite the passions of terror and pity.—Nor even directly the moral and religious sentiment.—The proper and direct object of art is to produce the idea and the sentiment of the beautiful; this idea and this sentiment purify and elevate the soul by the affinity between the beautiful and the good, and by the relation of ideal beauty to its principle, which is God.—True mission of art.

Man is not made only to know and love the beautiful in the works of nature, he is endowed with the power of reproducing it. At the sight of a natural beauty, whatever it may be, physical or moral, his first need is to feel and admire. He is penetrated, ravished, as it were overwhelmed with the sentiment of beauty. But when the sentiment is energetic, he is not a long time sterile. We wish to see again, we wish to feel again what caused us so vivid a pleasure, and for that end we attempt to revive the beauty that charmed us, not as it was, but as our imagination represents it to us. Hence a work original and peculiar to man, a work of art. Art is the free reproduction of beauty, and the power in us capable of reproducing it is called genius.

What faculties are used in this free reproduction of the beautiful? The same that serve to recognize and feel it. Taste carried to the highest degree, if you always join to it an additional element, is genius. What is this element?

Three faculties enter into that complex faculty that is called taste,—imagination, sentiment, reason.

These three faculties are certainly necessary for genius, but they are not sufficient for it. What essentially distinguishes genius from taste is the attribute of creative power. Taste feels, judges, discusses, analyzes, but does not invent. Genius is, before all, inventive and creative. The man of genius is not the master of the power that is in him; it is by the ardent, irresistible need of expressing what he feels, that he is a man of genius. He suffers by withholding the sentiments, or images, or thoughts, that agitate his breast. It has been said that there is no superior man without some grain of folly; but this folly, like that of the cross, is the divine part of reason. This mysterious power Socrates called his demon. Voltaire called it the devil in the body; he demanded it even in a comedian in order to be a comedian of genius. Give to it what name you please, it is certain that there is a I-know-not-what that inspires genius, that also torments it until it has delivered itself of what consumes it; until, by expressing them, it has solaced its pains and its joys, its emotions, its ideas; until its reveries have become living works. Thus two things characterize genius; at first, the vivacity of the need it has of producing, then the power of producing; for the need without the power is only a malady that resembles genius, but is not it. Genius is above all, is essentially, the power of doing, of inventing, of creating. Taste is contented with observing, with admiring. False genius, ardent and impotent imagination, consumes itself in sterile dreams and produces nothing, at least nothing great. Genius alone has the power to convert conceptions into creations.

If genius creates it does not imitate.

But genius, it is said, is then superior to nature, since it does not imitate it. Nature is the work of God; man is then the rival of God.

The answer is very simple. No, genius is not the rival of God; but it is the interpreter of him. Nature expresses him in its way, human genius expresses him in its own way.

Let us stop a moment at that question so much discussed,— whether art is any thing else than the imitation of nature.

Doubtless, in one sense, art is an imitation; for absolute creation belongs only to God. Where can genius find the elements upon which it works, except in nature, of which it forms a part? But does it limit itself to the reproduction of them as nature furnishes them to it, without adding any thing to them which belongs to itself? Is it only a copier of reality? Its sole merit, then, is that of the fidelity of the copy. And what labor is more sterile than that of copying works essentially inimitable on account of the life with which they are endowed, in order to obtain an indifferent image of them? If art is a servile pupil, it is condemned never to be any thing but an impotent pupil.

The true artist feels and profoundly admires nature; but every thing in nature is not equally admirable. As we have just said, it has something by which it infinitely surpasses art—its life. Besides that, art can, in its turn, surpass nature, on the condition of not wishing to imitate it too closely. Every natural object, however beautiful, is defective on some side. Every thing that is real is imperfect. Here, the horrible and the hideous are united to the sublime; there, elegance and grace are separated from grandeur and force. The traits of beauty are scattered and diverse. To reunite them arbitrarily, to borrow from such a face a mouth, eyes from such another, without any rule that governs this choice and directs these borrowings, is to compose monsters; to admit a rule, is already to admit an ideal different from all individuals. It is this ideal that the true artist forms to himself in studying nature. Without nature, he never would have conceived this ideal; but with this ideal, he judges nature herself, rectifies her, and dares undertake to measure himself with her.

The ideal is the artist's object of passionate contemplation. Assiduously and silently meditated, unceasingly purified by reflection and vivified by sentiment, it warms genius and inspires it with the irresistible need of seeing it realized and living. For this end, genius takes in nature all the materials that can serve it, and applying to them its powerful hand, as Michael Angelo impressed his chisel upon the docile marble, makes of them works that have no model in nature, that imitate nothing else than the ideal dreamed of or conceived, that are in some sort a second creation inferior to the first in individuality and life, but much superior to it, we do not fear to say, on account of the intellectual and moral beauty with which it is impressed.

Moral beauty is the foundation of all true beauty. This foundation is somewhat covered and veiled in nature. Art disengages it, and gives to it forms more transparent. On this account, art, when it knows well its power and its resources, institutes with nature a contest in which it may have the advantage.

Let us establish well the end of art: it is precisely where its power lies. The end of art is the expression of moral beauty, by the aid of physical beauty. The latter is only a symbol of the former. In nature, this symbol is often obscure: art in bringing it to light attains effects that nature does not always produce. Nature may please more, for, once more, it possesses in an incomparable degree what makes the great charm of imagination and sight—life; art touches more, because in expressing, above all, moral beauty, it addresses itself more directly to the source of profound emotions. Art can be more pathetic than nature, and the pathetic is the sign and measure of great beauty.

Two extremes are equally dangerous—a lifeless ideal, or the absence of the ideal. Either we copy the model, and are wanting in true beauty, or we work *de tête*, and fall into an ideality without character. Genius is a ready and sure perception of the right proportion in which the ideal and the natural, form and thought, ought to be united. This union is the perfection of art: *chefs-d'œuvre* are produced by observing it.

It is important, in my opinion, to follow this rule in teaching art. It is asked whether pupils should begin with the study of the ideal or the real. I do not hesitate to answer,—by both. Nature herself never offers the general without the individual, nor the individual without the general. Every figure is composed of individual traits which distinguish it from all others, and make its own looks, and, at the same time, it has general traits which constitute what is called the human figure. These general traits are the constitutive lineaments, and this figure is the type, that are given to the pupil that is beginning in the art of design to trace. It would also be good, I believe, in order to preserve him from the dry and abstract, to exercise him early in copying some natural object, especially a living figure. This would be putting pupils to the true school of nature. They would thus become accustomed never to sacrifice either of the two essential elements of the beautiful, either of the two imperative conditions of art.

But, in uniting these two elements, these two conditions, it is necessary to distinguish them, and to know how to put them in their place. There is no true ideal without determinate form, there is no unity without variety, no genus without individuals, but, in fine, the foundation of the beautiful is the idea; what makes art is before all, the realization of the idea, and not the imitation of such or such a particular form.

At the commencement of our century, the Institute of France offered a prize for the best answer to the following question: *What were the causes of the perfection of the antique sculpture, and what would be the best means of attaining it?* The successful competitor, M. Emeric David,[112] maintained the opinion then dominant, that the assiduous study of natural beauty had alone conducted the antique art to perfection, and that thus the imitation of nature was the only route to reach the same perfection. A man whom I do not fear to compare with Winkelmann, the future author of the *Olympic Jupiter*,[113] M. Quatremère de Quincy, in some ingenious and profound disquisitions,[114] combated the doctrine of the laureate, and defended the cause of ideal beauty. It is impossible to demonstrate more decidedly, by the entire history of Greek sculpture, and by authentic texts from the greatest critiques of antiquity, that the process of art among the Greeks was not the imitation of nature, either by a particular model, or by several, the most beautiful model being always very imperfect, and several models not being able to compose a single beauty. The true process of the Greek art was the representation of an ideal beauty

---
[112] Recherches sur l'Art Statuaire. Paris, 1805.
[113] Paris, 1815, in folio, an eminent work that will subsist even when time shall have destroyed some of its details.
[114] Since reprinted under the title of Essais sur l'Ideal dans ses Applications Pratiques. Paris, 1837.

which nature scarcely possessed more in Greece than among us, which it could not then offer to the artist. We regret that the honorable laureate, since become a member of the Institute, pretended that this expression of ideal beauty, if it had been known by the Greeks, would have meant *visible beauty*, because ideal comes from εἶδος, which signifies only, according to M. Emeric David, a form seen by the eye. Plato would have been much surprised at this exclusive interpretation of the word εἶδος. M. Quatremère de Quincy confounds his unequal adversary by two admirable texts, one from the *Timæus*, where Plato marks with precision in what the true artist is superior to the ordinary artist, the other at the commencement of the *Orator*, where Cicero explains the manner in which great artists work, in referring to the manner of Phidias, that is to say, the most perfect master of the most perfect epoch of art.

"The artist,[115] who, with eye fixed upon the immutable being, and using such a model, reproduces its idea and its excellence, cannot fail to produce a whole whose beauty is complete, whilst he who fixes his eye upon what is transitory, with this perishable model will make nothing beautiful."

"Phidias,[116] that great artist, when he made the form of Jupiter or Minerva, did not contemplate a model a resemblance of which he would express; but in the depth of his soul resided a perfect type of beauty, upon which he fixed his look, which guided his hand and his art."

Is not this process of Phidias precisely that which Raphael describes in the famous letter to Castiglione, which he declares that he followed himself for the Galatea?[117] "As," he says, "I am

---

[115] Translation of Plato, vol. xii., Timæus, p. 116.

[116] Orator: "Neque enim ille artifex (Phidias) cum faceret Jovis formam aut Minervæ, contemplabatur aliquem a quo similitudinem duceret; sed ipsius in mente insidebat species pulchritudinis eximia quædam, quam intuens, in ea que defixus, ad illius similitudinem artem et manum dirigebat."

[117] Raccolta di lett. Sulla pitt., i., p. 83. "Essendo carestia e de' buoni giudici e di belle donne, io mi servo di certa idea che mi viene alla mente."

destitute of beautiful models, I use a certain ideal which I form for myself."

There is another theory which comes back, by a circuit, to imitation: it is that which makes illusion the end of art. If this theory be true, the ideal beauty of painting is a *tromp-l'œil*,[118] and its master-piece is the grapes of Zeuxis that the birds came and pecked at. The height of art in a theatrical piece would be to persuade you that you are in the presence of reality. What is true in this opinion is, that a work of art is beautiful only on the condition of being life-like, and, for example, the law of dramatic art is not to put on the stage pale phantoms of the past, but personages borrowed from imagination or history, as you like, but animated, endowed with passion, speaking and acting like men and not like shades. It is human nature that is to be represented to itself under a magic light that does not disfigure it, but ennobles it. This magic is the very genius of art. It lifts us above the miseries that besiege us, and transports us to regions where we still find ourselves, for we never wish to lose sight of ourselves, but where we find ourselves transformed to our advantage, where all the imperfections of reality have given place to a certain perfection, where the language that we speak is more equal and elevated, where persons are more beautiful, where the ugly is not admitted, and all this while duly respecting history, especially without ever going beyond the imperative conditions of human nature. Has art forgotten human nature? it has passed beyond its end, it has not attained it; it has brought forth nothing but chimeras without interest for our soul. Has it been too human, too real, too nude? it has fallen short of its end; it has then attained it no better.

Illusion is so little the end of art, that it may be complete and have no charm. Thus, in the interest of illusion, theatrical men have taken great pains in these latter times to secure historical accuracy of costume. This is all very well; but it is not the most important thing. Had you found, and lent to the actor

---

[118] "A picture representing a broken glass over several subjects painted on the canvas, by which the eye is deceived."

who plays the part of Brutus, the very costume that of old the Roman hero wore, it would touch true connoisseurs very little. This is not all; when the illusion goes too far, the sentiment of art disappears in order to give place to a sentiment purely natural, sometimes insupportable. If I believed that Iphegenia were in fact on the point of being immolated by her father at a distance of twenty paces from me, I should leave the theatre trembling with horror. If the Ariadne that I see and hear, were the true Ariadne who is about to be betrayed by her sister, in that pathetic scene where the poor woman, who already feels herself less loved, asks who then robs her of the heart, once so tender, of Theseus, I would do as the young Englishman did, who cried out, sobbing and trying to spring upon the stage, "It is Phèdre, it is Phèdre!" as if he would warn and save Ariadne.

But, it is said, is it not the aim of the poet to excite pity and terror? Yes; but at first in a certain measure; then he must mix with them some other sentiment that tempers them, or makes them serve another end. If the aim of dramatic art were only to excite in the highest degree pity and terror, art would be the powerless rival of nature. All the misfortunes represented on the stage are very feeble in comparison with those sad spectacles which we may see every day. The first hospital is fuller of pity and terror than all the theatres in the world. What should the poet do in the theory that we combat? He should transfer to the stage the greatest possible reality, and move us powerfully by shocking our senses with the sight of frightful pains. The great resort of the pathetic would then be the representation of death, especially that of the greatest torture. Quite on the contrary, there is an end of art when sensibility is too much excited. To take, again, an example that we have already employed, what constitutes the beauty of a tempest, of a shipwreck? What attracts us to those great scenes of nature? It is certainly not pity and terror,—these poignant and lacerating sentiments would much sooner keep us away. An emotion very different from these is necessary, which triumphs over us, in order to retain us by the shore; this emotion is the pure sentiment of the beautiful and the sublime, excited and kept alive by the grandeur of the spectacle, by the vast extent of the sea, the rolling of the foaming waves, and the imposing sound of the thunder. But do we think for a single instant that there are in the midst of the sea the unfortunate who are suffering, and are, perhaps, about to perish? From that moment the spectacle becomes to us insupportable. It is so in art. Whatever sentiment it proposes to excite in us, must always be tempered and governed by that of the beautiful. If it only produces pity or terror beyond a certain limit, especially physical pity or terror, it revolts, and no longer charms; it loses the effect that belongs to it in exchange for a foreign and vulgar effect.

For this same reason, I cannot accept another theory, which, confounding the sentiment of the beautiful with the moral and religious sentiment, puts art in the service of religion and morals, and gives it for its end to make us better and elevate us to God. There is here an essential distinction to be made. If all beauty covers a moral beauty, if the ideal mounts unceasingly towards the infinite, art, which expresses ideal beauty, purifies the soul in elevating it towards the infinite, that is to say, towards God. Art, then, produces the perfection of the soul, but it produces it indirectly. The philosopher who investigates effects and causes, knows what is the ultimate principle of the beautiful and its certain, although remote, effects. But the artist is before all things an artist; what animates him is the sentiment of the beautiful; what he wishes to make pass into the soul of the spectator is the same sentiment that fills his own. He confides himself to the virtue of beauty; he fortifies it with all the power, all the charm of the ideal; it must then do its own work; the artist has done his when he has procured for some noble souls the exquisite sentiment of beauty. This pure and disinterested sentiment is a noble ally of the moral and religious sentiments; it awakens, preserves, and develops them, but it is a distinct and special sentiment. So art, which is founded on this sentiment, which is inspired by it, which expands it, is in its turn an independent power. It is naturally associated with all that ennobles the soul, with morals and religion; but it springs only from itself.

Let us confine our thought strictly within its proper limits. In vindicating the independence, the proper dignity, and the particular end of art, we do not intend to separate it from religion, from morals, from country. Art draws its inspirations from these profound sources, as well as from the ever open source of nature. But it is not less true that art, the state, religion, are powers which have each their world apart and their own effects; they mutually help each other; they should not serve each other. As soon as one of them wanders from its end, it errs, and is degraded. Does art blindly give itself up to the orders of religion and the state? In losing its liberty, it loses its charm and its empire.

Ancient Greece and modern Italy are continually cited as triumphant examples of what the alliance of art, religion, and the state can do. Nothing is more true, if the question is concerning their union; nothing is more false, if the question is concerning the servitude of art. Art in Greece was so little the slave of religion, that it little by little modified the symbols, and, to a certain extent, the spirit itself, by its free representations. There is a long distance between the divinities that Greece received from Egypt and those of which it has left immortal exemplars. Are those primitive artists and poets, as Homer and Dedalus are called, strangers to this change? And in the most beautiful epoch of art, did not Æschylus and Phidias carry a great liberty into the religious scenes which they exposed to the gaze of the people, in the theatre, or in front of the temples? In Italy as in Greece, as everywhere, art is at first in the hands of priesthoods and governments; but, as it increases its importance and is developed, it more and more conquers its liberty. Men speak of the faith that animated the artists and vivified their works; that is true of the time of Giotto and Ciambuë; but after Angelico de Fiesole, at the end of the fifteenth century, in Italy, I perceive especially the faith of art in itself and the worship of beauty. Raphael was about to become a cardinal;[119] yes, but always painting Galatea, and

---

[119] Vassari, Vie de Raphael.

without quitting Fornarine. Once more, let us exaggerate nothing; let us distinguish, not separate; let us unite art, religion, and country, but let not their union injure the liberty of each. Let us be thoroughly penetrated with the thought, that art is also to itself a kind of religion. God manifests himself to us by the idea of the true, by the idea of the good, by the idea of the beautiful. Each one of them leads to God, because it comes from him. True beauty is ideal beauty, and ideal beauty is a reflection of the infinite. So, independently of all official alliance with religion and morals, art is by itself essentially religious and moral; for, far from wanting its own law, its own genius, it everywhere expresses in its works eternal beauty. Bound on all sides to matter by inflexible laws, working upon inanimate stone, upon uncertain and fugitive sounds, upon words of limited and finite signification, art communicates to them, with the precise form that is addressed to such or such a sense, a mysterious character that is addressed to the imagination and the soul, takes them away from reality, and bears them sweetly or violently into unknown regions. Every work of art, whatever may be its form, small or great, figured, sung, or uttered,—every work of art, truly beautiful or sublime, throws the soul into a gentle or severe reverie that elevates it towards the infinite. The infinite is the common limit after which the soul aspires upon the wings of imagination as well as reason, by the route of the sublime and the beautiful, as well as by that of the true and the good. The emotion that the beautiful produces turns the soul from this world; it is the beneficent emotion that art produces for humanity.

LECTURE IX.

THE DIFFERENT ARTS.

Expression is the general law of art.—Division of arts.—Distinction between liberal arts and trades.—Eloquence itself, philosophy, and history do not make a part of the fine arts.—That the arts gain nothing by encroaching upon each other, and usurping each other's means and processes.—Classification of the arts:—its true principle is expression.—Comparison of arts with each other.—Poetry the first of arts.

A *résumé* of the last lecture would be a definition of art, of its end and law. Art is the free reproduction of the beautiful, not of a single natural beauty, but of ideal beauty, as the human imagination conceives it by the aid of data which nature furnishes it. The ideal beauty envelops the infinite:—the end of art is, then, to produce works that, like those of nature, or even in a still higher degree, may have the charm of the infinite. But how and by what illusion can we draw the infinite from the finite? This is the difficulty of art, and its glory also. What bears us towards the infinite in natural beauty? The ideal side of this beauty. The ideal is the mysterious ladder that enables the soul to ascend from the finite to the infinite. The artist, then, must devote himself to the representation of the ideal. Every thing has its ideal. The first care of the artist will be, then, whatever he does, to penetrate at first to the concealed ideal of his subject, for his subject has an ideal,—in order to render it, in the next place, more or less striking to the senses and the soul, according to the conditions which the very materials that he employs—the stone, the color, the sound, the language—impose on him.

So, to express the ideal of the infinite in one way or another, is the law of art; and all the arts are such only by their relation to the sentiment of the beautiful and the infinite which they awaken in the soul, by the aid of that high quality of every work of art that is called expression.

Expression is essentially ideal: what expression tries to make felt, is not what the eye can see and the hand touch, evidently it is something invisible and impalpable.

The problem of art is to reach the soul through the body. Art offers to the senses forms, colors, sounds, words, so arranged that they excite in the soul, concealed behind the senses, the inexpressible emotion of beauty.

Expression is addressed to the soul as form is addressed to the senses. Form is the obstacle of expression, and, at the same time, is its imperative, necessary, only means. By working upon form, by bending it to its service, by dint of care, patience, and genius, art succeeds in converting an obstacle into a means.

By their object, all arts are equal; all are arts only because they express the invisible. It cannot be too often repeated, that expression is the supreme law of art. The thing to express is always the same,—it is the idea, the spirit, the soul, the invisible, the infinite. But, as the question is concerning the expression of this one and the same thing, by addressing ourselves to the senses which are diverse, the difference of the senses divides art into different arts.

We have seen, that, of the five senses which have been given to man,[120] three—taste, smell, and touch—are incapable of producing in us the sentiment of beauty. Joined to the other two, they may contribute to the understanding of this sentiment; but alone and by themselves they cannot produce it. Taste judges of the agreeable, not of the beautiful. No sense is less allied to the soul and more in the service of the body; it flatters, it serves the grossest of all masters, the stomach. If smell sometimes seems to participate in the sentiment of the beautiful, it is because the odor is exhaled from an object that is already beautiful, that is beautiful for some other reason. Thus the rose is beautiful for its graceful form, for the varied splendor of its colors; its odor is agreeable, it is not beautiful. Finally, it is not touch alone that judges of the regularity of forms, but touch enlightened by sight.

---

[120] Lecture 6.

There remain two senses to which all the world concedes the privilege of exciting in us the idea and the sentiment of the beautiful. They seem to be more particularly in the service of the soul. The sensations which they give have something purer, more intellectual. They are less indispensable for the material preservation of the individual. They contribute to the embellishment rather than to the sustaining of life. They procure us pleasures in which our personality seems less interested and more self-forgetful. To these two senses, then, art should be addressed, is addressed, in fact, in order to reach the soul. Hence the division of arts into two great classes,—arts addressed to hearing, arts addressed to sight; on the one hand, music and poetry; on the other, painting, with engraving, sculpture, architecture, gardening.

It will, perhaps, seem strange that we rank among the arts neither eloquence, nor history, nor philosophy.

The arts are called the fine arts, because their sole object is to produce the disinterested emotion of beauty, without regard to the utility either of the spectator or the artist. They are also called the liberal arts, because they are the arts of free men and not of slaves, which affranchise the soul, charm and ennoble existence; hence the sense and origin of those expressions of antiquity, *artes liberales, artes ingenuæ*. There are arts without nobility, whose end is practical and material utility; they are called trades, such as that of the stove-maker and the mason. True art may be joined to them, may even shine in them, but only in the accessories and the details.

Eloquence, history, philosophy, are certainly high employments of intelligence; they have their dignity, their eminence, which nothing surpasses, but rigorously speaking, they are not arts.

Eloquence does not propose to itself to produce in the soul of the auditors the disinterested sentiment of beauty. It may also produce this effect, but without having sought it. Its direct end, which it can subordinate to no other, is to convince, to persuade. Eloquence has a client which before all it must save or make triumph. It matters little, whether this client be a man, a people, or an idea. Fortunate is the orator if he elicits the expression: That is beautiful! for it is a noble homage rendered to his talent; unfortunate is he if he does not elicit this, for he has missed his end. The two great types of political and religious eloquence, Demosthenes in antiquity, Bossuet among the moderns, think only of the interest of the cause confided to their genius, the sacred cause of country and that of religion; whilst at bottom Phidias and Raphael work to make beautiful things. Let us hasten to say, what the names of Demosthenes and Bossuet command us to say, that true eloquence, very different from that of rhetoric, disdains certain means of success; it asks no more than to please, but without any sacrifice unworthy of it; every foreign ornament degrades it. Its proper character is simplicity, earnestness—I do not mean affected earnestness, a designed and artful gravity, the worst of all deceptions—I mean true earnestness, that springs from sincere and profound conviction. This is what Socrates understood by true eloquence.[121]

As much must be said of history and philosophy. The philosopher speaks and writes. Can he, then, like the orator, find accents which make truth enter the soul, colors and forms that make it shine forth evident and manifest to the eyes of intelligence? It would be betraying his cause to neglect the means that can serve it; but the profoundest art is here only a means, the aim of philosophy is elsewhere; whence it follows that philosophy is not an art. Without doubt, Plato is a great artist; he is the peer of Sophocles and Phidias, as Pascal is sometimes the rival of Demosthenes and Bossuet;[122] but both would have blushed if they had discovered at the bottom of their soul another design, another aim than the service of truth and virtue.

History does not relate for the sake of relating; it does not paint for the sake of painting; it relates and paints the past that it

---

[121] See the Gorgias, with the Argument, vol. iii. of our translation of Plato.
[122] There is a Provincial that for vehemence can be compared only to the Philipics, and its fragment on the infinite has the grandeur and magnificence of Bossuet. See our work on the Thoughts of Pascal, 4th Series, Literature, vol. i.

may be the living lesson of the future. It proposes to instruct new generations by the experience of those who have gone before them, by exhibiting to them a faithful picture of great and important events, with their causes and their effects, with general designs and particular passions, with the faults, virtues, and crimes that are found mingled together in human things. It teaches the excellence of prudence, courage, and great thoughts profoundly meditated, constantly pursued, and executed with moderation and force. It shows the vanity of immoderate pretensions, the power of wisdom and virtue, the impotence of folly and crime. Thucydides, Polybius, and Tacitus undertake any thing else than procuring new emotions for an idle curiosity or a worn-out imagination; they doubtless desire to interest and attract, but more to instruct; they are the avowed masters of statesmen and the preceptors of mankind.

The sole object of art is the beautiful. Art abandons itself as soon as it shuns this. It is often constrained to make concessions to circumstances, to external conditions that are imposed upon it; but it must always retain a just liberty. Architecture and the art of gardening are the least free of arts; they are subjected to unavoidable obstacles; it belongs to the genius of the artist to govern these obstacles, and even to draw from them happy effects, as the poet turns the slavery of metre and rhyme into a source of unexpected beauties. Extreme liberty may carry art to a caprice which degrades it, as chains too heavy crush it. It is the death of architecture to subject it to convenience, to *comfort*. Is the architect obliged to subordinate general effect and the proportions of the edifice to such or such a particular end that is prescribed to him? He takes refuge in details, in pediments, in friezes, in all the parts that have not utility for a special object, and in them he becomes a true artist. Sculpture and painting, especially music and poetry, are freer than architecture and the art of gardening. One can also shackle them, but they disengage themselves more easily.

Similar by their common end, all the arts differ by the particular effects which they produce, and by the processes which they employ. They gain nothing by exchanging their means and confounding the limits that separate them. I bow before the authority of antiquity; but, perhaps, through habit and a remnant of prejudice, I have some difficulty in representing to myself with pleasure statues composed of several metals, especially painted statues.[123] Without pretending that sculpture has not to a certain point its color, that of perfectly pure matter, that especially which the hand of time impresses upon it, in spite of all the seductions of a contemporaneous[124] artist of great talent, I have little taste, I confess, for that artifice that is forced to give to marble the *morbidezza* of painting. Sculpture is an austere muse; it has its graces, but they are those of no other art. Flesh-color must remain a stranger to it: there would nothing more remain to communicate to it but the movement of poetry and the indefiniteness of music! And what will music gain by aiming at the picturesque, when its proper domain is the pathetic? Give to the most learned symphonist a storm to render. Nothing is easier to imitate than the whistling of the winds and the noise of thunder. But by what combinations of harmony will he exhibit to the eyes the glare of the lightning rending all of a sudden the veil of the night, and what is most fearful in the tempest, the movement of the waves that now ascend like a mountain, now descend and seem to precipitate themselves into bottomless abysses? If the auditor is not informed of the subject, he will never suspect it, and I defy him to distinguish a tempest from a battle. In spite of science and genius, sounds cannot paint forms. Music, when well guided, will guard itself from contending against the impossible; it will not undertake to express the tumult and strife of the waves and other similar phenomena; it will do more: with sounds it will fill the soul with the sentiments that succeed each other in us during the different scenes of the tempest. Haydn will thus become[125] the rival, even the vanquisher

---

[123] See the Jupiter Olympien of M. Quatremère de Quincy.

[124] Allusion to the Magdeleine of Canova, which was then to be seen in the gallery of M. de Sommariva.

[125] See the Tempest of Haydn, among the pianoforte works of this master.

of the painter, because it has been given to music to move and agitate the soul more profoundly than painting.

Since the *Laocoon* of Lessing, it is no longer permitted to repeat, without great reserve, the famous axiom,—*Ut pictura poesis*; or, at least, it is very certain that painting cannot do every thing that poetry can do. Everybody admires the picture of Rumor, drawn by Virgil; but let a painter try to realize this symbolic figure; let him represent to us a huge monster with a hundred eyes, a hundred mouths, and a hundred ears, whose feet touch the earth, whose head is lost in the clouds, and such a figure will become very ridiculous.

So the arts have a common end, and entirely different means. Hence the general rules common to all, and particular rules for each. I have neither time nor space to enter into details on this point. I limit myself to repeating, that the great law which governs all others, is expression. Every work of art that does not express an idea signifies nothing; in addressing itself to such or such a sense, it must penetrate to the mind, to the soul, and bear thither a thought, a sentiment capable of touching or elevating it. From this fundamental rule all the others are derived; for example, that which is continually and justly recommended,—composition. To this is particularly applied the precept of unity and variety. But, in saying this, we have said nothing so long as we have not determined the nature of the unity of which we would speak. True unity, is unity of expression, and variety is made only to spread over the entire work the idea or the single sentiment that it should express. It is useless to remark, that between composition thus defined, and what is often called composition, as the symmetry and arrangement of parts according to artificial rules, there is an abyss. True composition is nothing else than the most powerful means of expression.

Expression not only furnishes the general rules of art, it also gives the principle that allows of their classification.

In fact, every classification, supposes a principle that serves as a common measure.

Such a principle has been sought in pleasure, and the first of arts has seemed that which gives the most vivid joys. But we have proved that the object of art is not pleasure:—the more or less of pleasure that an art procures cannot, then, be the true measure of its value.

This measure is nothing else than expression. Expression being the supreme end, the art that most nearly approaches it is the first of all.

All true arts are expressive, but they are diversely so. Take music; it is without contradiction the most penetrating, the profoundest, the most intimate art. There is physically and morally between a sound and the soul a marvellous relation. It seems as though the soul were an echo in which the sound takes a new power. Extraordinary things are recounted of the ancient music. And it must not be believed that the greatness of effect supposes here very complicated means. No, the less noise music makes, the more it touches. Give some notes to Pergolese, give him especially some pure and sweet voices, and he returns a celestial charm, bears you away into infinite spaces, plunges you into ineffable reveries. The peculiar power of music is to open to the imagination a limitless career, to lend itself with astonishing facility to all the moods of each one, to arouse or calm, with the sounds of the simplest melody, our accustomed sentiments, our favorite affections. In this respect music is an art without a rival:—however, it is not the first of arts.

Music pays for the immense power that has been given it; it awakens more than any other art the sentiment of the infinite, because it is vague, obscure, indeterminate in its effects. It is just the opposite art to sculpture, which bears less towards the infinite, because every thing in it is fixed with the last degree of precision. Such is the force and at the same time the feebleness of music, that it expresses every thing and expresses nothing in particular. Sculpture, on the contrary, scarcely gives rise to any reverie, for it clearly represents such a thing and not such another. Music does not paint, it touches; it puts in motion imagination, not the imagination that reproduces images, but that which makes the heart beat, for it is absurd to limit imagination to the domain of images.[126] The heart, once touched, moves all the rest of our being; thus music, indirectly, and to a certain point, can recall images and ideas; but its direct and natural power is neither on the representative imagination nor intelligence, it is on the heart, and that is an advantage sufficiently beautiful.

The domain of music is sentiment, but even there its power is more profound than extensive, and if it expresses certain sentiments with an incomparable force, it expresses but a very small number of them. By way of association, it can awaken them all, but directly it produces very few of them, and the simplest and the most elementary, too,—sadness and joy with their thousand shades. Ask music to express magnanimity, virtuous resolution, and other sentiments of this kind, and it will be just as incapable of doing it, as of painting a lake or a mountain. It goes about it as it can; it employs the slow, the rapid, the loud, the soft, etc., but imagination has to do the rest, and imagination does only what it pleases. The same measure reminds one of a mountain, another of the ocean; the warrior finds in it heroic inspirations, the recluse religious inspirations. Doubtless, words determine musical expression, but the merit then is in the word, not in the music; and sometimes the word stamps the music with a precision that destroys it, and deprives it of its proper effects— vagueness, obscurity, monotony, but also fulness and profundity, I was about to say infinitude. I do not in the least admit that famous definition of song:—a noted declamation. A simple declamation rightly accented is certainly preferable to stunning accompaniments; but to music must be left its character, and its defects and advantages must not be taken away from it. Especially it must not be turned aside from its object, and there must not be demanded from it what it could not give. It is not made to express complicated and factitious sentiment, nor terrestrial and vulgar sentiments. Its peculiar charm is to elevate the soul towards the infinite. It is therefore naturally allied to religion, especially to

---

[126] See lecture 6.

that religion of the infinite, which is at the same time the religion of the heart; it excels in transporting to the feet of eternal mercy the soul trembling on the wings of repentance, hope, and love. Happy are those, who, at Rome, in the Vatican,[127] during the solemnities of the Catholic worship, have heard the melodies of Leo, Durante, and Pergolese, on the old consecrated text! They have entered heaven for a moment, and their souls have been able

---

[127] I have not myself had the good fortune to hear the religious music of the Vatican. Therefore, I shall let a competent judge, M. Quatremère de Quincy, speak, Considérations Morales sur les Destination des Ouvrages de l'Art, Paris, 1815, p. 98: "Let one call to mind those chants so simple and so touching, that terminate at Rome the funeral solemnities of those three days which the Church particularly devotes to the expression of its grief, in the last week of Lent. In that nave where the genius of Michael Angelo has embraced the duration of ages, from the wonders of creation to the last judgment that must destroy its works, are celebrated, in the presence of the Roman pontiff, those nocturnal ceremonies whose rites, symbols, and plaintive liturgies seem to be so many figures of the mystery of grief to which they are consecrated. The light decreasing by degrees, at the termination of each psalm, you would say that a funeral veil is extended little by little over those religious vaults. Soon the doubtful light of the last lamp allows you to perceive nothing but Christ in the distance, in the midst of clouds, pronouncing his judgments, and some angel executors of his behests. Then, at the bottom of a tribune interdicted to the regard of the profane, is heard the psalm of the penitent king, to which three of the greatest masters of the art have added the modulations of a simple and pathetic chant. No instrument is mingled with those accents. Simple harmonies of voice execute that music; but these voices seem to be those of angels, and their effect penetrates the depths of the soul."

We have cited this beautiful passage—and we could have cited many others, even superior to it—of a man now forgotten, and almost always misunderstood, but whom posterity will put in his place. Let us indicate, at least, the last pages of the same production, on the necessity of leaving the works of art in the place for which they were made, for example, the portrait of Mlle. de Vallière in the Madeleine aux Carmélites, instead of transferring it to, and exposing it in the apartments of Versailles, "the only place in the world," eloquently says M. Quatremère, "which never should have seen it."

to ascend thither without distinction of rank, country, even belief, by those invisible and mysterious steps, composed, thus to speak, of all the simple, natural, universal sentiments, that everywhere on earth draw from the bosom of the human creature a sigh towards another world!

Between sculpture and music, those two opposite extremes, is painting, nearly as precise as the one, nearly as touching as the other. Like sculpture, it marks the visible forms of objects, but adds to them life; like music, it expresses the profoundest sentiments of the soul, and expresses them all. Tell me what sentiment does not come within the province of the painter? He has entire nature at his disposal, the physical world, and the moral world, a churchyard, a landscape, a sunset, the ocean, the great scenes of civil and religious life, all the beings of creation, above all, the figure of man, and its expression, that living mirror of what passes in the soul. More pathetic than sculpture, clearer than music, painting is elevated, in my opinion, above both, because it expresses beauty more under all its forms, and the human soul in all the richness and variety of its sentiments.

But the art *par excellence*, that which surpasses all others, because it is incomparably the most expressive, is poetry.

Speech is the instrument of poetry; poetry fashions it to its use, and idealizes it, in order to make it express ideal beauty. Poetry gives to it the charm and power of measure; it makes of it something intermediary between the ordinary voice and music, something at once material and immaterial, finite, clear, and precise, like contours and forms the most definite, living and animated like color, pathetic and infinite like sound. A word in itself, especially a word chosen and transfigured by poetry, is the most energetic and universal symbol. Armed with this talisman, poetry reflects all the images of the sensible world, like sculpture and painting; it reflects sentiment like painting and music, with all its varieties, which music does not attain, and in their rapid succession that painting cannot follow, as precise and immobile as sculpture; and it not only expresses all that, it expresses what is inaccessible to every other art, I mean thought, entirely distinct from the senses and even from sentiment,—thought that has no forms,—thought that has no color, that lets no sound escape, that does not manifest itself in any way,—thought in its highest flight, in its most refined abstraction.

Think of it. What a world of images, of sentiments, of thoughts at once distinct and confused, are excited within us by this one word—country! and by this other word, brief and immense,—God! What is more clear and altogether more profound and vast!

Tell the architect, the sculptor, the painter, even the musician, to call forth also by a single stroke all the powers of nature and the soul! They cannot, and by that they acknowledge the superiority of speech and poetry.

They proclaim it themselves, for they take poetry for their own measure; they esteem their own works, and demand that they should be esteemed, in proportion as they approach the poetic ideal. And the human race does as artists do: a beautiful picture, a noble melody, a living and expressive statue, gives rise to the exclamation—How poetical! This is not an arbitrary comparison; it is a natural judgment which makes poetry the type of the perfection of all the arts,—the art *par excellence*, which comprises all others, to which they aspire, which none can reach.

When the other arts would imitate the works of poetry, they usually err, losing their own genius, without robbing poetry of its genius. But poetry constructs according to its own taste palaces and temples, like architecture; it makes them simple or magnificent; all orders, as well as all systems, obey it; the different ages of art are the same to it; it reproduces, if it pleases, the classic or the Gothic, the beautiful or the sublime, the measured or the infinite. Lessing has been able, with the exactest justice, to compare Homer to the most perfect sculptor; with such precision are the forms which that marvellous chisel gives to all beings determined! And what a painter, too, is Homer! and, of a different kind, Dante! Music alone has something more penetrating than poetry, but it is vague, limited, and fugitive. Besides its clearness, its variety, its durability, poetry has also the most pathetic accents. Call to mind the words that Priam utters at the feet of Achilles while asking him for the dead body of his son, more than one verse of Virgil, entire scenes of the *Cid* and the *Polyeucte*, the prayer of Esther kneeling before the Lord, the choruses of *Esther* and *Athalie*. In the celebrated song of Pergolese, *Stabat Mater Dolorosa*, we may ask which moves most, the music or the words. The *Dies iræ, Dies illa*, recited only, produces the most terrible effect. In those fearful words, every blow tells, so to speak; each word contains a distinct sentiment, an idea at once profound and determinate. The intellect advances at each step, and the heart rushes on in its turn. Human speech idealized by poetry has the depth and brilliancy of musical notes; it is luminous as well as pathetic; it speaks to the mind as well as to the heart; it is in that inimitable, unique, and embraces all extremes and all contraries in a harmony that redoubles their reciprocal effect, in which, by turns, appear and are developed, all images, all sentiments, all ideas, all the human faculties, all the inmost recesses of the soul, all the forms of things, all real and all intelligible worlds!

LECTURE X.

FRENCH ART IN THE SEVENTEENTH CENTURY.

Expression not only serves to appreciate the different arts, but the different schools of art. Example:—French art in the seventeenth century. French poetry:—Corneille. Racine. Molière. La Fontaine. Boileau.—Painting:—Lesueur. Poussin. Le Lorrain. Champagne.—Engraving.—Sculpture:—Sarrazin. The Anguiers. Girardon. Pujet.—Le Nôtre.—Architecture.

We believe that we have firmly established that all kinds of beauty, although most dissimilar in appearance, may, when subjected to a serious examination, be reduced to spiritual and moral beauty; that expression, therefore, is at once the true object and the first law of art; that all arts are such only so far as they express the idea concealed under the form, and are addressed to the soul through the senses; finally, that in expression the different arts find the true measure of their relative value, and the most expressive art must be placed in the first rank.

If expression judges the different arts, does it not naturally follow, that by the same title it can also judge the different schools which, in each art, dispute with each other the empire of taste?

There is not one of these schools that does not represent in its own way some side of the beautiful, and we are disposed to embrace all in an impartial and kindly study. We are eclectics in the arts as well as in metaphysics. But, as in metaphysics, the knowledge of all systems, and the portion of truth that is in each, enlightens without enfeebling our convictions; so, in the history of arts, while holding the opinion that no school must be disdained, that even in China some shade of beauty can be found, our eclecticism does not make us waver in regard to the sentiment of true beauty and the supreme rule of art. What we demand of the different schools, without distinction of time or place, what we see in the south as well as in the north, at Florence, Rome, Venice, and Seville, as well as at Antwerp, Amsterdam, and Paris,—wherever there are men, is something human, is the expression of a sentiment or an idea.

A criticism that should be founded on the principle of expression, would somewhat derange, it must be confessed, received judgments, and would carry some disorder into the hierarchy of the renowned. We do not undertake such a revolution; we only propose to confirm, or at least elucidate our principle by an example, and by an example that is at our hand.

There is in the world a school formerly illustrious, now very lightly treated:—this school is the French school of the seventeenth century. We would replace it in honor, by recalling attention to the qualities that make its glory.

We have worked with constancy to reinstate among us the philosophy of Descartes, unworthily sacrificed to the philosophy of Locke, because with its defects it possesses in our view the incomparable merit of subordinating the senses to the mind, of elevating and ennobling man. So we profess a serious and reflective admiration for our national art of the seventeenth century, because, without disguising what is wanting to it, we find in it what we prefer to every thing else, grandeur united to good sense and reason, simplicity and force, genius of composition, especially that of expression.

France, careless of her glory, does not appear to have the least notion that she reckons in her annals perhaps the greatest century of humanity, that which embraces the greatest number of extraordinary men of every kind. When, I pray you, have politicians like Henry IV., Richelieu, Mazarin, Colbert, Louis XIV. been seen giving each other the hand? I do not pretend that each of them has no rival, even superiors. Alexander, Cæsar, Charlemagne, perhaps excel them. But Alexander has but a single contemporary that can be compared with him, his father Philip; Cæsar cannot even have suspected that Octavius would one day be worthy of him; Charlemagne is a colossus in a desert; whilst among us these five men succeed each other without an interval, press upon each other, and have, thus to speak, a single soul. And by what officers were they served! Is Condé really inferior to Alexander, Hannibal, and Cæsar; for among his predecessors we must not look for other rivals? Who among them surpasses him in the extent and justness of his conceptions, in quickness of sight, in rapidity of manœuvres, in the union of impetuosity and firmness, in the double glory of taker of cities and gainer of battles? Add that he dealt with generals like Merci and William, that he had under him Turenne and Luxemburg, without speaking of so many other soldiers who were reared in that admirable school, and at the hour of reverse still sufficed to save France.

What other time, at least among the moderns, has seen flourishing together so many poets of the first order? We have, it is true, neither Homer, nor Dante, nor Milton, nor even Tasso. The epic, with its primitive simplicity, is interdicted us. But in the drama we scarcely have equals. It is because dramatic poetry is the poetry that is adapted to us, moral poetry *par excellence*, which represents man with his different passions armed against each other, the violent contentions between virtue and crime, the freaks of fortune, the lessons of providence, and in a narrow compass, too, in which the events press upon each other without confusion, in which the action rapidly progresses towards the crisis that must reveal what is most intimate to the heart of the personages.

Let us dare to say what we think, that, in our opinion, Æschylus, Sophocles, and Euripides, together, do not equal Corneille; for none of them has known and expressed like him what is of all things most truly touching, a great soul at war with itself, between a generous passion and duty. Corneille is the creator of a new pathetic unknown to antiquity and to all the moderns before him. He disdains to address common and subaltern passions; he does not seek to rouse terror and pity, as demands Aristotle, who limits himself to erecting into maxims the practice of the Greeks. Corneille seems to have read Plato, and followed his precepts:—he addresses a most elevated part of human nature, the noblest passion, the one nearest virtue,—

admiration; and from admiration carried to its culmination he draws the most powerful effects. Shakspeare, we admit, is superior to Corneille in extent and richness of dramatic genius. Entire human nature seems at his disposal, and he reproduces the different scenes of life in their beauty and deformity, in their grandeur and baseness. He excels in painting the terrible or the gentle passions. Othello is jealousy, Lady Macbeth is ambition, as Juliet and Desdemona are the immortal names of youthful and unfortunate love. But if Corneille has less imagination, he has more soul. Less varied, he is more profound. If he does not put upon the stage so many different characters, those that he does put on it are the greatest that can be offered to humanity. The scenes that he gives are less heart-rending, but at once more delicate and more sublime. What is the melancholy of Hamlet, the grief of King Lear, even the disdainful intrepidity of Cæsar, in comparison with the magnanimity of Augustus striving to be master of himself as well as the universe, in comparison with Chimène sacrificing love to honor, especially in comparison with Pauline, not suffering even at the bottom of her heart an involuntary sigh for the one that she must not love? Corneille always confines himself to the highest regions. He is by turns Roman and Christian. He is the interpreter of heroes, the chanter of virtue, the poet of warriors and politicians.[128] And it must not be forgotten that Shakspeare is almost alone in his times, whilst after Corneille comes Racine, who would suffice for the poetical glory of a nation.

Racine assuredly cannot be compared with Corneille for dramatic genius; he is more the man of letters; he has not the tragic soul; he neither loves nor understands politics and war. When he imitates Corneille, for example, in Alexander, and even in Mithridates, he imitates him badly enough. The scene, so vaunted, of Mithridates exposing his plan of campaign to his sons is a morsel of the finest rhetoric, which cannot be compared with the political and military scenes of Cinna and Sertorius, especially

---

[128] One is reminded of the expression of the great Condé: "Where then has Corneille learned politics and war?"

with that first scene of the Death of Pompey, in which you witness a counsel as true, as grand, as profound as ever could have been one of the counsels of Richelieu or Mazarin. Racine was not born to paint heroes, but he paints admirably man with his natural passions, and the most natural as well as the most touching of all, love. So he particularly excels in feminine characters. For men he has need of being sustained by Tacitus or holy Scripture.[129] With woman he is at his ease, and he makes them think and speak with perfect truth, set off by exquisite art. Demand of him neither Emilie, Cornélie, nor Pauline; but listen to Andromaque, Monime, Bérénice, and Phèdre! There, even in imitating, he is original, and leaves the ancients very far behind him. Who has taught him that charming delivery, those graceful troubles, that purity even in feebleness, that melancholy, sometimes even that depth, with that marvellous language which seems the natural accent of woman's heart? It is continually repeated that Racine wrote better than Corneille:—say only that the two wrote very differently, and like men in very different epochs. One has two sovereign qualities, which belong to his own nature and his times, a *naïveté* and grandeur, the other is not *naïve*, but he has too much taste not to be always simple, and he supplies the place of grandeur, forever lost, with consummate elegance. Corneille speaks the language of statesmen, soldiers,

---

[129] It would be a curious and useful study, to compare with the original all the passages of Britannicus imitated from Tacitus; in them Racine would almost always be found below his model. I will give a single example. In the account of the death of Britannicus, Racine thus expresses the different effects of the crime on the spectators:

Juez combien ce coup frappe tous les esprits; La moitié s'épouvante et sort avec des cris; Mais ceux qui de la cour ont un plus long usage Sur les yeux de César composent leur visage.

Certainly the style is excellent; but it pales and seems nothing more than a very feeble sketch in comparison with the rapid and sombre pencil-strokes of the great Roman painter: "Trepidatur a circumsedentibus, diffugiunt imprudentes; at, quibus altior intellectus, resistunt defixi et Neronem intuentes."

theologians, philosophers, and clever women; of Richelieu, Rohan, Saint-Cyran, Descartes, and Pascal; of mother Angélique Arnaud and mother Madeleine de Saint-Joseph; the language which Molière still spoke, which Bossuet preserved to his last breath. Racine speaks that of Louis XIV. and the women who were the ornament of his court. I suppose that thus spoke Madame, the amiable, sprightly, and unfortunate Henriette; thus wrote the author of the *Princesse de Clèves* and the author of *Télémaque*. Or, rather, this language is that of Racine himself, of that feeble and tender soul, which passed quickly from love to devotion, which uttered its complaints in lyric poetry, which was wholly poured out in the choruses of *Esther* and *Athalie*, and in the *Cantiques Spirituels*; that soul, so easy to be moved, that a religious ceremony or a representation of *Esther* at Saint-Cyr touched to tears, that pitied the misfortunes of the people, that found in its pity and its charity the courage to speak one day the truth to Louis XIV., and was extinguished by the first breath of disgrace.

Molière is, in comparison with Aristophanes, what Corneille is, in comparison with Shakspeare. The author of *Plutus*, the *Wasps*, and the *Clouds*, has doubtless an imagination, an explosive buffoonery, a creative power, above all comparison. Molière has not as great poetical conceptions: he has more, perhaps; he has characters. His coloring is less brilliant, his graver is more penetrating. He has engraved in the memory of men a certain number of irregularities and vices which will ever be called *l'Avare* (*the Miser*), *le Malade Imaginaire* (the *Hypochondriac*), *les Femmes Savantes* (the *Learned Women*), *le Tartufe* (the *Hypocrite*), and *Don Juan*, not to speak of the *Misanthrope*, a piece apart, touching as pleasant, which is not addressed to the crowd, and cannot be popular, because it expresses a ridicule rare enough, excess in the passion of truth and honor.

Of all fabulists, ancient and modern, does any one, even the ingenious, the pure, the elegant Phædrus, approach our La Fontaine? He composes his personages, and puts them in action with the skill of Molière; he knows how to take on occasion the tone of Horace, and mingle an ode with a fable; he is at once the most naïve, and the most refined of writers, and his art disappears in its very perfection. We do not speak of the tales, first, because we condemn the kind, then, because La Fontaine displays in them qualities more Italian than French, a narrative full of nature, malice, and grace, but without any of those profound, tender, melancholy traits, that place among the greatest poets of all time the author of the *Two Pigeons* (*Deux Pigeons*), the *Old Man* (*Vieillard*), and the *Three Young Persons* (*Gens*).

We do not hesitate to put Boileau among these great men. He comes after them, it is true, but he belongs to their company: he comprehends them, loves them, sustains them. It was he, who, in 1663, after the *School of Women* (*l'Ecole des Femmes*) and long before the *Hypocrite* (*le Tartufe*), and the *Misanthrope*, proclaimed Molière the master in the art of verse. It was he who, in 1677, after the failure of *Phèdre*, defended the vanquisher of Euripides against the successes of Pradon. It was he who, in advance of posterity, first put in light what is new and entirely original in the plays of Corneille.[130] He saved the pension of the old tragedian by offering the sacrifice of his own. Louis XIV. asking him what writer most honored his reign, Boileau answered, that it was Molière; and when the great king in his decline persecuted Port-Royal, and wished to lay hands on Arnaud, he encountered a man of letters, who said to the face of the imperious monarch,—"Your Majesty in vain seeks M. Arnaud, you are too fortunate to find him." Boileau is somewhat wanting in imagination and invention; but he is great in the energetic sentiment of truth and justice; he carries to the extent of passion taste for the beautiful and the honest; he is a poet by force of soul and good sense. More than once his heart dictated to him the most pathetic verses:

---

[130] See the letter to Perrault.

"In vain against the Cid a minister is leagued,[131] All Paris for Chimène the eyes of Rodrique," etc.

*   *   *   *   *

"After a little spot of earth, obtained by prayer, Forever in the tomb had inclosed Molière," etc.

And this epitaph of Arnaud, so simple and so grand:[132]

"At the feet of this altar of structure gross, Lies without pomp, inclosed in a coffin vile, The most learned mortal that ever wrote; Arnaud, who in grace instructed by Jesus Christ, Combating for the Church, has, in the Church itself, Suffered more than one outrage and more than one anathema," etc.

*   *   *   *   *

"Wandering, poor, banished, proscribed, persecuted; And even by his death their ill-extinguished rage Had never left his ashes in repose, If God himself here by his holy flock From these devouring wolves had not concealed his bones."[133]

These are, I think, poets sufficiently great, and we have more of them still: I mean those charming or sublime minds who have

---

[131] En vain contre le Cid ministre se ligue, Tout Paris pour Chimène a les yeux de Rodrique, etc.

*   *   *   *   *

Après qu'un peu de terre, obtenu par prière, Pour jamais dans la tombe eut enfermé Molière, etc.

*   *   *   *   *

[132] Aux pieds de cet autel de structure grossière, Git sans pompe, enfermé dans une vile bière, Le plus savant mortel qui jamais ait écrit; Arnaud, qui sur la grâce instruit par Jésus-Christ, Combattant pour l'Eglise, a, dans l'Eglise même, Souffert plus d'un outrage et plus d'un anathème, etc.

*   *   *   *   *

Errant, pauvre, banni, proscrit, persécuté; Et même par sa mort leur fureur mal éteinte N'aurait jamais laissé ses cendres en repos, Si Dieu lui-même ici de son ouaille sainte A ces loups dévorants n'avait caché les os.

[133] These verses did not appear till after the death of Boileau, and they are not well known. Jean-Baptiste Rousseau, in a letter to Brossette, rightly said that these are "the most beautiful verses that M. Despréaux ever made."

elevated prose to poetry. Greece alone, in her most beautiful days, offers, perhaps, such a variety of admirable prose writers. Who can enumerate them? At first, Rabelais and Montaigne; later, Descartes, Pascal, and Malebranche; La Rochefoucauld and La Bruyère; Retz and Saint-Simon; Bourdaloue, Fléchier, Fénelon, and Bossuet; add to these so many eminent women, at their head

Madame de Sévigné; while Montesquieu, Voltaire, Rousseau, and Buffon are still to come.[134]

By what strange diversity could a country, in which the mental arts were carried to such perfection, remain ordinary in the other arts? Was the sentiment of the beautiful wanting, then, to

---

[134] 4th Series of our works, Literature, book i., Preface, p. 3: "It is in prose, perhaps, that our literary glory is most certain.... What modern nation reckons prose writers that approach those of our nation? The country of Shakspeare and Milton does not possess, since Bacon, a single prose writer of the first order [?]; that of Dante, Petrarch, Ariosto, and Tasso, is in vain proud of Machiavel, whose sound and manly diction, like the thought that it expresses, is destitute of grandeur. Spain, it is true, has produced Cervantes, an admirable writer, but he is alone.... France can easily show a list of more than twenty prose writers of genius: Froissard, Rabelais, Montaigne, Descartes, Pascal, La Rochefoucauld, Molière, Retz, La Bruyère, Malebranche, Bossuet, Fénelon, Fléchier, Bourdaloue, Massillon, Mme. de Sévigné, Saint-Simon, Montesquieu, Voltaire, Buffon, J. J. Rousseau; without speaking of so many more that would be in the first rank everywhere else,—Amiot, Calvin, Pasquier, D'Aubigné, Charron, Balzac, Vaugelas, Pélisson, Nicole, Fleury, Bussi, Saint-Evremont, Mme. de Lafayette, Mme. de Maintenon, Fontenelle, Vauvenargues, Hamilton, Le Sage, Prévost, Beaumarchais, etc. It may be said with the exactest truth, that French prose is without a rival in modern Europe; and, even in antiquity, superior to the Latin prose, at least in the quantity and variety of models, it has no equal but the Greek prose, in its palmiest days, in the days of Herodotus and Demosthenes. I do not prefer Demosthenes to Pascal, and it would be difficult for me to put Plato himself above Bossuet. Plato and Bossuet, in my opinion, are the two greatest masters of human language, with manifest differences, as well as more than one trait of resemblance; both ordinarily speak like the people, with the last degree of simplicity, and at moments ascending without effort to a poetry as magnificent as that of Homer, ingenious and polished to the most charming delicacy, and by instinct majestic and sublime. Plato, without doubt, has incomparable graces, the supreme serenity, and, as it were, the demi-smile of the divine sage. Bossuet, on his side, has the pathetic, in which he has no rival but the great Corneille. When such writers are possessed, is it not a religion to render them the honor that is their due, that of a regular and profound study?"

that society so polished, to that magnificent court, to those great lords and those great ladies passionately loving luxury and elegance, to that public of the *élite*, enamored of every kind of glory, whose enthusiasm defended the *Cid* against Richelieu? No; France in the seventeenth century was a whole, and produced artists that she can place by the side of her poets, her philosophers, her orators.

But, in order to admire our artists, it is necessary to comprehend them.

We do not believe that imagination has been less freely imparted to France than to any other nation of Europe. It has even had its reign among us. It is fancy that rules in the sixteenth century, and inspires the literature and the arts of the *Renaissance*. But a great revolution intervened at the commencement of the seventeenth century. France at that moment seems to pass from youth to virility. Instead of abandoning imagination to itself, we apply ourselves from that moment to restrain it without destroying it, to moderate it, as the Greeks did by the aid of taste; as in the progress of life and society we learn to repress or conceal what is too individual in character. An end is made of the literature of the preceding age. A new poetry, a new prose, begin to appear, which, during an entire century, bear fruits sufficiently beautiful. Art follows the general movement; after having been elegant and graceful, it becomes in its turn serious; it no longer aims at originality and extraordinary effects; it neither flashes nor dazzles; it speaks, above all, to the mind and the soul. Hence its good qualities and also its defects. In general, it is somewhat wanting in brilliancy and coloring, but it is in the highest degree expressive.

Some time since we have changed all that. We have discovered, somewhat late, that we have not sufficient imagination; we are in training to acquire it, it is true, at the expense of reason, alas! also at the expense of soul, which is forgotten, repudiated, proscribed. At this moment, color and form are the order of the day, in poetry, in painting, in every thing. We are beginning to run mad with Spanish painting. The

Flemish and Venetian schools are gaining ground on the schools of Florence and Rome. Rossini equals Mozart, and Gluck will soon seem to us insipid.

Young artists, who, rightly disgusted with the dry and inanimate manner of David, undertake to renovate French painting, who would rob the sun of its heat and splendor, remember that of all beings in the world, the greatest is still man, and that what is greatest in man is his intelligence, and above all, his heart; that it is this heart, then, which you must put and develop on your canvas. This is the most elevated object of art. In order to reach it, do not make yourselves disciples of Flemings, Venetians, and Spaniards; return, return to the masters of our great national school of the seventeenth century.

We bow with respectful admiration before the schools of Rome and Florence, at once ideal and living; but, those excepted, we maintain that the French school equals or surpasses all others. We prefer neither Murillo, Rubens, Corregio, nor Titian himself to Lesueur and Poussin, because, if the former have an incomparable hand and color, our two countrymen are much greater in thought and expression.

What a destiny was that of Eustache Lesueur![135] He was born at Paris about 1617, and he never went out of it. Poor and humble, he passed his life in the churches and convents where he worked. The only sweetness of his sad days, his only consolation was his wife: he loses her, and goes to die, at thirty-eight, in that cloister of Chartreux, which his pencil has immortalized. What resemblance at once, and what difference between his life and that of Raphael, who also died young, but in the midst of pleasures, in honors, and already almost in purple! Our Raphael was not the lover of Fornarina and the favorite of a pope: he was Christian; he is Christianity in art.

Lesueur is a genius wholly French. Scarcely having escaped from the hands of Simon Vouët, he formed himself according to the model which he had in the soul. He never saw the sky of Italy.

---

[135] See the Appendix, at the end of the volume.

He knew some fragments of the antique, some pictures of Raphael, and the designs that Poussin sent him. With these feeble resources, and guided by a happy instinct, in less than ten years he mounted by a continual progress to the perfection of his talent, and expired at the moment when, finally sure of himself, he was about to produce new and more admirable master-pieces. Follow him from the *St. Bruno* completed in 1648, through the *St. Paul* of 1649, to the *Vision of St. Benedict* in 1651, and to the *Muses*, scarcely finished before his death. Lesueur went on adding to his essential qualities which he owed to his own genius, and to the national genius, I mean composition and expression, qualities which he had dreamed of, or had caught glimpses of. His design from day to day became more pure, without ever being that of the Florentine school, and the same is true of his coloring.

In Lesueur every thing is directed towards expression, every thing is in the service of the mind, every thing is idea and sentiment. There is no affectation, no mannerism; there is a perfect *naïveté*; his figures sometimes would seem even a little common, so natural are they, if a Divine breath did not animate them. It must not be forgotten that his favorite subjects do not exact a brilliant coloring: he oftenest retraces scenes mournful or austere. But as in Christianity by the side of suffering and resignation is faith with hope, so Lesueur joins to the pathetic sweetness and grace; and this man charms me at the same time that he moves me.

The works of Lesueur are almost always great wholes that demanded profound meditation, and the most flexible talent, in order to preserve in them unity of subject, and to give them variety and harmony. The *History of St. Bruno*, the founder of the order *des Chartreux*, is a vast melancholy poem, in which are represented the different scenes of monastic life. The *History of St. Martin and St. Benedict* has not come down to us entire; but the two fragments of it that we possess, the *Mass of St. Martin*, and the *Vision of St. Benedict*, allow us to compare that great work with every better thing of the kind that has been done in

Italy, as, to speak sincerely, the *Muses* and the *History of Love,* appear to us to equal at least the Farnesina.

In the *History of St. Bruno,* it is particularly necessary to remark St. Bruno, prostrated before a crucifix, the saint reading a letter of the pope, his death, his apotheosis. Is it possible to carry meditation, humiliation, rapture farther? *St. Paul preaching at Ephesus* reminds one of the *School of Athens,* by the extent of the scene, the employment of architecture, and the skilful distribution of groups. In spite of the number of personages, and the diversity of episodes, the picture wholly centres in St. Paul. He preaches, and upon his words hang those who are listening, of every sex, of every age, in the most varied attitudes. In that we behold the grand lines of the Roman school, its design full of nobleness and truth at the same time. What charming and grave heads! What graceful, bold, and always natural movements! Here, that child with ringlets, full of *naïve* enthusiasm; there, that old man with bended knees, and hands joined. Are not all those beautiful heads, and those draperies, too, worthy of Raphael? But the marvel of the picture is the figure of St. Paul,[136]—it is that of the Olympic Jupiter, animated by a new spirit. The *Mass of St. Martin* carries into the soul an impression of peace and silence. The *Vision of St. Benedict* has the character of simplicity full of grandeur. A desert, the saint on his knees, contemplating his sister, St. Scholastique, who is ascending to heaven, borne up by angels, accompanied by two young girls, crowned with flowers, and bearing the palm, the symbol of virginity. St. Peter and St. Paul show St. Benedict the abode whither his sister is going to enjoy eternal peace. A slight ray of the sun pierces the cloud. St. Benedict is as it were lifted up from the earth by this ecstatic vision. One scarcely desires a more lively color, and the expression is divine. Those two virgins, a little too tall, perhaps, how beautiful and pure they are! How sweet are those forms! How grave and gentle are those faces! The person of the holy monk, with all the material accessories, is perfectly natural, for it remains

---

[136] See the Appendix.

on the earth; whilst his face, where his soul shines forth, is wholly ideal, and already in heaven.

But the *chef-d'œuvre* of Lesueur is, in our opinion, the *Descent from the Cross*, or rather the enshrouding of Jesus Christ, already descended from the cross, whom Joseph of Arimathea, Nicodemus, and St. John are placing in the shroud. On the left, Magdalen, in tears, kisses the feet of Jesus; on the right, are the holy women and the Virgin. It is impossible to carry the pathetic farther and preserve beauty. The holy women, placed in front, have each their particular grief. While one of them abandons herself to despair, an immense but internal and thoughtful sadness is upon the face of the mother of the crucified. She has comprehended the divine benefit of the redemption of the human race, and her grief, sustained by this thought, is calm and resigned. And then what dignity in that head! It, in some sort, sums up the whole picture, and gives to it its character, that of a profound and subdued emotion. I have seen many *Descents from the Cross*; I have seen that of Rubens at Antwerp, in which the sanctity of the subject has, as it were, constrained the great Flemish painter to join sensibility and sentiment to color; none of those pictures have touched me like that of Lesueur. All the parts of art are there in the service of expression. The drawing is severe and strong; even the color, without being brilliant, surpasses that of the *St. Bruno*, the *Mass of St. Martin*, the *St. Paul*, and even that of the *Vision of St. Benedict*; as if Lesueur had wished to bring together in it all the powers of his soul, all the resources of his talent![137]

Now, regard the *Muses*—other scenes, other beauties, the same genius. Those are Pagan pictures, but Christianity is in them also, by reason of the adorable chastity with which Lesueur has clothed them. All critics have emulously shown the mythological errors into which poor Lesueur fell, and they have not wanted occasion to deplore that he had not made the journey to Italy and

---

[137] This picture had been made for a chapel of the church of St. Gervais. It formed the altar-piece, and in the foreground there was the admirable Bearing of the Cross, which is still seen in the Museum.

studied antiquity more. But who can have the strange idea of searching in Lesueur for an archeology? I seek and find in him the very genius of painting. Is not that Terpsichore, well or ill named, with a harp a little too strong, it is said, as if the Muse had no particular gift, in her modest attitude the symbol of becoming grace? In that group of three Muses, to which one may give what name he pleases, is not the one that holds upon her knees a book of music, who sings or is about to sing, the most ravishing creature, a St. Cecilia that preludes just before abandoning herself to the intoxication of inspiration? And in those pictures there is brilliancy and coloring; the landscape is beautifully lighted, as if Poussin had guided the hand of his friend.

Poussin! What a name I pronounce. If Lesueur is the painter of sentiment, Poussin is the painter of thought. He is in some sort the philosopher of painting. His pictures are religious or moral lectures that testify a great mind as well as a great heart. It is sufficient to recall the *Seven Sacraments*, the *Deluge*, the *Arcadia*, the *Truth that Time frees from the Taints of Envy*, the *Will of Eudamidas*, and the *Dance of Human Life*. And the style is equal to the conception. Poussin draws like a Florentine, composes like a Frenchman, and often equals Lesueur in expression; coloring alone is sometimes wanting to him. As well as Racine, he is smitten with the antique beauty, and imitates it; but, like Racine, he always remains original. In place of the naïveté and unique charm of Lesueur, he has a severe simplicity, with a correctness that never abandons him. Remember, too, that he cultivated every kind of painting. He is at once a great historical painter and a great landscape painter,—he treats religious subjects as well as profane subjects, and by turns is inspired by antiquity and the Bible. He lived much at Rome, it is true, and died there; but he also worked in France, and almost always for France. Scarcely had he become known, when Richelieu attracted him to Paris and retained him there, loading him with honors, and giving him the commission of first painter in ordinary to the king, with the general direction of all the works of painting, and all the ornaments of the royal houses. During that sojourn of two years in Paris, he made the *Last Supper (Cène)*, the *St. François Xavier*, the *Truth that Time frees from the Taints of Envy*. It was also to France, to his friend M. de Chantelou, that from Rome he addressed the *Inspiration of St. Paul*, as well as the second series of the *Seven Sacraments*, an immense composition that, for grandeur of thought, can vie with the *Stanze* of Raphael. I speak of it from the engravings; for the *Seven Sacraments* are no longer in France. Eternal shame of the eighteenth century! It was at least necessary to wrest from the Greeks the pediments of the Parthenon,—we, we delivered up to strangers, we sold all those monuments of French genius which Richelieu and Mazarin, with religious care, had collected. Public indignation did not avert the act! And there has not since been found in France a king, a statesman, to interdict letting the master-pieces of art that honor the nation depart without authorization from the national territory![138] There has not been found a government which has undertaken at least to repurchase those that we have lost, to get back again the great works of Poussin, Lesueur, and so many others, scattered in Europe, instead of squandering millions to acquire the baboons of Holland, as Louis XIV. said, or Spanish canvasses, in truth of an admirable color, but without nobleness and moral expression.[139] I know and I love the Dutch pastorals and the cows of Potter; I am not insensible to the sombre and ardent coloring of Zurbaran, to the brilliant Italian imitations of Murillo and Velasquez; but in fine, what is all that in comparison with serious and powerful compositions like the *Seven Sacraments*, for example, that profound representation of Christian rites, a work of the highest faculties of the intellect and the soul, in which the intellect and the soul will ever find an exhaustless subject of study and meditation! Thank God, the graver of Pesne has saved them from our ingratitude and barbarity. Whilst the originals decorate the gallery of a great

---

[138] Such a law was the first act of the first assembly of affranchised Greece, and all the friends of art have applauded it from end to end of civilized Europe.

[139] See the Appendix.

English lord,[140] the love and the talent of a Pesne, of a Stella, have preserved for us faithful copies in those expressive engravings that one never grows tired of contemplating, that every time we examine them, reveal to us some new side of the genius of our great countryman. Regard especially the *Extreme Unction!* What a sublime and at the same time almost graceful scene! One would call it an antique bas-relief, so many groups are properly distributed in it, with natural and varied attitudes. The draperies are as admirable as those of a fragment of the *Panathenæa*, which is in the Louvre. The figures are all beautiful. Beauty of figures belongs to sculpture, one is about to say:—yes, but it also belongs to painting, if you have yourself the eye of the painter, if you have been struck with the expression of those postures, those heads, those gestures, and almost those looks; for every thing lives, every thing breathes, even in those engravings, and if it were the place, we would endeavor to make the reader penetrate with us into those secrets of Christian sentiment which are also the secrets of art.

We endeavor to console ourselves for having lost the *Seven Sacraments*, and for not having known how to keep from England and Germany so many productions of Poussin, now buried in foreign collections,[141] by going to see at the Louvre what remains to us of the great French artist,—thirty pictures produced at different epochs of his life, which, for the most part, worthily sustain his renown,—the portrait of *Poussin*, one of the *Bacchanals* made for Richelieu, *Mars and Venus*, the *Death of Adonis*, the *Rape of the Sabines*,[142] *Eliezer and Rebecca*, *Moses saved from the Waters*, the *Infant Jesus on the Knees of the*

---

[140] The Seven Sacraments of Poussin are now in the Bridgewater Gallery. See the Appendix.
[141] See the Appendix.
[142] In the midst of this scene of brutal violence, everybody has remarked this delicate trait—a Roman quite young, almost juvenile, while possessing himself by force of a young girl taking refuge in the arms of her mother, asks her from her mother with an air at once passionate and restrained. In order to appreciate this picture, compare it with that of David in the ensemble and in the details.

Virgin and St. Joseph standing by,[143] especially the *Manna in the Desert*, the *Judgment of Solomon*, the *Blind Men of Jericho*, the *Woman taken in Adultery*, the *Inspiration of St. Paul*, the *Diogenes*, the *Deluge*, the *Arcadia*. Time has turned the color, which was never very brilliant; but it has not been able to disturb what will make them live forever,—the design, the composition, and the expression. The *Deluge* has remained, and in fact will always be, the most striking. After so many masters who have treated the same subject, Poussin has found the secret of being original, and more pathetic than his predecessors, in representing the solemn moment when the race is about to disappear. There are few details; some dead bodies are floating upon the abyss; a sinister-looking moon has scarcely risen; a few moments and mankind will be no more; the last mother uselessly extends her last child to the last father, who cannot take it, and the serpent that has destroyed mankind darts forth triumphant. We try in vain to find in the Deluge some signs of a trembling hand: the soul that sustained and conducted that hand makes itself felt by our soul, and profoundly moves it. Stop at that scene of mourning, and almost by its side let your eyes rest upon that fresh landscape and upon those shepherds that surround a tomb. The most aged, with a knee on the ground, reads these words graven upon the stone: *Et in Arcadia ego*, and I also lived in Arcadia. At the left a shepherd listens with serious attention. At the right is a charming group, composed of a shepherd in the spring-time of life, and a young girl of ravishing beauty. An artless admiration is painted on the face of the young peasant, who looks with happiness on his beautiful companion. As for her, her adorable face is not even veiled with the slightest shade; she smiles, her hand resting carelessly upon the shoulder of the young man, and she has no appearance of comprehending that lecture given to beauty, youth, and love. I confess that, for this picture alone, of so touching a philosophy, I would give many master-pieces of

---

[143] In fact, the St. Joseph is here the important personage. He governs the whole scene; he prays, he is as it were in ecstasy.

coloring, all the pastorals of Potter, all the badinages of Ostade, all the buffooneries of Teniers.

Lesueur and Poussin, by very different but nearly equal titles, are at the head of our great painting of the seventeenth century. After them, what artists again are Claude Lorrain and Philippe de Champagne?

Do you know in Italy or Holland a greater landscape painter than Claude? And seize well his true character. Look at those vast and beautiful solitudes, lighted by the first or last rays of the sun, and tell me whether those solitudes, those trees, those waters, those mountains, that light, that silence,—whether all that nature has a soul, and whether those luminous and pure horizons do not lift you involuntarily, in ineffable reveries, to the invisible source of beauty and grace! Lorrain is, above all, the painter of light, and his works might be called the history of light and all its combinations, in small and great, when it is poured out over large plains or breaks in the most varied accidents, on land, on waters, in the heavens, in its eternal source. The human scenes thrown into one corner have no other object than to relieve and make appear to advantage the scenes of nature by harmony or contrast. In the *Village Fête*, life, noise, movement are in front,—peace and grandeur are at the foundation of the landscape, and that is truly the picture. The same effect is in the *Cattle Crossing a River*. The landscape placed immediately under your eyes has nothing in it very rare, we can find such a one anywhere; but follow the perspective,—it leads you across flowering fields, a beautiful river, ruins, mountains that overlook these ruins, and you lose yourself in infinite distances. That Landscape crossed by a river, where a peasant waters his herd, means nothing great at first sight. Contemplate it some time, and peace, a sort of meditativeness in nature, a well-graduated perspective, will, little by little, gain your heart, and give you in that small picture a penetrating charm. The picture called a *Landscape* represents a vast champagne filled with trees, and lighted by the rising sun,—in it there is freshness and—already—warmth, mystery, and splendor, with skies of the sweetest harmony. *A Dance at Sunset* expresses the close of a beautiful day. One sees in it, one feels in it the decline of the heat of the day; in the foreground are some shepherds and shepherdesses dancing by the side of their flocks.[144]

Is it not strange, that Champagne has been put in the Flemish school?[145] He was born at Brussels, it is true, but he came very early to Paris, and his true master was Poussin, who counselled him. He devoted his talent to France, lived there, died there, and what is decisive, his manner is wholly French. Will it be said that he owes to Flanders his color? We respond that this quality is balanced by a grave defect that he also owes to Flanders, the want of ideality in the figures; and it was from France that he learned how to repair this defect by beauty of moral expression. Champagne is inferior to Lesueur and Poussin, but he is of their family. He was, also, of those artists contemporaneous with Corneille, simple, poor, virtuous, Christian.[146] Champagne worked both for the convent of the Carmelites in the *Rue St. Jacques*, that venerable abode of ardent and sublime piety, and Port-Royal, that place of all others that contained in the smallest space the most virtue and genius, so many admirable men and women

---

[144] The pictures of Claude Lorrain, of which we have just spoken, are in the Museum of Paris. In all there are thirteen, whilst the Museum of Madrid alone possesses almost as many, while there are in England more than fifty, and those the most admirable. See the Appendix.

[145] The last Notice of the Pictures exhibited in the Gallery of the National Museum of the Louvre, 1852, although its author, M. Villot, is surely a man of incontestable knowledge and taste, persists in placing Champagne in the Flemish school. En revanche, a learned foreigner, M. Waagen, claims him for the French school. Kunstwerke und Künstler in Paris, Berlin, 1839, p. 651.

[146] Well appreciated by Richelieu, he preferred his esteem to his benefits. One day when an envoy of Richelieu said to him that he had only to ask freely what he wished for the advancement of his fortune, Champagne responded that if M. the Cardinal could make him a more skilful painter than he was, it was the only thing that he asked of his Eminence; but that being impossible, he only desired the honor of his good graces. Félibien, Entretiens, 1st edition, 4to., part v., p. 171; and de Piles, Abrégé de la Vie des Peintres, 2d edition, p. 500.— "As he had much love for justice and truth, provided he satisfied what they both demanded, he easily passed over all the rest."—Nécrologe de Port-Royal, p. 336.

worthy of them. What has become of that famous crucifix that he painted for the Church of the Carmelites, a master-piece of perspective that upon a horizontal plane appeared perpendicular? It perished with the holy house. The *Last Supper* (*Cène*) is a living picture, on account of the truth of all the figures, movements, and postures, but to my eyes it is blemished by the absence of the ideal. I am obliged to say as much of the *Repast with Simon the Pharisee*. The *chef-d'œuvre* of Champagne is the *Apparition of St. Gervais and St. Protais to St. Ambrose in a Basilica of Milan*. All the qualities of French art are seen in it,— simplicity and grandeur in composition, with a profound expression. On that canvas are only four personages, the two martyrs and St. Paul, who presents them to St. Ambrose. Those four figures fill the temple, lighted above all in the obscurity of the night, by the luminous apparition. The two martyrs are full of majesty. St. Ambrose, kneeling and in prayer, is, as it were, seized with terror.[147]

I certainly admire Champagne as an historical painter, and even as a landscape painter; but he is perhaps greatest as a portrait painter. In portraits truth and nature are particularly in their place, relieved by coloring, and idealized in proper measure by expression. The portraits of Champagne are so many monuments in which his most illustrious contemporaries will live forever. Every thing about them is strikingly real, grave, and severe, with a penetrating sweetness. Should the records of Port-Royal be lost, all Port-Royal might be found in Champagne. Among those portraits we see the inflexible Saint-Cyran,[148] as well as his persecutor, the imperious Richelieu.[149] We see, too, the learned, the intrepid Antoine Arnaud, to whom the contemporaries of Bossuet decreed the name of Great;[150] and Mme. Angélique

---

[147] See the Appendix.

[148] The original is in the Museum of Grenoble; but see the engraving of Morin; see also that of Daret, after the beautiful design of Demonstier.

[149] In the Museum of the Louvre; see also the engraving of Morin.

[150] The original is now in the Château of Sablé, belonging to the Marquis of Rougé; see the engraving of Simonneau in Perrault. The beautiful engraving of

Arnaud, with her naïve and strong figure.[151] Among them is mother Agnes and the humble daughter of Champagne himself, sister St. Suzanne.[152] She has just been miraculously cured, and her whole prostrated person bears still the impress of a relic of suffering. Mother Agnes, kneeling before her, regards her with a look of grateful joy. The place of the scene is a poor cell; a wooden cross hanging on the wall, and some straw chairs, are all the ornaments. On the picture is the inscription,—*Christo uni medico animarum et corporum*, etc. There is possessed the Christian stoicism of Port-Royal in its imposing austerity. Add to all these portraits that of Champagne;[153] for the painter may be put by the side of his personages.

Had France produced in the seventeenth century only these four great artists, it would be necessary to give an important place to the French school; but she counts many other painters of the greatest merit. Among these we may distinguish P. Mignard, so much admired in his times, so little known now, and so worthy of being known. How have we been able to let fall into oblivion the author of the immense fresco of *Val-de-grâce*, so celebrated by Molière, which is perhaps the greatest page of painting in the world![154] What strikes at first, in this gigantic work, is the order

---

Edelinck was made after a different original, attributed to a nephew of Champagne.

[151] The original is also in the possession of the Marquis of Rougé; the admirable engraving of Van Schupen may take its place.

[152] In the Museum.

[153] In the Museum, and engraved by Gérard Edelinck.

[154] La Gloire du Val-de-Grâce, in 4to, 1669, with a frontispiece and vignettes. Molière there enters into infinite details on all the parts of the art of painting and the genius of Mignard. He pushes eulogy perhaps to the extent of hyperbole; afterwards, hyperbole gave place to the most shameful indifference. The fresco of the dome of Val-de-grâce is composed of four rows of figures, which rise in a circle from the base to the vertex of the arch. In the upper part is the Trinity, above which is raised a resplendent sky. Below the Trinity are the celestial powers. Descending a degree, we see the Virgin and the holy personages of the Old and New Testament. Finally, at the lower extremity is Anne of Austria, introduced into paradise by St. Anne and St. Louis, and these three figures are accompanied by a multitude of personages pertaining to the

and harmony. Then come a thousand charming details and innumerable episodes which form themselves important compositions. Remark also the brilliant and sweet coloring which should at least obtain favor for so many other beauties of the first order. Again, it is to the pencil of Mignard that we owe that ravishing ceiling of a small apartment of the King at Versailles, a master-piece now destroyed, but of which there remains to us a magnificent translation in the beautiful engraving of Gerard Audran. What profound expression in the *Plague of Æacus*,[155] and in the *St. Charles giving the Communion to the Plague-infected of Milan*! Mignard is recognized as one of our best portrait painters: grace, sometimes a little too refined, is joined in him to sentiment. The French school can also present with pride Valentin, who died young and was so full of promise; Stella, the worthy friend of Poussin, the uncle of Claudine, Antoinette, and Françoise Stella; Lahyre, who has so much spirit and taste;[156] Sébastien Bourdon, so animated and elevated;[157] the Lenains, who sometimes have the *naïveté* of Lesueur and the color of Champagne; Bourguignon, full of fire and enthusiasm; Jouvenet, whose composition is so good;[158] finally, besides so many others, Lebrun, whom it is now the fashion to treat cavalierly, who received from nature, with perhaps an immoderate passion for fame, passion for the beautiful of every kind, and a talent of admirable flexibility,—the true painter of a great king by the

---

history of France, among whom are distinguished Joan of Arc, Charlemagne, etc.

[155] Engraved by Gerard Audran under the name of the Plague of David (la Peste de David). What has become of the original?

[156] See his Landscape at Sunset, and the Bathers (les Baigneuses), an agreeable scene somewhat blemished by careless drawing.

[157] It would be necessary to cite all his compositions. In his Holy Family the figure of the Virgin, without being celestial, admirably expresses meditation and reflection. We lost some time ago the most important work of S. Bourdon, the Sept Œuvres de Miséricorde. See the Appendix.

[158] See especially his Extreme Unction.

richness and dignity of his manner, who, like Louis XIV., worthily closes the seventeenth century.[159]

Since we have spoken somewhat extensively of painting, would it not be unjust to pass in silence over engraving, its daughter, or its sister? Certainly it is not an art of ordinary importance; we have excelled in it; we have above all carried it to its perfection in portraits. Let us be equitable to ourselves. What school—and we are not unmindful of those of Marc' Antonio, Albert Durer, and Rembrandt—can present such a succession of artists of this kind? Thomas de Leu and Léonard Gautier make in some sort the passage from the sixteenth to the seventeenth century. Then come a crowd of men of the most diverse talents,—Mellan, Michel Lasne, Morin, Daret, Huret, Masson, Nanteuil, Drevet, Van Schupen, the Poillys, the Edelincks, and the Audrans. Gérard Edelinck and Nanteuil alone have a popular renown, and they merit it by the delicacy, splendor, and charm of their graver. But the connoisseurs of elevated taste find at least their rivals in engravers now less admired, because they do not flatter the eye so much, but have, perhaps, more truth and vigor. It must also be said, that the portraits of these two masters have not the historic importance of those of their predecessors. The *Condé* of Nanteuil is justly admired; but if we wish to know the great Condé, the conqueror of Rocroy and Lens, we must not demand him from Nanteuil, but from Huret, Michel Lasne, and Daret,[160] who designed and engraved him in all his force and

---

[159] The picture that is called le Silence, which represents the sleep of the infant Jesus, is not unworthy of Poussin. The head of the infant is of superhuman power. The Battles of Alexander, with their defects, are pages of history of the highest order; and in the Alexander visiting with Ephestion the Mother and the Wife of Darius, one knows not which to admire most, the noble ordering of the whole or the just expression of the figures.

[160] It seems that Lesueur sometimes furnished Daret with designs. It is indeed to Lesueur that Daret owes the idea and the design of his chef-d'œuvre, the portrait of Armand de Bourbon, prince de Conti, represented in his earliest youth, and in an abbé, sustained and surrounded by angels of different size, forming a charming composition. The drawing is completely pure, except some

190

heroic beauty. Edelinck and Nanteuil himself scarcely knew and retraced the seventeenth century, except at the approach of its decline.[161] Morin and Mellan were able to see it, and transmit it in its glorious youth. Morin is the Champagne of engraving: he does not engrave, he paints. It is he who represents and transmits to posterity the illustrious men of the first half of the great century—Henry IV., Louis XIII., the de Thous, Bérulle, Jansenius, Saint-Cyran, Marillac, Bentivoglio, Richelieu, Mazarin, still young, and Retz, when he was only a coadjutor.[162] Mellan had the same advantage. He is the first in date of all the engravers of the seventeenth century, and perhaps is also the most expressive. With a single line, it seems that from his hands only shades can spring; he does not strike at first sight; but the more we regard him, the more he seizes, penetrates, and touches, like Lesueur.[163]

Christianity, that is to say, the reign of the spirit, is favorable to painting, is particularly expressive. Sculpture seems to be a pagan art; for, if it must also contain moral expression, it is always under the imperative condition of beauty of form. This is the reason why sculpture is as it were natural to antiquity, and appeared there with an incomparable splendor, before which

---

imperfect fore-shortenings. The little angels that sport with the emblems of the future cardinal are full of spirit, and, at the same time, sweetness.

[161] Edelinck saw only the reign of Louis XIV. Nanteuil was able to engrave very few of the great men of the time of Louis XIII., and the regency, and in the latter part of their life; Mazarin, in his last five or six years; Condé, growing old; Turenne, old; Fouquet and Matthieu Molé, some years before the fall of the one and the death of the other; and he was too often obliged to waste his talent upon a crowd of parliamentarians, ecclesiastics, and obscure financiers.

[162] If I wished to make any one acquainted with the greatest and most neglected portion of the seventeenth century, that which Voltaire almost wholly omitted, I would set him to collecting the works of Morin.

[163] Mellan not only made portraits after the celebrated painters of his time, he is himself the author of great and charming compositions, many of which serve as frontispieces to books. I willingly call attention to that one which is at the head of a folio edition of the Introduction à la Vie Dévote, and to the beautiful frontispieces of the writings of Richelieu, from the press of the Louvre.

painting somewhat paled,[164] whilst among the moderns it has been eclipsed by painting, and has remained very inferior to it, by reason of the extreme difficulty of bringing stone and marble to express Christian sentiment, without which, material beauty suffers; so that our sculpture is too insignificant to be beautiful, too mannered to be expressive. Since antiquity, there have scarcely been two schools of sculpture:[165]—one at Florence, before Michael Angelo, and especially with Michael Angelo; the other in France, at the *Renaissance*, with Jean Cousin, Goujon, Germain Pilon. We may say that these three artists have, as it were, shared among themselves grandeur and grace: to the first belong nobility and force, with profound knowledge;[166] to the other two, an elegance full of charm. Sculpture changes its character in the seventeenth century as well as every thing else: it no longer has the same attraction, but it finds moral and religious inspiration, which the skilful masters of the *Renaissance* too much lacked. Jean Cousin excepted, is there one of them that is superior to Jacques Sarazin? That great artist, now almost forgotten, is at once a disciple of the French school and the Italian school, and to the qualities that he borrows from his predecessors, he adds a moral expression, touching and elevated, which he owes to the spirit of the new school. He is, in sculpture, the worthy contemporary of Lesueur and Poussin, of Corneille, Descartes,

---

[164] This was the opinion of Winkelmann at the end of the eighteenth century; it is our opinion now, even after all the discoveries that have been made during fifty years, that may be seen in great part retraced and described in the Musio real Barbonico.

[165] There was doubtless sculpture in the middle age: the innumerable figures at the portals of our cathedrals, and the statues that are discovered every day sufficiently testify it. The imagers of that time certainly had much spirit and imagination; but, at least in everything that we have seen, beauty is absent, and taste wanting.

[166] Go and see at the Museum of Versailles the statue of Francis I., and say whether any Italian, except the author of the Laurent de Medicis, has made any thing like it. See also in the Museum of the Louvre, the statue of Admiral Chabot.

and Pascal. He belongs entirely to the reign of Louis XIII., Richelieu, and Mazarin; he did not even see that of Louis XIV.[167] Called into France by Richelieu, who had also called there Poussin and Champagne, Jacques Sarazin in a few years produced a multitude of works of rare elegance and great character. What has become of them? The eighteenth century passed over them without regarding them. The barbarians that destroyed or scattered them, were arrested before the paintings of Lesueur and Poussin, protected by a remnant of admiration: while breaking the master-pieces of the French chisel, they had no suspicion of the sacrilege they were committing against art as well as their country. I was at least able to see, some years ago, at the Museum of French Monuments, collected by the piety of a friend of the arts, beautiful parts of a superb mausoleum erected to the memory of Henri de Bourbon, second of the name, Prince of Condé, father of the great Condé, the worthy support, the skilful fellow-laborer of Richelieu and Mazarin. This monument was supported by four figures of natural grandeur,—*Faith, Prudence, Justice, Charity*. There were four bas-reliefs in bronze, representing the *Triumphs of Renown, Time, Death*, and *Eternity*. In the *Triumph of Death*, the artist had represented a certain number of illustrious moderns, among whom he had placed himself by the side of Michael Angelo.[168] We can still contemplate in the court of the Louvre, in the pavilion of the Horloge, those caryatides of Sarazin at once so

---

[167] Sarazin died in 1660, Lesueur in 1655, Poussin in 1665, Descartes in 1650, Pascal in 1662, and the genius of Corneille did not extend beyond that epoch.

[168] Lenoir, Musée des Monuments Français, vol. v., p. 87-91, and the Musée Royale des Monuments Français of 1815, p. 98, 99, 108, 122, and 140. This wonderful monument, erected to Henri de Bourbon, at the expense of his old intendant Perrault, president of the Chambre des Comptes, was placed in the Church of the Jesuits, and was wholly in bronze. It must not be confounded with the other monument that the Condés erected to the same prince in their family burial-ground at Vallery, near Montereau, in Yonne. This monument is in marble, and by the hand of Michel Anguier; see the description in Lenoir, vol. v., p. 23-25, and especially in the Annuaire de l'Yonne pour 1842, p. 173, etc.

majestic and so graceful, which are detached with admirable relief and lightness. Have Jean Goujon and Germain Pilon done any thing more elegant and lifelike? Those females breathe, and are about to move. Take the pains to go a short distance[169] to visit the humble chapel that now occupies the place of that magnificent church of the Carmelites, once filled with the paintings of Champagne, Stella, Lahire, and Lebrun; where the voice of Bossuet was heard, where Mlle. de Lavallière and Mme. de Longueville were so often seen prostrated, their long hair shorn, and their faces bathed in tears. Among the relics that are preserved of the past splendor of the holy monastery, consider the noble statue of the kneeling Cardinal de Bérulle. On those meditative and penetrating features, in those eyes raised to heaven, breathes the soul of that great servant of God, who died at the altar like a warrior on the field of honor. He prays God for his dear Carmelites. That head is perfectly natural, as Champagne might have painted it, and has a severe grace that reminds one of Lesueur and Poussin.[170]

Below Sarazin, the Anguiers are still artists that Italy would admire, and to whom there is wanting, since the great century, nothing but judges worthy of them. These two brothers covered Paris and France with the most precious monuments. Look at the tomb of Jacques-Auguste de Thou, by François Anguier: the face of the great historian is reflective and melancholy, like that of a man weary of the spectacle of human things; and nothing is more amiable than the statues of his two wives, Marie Barbançon de Cany, and Gasparde de la Châtre.[171] The mausoleum of Henri de

---

[169] Rue d'Enfer, No. 67.

[170] The Museum of the Louvre possesses only a very small number of Sarazin's works, and those of very little importance:—a bust of Pierre Séguier, strikingly true, two statuettes full of grace, and the small funeral monument of Hennequin, Abbé of Bernay, member of Parliament, who died in 1651, which is a chef-d'œuvre of elegance.

[171] These three statues were united in the Museum des Petits-Augustins, Lenoir, Musée-royal, etc., p. 94; we know not why they have been separated; Jacques-Auguste de Thou has been placed in the Louvre, and his two wives at Versailles.

Montmorency, beheaded at Toulouse in 1632, which is still seen at Moulins, in the church of the ancient convent of the daughters of Sainte-Marie, is an important work of the same artist, in which force is manifest, with a little heaviness.[172] To Michel Anguier are attributed the statues of the duke and duchess of Tresmes, and that of their illustrious son, Potier, Marquis of Gêvres.[173] Behold in him the intrepid companion of Condé, arrested in his course at thirty-two years of age before Thionville, after the battle of Rocroy, already lieutenant-general, and when Condé was demanding for him the bâton of a marshal of France, deposited on his tomb; behold him young, beautiful, brave, like his comrades cut down also in the flower of life, Laval, Châtillon, La Moussaye. One of the best works of Michel Anguier is the monument of Henri de Chabot, that other companion, that faithful friend of Condé, who by the splendor of his valor, especially by the graces of his person, knew how to gain the heart, the fortune, and the name of the beautiful Marguerite, the daughter of the great Duke of Rohan. The new duke died, still young, in 1655, at thirty-nine years of age. He is represented lying down, the head inclined and supported by an angel; another angel is at his feet. The whole is striking, and the details are exquisite. The face of Chabot has every beauty, as if to answer to its reputation, but the beauty is that of one dying. The body has already the languor of death, *longuescit moriens*, with I know not what antique grace. This morsel, if the drawing were more severe,

---

[172] François Anguier had made a marble tomb of Cardinal de Bérulle, which was in the oratory of Rue St. Honoré. It would have been interesting to compare this statue with that of Sarazin, which is still at the Carmelites. François is also the author of the monument of the Longuevilles, which, before the Revolution, was at the Célestins, and was seen in 1815 at the museum des Petits-Augustins, Lenoir, ibid., p. 103; it is now in the Louvre. It is an obelisk, the four sides of which are covered with allegorical bas-reliefs. The pedestal, also ornamented with bas-reliefs, has four female figures in marble, representing the cardinal virtues.

[173] Now at Versailles. Lenoir, p. 97 and 100. See his portrait, painted by Champagne, and engraved by Morin.

would rival the *Dying Gladiator*, of which it reminds one, which it perhaps even imitates.[174]

In truth, I wonder that men now dare speak so lightly of Puget and Girardon. To Puget qualities of the first order cannot be refused. He has the fire, the enthusiasm, the fecundity of genius. The caryatides of the Hôtel de Ville of Toulon, which have been brought to the Museum of Paris, attest a powerful chisel. The *Milon* reminds one of the manner of Michael Angelo; it is a little overstrained, but it cannot be denied that the effect is striking. Do you want a talent more natural, and still having force and elevation? Take the trouble to search in the Tuileries, in the gardens of Versailles, in several churches of Paris, for the scattered works of Girardon, here for the mausoleum of the Gondis,[175] there for that of the Castellans,[176] that of Louvois,[177] etc.; especially go to see in the church of the Sorbonne the mausoleum of Richelieu. The formidable minister is there represented in his last moments, sustained by religion and wept by his country. The whole person is of a perfect nobility, and the figure has the fineness, the severity, the superior distinction given to it by the pencil of Champagne, and the gravers of Morin, Michel Lasne, and Mellan.

Finally, I do not regard as a vulgar sculptor Coysevox, who, under the influence of Lebrun, unfortunately begins the theatrical style, who still has the facility, movement, and elegance of Lebrun

---

[174] Group in white marble which was at the Célestins, a church near the hôtel of Rohan-Chabot in the Place Royale; re-collected in the Museum des Petits-Augustins, Lenoir, ibid., p. 97; it is now at Versailles. We must not pass over that beautiful production, the mausoleum of Jacques de Souvré, Grand Prior of France, the brother of the beautiful Marchioness de Sablé; a mausoleum that came from Saint-Jean de Latran, passed through the Museum des Petits-Augustins, and is now found in the Louvre. The sculptures of the porte Saint-Denis are also owed to Michel Anguier, as well as the admirable bust of Colbert, which is in the museum.

[175] At first at Notre-Dame, the natural place for the tombs of the Gondis, then at the Augustins, now at Versailles.

[176] In the Church St. Germain des Prés.

[177] At the Capuchins, then at the Augustins, then at Versailles.

himself. He reared worthy monuments to Mazarin, Colbert, and Lebrun,[178] and thus to speak, sowed busts of the illustrious men of his time. For, remark it well, artists then took scarcely any arbitrary and fanciful subjects. They worked upon contemporaneous subjects, which, while giving them proper liberty, inspired and guided them, and communicated a public interest to their works. The French sculpture of the seventeenth century, like that of antiquity, is profoundly natural. The churches and the monasteries were filled with the statues of those who loved them during life, and wished to rest in them after death. Each church of Paris was a popular museum. The sumptuous residences of the aristocracy—for at that period, there was one in France, like that of England at the present time—possessed their secular tombs, statues, busts, and portraits of eminent men whose glory belonged to the country as well as their own family. On its side, the state did not encourage the arts in detail, and, thus to speak, in a small way; it gave them a powerful impulse by demanding of them important works, by confiding to them vast enterprises. All great things were thus mingled together, reciprocally inspired and sustained each other.

One man alone in Europe has left a name in the beautiful art that surrounds a chateau or a palace with graceful gardens or magnificent parks,—that man is a Frenchman of the seventeenth century, is Le Nôtre. Le Nôtre may be reproached with a regularity that is perhaps excessive, and a little mannerism in details; but he has two qualities that compensate for many defects, grandeur and sentiment. He who designed the park of Versailles, who to the proper arrangement of parterres, to the movement of fountains, to the harmonious sound of waterfalls, to the mysterious shades of groves, has known how to add the magic of

---

[178] See, on these monuments, Lenoir, p. 98, 101, 102. That of Mazarin is now at the Louvre; that of Colbert has been restored to the Church of St. Eustache, and that of Lebrun to the Church St. Nicholas du Chardonnet, as well as the mausoleum, so expressive but a little overstrained, of the mother of Lebrun, by Tuby, and the mausoleum of Jerome Bignon, the celebrated Councillor of State, who died in 1656.

infinite perspective by means of that spacious walk where the view is extended over an immense sheet of water to be lost in the limitless distances,—he is a landscape-painter worthy of having a place by the side of Poussin and Lorrain.

We had in the middle age our Gothic architecture, like all the nations of northern Europe. In the sixteenth century what architects were Pierre Lescot, Jean Bullant, and Philibert Delorme! What charming palaces, what graceful edifices, the Tuileries, the Hotel de Ville of Paris, Chambord, and Ecouen! The seventeenth century also had its original architecture, different from that of the middle age and that of the *Renaissance*, simple, austere, noble, like the poetry of Corneille and the prose of Descartes. Study without scholastic prejudice the Luxembourg of de Brosses,[179] the portal of Saint-Gervais, and the great hall of the Palais de Justice, by the same architect; the Palais Cardinal and the Sorbonne of Lemercier;[180] the cupola of Val-de-Grâce by Lemuet;[181] the triumphal arch of the Porte Saint-Denis by François Blondel; Versailles, and especially the Invalides, of Mansart.[182] Consider with attention the last edifice, let it make its impression on your mind and soul, and you will easily succeed in recognizing in it a particular beauty. It is not a Gothic monument, neither is it an

---

[179] Quatremère de Quincy, Histoire de la Vie et des Ouvrages de plus Célèbres Architectes, vol. ii., p. 145:—"There could scarcely be found in any country an ensemble so grand, which offers with so much unity and regularity an aspect at once more varied and picturesque, especially in the façade of the entrance." Unfortunately this unity has disappeared, thanks to the constructions that have since been added to the primitive work.

[180] In order to appreciate the beauty of the Sorbonne, one must stand in the lower part of the great court, and from that point consider the effect of the successive elevation, at first of the other part of the court, then of the different stories of the portico, then of the portico itself, of the church, and, finally, of the dome.

[181] Quatremère de Quincy, Ibid., p. 257:—"The cupola of this edifice is one of the finest in Europe."

[182] We do not speak of the colonnade of the Louvre by Perrault, because in spite of its grand qualities, it begins the decline and marks the passage from the serious to the academic style, from originality to imitation, from the seventeenth century to the eighteenth.

almost Pagan monument of the sixteenth century,—it is modern, and also Christian; it is vast with measure, elegant with gravity. Contemplate at sunset that cupola reflecting the last rays of day, elevating itself gently towards the heavens in a slight and graceful curve; cross that imposing esplanade, enter that court admirably lighted in spite of its covered galleries, bow beneath the dome of that church where Vauban and Turenne sleep,—you will not be able to guard yourself from an emotion at once religious and military; you will say to yourself that this is indeed the asylum of warriors who have reached the evening of life and are prepared for eternity!

Since then, what has French architecture become? Once having left tradition and national character, it wanders from imitation to imitation, and without comprehending the genius of antiquity, it unskilfully reproduces its forms. This bastard architecture, at once heavy and mannered, is, little by little, substituted for the beautiful architecture of the preceding century, and everywhere effaces the vestiges of the French spirit. Do you wish a striking example of it? In Paris, near the Luxembourg, the Condés had their *hôtel*,[183] magnificent and severe, with a military aspect, as it was fitting for the dwelling-place of a family of warriors, and within of almost royal splendor. Beneath those lofty ceilings had been some time suspended the Spanish flags taken at Rocroy. In those vast saloons had been assembled the *élite* of the grandest society that ever existed. In those beautiful gardens had been seen promenading Corneille and Madame de Sévigné, Molière, Bossuet, Boileau, Racine, in the company of the great Condé. The oratory had been painted by the hand of Lesueur.[184]

---

[183] See the engraving of Pérelle. Sauval, vol. ii., p. 66 and p. 131, says that the hôtel of Condé was magnificently built, that it was the most magnificent of the time.

[184] Notice of Guillet de St. Georges, recently published (see the Appendix):— "Nearly at the same time the Princess-dowager de Condé, Charlotte-Marguerite de Montmorency, mother of the late prince, had an oratory painted by Lesueur in the hôtel of Condé. The altar-piece represents a Nativity, that of the ceiling a Celestial Glory. The wainscot is enriched with several figures and with a quantity of ornaments worked with great care."

It had been easy to repair and preserve the noble habitation. At the end of the eighteenth century, a descendant of the Condés sold it to a dismal company to build that palace without character and taste which is called the Palais-Bourbon. Almost at the same epoch there was a movement made to construct a church to the patroness of Paris, to that Geneviève, whose legend is so touching and so popular. Was there ever a better chance for a national and Christian monument? It was possible to return to the Gothic style and even to the Byzantine style. Instead of that there was made for us an immense Roman basilica of the Decline. What a dwelling for the modest and holy virgin, so dear to the fields that bordered upon Lutèce, whose name is still venerated by the poor people who inhabit these quarters! Behold the church which has been placed by the side of that of Saint-Etienne du Mont, as if to make felt all the differences between Christianity and Paganism! For here, in spite of a mixture of the most different styles, it is evident that the Pagan style predominates. Christian worship cannot be naturalized in this profane edifice, which has so many times changed its destination. It is in vain to call it anew Saint-Geneviève,—the revolutionary name of Pantheon will stick to it.[185] The eighteenth century treated the Madeleine no better than Saint-Geneviève. In vain the beautiful sinner wished to renounce the joys of the world and attach herself to the poverty of Jesus Christ. She has been brought back to the pomp and luxury that she repudiated; she has been put in a rich palace, all shining with gold, which might very well be a temple of Venus, for certainly it has not the severe grace of the Pantheon, of which it is the most vulgar copy. How far we are from the Invalides, from Val-de-Grâce, and the Sorbonne, so admirably appropriated to their

---

[185] The Pantheon is an imitation of the St. Paul's of London, which is itself a very sad imitation of St. Peter's of Rome. The only merit of the Pantheon is its situation on the summit of the hill of St. Geneviève, from which it overlooks that part of the town, and is seen on different sides to a considerable distance. Put in its place the Val-de-Grâce of Lemercier with the dome of Lemuet, and judge what would be the effect of such an edifice!

object, wherein appears so well the hand of the century and the country which reared them!

While architecture thus strays, it is natural that painting should seek above every thing color and brilliancy, that sculpture should apply itself to become Pagan again, that poetry itself, receding for two centuries, should abjure the worship of thought for that of fancy, that it should everywhere go borrowing images from Spain, Italy, and Germany, that it should run after subaltern and foreign qualities which it will not attain, and abandon the grand qualities of the French genius.

It will be said that the Christian sentiment which animated Lesueur and the artists of the seventeenth century is wanting to those of ours; it is extinguished, and cannot be rekindled. In the first place, is that very certain? Native faith is dead, but cannot reflective faith take its place? Christianity is exhaustless; it has infinite resources, and admirable flexibility; there are a thousand ways of arriving at it and returning to it, because it has itself a thousand phases that answer to the most different dispositions, to all the wants, to all the mobility of the heart. What it loses on one side, it gains on another; and as it has produced our civilization, it is called to follow it in all its vicissitudes. Either every religion will perish in this world, or Christianity will endure, for it is not in the power of thought to conceive a more perfect religion. Artists of the nineteenth century, do not despair of God and yourselves. A superficial philosophy has thrown you far from Christianity considered in a strict sense; another philosophy can bring you near it again by making you see it with another eye. And then, if the religious sentiment is weakened, are there not other sentiments that can make the heart of man beat, and fecundate genius? Plato has said, that beauty is always old and always new. It is superior to all its forms, it belongs to all countries and all times; it belongs to all beliefs, provided these beliefs be serious and profound, and the need be felt of expressing and spreading them. If, then, we have not arrived at the boundary assigned to the grandeur of France, if we are not beginning to descend into the shade of death, if we still truly live, if there remain to us convictions, of whatever kind they may be, thereby even remains to us, or at least may remain to us, what made the glory of our fathers, what they did not carry with them to the tomb, what had already survived all revolutions, Greece, Rome, the Middle Age, what does not belong to any temporary or ephemeral accident, what subsists and is continually found in the focus of consciousness—I mean moral inspiration, immortal as the soul.

Let us terminate here, and sum up this defence of the national art. There are in arts, as well as in letters and philosophy, two contrary schools. One tends to the ideal in all things,—it seeks, it tries to make appear the spirit concealed under the form, at once manifested and veiled by nature; it does not so much wish to please the senses and flatter the imagination as to enlarge the intellect and move the soul. The other, enamored of nature, stops there and devotes itself to imitation,—its principal object is to reproduce reality, movement, life, which are for it the supreme beauty. The France of the seventeenth century, the France of Descartes, Corneille, and Bossuet, highly spiritual in philosophy, poetry, and eloquence, was also highly spiritual in the arts. The artists of that great epoch participate in its general character, and represent it in their way. It is not true that they lacked imagination, more than Pascal and Bossuet lacked it. But inasmuch as they do not suffer imagination to usurp the dominion that does not belong to it, inasmuch as they subject its order, even its impetuosity, to the reign of reason and the inspirations of the heart, it seems that it is not so strong when it is only disciplined and regulated. As we have said, they excel in composition, especially in expression. They always have a thought, and a moral and elevated thought. For this reason they are dear to us, their cause interests us, is in some sort our own cause, and so this homage rendered to their misunderstood glory naturally crowns these lectures devoted to true beauty, that is to say, moral beauty.

May these lectures be able to make it known, and, above all, loved! May they be able also to inspire some one of you with the idea of devoting himself to studies so beautiful, of devoting to them his life, and attaching to them his name! The sweetest recompense of a professor who is not too unworthy of that title, is to see rapidly following in his footsteps young and noble spirits who easily pass him and leave him far behind them.[186]

---

[186] In the first rank of the intelligent auditors of this course was M. Jouffroy, who already under our auspices, had presented to the faculté des lettres, in order to obtain the degree of doctor, a thesis on the beautiful. M. Jouffroy had cultivated, with care and particular taste, the seeds that our teaching might have planted in his mind. But of all those who at that epoch or later frequented our lectures, no one was better fitted to embrace the entire domain of beauty or art than the author of the beautiful articles on Eustache Lesueur, the Cathedral of Noyon, and the Louvre. M. Vitet possesses all the knowledge, and, what is more, all the qualities requisite for a judge of every kind of beauty, for a worthy historian of art. I yield to the necessity of addressing to him the public petition that he may not be wanting to a vocation so marked and so elevated.

PART THIRD
THE GOOD.

LECTURE XI.

PRIMARY NOTIONS OF COMMON SENSE.

Extent of the question of the good.—Position of the question according to the psychological method: What is, in regard to the good, the natural belief of mankind?—The natural beliefs of humanity must not be sought in a pretended state of nature.—Study of the sentiments and ideas of men in languages, in life, in consciousness.—Disinterestedness and devotedness.—Liberty.—Esteem and contempt.—Respect.—Admiration and indignation.—Dignity.—Empire of opinion.—Ridicule.—Regret and repentance.—Natural and necessary foundations of all justice.—Distinction between fact and right.—Common sense, true and false philosophy.

The idea of the true in its developments, comprises psychology, logic, and metaphysics. The idea of the beautiful begets what is called æsthetics. The idea of the good is the whole of ethics.

It would be forming a false and narrow idea of ethics to confine them within the inclosure of individual consciousness. There are public ethics, as well as private ethics, and public ethics embrace, with the relations of men among themselves, so far as men, their relations as citizens and as members of a state. Ethics extend wherever is found in any decree the idea of the good. Now, where does this idea manifest itself more, and where do justice and injustice, virtue and crime, heroism and weakness appear more openly, than on the theatre of civil life? Moreover, is there any thing that has a more decisive influence over manners, even of individuals, than the institutions of peoples and the constitutions of states? If the idea of the good goes thus far, it must be followed thither, as recently the idea of the beautiful has introduced us into the domain of art.

Philosophy usurps no foreign power; but it is not disposed to relinquish its right of examination over all the great manifestations of human nature. All philosophy that does not terminate in ethics, is hardly worthy of the name, and all ethics that do not terminate at least in general views on society and government, are powerless ethics, that have neither counsels nor rules to give humanity in its most difficult trials.

It seems that at the point where we have arrived, the metaphysics and æsthetics that we have taught evidently involve such a doctrine of morality and not such another, that, accordingly, the question of the good, that question so fertile and so vast, is for us wholly solved, and that we can deduce, by way of reasoning, the moral theory that is derived from our theory of the beautiful and our theory of the true. We might do this, perhaps, but we will not. This would be abandoning the method that we have hitherto followed, that method that proceeds by observation, and not by deduction, and makes consulting experience a law to itself. We do not grow weary of experience. Let us attach ourselves faithfully to the psychological method; it has its delays; it condemns us to more than one repetition, but it places us in the beginning, and a long time retains us at the source of all reality, and all light.

The first maxim of the psychological method is this: True philosophy invents nothing, it establishes and describes what is. Now here, what is, is the natural and permanent belief of the being that we are studying, to wit, man. What is, then, in relation to the good, the natural and permanent belief of the human race? Such is, in our eyes, the first question.

With us, in fact, the human race does not take one side, and philosophy the other. Philosophy is the interpreter of the human race. What the human race thinks and believes, often unconsciously, philosophy re-collects, explains, establishes. It is the faithful and complete expression of human nature, and human nature is entire in each of us philosophers, and in every other man. Among us, it is attained by consciousness; among other men, it manifests itself in their words and actions. Let us, then, interrogate the latter and the former; let us especially interrogate our own consciousness; let us clearly recognize what the human race thinks; we shall then see what should be the office of philosophy.

Is there a human language known to us that has not different expressions for good and evil, for just and unjust? Is there any language, in which, by the side of the words pleasure, interest, utility, happiness, are not also found the words sacrifice, disinterestedness, devotedness, virtue? Do not all languages, as well as all nations, speak of liberty, duty, and right?

Here, perhaps, some disciple of Condillac and Helvetius will ask us whether, in this regard, we possess authentic dictionaries of the language of savage tribes found by voyagers in the isles of the ocean? No; but we have not made our philosophic religion out of the superstitions and prejudices of a certain school. We absolutely deny that it is necessary to study human nature in the famous savage of Aveyron, or in the like of him of the isles of the ocean, or the American continent. The savage state offers us humanity in swaddling-clothes, thus to speak, the germ of humanity, but not humanity entire. The true man is the perfect man of his kind; true human nature is human nature arrived at its development, as true society is also perfected society. We do not think it worth the while to ask a savage his opinion on the Apollo Belvidere, neither will we ask him for the principles that constitute the moral nature of man, because in him this moral nature is only sketched and not completed. Our great philosophy of the seventeenth century was sometimes a little too much pleased with hypotheses in which God plays the principal part, and crushes human liberty.[187] The philosophy of the eighteenth century threw itself into the opposite extreme; it had recourse to hypotheses of a totally different character, among others, to a pretended natural state, whence it undertook, with infinite pains, to draw society and man

---

[187] See 2d Series, vol. ii., lect. 11 and 12; 4th Series, vol. ii., last pages of Jacqueline Pascal, and the Fragments of the Cartesian Philosophy, p. 469.

as we now see them. Rousseau plunged into the forests, in order to find there the model of liberty and equality. That is the commencement of his politics. But wait a little, and soon you will see the apostle of the natural state, driven, by a necessary inconsequence, from one excess to an opposite excess, instead of the sweets of savage liberty, proposing to us the *Contrat Social and Lacédémone*. Condillac[188] studies the human mind in a statue whose senses enter into exercise under the magic wand of a systematic analysis, and are developed in the measure and progress that are convenient to him. The statue successively acquires our five senses, but there is one thing that it does not acquire, that is, a mind like the human mind, and a soul like ours. And this was what was then called the experimental method! Let us leave there all those hypotheses. In order to understand reality, let us study it, and not imagine it. Let us take humanity as it is incontestably shown to us in its actual characters, and not as it may have been in a primitive, purely hypothetical state, in those unformed lineaments or that degradation which is called the savage state. In that, without doubt, may be found signs or *souvenirs* of humanity, and, if this were the plea, we might, in our turn, examine the recitals of voyages, and find, even in that darkness of infancy or decrepitude, admirable flashes of light, noble instincts, which already appear, or still subsist, presaging or recalling humanity. But, for the sake of exactness of method and true analysis, we turn our eyes from infancy and the savage state, in order to direct them towards the being who is the sole object of our studies, the actual man, the real and completed man.

Do you know a language, a people, which does not possess the word disinterested virtue? Who is especially called an honest man? Is it the skilful calculator, devoting himself to making his own affairs the best possible, or he who, under all circumstances, is disposed to observe justice against his apparent or real interest? Take away the idea that an honest man is capable, to a certain degree, of resisting the attractions of personal interest, and of

---

[188] Ist Series, vol. iii., lectures 2 and 3, Condillac.

making some sacrifices for opinion, for propriety, for that which is or appears honest, and you take away the foundation of that title of honest man, even in the most ordinary sense. That disposition to prefer what is good to our pleasure, to our personal utility, in a word, to interest—that disposition more or less strong, more or less constant, more or less tested, measures the different degrees of virtue. A man who carries disinterestedness as far as devotion, is called a hero, let him be concealed in the humblest condition, or placed on a public stage. There is devotedness in obscure as well as in exalted stations. There are heroes of probity, of honor, of loyalty, in the relations of ordinary life, as well as heroes of courage and patriotism in the counsels of peoples and at the head of armies. All these names, with their meaning well recognized, are in all languages, and constitute a certain and universal fact. We may explain this fact, but on one imperative condition, that in explaining we do not destroy it. Now, is the idea and the word disinterestedness explained to us by reducing disinterestedness to interest? This is what common sense invincibly repels.

Poets have no system,—they address themselves to men as they really are, in order to produce in them certain effects. Is it skilful selfishness or disinterested virtue that poets celebrate? Do they demand our applause for the success of fortunate address, or for the voluntary sacrifices of virtue? The poet knows that there is at the foundation of the human soul I know not what marvellous power of disinterestedness and devotedness. In addressing himself to this instinct of the heart, he is sure of awakening a sublime echo, of opening every source of the pathetic.

Consult the annals of the human race, and you will find in them man everywhere, and more and more, claiming his liberty. This word liberty is as old as man himself. What then! Men wish to be free, and man himself should not be free! The word nevertheless exists with the most determined signification. It signifies that man believes himself a free being, not only animated and sensible, but endowed with will, a will that belongs to him, that consequently cannot admit over itself the tyranny of another will which would make, in regard to him, the office of fatality, even were it that of the most beneficent fatality. Do you suppose that the word liberty could ever have been formed, if the thing itself did not exist? None but a free being could possess the idea of liberty. Will it be said that the liberty of man is only an illusion? The wishes of the human race are then the most inexplicable extravagance. In denying the essential distinction between liberty and fatality, we contradict all languages and all received notions; we have, it is true, the advantage of absolving tyrants, but we degrade heroes. They have, then, fought and died for a chimera!

All languages contain the words esteem and contempt. To esteem, to despise,—these are universal expressions, certain phenomena, from which an impartial analysis can draw the highest notions. Can we despise a being who, in his acts, should not be free, a being who should not know the good, and should not feel himself obligated to fulfil it? Suppose that the good is not essentially different from the evil, suppose that there is in the world only interest more or less well understood, that there is no real duty, and that man is not essentially a free being,—it is impossible to explain rationally the word contempt. It is the same with the word esteem.

Esteem is a fact which, faithfully expressed, contains a complete philosophy as solid as generous. Esteem has two certain characters: 1st, It is a disinterested sentiment in the soul of him who feels it; 2d, It is applied only to disinterested acts. We do not esteem at will, and because it is our interest to esteem. Neither do we esteem an action or a person because they have been successful. Success, fortunate calculation, may make us envied; it does not bring esteem, which has another price.

Esteem in a certain degree, and under certain circumstances, is respect,—respect, a holy and sacred word which the most subtle or the loosest analysis will never degrade to expressing a sentiment that is related to ourselves, and is applied to actions crowned by fortune.

Take again these two words, these two facts analogous to the first two, admiration and indignation. Esteem and contempt are rather judgments; indignation and admiration are sentiments, but sentiments that pertain to intelligence and envelop a judgment.[189]

Admiration is an essentially disinterested sentiment. See whether there is any interest in the world that has the power to give you admiration for any thing or any person. If you were interested, you might feign admiration, but you would not feel it. A tyrant with death in his hand, may constrain you to appear to admire, but not to admire in reality. Even affection does not determine admiration; whilst a heroic trait, even in an enemy, compels you to admire.

The phenomenon opposed to admiration is indignation. Indignation is no more anger than admiration is desire. Anger is wholly personal. Indignation is never directly related to us; it may have birth in the midst of circumstances wherein we are engaged, but the foundation and the dominant character of the phenomenon in itself is to be disinterested. Indignation is in its nature generous. If I am a victim of an injustice, I may feel at once anger and indignation, anger against him that injures me, indignation towards him who is unjust to one of his fellow-men. We may be indignant towards ourselves; we are indignant towards every thing that wounds the sentiment of justice. Indignation covers a judgment, the judgment that he who commits such or such an action, whether against us, or even for us, does an action unworthy, contrary to our dignity, to his own dignity, to human dignity. The injury sustained is not the measure of indignation, as the advantage received is not that of admiration. We felicitate ourselves on possessing or having acquired a useful thing; but we never admire, on that account, either ourselves or the thing that we have just acquired. So we repel the stone that wounds us, we do not feel indignant towards it.

---

[189] See the Theory of Sentiment, part i., lecture 5.

Admiration elevates and ennobles the soul. The generous parts of human nature are disengaged and exalted in presence of, and as it were in contact with, the image of the good. This is the reason why admiration is already by itself so beneficent, even should it be deceived in its object. Indignation is the result of these same generous parts of the soul, which, wounded by injustice, are highly roused and protest in the name of offended human dignity.

Look at men in action, and you will see them imposing upon themselves great sacrifices in order to conquer the suffrages of their fellows. The empire of opinion is immense,—vanity alone does not explain it; it doubtless also pertains to vanity, but it has deeper and better roots. We judge that other men are, like us, sensible to good and evil, that they distinguish between virtue and vice, that they are capable of being indignant and admiring, of esteeming and respecting, as well as despising. This power is in us, we have consciousness of it, we know that other men possess it as well as we, and it is this power that frightens us. Opinion is our own consciousness transferred to the public, and there disengaged from all complaisance and armed with an inflexible severity. To the remorse in our own hearts, responds the shame in that second soul which we have made ourselves, and is called public opinion. We must not be astonished at the sweets of popularity. We are more sure of having done well, when to the testimony of our consciousness we are able to join that of the consciousness of our fellow-men. There is only one thing that can sustain us against opinion, and even place us above it: it is the firm and sure testimony of our consciousness, because, in fine, the public and the whole human race are compelled to judge us according to appearance, whilst we judge ourselves infallibly and by the most certain of all knowledge.

Ridicule is the fear of opinion in small things. The force of ridicule is wholly in the supposition that there is a common taste, a common type of what is proper, that directs men in their judgments, and even in their pleasantries, which in their way are also judgments. Without this supposition, ridicule falls of itself, and pleasantry loses its sting. But it is immortal, as well as the distinction between good and evil, between the beautiful and the ugly, between what is proper and what is improper.

When we have not succeeded in any measure undertaken for our interest and prosperity, we experience a sentiment of pain that is called regret. But we do not confound regret with that other sentiment that rises in the soul when we are conscious of having done something morally bad. This sentiment is also a pain, but of quite a different nature,—it is remorse, repentance. That we have lost in play, for example, is disagreeable to us; but if, in gaining, we have the consciousness of having deceived our adversary, we experience a very different sentiment.

We might prolong and vary these examples. We have said enough to be entitled to conclude that human language and the sentiments that it expresses are inexplicable, if we do not admit the essential distinction between good and evil, between virtue and crime, crime founded on interest, virtue founded on disinterestedness.

Disturb this distinction, and you disturb human life and entire society. Permit me to take an extreme, tragic, and terrible example. Here is a man that has just been judged. He has been condemned to death, and is about to be executed—to be deprived of life. And why? Place yourself in the system that does not admit the essential distinction between good and evil, and ponder on what is stupidly atrocious in this act of human justice. What has the condemned done? Evidently a thing indifferent in itself. For if there is no other outward distinction than that of pleasure and pain, I defy any one to qualify any human action, whatever it may be, as criminal, without the most absurd inconsequence. But this thing, indifferent in itself, a certain number of men, called legislators, have declared to be a crime. This purely arbitrary declaration has found no echo in the heart of this man. He has not been able to feel the justice of it, since there is nothing in itself just. He has therefore done, without remorse, what this declaration arbitrarily interdicted. The court proceeds to prove to him that he has not succeeded, but not that he has done contrary to justice, for there is no justice. I maintain that every condemnation, be it to death, or to any punishment whatever, imperatively supposes, in order to be any thing else than a repression of violence by violence, the four following points:—1st, That there is an essential distinction between good and evil, justice and injustice, and that to this distinction is attached, for every intelligent and free being, the obligation of conforming to good and justice; 2d, That man is an intelligent and free being, capable of comprehending this distinction, and the obligation that accompanies it, and of adhering to it naturally, independently of all convention, and every positive law; capable also of resisting the temptations that bear him towards evil and injustice, and of fulfilling the sacred law of natural justice; 3d, That every act contrary to justice deserves to be repressed by force, and even punished in reparation of the fault committed, and independently too of all law and all convention; 4th, That man naturally recognizes the distinction between the merit and demerit of actions, as he recognizes the distinction between the just and the unjust, and knows that every penalty applied to an unjust act is itself most strictly just.

Such are the foundations of that power of judging and punishing which is entire society. Society has not made those principles for its own use; they are much anterior to it, they are contemporaneous with thought and the soul, and upon these rests society, with its laws and its institutions. Laws are legitimate by their relation to these eternal laws. The surest power of institutions resides in the respect that these principles bear with them and extend to every thing that participates in them. Education develops them, it does not create them. They direct the legislator who makes the law, and the judge who applies it. They are present to the accused brought before the tribunal, they inspire every just sentence, they give it authority in the soul of the condemned, and in that of the spectator, and they consecrate the employment of force necessary for his execution. Take away a single one of these principles, and all human justice is overthrown, no longer is there any thing but a mass of arbitrary conventions which no one in conscience is bound to respect, which may be violated without remorse, which are sustained only by the display of extreme punishments. The decisions of such a justice are not true judgments, but acts of force, and civil society is only an arena where men contend with each other without duties and rights, without any other object than that of procuring for themselves the greatest possible amount of enjoyment, of procuring it by conquest and preserving it by force or cunning, save throwing over all that the cloak of hypocritical laws.

It is true, such is the aspect under which skepticism makes us consider society and human justice, driving us through despair to revolt and disorder, and bringing us back through despair again to quite another yoke than that of reason and virtue, to that regulated disorder which is called despotism. The spectacle of human things, viewed coolly, and without the spirit of system, is, thank God, less sombre. Without doubt, society and human justice have still many imperfections which time discovers and corrects; but it may be said, that in general they rest on truth and natural equity. The proof of it is, that society everywhere subsists, and is even developed. Moreover, facts, were they such as the melancholy pen of a Pascal or a Rousseau represent them to be, facts are not all,—before facts is right; and this idea of right alone, if it is real, suffices to overturn an abasing system, and save human dignity. Now, is the idea of right a chimera? I again appeal to languages, to individual consciousness, to the human race,—is it not true that fact is everywhere distinguished from right, fact which too often, perhaps, but not always, as it is said, is opposed to right; and right that subdues and rules fact, or protests against it? What word is it that restrains most in human societies? Is it not that of right? Look for a language that does not contain it. On all sides, society is bristling with rights. There is even a distinction made between natural right and positive right, between what is legal and what is equitable. It is proclaimed that force should be in the service of right, and not right at the mercy of force. The triumphs of force, wherever we perceive them, either under our eyes, or by the aid of history in bygone centuries, or by favor of universal publicity beyond the ocean, and in foreign continents, rouse indignation in the disinterested spectator or reader. On the contrary, he who inscribes on his banner the name of right, by that alone interests us; the cause of right, or what we suppose to be the cause of right, is for us the cause of humanity. It is also a fact, and an incontestable fact, that in the eyes of man fact is not every thing, and that the idea of right is a universal idea, graven in shining and ineffaceable characters, if not in the visible world, at least in that of thought and the soul; concerning that is the question; it is also that which in the long run reforms and governs the other.

Individual consciousness, conceived and transferred to the entire species, is called common sense. It is common sense that has made, that sustains, that develops languages, natural and permanent beliefs, society and its fundamental institutions. Grammarians have not invented languages, nor legislators societies, nor philosophers general beliefs. All these things have not been personally done, but by the whole world,—by the genius of humanity.

Common sense is deposited in its works. All languages, and all human institutions contain the ideas and the sentiments that we have just called to mind and described, and especially the distinction between good and evil, between justice and injustice, between free will and desire, between duty and interest, between virtue and happiness, with the profoundly rooted belief that happiness is a recompense due to virtue, and that crime in itself deserves to be punished, and calls for the reparation of a just suffering.

These things are attested by the words and actions of men. Such are the sincere and impartial, but somewhat confused, somewhat gross notions of common sense.

Here begins the part of philosophy. It has before it two different routes; it can do one of two things: either accept the notions of common sense, elucidate them, thereby develop and increase them, and, by faithfully expressing them, fortify the natural beliefs of humanity; or, preoccupied with such or such a principle, impose it upon the natural data of common sense, admit those that agree with this principle, artificially bend the others to these, or openly deny them; this is what is called making a system.

Philosophic systems are not philosophy; they try to realize the idea of it, as civil institutions try to realize that of justice, as the arts express in their way infinite beauty, as the sciences pursue universal science. Philosophic systems are necessarily very imperfect, otherwise there never would have been two systems in the world. Fortunate are those that go on doing good, that expand in the minds and souls of men, with some innocent errors, the sacred love of the true, the beautiful, and the good! But philosophic systems follow their times much more than they direct them; they receive their spirit from the hands of their age. Transferred to France towards the close of the regency and under the reign of Louis XV., the philosophy of Locke gave birth there to a celebrated school, which for a long time governed and still subsists among us, protected by ancient habits, but in radical opposition to our new institutions and our new wants. Sprung from the bosom of tempests, nourished in the cradle of a revolution, brought up under the bad discipline of the genius of war, the nineteenth century cannot recognize its image and find its instincts in a philosophy born under the influence of the voluptuous refinements of Versailles, admirably fitted for the decrepitude of an arbitrary monarchy, but not for the laborious life of a young liberty surrounded with perils. As for us, after having combated the philosophy of sensation in the metaphysics which it substituted for Cartesianism, and in the deplorable æsthetics, now too accredited, under which succumbed our great national art of the seventeenth century, we do not hesitate to combat it again in the ethics that were its necessary product, the ethics of interest.

The exposition and refutation of these pretended ethics will be the subject of the next lecture.

LECTURE XII.

THE ETHICS OF INTEREST.[190]

Exposition of the doctrine of interest.—What there is of truth in this doctrine.—Its defects. 1st. It confounds liberty and desire, and thereby abolishes liberty. 2d. It cannot explain the fundamental distinction between good and evil. 3d. It cannot explain obligation and duty. 4th. Nor right. 5th. Nor the principle of merit and demerit.—Consequences of the ethics of interest: that they cannot admit a providence, and lead to despotism.

The philosophy of sensation, setting out from a single fact, agreeable or painful sensation, necessarily arrives in ethics at a single principle,—interest. The whole of the system may be explained as follows:

Man is sensible to pleasure and pain: he shuns the one and seeks the other. That is his first instinct, and this instinct will never abandon him. Pleasure may change so far as its object is concerned, and be diversified in a thousand ways: but whatever form it takes,—physical pleasure, intellectual pleasure, moral pleasure, it is always pleasure that man pursues.

The agreeable generalized is the useful; and the greatest possible sum of pleasure, whatever it may be, no longer concentrated within such or such an instant, but distributed over a certain extent of duration, is happiness.[191]

---

[190] On the ethics of interest, to this lecture may be joined those of vol. iii. of the 1st Series, on the doctrine of Helvetius and St. Lambert.

[191] The word bonheur, which has no exact English equivalent, which M. Cousin uses in his ethical discussions in the precise sense of the definition given above, we have sometimes translated happiness, sometimes good fortune, sometimes prosperity, sometimes fortune. When one has in mind the thing, he will not be troubled by the more or less exact word that indicates it:—all language, at best, is only symbolic; it bears the same relation to thought as the

Happiness, like pleasure, is relative to him who experiences it; it is essentially personal. Ourselves, and ourselves alone we love, in loving pleasure and happiness.

Interest is that which prompts us to seek in every thing our pleasure and our happiness.

If happiness is the sole end of life, interest is the sole motive of all our actions.

Man is only sensible to his interest, but he understands it well or ill. Much art is necessary in order to be happy. We are not ready to give ourselves up to all the pleasures that are offered on the highway of life, without examining whether these pleasures do not conceal many a pain. Present pleasure is not every thing,—it is necessary to take thought for the future; it is necessary to know how to renounce joys that may bring regret, and sacrifice pleasure to happiness, that is to say, to pleasure still, but pleasure more enduring and less intoxicating. The pleasures of the body are not the only ones,—there are other pleasures, those of mind, even those of opinion: the sage tempers them by each other.

The ethics of interest are nothing else than the ethics of perfected pleasure, substituting happiness for pleasure, the useful for the agreeable, prudence for passion. It admits, like the human race, the words good and evil, virtue and vice, merit and demerit, punishment and reward, but it explains them in its own way. The good is that which in the eyes of reason is conformed to our true interest; evil is that which is contrary to our true interest. Virtue is that wisdom which knows how to resist the enticement of passions, discerns what is truly useful, and surely proceeds to happiness. Vice is that aberration of mind and character that sacrifices happiness to pleasures without duration or full of dangers. Merit and demerit, punishment and reward, are the consequences of virtue and vice:—for not knowing how to seek happiness by the road of wisdom, we are punished by not attaining it. The ethics of interest do not pretend to destroy any of the duties consecrated by public opinion; it establishes that all

---

forms of nature do to the laws that produce and govern them. The true reader never mistakes the symbol for the thing symbolized, the shadow for the reality.

are conformed to our personal interest, and it is thereby that they are duties. To do good to men is the surest means of making them do good to us; and it is also the means of acquiring their esteem, their good will, and their sympathy,—always agreeable, and often useful. Disinterestedness itself has its explanation. Doubtless there is no disinterestedness in the vulgar sense of the word, that is to say, a real sacrifice of self, which is absurd, but there is the sacrifice of present interest to future interest, of gross and sensual passion to a nobler and more delicate pleasure. Sometimes one renders to himself a bad account of the pleasure that he pursues, and in fault of seeing clearly into his own heart, invents that chimera of disinterestedness of which human nature is incapable, which it cannot even comprehend.

It will be conceded that this explanation of the ethics of interest is not overcharged, that it is faithful.

We go further,—we acknowledge that these ethics are an extreme, but, up to a certain point, a legitimate reaction against the excessive rigor of stoical ethics, especially ascetic ethics that smother sensibility instead of regulating it, and, in order to save the soul from passions, demands of it a sacrifice of all the passions of nature that resembles a suicide.

Man was not made to be a sublime slave, like Epictetus, employed in supporting bad fortune well without trying to surmount it, nor, like the author of the *Imitation*, the angelic inhabitant of a cloister, calling for death as a fortunate deliverance, and anticipating it, as far as in him lies, by continual penitence and in mute adoration. The love of pleasure, even the passions, have a place among the needs of humanity. Suppress the passions, and it is true there is no more excess; neither is there any mainspring of action,—without winds the vessel no longer proceeds, and soon sinks in the deep. Suppose a being that lacks love of self, the instinct of preservation, the horror of suffering, especially the horror of death, who has neither the love of pleasure nor the love of happiness, in a word, destitute of all personal interest,—such a being will not long resist the innumerable causes of destruction that surround and besiege him;

he will not remain a day. Never can a single family, nor the least society be formed or maintained. He who has made man has not confided the care of his work to virtue alone, to devotedness and sublime charity,—he has willed that the duration and development of the race and human society should be placed upon simpler and surer foundations; and this is the reason why he has given to man the love of self, the instinct of preservation, the taste of pleasure and happiness, the passions that animate life, hope and fear, love, ambition, personal interest, in fine, a powerful, permanent, universal motive that urges us on to continually ameliorate our condition upon the earth.

So we do not contest with the ethics of interest the reality of their principle,—we are convinced that this principle exists, that it has a right to be. The only question that we raise is the following:—The principle of interest is true in itself, but are there not other principles quite as true, quite as real? Man seeks pleasure and happiness, but are there not in him other needs, other sentiments as powerful, as vital? The first and universal principle of human life is the need of the individual to preserve himself; but would this principle suffice to support human life and society entire and as we behold it?

Just as the existence of the body does not hinder that of the soul, and reciprocally, so in the ample bosom of humanity and the profound designs of divine Providence, the principles that differ most do not exclude each other.

The philosophy of sensation continually appeals to experience. We also invoke experience; and it is experience that has given us certain facts mentioned in the preceding lecture, which constitute the primary notions of common sense. We admit the facts that serve as a foundation for the system of interest, and reject the system. The facts are true in their proper bearing,—the system is false in attributing to them an excessive, limitless bearing; and it is false again in denying other facts quite as incontestable. A sound philosophy holds for its primary law to collect all real facts and respect the real differences that also distinguish them. What it pursues before all, is not unity, but truth.[192] Now the ethics of interest mutilate truth,—they choose among facts those that agree with them, and reject all the others, which are precisely the very facts of morality. Exclusive and intolerant, they deny what they do not explain,—they form a whole well united, which, as an artificial work, may have its merit, but is broken to pieces as soon as it comes to encounter human nature with its grand parts.

We are about to show that the ethics of interest, an offspring of the philosophy of sensation, are in contradiction with a certain number of phenomena, which human nature presents to whomsoever interrogates it without the spirit of system.

1st. We have established, not in the name of a system, but in the name of the most common experience, that entire humanity believes in the existence, in each of its members, of a certain force, a certain power that is called liberty. Because it believes in liberty in the individual, it desires that this liberty should be respected and protected in society. Liberty is a fact that the consciousness of each of us attests to him, which, moreover, is enveloped in all the moral phenomena that we have signalized, in moral approbation and disapprobation, in esteem and contempt, in admiration and indignation, in merit and demerit, in punishment and reward. We ask the philosophy of sensation and the ethics of interest what they do with this universal phenomena which all the beliefs of humanity suppose, on which entire life, private and public, turns.

Every system of ethics, whatever it may be, which contains, I do not say a rule, but a simple advice, implicitly admits liberty. When the ethics of interest advise a man to sacrifice the agreeable to the useful, it apparently admits that man is free to follow or not to follow this advice. But in philosophy it does not suffice to admit a fact, there must be the right to admit it. Now, most moralists of interest deny the liberty of man, and no one has the right to admit it in a system that derives the entire human soul, all

---

[192] On the danger of seeking unity before all, see in the 3d Series, Fragments Philosophiques, vol. iv., our Examination of the Lectures of M. Laromeguière.

its faculties as well as all its ideas, from sensation alone and its developments.

When an agreeable sensation, after having charmed our soul, quits it and vanishes, the soul experiences a sort of suffering, a want, a need,—it is agitated, disquieted. This disquietude, at first vague and indecisive, is soon determined; it is borne towards the object that has pleased us, whose absence makes us suffer. This movement of the soul, more or less vivid, is desire.

Is there in desire any of the characters of liberty? What is it called to be free? Each one knows that he is free, when he knows that he is master of his action, that he can begin it, arrest it, or continue it as he pleases. We are free, when before acting we have taken the resolution to act, knowing well that we are able to take the opposite resolution. A free act is that of which, by the infallible testimony of my consciousness, I know that I am the cause, for which, therefore, I regard myself as responsible. God, the world, the body, can produce in me a thousand movements; these movements may seem to the eyes of an external observer to be voluntary acts; but any error is impossible to consciousness,— it distinguishes every movement not voluntary, whatever it may be, from a voluntary act.

True activity is voluntary and free activity. Desire is just the opposite. Desire, carried to its culmination, is passion; but language, as well as consciousness, says that man is passive in passion; and the more vivid passion is, the more imperative are its movements, the farther is it from the type of true activity in which the soul possesses and governs itself.

I am no more free in desire than in the sensation that precedes and determines it. If an agreeable object is presented to me, am I able not to be agreeably moved? If it is a painful object, am I able not to be painfully moved? And so, when this agreeable sensation has disappeared, if memory and imagination remind me of it, is it in my power not to suffer from no longer experiencing it, is it in my power not to feel the need of experiencing it again, and to desire more or less ardently the object that alone can appease the disquietude and suffering of my soul?

Observe well what takes place within you in desire; you recognize in it a blind emotion, that, without any deliberation on your part, and without the intervention of your will, rises or falls, increases or diminishes. One does not desire, and cease to desire, according to his will.

Will often combats desire, as it often also yields to it; it is not, therefore, desire. We do not reproach the sensations that objects produce, nor even the desires that these sensations engender; we do reproach ourselves for the consent of the will to these desires, and the acts that follow, for these acts are in our power.

Desire is so little will, that it often abolishes it, and leads man into acts that he does not impute to himself, for they are not voluntary. It is even the refuge of many of the accused; they lay their faults to the violence of desire and passion, which have not left them masters of themselves.

If desire were the basis of will, the stronger the desire the freer we should be. Evidently the contrary is true. As the violence of desire increases, the dominion of man over himself decreases; and as desire is weakened and passion extinguished, man repossesses himself.

I do not say that we have no influence over our desires. That two facts differ, it does not follow that they must be without relation to each other. By removing certain objects, or even by merely diverting our thoughts away from the pleasure that they can give us, we are able, to a certain extent, to turn aside and elude the sensible effects of these objects, and escape the desire which they might excite in us. One may also, by surrounding himself with certain objects, in some sort manage himself, and produce in himself sensations and desires which for that are not more voluntary than would be the impression made upon us by a stone with which we should strike ourselves. By yielding to these desires, we lend them a new force, and we moderate them by a skilful resistance. One even has some power over the organs of the body, and, by applying to them an appropriate regimen, he goes so far as to modify their functions. All this proves that there is in us a power different from the senses and desire, which, without disposing of them, sometimes exercises over them an indirect authority.

Will also directs intelligence, although it is not intelligence. To will and to know are two things essentially different. We do not judge as we will, but according to the necessary laws of the judgment and the understanding. The knowledge of truth is not a resolution of the will. It is not the will that declares, for example, that body is extended, that it is in space, that every phenomenon has a cause, etc. Yet the will has much power over intelligence. It is freely and voluntarily that we work, that we give attention, for a longer or a shorter time, more or less intense, to certain things; consequently, it is the will that develops and increases intelligence, as it might let it languish and become extinguished. It must, then, be avowed that there is in us a supreme power that presides over all our faculties, over intelligence as well as sensibility, which is distinguished from them, and is mingled with them, governs them, or leaves them to their natural development, making appear, even in its absence, the character that belongs to it, since the man that is deprived of it avows that he is no longer master of himself, that he is not himself, so true is it that human personality resides particularly in that prominent power that is called the will.[193]

Singular destiny of that power, so often misconceived, and yet so manifest! Strange confounding of will and desire, wherein the most opposite schools meet each other, Spinoza, Malebranche, and Condillac, the philosophy of the seventeenth century, and that of the eighteenth! One, a despiser of humanity, by an extreme and ill-understood piety, strips man of his own activity, in order to concentrate it in God; the other transfers it to nature. In both man is a mere instrument, nothing else than a mode of God or a product of nature. When desire is once taken as the type of human activity, there is an end of all liberty and personality. A philosophy, less systematic, by conforming itself to facts, carries through common sense to better results. By

---

[193] On the difference between desire, intelligence, and will, see the Examination, already cited, of the Lectures of M. Laromeguière.

distinguishing between the passive phenomenon of desire and the power of freely determining self, it restores the true activity that characterizes human personality. The will is the infallible sign and the peculiar power of a real and effective being; for how could he who should be only a mode of another being find in his own borrowed being a power capable of willing and producing acts of which he should feel himself the cause, and the responsible cause?

If the philosophy of sensation, by setting out from passive phenomena, cannot explain true activity, voluntary and free activity, we might regard it as demonstrated that this same philosophy cannot give a true doctrine of morality, for all ethics suppose liberty. In order to impose rules of action on a being, it is necessary that this being should be capable of fulfilling or violating them. What makes the good and evil of an action is not the action itself, but the intention that has determined it. Before every equitable tribunal, the crime is in the intention, and to the intention the punishment is attached. Where, then, liberty is wanting, where there is nothing but desire and passion, not even a shade of morality subsists. But we do not wish to reject, by the previous question, the ethics of sensation. We proceed to examine in itself the principle that they lay down, and to show that from this principle can be deduced neither the idea of good and evil, nor any of the moral ideas that are attached to it.

2d. According to the philosophy of sensation, the good is nothing else than the useful. By substituting the useful for the agreeable, without changing the principle, there has been contrived a convenient refuge against many difficulties; for it will always be possible to distinguish interest well understood from apparent and vulgar interest. But even under this somewhat refined form, the doctrine that we are examining none the less destroys the distinction between good and evil.

If utility is the sole measure of the goodness of actions, I must consider only one thing when an action is proposed to me to do,—what advantages can result from it to me?

So I make the supposition that a friend, whose innocence is known to me, falls into disfavor with a king, or opinion—a mistress more jealous and imperious than all kings,—and that there is danger in remaining faithful to him and advantage in separating myself from him; if, on one side, the danger is certain, and on the other the advantage is infallible, it is clear that I must either abandon my unfortunate friend, or renounce the principle of interest—of interest well understood.

But it will be said to me:—think on the uncertainty of human things; remember that misfortune may also overtake you, and do not abandon your friend, through fear that you may one day be abandoned.

I respond that, at first, it is the future that is uncertain, but the present is certain; if I can reap great and unmistakable advantages from an action, it would be absurd to sacrifice them to the chance of a possible misfortune. Besides, according to my supposition, all the chances of the future are in my favor,—this is the hypothesis that we have made.

Do not speak to me of public opinion. If personal interest is the only rational principle, the public reason must be with me. If it were against me, it would be an objection against the truth of the principle. For how could a true principle, rationally applied, be revolting to the public conscience?

Neither oppose to me remorse. What remorse can I feel for having followed the truth, if the principle of interest is in fact moral truth? On the contrary, I should feel satisfaction on account of it.

The rewards and punishments of another life remain. But how are we to believe in another life, in a system that confines human consciousness within the limits of transformed sensation?

I have, then, no motive to preserve fidelity to a friend. And mankind nevertheless imposes on me this fidelity; and, if I am wanting in it, I am dishonored.

If happiness is the highest aim, good and evil are not in the act itself, but in its happy or unhappy results.

Fontenelle seeing a man led to punishment, said, "There is a man who has calculated badly." Whence it follows that, if this man, in doing what he did, could have escaped punishment, he would have calculated well, and his conduct would have been laudable. The action then becomes good or ill according to the issue. Every act is of itself indifferent, and it is lot that qualifies it.

If the honest is only the useful, the genius of calculation is the highest wisdom; it is even virtue!

But this genius is not within the reach of everybody. It supposes, with long experience of life, a sure insight, capable of discerning all the consequences of actions, a head strong and large enough to embrace and weigh their different chances. The young man, the ignorant, the poor in mind, are not able to distinguish between the good and the evil, the honest and the dishonest. And even in supposing the most consummate prudence, what place remains, in the profound obscurity of human things, for chance and the unforeseen! In truth, in the system of interest well understood, there must be great knowledge in order to be an honest man. Much less is requisite for ordinary virtue, whose motto has always been: Do what you ought, let come what may.[194]

---

[194] 1st Series, vol. iii., p. 193: "In the doctrine of interest, every man seeks the useful, but he is not sure of attaining it. He may, by dint of prudence and profound combinations, increase in his favor the chances of success; it is impossible that there should not remain some chances against him; he never pursues, then, any thing but a probable result. On the contrary, in the doctrine of duty, I am always sure of obtaining the last end that I propose to myself, moral good. I risk my life to save my fellow; if, through mischance, I miss this end, there is another which does not, which cannot, escape me,—I have aimed at the good, I have been successful. Moral good, being especially in the virtuous intention, is always in my power and within my reach; as to the material good that can result from the action itself, Providence alone disposes of it. Let us felicitate ourselves that Providence has placed our moral destiny in our own hands, by making it depend upon the good and not upon the useful. The will, in order to act in the sad trials of life, has need of being sustained by certainty. Who would be disposed to give his blood for an uncertain end? Success is a complicated problem, that, in order to be solved, exacts all the power of the calculus of probabilities. What labor and what uncertainties does such a calculus involve! Doubt is a very sad preparation for action. But when one proposes before all to do his duty, he acts without any perplexity. Do what

But this principle is precisely the opposite of the principle of interest. It is necessary to choose between them. If interest is the only principle avowed by reason, disinterestedness is a lie and madness, and literally an incomprehensible monster in well-ordered human nature.

Nevertheless humanity speaks of disinterestedness, and thereby it does not simply mean that wise selfishness that deprives itself of a pleasure for a surer, more delicate, or more durable pleasure. No one has ever believed that it was the nature or the degree of the pleasure sought that constituted disinterestedness. This name is awarded only to the sacrifice of an interest, whatever it may be, to a motive free from all interest. And the human race, not only thus understands disinterestedness, but it believes that such a disinterestedness exists; it believes the human soul capable of it. It admires the devotedness of Regulus, because it does not see what interest could have impelled that great man to go far from his country to seek, among cruel enemies, a frightful death, when he might have lived tranquil and even honored in the midst of his family and his fellow-citizens.

But glory, it will be said, the passion of glory inspired Regulus; it is, then, interest still that explains the apparent heroism of the old Roman. Admit, then, that this manner of understanding his interest is even ridiculously absurd, and that heroes are very unskilful and inconsistent egoists. Instead of erecting statues, with the deceived human race, to Regulus, d'Assas, and St. Vincent de Paul, true philosophy must send them to the Petites-Maisons, that a good regime may cure them of generosity, charity, and greatness of soul, and restore them to the sane state, the normal state, the state in which man only thinks of himself, and knows no other law, no other principle of action than his interest.

---

you ought, let come what may, is a motto that does not deceive. With such an end, we are sure of never pursuing it in vain."

3d. If there is no liberty, if there is no essential distinction between good and evil, if there is only interest well or ill understood, there can be no obligation.

It is at first very evident that obligation supposes a being capable of fulfilling it, that duty is applied only to a free being. Then the nature of obligation is such, that if we are delinquent in fulfilling it, we feel ourselves culpable, whilst if, instead of understanding our interest well, we have understood it ill, there follows only a single thing, that we are unfortunate. Are, then, being culpable and being unfortunate the same thing? These are two ideas radically different. You may advise me to understand my interest well, under penalty of falling into misfortune; you cannot command me to see clearly in regard to my interest under penalty of crime.

Imprudence has never been considered a crime. When it is morally accused, it is much less as being wrong than as attesting vices of the soul, lightness, presumption, feebleness.

As we have said, our true interest is often most difficult of discernment. Obligation is always immediate and manifest. In vain passion and desire combat it; in vain the reasoning that passion trains for its attendance, like a docile slave, tries to smother it under a mass of sophisms: the instinct of conscience, a cry of the soul, an intuition of reason, different from reasoning, is sufficient to repel all sophisms, and make obligation appear.

However pressing may be the solicitations of interest, we may always enter into contest and arrangement with it. There are a thousand ways of being happy. You assure me that, by conducting myself in such a manner, I shall arrive at fortune. Yes, but I love repose more than fortune, and with happiness alone in view, activity is not better than sloth. Nothing is more difficult than to advise any one in regard to his interest, nothing is easier than to advise him in regard to honor.

After all, in practice, the useful is resolved into the agreeable, that is to say, into pleasure. Now, in regard to pleasure, every thing depends on humor and temperament. When there is neither good nor evil in itself, there are no pleasures more or less noble, more or less elevated; there are only pleasures that are more or less agreeable to us. Every thing depends on the nature of each one. This is the reason why interest is so capricious. Each one understands it as it pleases him, because each one is the judge of what pleases him. One is more moved by pleasures of the senses; another by pleasures of mind and heart. To the latter, the passion of glory takes the place of pleasures of the senses; to the former, the pleasure of dominion appears much superior to that of glory. Each man has his own passions, each man, then, has his own way of understanding his interest; and even my interest of to-day is not my interest of to-morrow. The revolutions of health, age, and events greatly modify our tastes, our humors. We are ourselves perpetually changing, and with us change our desires and our interests.

It is not so with obligation. It exists not, or it is absolute. The idea of obligation implies that of something inflexible. That alone is a duty from which one cannot be loosed under any pretext, and is, by the same title, a duty for all. There is one thing before which all the caprices of my mind, of my imagination, of my sensibility must disappear,—the idea of the good with the obligation which it involves. To this supreme command I can oppose neither my humor, nor circumstances, nor even difficulties. This law admits of no delay, no accommodation, no excuse. When it speaks, be it to you or me, in whatever place, under whatever circumstance, in whatever disposition we may be, it only remains for us to obey. We are able not to obey, for we are free; but every disobedience to the law appears to ourselves a fault more or less grave, a bad use of our liberty. And the violated law has its immediate penal sanction in the remorse that it inflicts upon us.

The only penalty that is brought upon us by the counsels of prudence, comprehended more or less well, followed more or less well, is, in the final account, more or less happiness or unhappiness. Now I pray you, am I obligated to be happy? Can obligation depend upon happiness, that is to say, on a thing that it is equally impossible for me to always seek and obtain at will? If

I am obligated, it must be in my power to fulfil the obligation imposed. But my liberty has but little power over my happiness, which depends upon a thousand circumstances independent of me, whilst it is all in all in regard to virtue, for virtue is only an employment of liberty. Moreover, happiness is in itself, morally, neither better nor worse than unhappiness. If I understand my interest badly, I am punished for it by regret, not by remorse. Unhappiness can overwhelm me; it does not disgrace me, if it is not the consequence of some vice of the soul.

Not that I would renew stoicism and say to suffering, Thou art no evil. No, I earnestly advise man to escape suffering as much as he can, to understand well his interest, to shun unhappiness and seek happiness. I only wish to establish that happiness is one thing and virtue another, that man necessarily aspires after happiness, but that he is only obligated to virtue, and that consequently, by the side of and above interest well understood is a moral law, that is to say, as consciousness attests, and the whole human race avows, an imperative prescription of which one cannot voluntarily divest himself without crime and shame.

4th. If interest does not account for the idea of duty, by a necessary consequence, it does not more account for that of right; for duty and right reciprocally suppose each other.

Might and right must not be confounded. A being might have immense power, that of the whirlwind, of the thunderbolt, that of one of the forces of nature; if liberty is not joined to it, it is only a fearful and terrible thing, it is not a person,—it may inspire, in the highest degree, fear and hope,—it has no right to respect; one has no duties towards it.

Duty and right are brothers. Their common mother is liberty.

They are born at the same time, are developed and perish together. It might even be said that duty and right make one, and are the same being, having a face on two different sides. What, in fact, is my right to your respect, except the duty you have to respect me, because I am a free being? But you are yourself a free being, and the foundation of my right and your duty becomes for you the foundation of an equal right, and in me of an equal duty.[195]

I say equal with the exactest equality, for liberty, and liberty alone, is equal to itself. All the rest is diverse; by all the rest men differ; for resemblance implies difference. As there are no two leaves that are the same, there are no two men absolutely the same in body, senses, mind, heart. But it is impossible to conceive of difference between the free will of one man and the free will of another. I am free or I am not free. If I am free, I am free as much as you, and you are as much as I. There is not in this more or less. One is a moral person as much as, and by the same title as another moral person. Volition, which is the seat of liberty, is the same in all men. It may have in its service different instruments, powers different, and consequently unequal, whether material or spiritual. But the powers of which will disposes are not it,[196] for it does not dispose of them in an absolute manner. The only free power is that of will, but that is essentially so. If will recognizes laws, these laws are not motives, springs that move it,—they are ideal laws, that of justice, for example; will recognizes this law, and at the same time it has the consciousness of the ability to fulfil it or to break it, doing the one only with the consciousness of the ability to do the other, and reciprocally. Therein is the type of liberty, and at the same time of true equality; every thing else is false. It is not true that men have the right to be equally rich, beautiful, robust, to enjoy equally, in a word, to be equally fortunate; for they originally and necessarily differ in all those points of their nature that correspond to pleasure, to riches, to good fortune. God has made us with powers unequal in regard to all these things. Here equality is against nature and eternal order; for diversity and difference, as well as harmony, are the law of creation. To dream of such an equality is a strange mistake, a deplorable error. False equality is the idol of ill-formed minds and hearts, of disquiet and ambitious egoism. True equality accepts without shame all the exterior inequalities that God has made,

---

[195] See the development of the idea of right, lectures 14 and 15.
[196] See lecture 14, Theory of liberty.

and that it is not in the power of man not only to efface, but even to modify. Noble liberty has nothing to settle with the furies of pride and envy. As it does not aspire to domination, so, and by virtue of the same principle, it does not more aspire to a chimerical equality of mind, of beauty, of fortune, of enjoyments. Moreover, such an equality, were it possible, would be of little value in its own eyes; it asks something much greater than pleasure, fortune, rank, to wit, respect. Respect, an equal respect of the sacred right of being free in every thing that constitutes the person, that person which is truly man; this is what liberty and with it true equality claim, or rather imperatively demand. Respect must not be confounded with homage. I render homage to genius and beauty. I respect humanity alone, and by that I mean all free natures, for every thing that is not free in man is foreign to him. Man is therefore the equal of man precisely in every thing that makes him man, and the reign of true equality exacts on the part of all only the same respect for what each one possesses equally in himself, both young and old, both ugly and beautiful, both rich and poor, both the man of genius and the mediocre man, both woman and man, whatever has consciousness of being a person and not a thing. The equal respect of common liberty is the principle at once of duty and right; it is the virtue of each and the security of all; by an admirable agreement, it is dignity among men, and accordingly peace on earth. Such is the great and holy image of liberty and equality, which has made the hearts of our fathers beat, and the hearts of all virtuous and enlightened men, of all true friends of humanity. Such is the ideal that true philosophy pursues across the ages, from the generous dreams of Plato to the solid conceptions of Montesquieu, from the first free legislation of the smallest city of Greece to our declaration of rights, and the immortal works of the constituent Assembly.

The philosophy of sensation starts with a principle that condemns it to consequences as disastrous as those of the principle of liberty are beneficent. By confounding will with desire, it justifies passion, which is desire in all its force—passion, which is precisely the opposite of liberty. It accordingly unchains all the desires and all the passions, it gives full rein to imagination and the heart; it renders each man much less happy on account of what he possesses, than miserable on account of what he lacks; it makes him regard his neighbors with an eye of envy and contempt, and continually pushes society towards anarchy or tyranny. Whither, in fact, would you have interest lead in the train of desire? My desire is certainly to be the most fortunate possible. My interest is to seek to be so by all means, whatever they may be, under the single reserve that they be not contrary to their end. If I am born the first of men, the richest, the most beautiful, the most powerful, etc., I shall do every thing to preserve the advantages I have received. If fate has given me birth in a rank little elevated, with a moderate fortune, limited talents, and immense desires—for it cannot too often be repeated, desire of every kind aspires after the infinite—I shall do every thing to rise above the crowd, in order to increase my power, my fortune, my joys. Unfortunate on account of my position in this world, in order to change it, I dream of, and call for revolutions, it is true, without enthusiasm and political fanaticism, for interest alone does not produce these noble follies, but under the sharp goad of vanity and ambition. Thereby, then, I arrive at fortune and power; interest, then, claims security, as before it invoked agitation. The need of security brings me back from anarchy to the need of order, provided order be to my profit; and I become a tyrant, if I can, or the gilt servant of a tyrant. Against anarchy and tyranny, those two scourges of liberty, the only rampart is the universal sentiment of right, founded on the firm distinction between good and evil, the just and the useful, the honest and the agreeable, virtue and interest, will and desire, sensation and conscience.

5. Let us again signalize one of the necessary consequences of the doctrine of interest.

A free being, in possession of the sacred rule of justice, cannot violate it, knowing that he should and may follow it, without immediately recognizing that he merits punishment. The idea of punishment is not an artificial idea, borrowed from the profound calculations of legislators; legislations rest upon the natural idea of punishment. This idea, corresponding to that of liberty and justice, is necessarily wanting where the former two do not exist. Does he who obeys, and fatally obeys his desires, by the attraction of pleasure and happiness, supposing that, without any other motive than that of interest, he does an act conformed, externally at least, to the rule of justice, merit any thing by doing such an action? Not the least in the world. Conscience attributes to him no merit, and no one owes him thanks or recompense, for he only thinks of himself. On the other hand, if he injures others in wishing to serve himself, he does not feel culpable, and no one can say to him that he has merited punishment. A free being who wills what he does, who has a law, and can conform to it, or break it, is alone responsible for his acts. But what responsibility can there be in the absence of liberty and a recognized and accepted rule of justice? The man of sensation and desire tends to his own good under the law of interest, as the stone is drawn towards the centre of the earth under the law of gravitation, as the needle points to the pole. Man may err in the pursuit of his interest. In this case, what is to be done! As it seems, to put him again in the right way. Instead of that, he is punished. And for what, I pray you? For being deceived. But error merits advice, not punishment. Punishment has, in the system of interest, no more the sanction of moral sense than recompense. Punishment is only an act of personal defence on the part of society; it is an example which it gives, in order to inspire a salutary terror. These motives are excellent, if it be added that this punishment is just in itself, that it is merited, and that it is legitimately applied to the action committed. Omit that, and the other motives lose their authority, and there remains only an exercise of force, destitute of all morality. Then the culprit is not punished; he is smitten, or even put to death, as the animal that injures instead of serving is put to death without scruple. The condemned does not bow his head to the wholesome reparation due to justice, but to the weight of irons or the stroke of the axe. The chastisement is not a legitimate satisfaction, an expiation which, comprehended by the culprit, reconciles him in his own eyes with the order that he has violated. It is a storm that he could not escape; it is the thunder-bolt that falls upon him; it is a force more powerful than his own, which compasses and overthrows him. The appearance of public chastisements acts, without doubt, upon the imagination of peoples; but it does not enlighten their reason and speak to their conscience; it intimidates them, perhaps; it does not soften them. So recompense is only an additional attraction, added to all the others. As, properly speaking, there is no merit, recompense is simply an advantage that one desires, that is striven for and obtained without attaching to it any moral idea. Thus is degraded and effaced the great institution, natural and divine, of the recompense of virtue by happiness, and of reparation for a fault by proportionate suffering.[197]

We may then draw the conclusion, without fear of its being contradicted either by analysis or dialectics, that the doctrine of interest is incompatible with the most certain facts, with the strongest convictions of humanity. Let us add, that this doctrine is not less incompatible with the hope of another world, where the principle of justice will be better realized than in this.

I will not seek whether the sensualistic metaphysics can arrive at an infinite being, author of the universe and man. I am well persuaded that it cannot. For every proof of the existence of God supposes in the human mind principles of which sensation renders no account,—for example, the universal and necessary principle of causality, without which I should have no need of seeking, no power of finding the cause of whatever exists.[198] All that I wish to establish here is, that in the system of interest, man, not possessing any truly moral attribute, has no right to put in God that of which he finds no trace either in the world or in himself. The God of the ethics of interest must be analogous to the man of these same ethics. How could they attribute to him the justice and the love—I mean disinterested love—of which they cannot have the least idea? The God that they can admit

---

[197] See the preceding lecture, and lectures 14 and 15.
[198] 1st part, lecture I.

loves himself, and loves only himself. And reciprocally, not considering him as the supreme principle of charity and justice, we can neither love nor honor him, and the only worship that we can render him, is that of the fear with which his omnipotence inspires us.

What holy hope could we then found upon such a God? And we who have some time grovelled upon this earth, thinking only of ourselves, seeking only pleasure and a pitiable happiness, what sufferings nobly borne for justice, what generous efforts to maintain and develop the dignity of our soul, what virtuous affections for other souls, can we offer to the Father of humanity as titles to his merciful justice? The principle that most persuades the human race of the immortality of the soul is still the necessary principle of merit and demerit, which, not finding here below its exact satisfaction, and yet under the necessity of finding it, inspires us to call upon God for its satisfaction, who has not put in our hearts the law of justice to violate it himself in regard to us.[199] Now, we have just seen that the ethics of interest destroy the principle of merit and demerit, both in this world, and above all, in the world to come. Accordingly, there is no regard beyond this world,—no recourse to an all-powerful judge, wholly just and wholly good, against the sports of fortune and the imperfections of human justice. Every thing is completed for man between birth and death, in spite of the instincts and presentiments of his heart, and even the principles of his reason.

The disciples of Helvetius will, perhaps, claim the glory of having freed humanity from the fears and hopes that turn it aside from its true interests. It is a service which mankind will appreciate. But since they confine our whole destiny to this world, let us demand of them what lot so worthy of envy they have in reserve for us here, what social order they charge with our good fortune, what politics, in fine, are derived from their ethics.[200]

---

[199] See lecture 16.
[200] On the politics that are derived from the philosophy of sensation, see the four lectures that we devoted to the exposition and refutation of the doctrine of Hobbes, vol. iii. of the 1st Series.

You already know. We have demonstrated that the philosophy of sensation knows neither true liberty nor true right. What, in fact, is will for this philosophy? It is desire. What, then, is right? The power of satisfying desires. On this score, man is not free, and right is might.

Once more, nothing pertains less to man than desire. Desire comes of need which man does not make, which he submits to. He submits in the same way to desire. To reduce will to desire is to annihilate liberty; it is worse still, it is to put it where it is not; it is to create a mendacious liberty that becomes an instrument of crime and misery. To call man to such a liberty is to open his soul to infinite desires, which it is impossible for him to satisfy. Desire is in its nature without limits, and our power is very limited. If we were alone in this world, we should even then be much troubled to satisfy our desires. But we press against each other with immense desires, and limited, diverse, and unequal powers. When right is the force that is in each of us, equality of rights is a chimera,—all rights are unequal, since all forces are unequal and can never cease to be so. It is, therefore, necessary to renounce equality as well as liberty; or if one invents a false equality as well as a false liberty, he puts humanity in pursuit of a phantom.

Such are the social elements that the ethics of interest give to politics. From such elements I defy all the politics of the school of sensation and interest to produce a single day of liberty and happiness for the human race.

When right is might, the natural state of men among themselves, is war. All desiring the same things, they are all necessarily enemies; and in this war, woe to the feeble, to the feeble in body and the feeble in mind! The stronger are the masters by perfect right. Since right is might, the feeble may complain of nature that has not made them strong, and not complain of the strong man who uses his right in oppressing them. The feeble then call deception to their aid; and it is in this strife between cunning and force that humanity combats with itself.

Yes, if there are only needs, desires, passions, interests, with different forces pitted against each other, war, a war sometimes declared and bloody, sometimes silent and full of meannesses, is in the nature of things. No social art can change this nature,—it may be more or less covered; it always reappears, overcomes and rends the veil with which a mendacious legislation envelops it. Dream, then, of liberty for beings that are not free, of equality between beings that are essentially different, of respect for rights where there is no right, and of the establishment of justice on an indestructible foundation of inimical passions! From such a foundation can spring only endless troubles or oppression, or rather all these evils together in a necessary circle.

This fatal circle can be broken only by the aid of principles which all the metamorphoses of sensation do not engender, and for which interest cannot account, which none the less subsist to the honor and for the safety of humanity. These principles are those that time has little by little drawn from Christianity in order to give them for the guidance of modern societies. You will find them written in the glorious declaration of rights that forever broke the monarchy of Louis XV., and prepared the constitutional monarchy. They are in the charter that governs us, in our laws, in our institutions, in our manners, in the air that we breathe. They serve at once as foundations for our society and the new philosophy necessary to a new order.[201]

Perhaps you will ask me how, in the eighteenth century, so many distinguished, so many honest souls could let themselves be seduced by a system that must have been revolting to all their

---

[201] These words sufficiently mark the generous epoch in which we pronounce them, without wounding the authority and the applauses of a noble youth, when M. de Châteaubriand covered the Restoration with his own glory, when M. Royer-Collard presided over public instruction, M. Pasquier, M. Lainé, M. de Serre over justice and the interior, Marshal St. Cyr over war, and the Duke de Richelieu over foreign affairs, when the Duke de Broglie prepared the true legislation of the press, and M. Decazes, the author of the wise and courageous ordinance of September 5, 1816, was at the head of the councils of the crown; when finally, Louis XVIII. separated himself, like Henry IV., from his oldest servants in order to be the king of the whole nation.

sentiments. I will answer by reminding you that the eighteenth century was an immoderate reaction against the faults into which had sadly fallen the old age of a great century and a great king, that is to say, the revocation of the edict of Nantes, the persecution of all free and elevated philosophy, a narrow and suspicious devotion, and intolerance, with its usual companion, hypocrisy. These excesses must have produced opposite excesses. Mme. de Maintenon opened the route to Mme. de Pompadour. After the mode of devotion comes that of license; it takes every thing by storm. It descends from the court to the nobility, to the clergy even, and accordingly to the people. It carried away the best spirits, even genius itself. It put a foreign philosophy in the place of the national philosophy, culpable, persecuted as it had been, for not being irreconcilable with Christianity. A disciple of Locke, whom Locke had discarded, Condillac, took the place of Descartes, as the author of *Candide* and *la Pucelle* had taken the place of Corneille and Bossuet, as Boucher and Vanloo had taken the place of Lesueur and Poussin. The ethics of pleasure and interest were the necessary ethics of that epoch. It must not be supposed from this that all souls were corrupt. Men, says M. Royer-Collard, are neither as good nor as bad as their principles[202]. No stoic has been as austere as stoicism, no epicurean as enervated as epicureanism. Human weakness practically baffles virtuous theories; in return, thank God, the instinct of the heart condemns to inconsistency the honest man who errs in bad theories. Accordingly, in the eighteenth century, the most generous and most disinterested sentiments often shone forth under the reign of the philosophy of sensation and the ethics of interest. But it is none the less true, that the philosophy

---

[202] Œuvres de Reid, vol. iv., p. 297: "Men are neither as good nor as bad as their principles; and, as there is no skeptic in the street, so I am sure there is no disinterested spectator of human actions who is not compelled to discern them as just and unjust. Skepticism has no light that does not pale before the splendor of that vivid internal light that lightens the objects of moral perception, as the light of day lightens the objects of sensible perception."

of sensation is false, and the ethics of interest destructive of all morality.

I should perhaps make an apology for so long a lecture; but it was necessary to combat seriously a doctrine of morality radically incompatible with that which I would make penetrate your minds and your souls. It was especially necessary for me to strip the ethics of interest of that false appearance of liberty which they usurp in vain. I maintain, on the contrary, that they are the ethics of slaves, and send them back to the time when they ruled. Now, the principle of interest being destroyed, I propose to examine other principles also, less false without doubt, but still defective, exclusive, and incomplete, upon which celebrated systems have pretended to found ethics. I will successively combat these principles taken in themselves, and will then bring them together, reduced to their just value, in a theory large enough to contain all the true elements of morality, in order to express faithfully common sense and entire human consciousness.

LECTURE XIII.

OTHER DEFECTIVE PRINCIPLES.

The ethics of sentiment.—The ethics founded on the principle of the interest of the greatest number.—The ethics founded on the will of God alone.—The ethics founded on the punishments and rewards of another life.

Against the ethics of interest, all generous souls take refuge in the ethics of sentiment. The following are some of the facts on which these ethics are supported, and by which they seem to be authorized.

When we have done a good action, is it not certain that we experience a pleasure of a certain nature, which is to us the reward of this action? This pleasure does not come from the senses—it has neither its principle nor its measure in an impression made upon our organs. Neither is it confounded with the joy of satisfied personal interest,—we are not moved in the same manner, in thinking that we have succeeded, and in thinking that we have been honest. The pleasure attached to the testimony of a good conscience is pure; other pleasures are much alloyed. It is durable, whilst the others quickly pass away. Finally, it is always within our reach. Even in the midst of misfortune, man bears in himself a permanent source of exquisite joys, for he always has the power of doing right, whilst success, dependent upon a thousand circumstances of which we are not the masters, can give only an occasional and precarious pleasure.

As virtue has its joys, so crime has its pains. The suffering that follows a fault is the just recompense for the pleasure that we have found in it, and is often born with it. It poisons culpable joys and the successes that are not legitimate. It wounds, rends, bites, thus to speak, and thereby receives its name.[203] To be man, is sufficient to understand this suffering,—it is remorse.

---

[203] Mordre—to bite, is the main root of remords—remorse.

Here are other facts equally incontestable:

I perceive a man whose face bears the marks of distress and misery. There is nothing in this that reaches and injures me; nevertheless, without reflection or calculation, the sight alone of this suffering man makes me suffer. This sentiment is pity, compassion, whose general principle is sympathy.

The sadness of one of my fellow-men inspires me with sadness, and a glad face disposes me to joy:

Ut ridentibus arrident, ita flentibus adflent Humani vultus.

The joy of others has an echo in our souls, and their sufferings, even their physical sufferings, communicate themselves to us almost physically. Not as exaggerated as it has been supposed was that expression of Mme. de Sévigné to her sick daughter: I have a pain in your breast.

Our soul feels the need of putting itself in unison, and, as it were, in equilibrium with that of others. Hence those electric movements, thus to speak, that run through large assemblies. One receives the counter-stroke of the sentiments of his neighbors,—admiration and enthusiasm are contagious, as well as pleasantry and ridicule. Hence again the sentiment with which the author of a virtuous action inspires us. We feel a pleasure analogous to that which he feels himself. But are we witnesses of a bad action? our souls refuse to participate in the sentiments that animate the culpable man,—they have for him a true aversion, what is called antipathy.

We do not forget a third order of facts that pertain to the preceding, but differ from them.

We not only sympathize with the author of a virtuous action, we wish him well, we voluntarily do good to him, in a certain degree we love him. This love goes as far as enthusiasm when it has for its object a sublime act and a hero. This is the principle of the homages, of the honors that humanity renders to great men. And this sentiment does not pertain solely to others,—we apply it to ourselves by a sort of return that is not egoism. Yes, it may be said that we love ourselves when we have done well. The sentiment that others owe us, if they are just, we accord to ourselves,—that sentiment is benevolence.

On the contrary, do we witness a bad action? We experience for the author of this action antipathy; moreover we wish him evil,—we desire that he should suffer for the fault that he has committed, and in proportion to the gravity of the fault. For this reason great culprits are odious to us, if they do not compensate for their crimes by deep remorse, or by great virtues mingled with their crimes. This sentiment is not malevolence. Malevolence is a personal and interested sentiment, which makes us wish evil to others, because they are an obstacle to us. Hatred does not ask whether such a man is virtuous or vicious, but whether he obstructs us, surpasses us, or injures us. The sentiment of which we are speaking is a sort of hatred, but a generous hatred that neither springs from interest nor envy, but from a shocked conscience. It is turned against us when we do evil, as well as against others.

Moral satisfaction is not sympathy, neither is sympathy, to speak rigorously, benevolence. But these three phenomena have the common character of all being sentiments. They give birth to three different and analogous systems of ethics.

According to certain philosophers, a good action is that which is followed by moral satisfaction, a bad action is that which is followed by remorse. The good or bad character of an action is at first attested to us by the sentiment that accompanies it. Then, this sentiment, with its moral signification, we attribute to other men; for we judge that they do as we do, that in presence of the same actions they feel the same sentiments.

Other philosophers have assigned the same part to sympathy or benevolence.

For these the sign and measure of the good is in the sentiments of affection and benevolence which we feel for a moral agent. Does a man excite in us by such or such an action a more or less vivid disposition to wish him well, a desire to see and even make him happy? we may say that this action is good. If, by a series of actions of the same kind, he makes this disposition and this desire permanent in us, we judge that he is a virtuous man. Does he excite an opposite desire, an opposite disposition? he appears to us a dishonest man.

For the former, the good is that with which we naturally sympathize. Has a man devoted himself to death through love for his country? this heroic action awakens in us, in a certain degree, the same sentiments that inspired him. Bad passions are not thus echoed in our hearts, unless they find us already very corrupt, and have interest for their accomplice; but even then there is something in us that revolts against these passions, and in the most depraved soul subsists a concealed sentiment of sympathy for the good, and antipathy for the evil.

These different systems may be reduced to a single one, which is called the ethics of sentiment.

It is not difficult to show the difference which separates these ethics from those of egoism. Egoism is the exclusive love of self, is the thoughtful and permanent search for our own pleasure and our own well-being.

What is there more opposed to interest than benevolence? In benevolence, far from wishing others well by reason of our interest, we will voluntarily risk something, we will make some sacrifice in order to serve an honest man who has coined our heart. If even in this sacrifice the soul feels a pleasure, this pleasure is only the involuntary accompaniment of sentiment, it is not the end proposed,—we feel it without having sought it. It is, indeed, permitted the soul to taste this pleasure, for it is nature herself that attaches it to benevolence.

Sympathy, like benevolence, is related to another than ourselves,—our interest is not its starting-point. The soul is so constituted that it is capable of suffering on account of the sufferings of an enemy. That a man does a noble action, although it opposes our interests, awakens in us a certain sympathy for that action and its author.

The attempt has been made to explain the compassion with which the suffering of one of our fellow-men inspires us by the fear that we have of feeling it in our turn. But the unhappiness for which we feel compassion, is often so far from us and threatens us so little, that it would be absurd to fear it. Doubtless, that sympathy may have existence it is necessary to experience suffering,—*non ignara mali.* For how do you suppose that I can be sensible to evils of which I form to myself no idea? But that is only the condition of sympathy. It is not at all necessary to conclude that it is only a remembrance of our own ills or the fear of ills to come.

No recurrence to ourselves can account for sympathy. In the first place, it is involuntary, like antipathy. Then it cannot be supposed that we sympathize with any one in order to win his benevolence; for he who is its object often knows not what we feel. What benevolence are we seeking, when we sympathize with men that we have never seen, that we never shall see, with men that are no more?

Egoism admits all pleasures; it repels none; it may, if it is enlightened, if it has become delicate and refined, recommend, as more durable and less alloyed, the pleasures of sentiment. The ethics of sentiment would then be confounded with those of egoism, if they should prescribe obedience to sentiment for the pleasure that we find in it. There would, then, be no disinterestedness in it,—the individual would be the centre and sole end of all his actions. But such is not the case. The charm of the pleasures of conscience comes from the very fact that we are forgetful of self in the action that has produced them. So if nature has joined to sympathy and benevolence a true enjoyment, it is on condition that these sentiments remain as they are, pure and disinterested; you must only think of the object of your sympathy and benevolence in order that benevolence and sympathy may receive their recompense in the pleasure which they give. Otherwise, this pleasure no longer has its reason for existence, and it is wanting as soon as it sought for itself. No metamorphose of interest can produce a pleasure attached to disinterestedness alone.

The ethics of egoism are only a perpetual falsehood,—they preserve the names consecrated by ethics, but they abolish ethics themselves; they deceive humanity by speaking to humanity its own language, concealing under this borrowed language a radical opposition to all the instincts, to all the ideas that form the treasure of mankind. On the contrary, if sentiment is not the good itself, it is its faithful companion and useful auxiliary. It is as it were the sign of the presence of the good, and renders the accomplishment of it more easy. We always have sophisms at our disposal, in order to persuade ourselves that our true interest is to satisfy present passion; but sophism has less influence over the mind when the mind is in some sort defended by the heart. Nothing is, therefore, more salutary than to excite and preserve in the soul those noble sentiments that lift us above the slavery of personal interest. The habit of participating in the sentiments of virtuous men disposes us to act like them. To cultivate in ourselves benevolence and sympathy is to fertilize the source of charity and love, is to nourish and develop the germ of generosity and devotion.

It is seen that we render sincere homage to the ethics of sentiment. These ethics are true,—only they are not sufficient for themselves; they need a principle which authorizes them.

I act well, and I feel on account of it an internal satisfaction: I do evil, and feel remorse on account of it. These two sentiments do not qualify the act that I have just done, since they follow it. Would it be possible for us to feel any internal satisfaction for having acted well if we did not judge that we had acted well?—any remorse for having done evil, if we did not judge that we had done evil? At the same time that we do such or such an act, a natural and instinctive judgment characterizes it, and it is in consequence of this judgment that our sensibility is moved. Sentiment is not this primitive and immediate judgment; far from forming the basis of the idea of the good, it supposes it. It is manifestly a vicious circle to derive the knowledge of the good from that which would not exist without this knowledge.[204]

---

[204] See 1st part, lecture 5, On Mysticism, and 2d part, lecture 6, On the Sentiment of the Beautiful. See, also, 1st Series, vol. iv., detailed refutation of the Theories of Hutcheson and Smith.

So is it not because we find a good action that we sympathize with it? Is it not because the dispositions of a man appear to us conformed to the idea of justice, that we are inclined to participate in them with him? Moreover, if sympathy were the true criterion of the good, every thing for which we feel sympathy would be good. But sympathy is not only related to things in their nature moral, we also sympathize with the grief and the joy that have nothing to do with virtue and crime. We even sympathize with physical sufferings. Moral sympathy is only a case of general sympathy. It must even be acknowledged that sympathy is not always in accordance with right. We sometimes sympathize with certain sentiments that we condemn, because, without being in themselves bad—which would prevent all sympathy—they give an inclination to the greatest faults; for example, love, which comes so near to irregularity, and emulation, that so quickly leads to ambition.

Benevolence also is not always determined by the good alone. And, again, when it is applied to a virtuous man, it supposes a judgment by which we pronounce that this man is virtuous. It is not because we wish the author of an action well that we judge that this action is good; it is because we judge that this action is good that we wish its author well. This is not all. In the sentiment of benevolence is enveloped a new judgment which is not in sympathy. This judgment is the following: the author of a good action deserves to be happy, as the author of a bad action deserves to suffer in order to expiate it. This is the reason why we desire happiness for the one and reparatory suffering for the other. Benevolence is little else than the sensible form of this judgment.

All these sentiments, therefore, suppose an anterior and superior judgment. Everywhere and always the same vicious circle. From the fact that the sentiments which we have just described have a moral character, it is concluded that they constitute the idea of the good, whilst it is the idea of the good that communicates to them the character that we perceive in them.

Another difficulty is, that sentiments pertain to sensibility, and borrow from it something of its relative and changing nature.

It is, then, very necessary that all men should be made to enjoy with the same delicacy the pleasures of the heart. There are gross natures and natures refined. If your desires are impetuous and violent, will not the idea of the pleasures of virtue be in you much more easily overcome by the force of passion than if nature had given you a tranquil temperament? The state of the atmosphere, health, sickness, calm or rouse our moral sensibility. Solitude, by delivering man up to himself, leaves to remorse all its energy, the presence of death redoubles it; but the world, noise, force of example, habit, without power to smother it, in some sort stun it. The spirit has a little season of rest. We are not always in the vein of enthusiasm. Courage itself has its intermissions. We know the celebrated expression: He was one day brave. Humor has its vicissitudes that influence our most intimate sentiments. The purest, the most ideal sentiment still pertains on some side to organization. The inspiration of the poet, the passion of the lover, the enthusiasm of the martyr, have their languors and shortcomings that often depend on very pitiable material causes. On those perpetual fluctuations of sentiment, is it possible to ground a legislation equal for all?

Sympathy and benevolence do not escape the conditions of all the phenomena of sensibility. We do not all possess in the same degree the power of feeling what others experience. Those who have suffered most best comprehend suffering, and consequently feel for it the most lively compassion. With mere imagination one also represents to himself better and feels more what passes in the souls of his fellow-man. One feels more sympathy for physical pleasures and pains, another for pleasures and pains of soul; and each of these sympathies has in each of us its degrees and variations. They not only differ, they often oppose each other. Sympathy for talent weakens the indignation that outraged virtue produces. We overlook many things in Voltaire, in Rousseau, in Mirabeau, and we excuse them on account of the corruption of their century. The sympathy caused by the pain of a condemned person renders less lively the just antipathy excited by his crime. Thus turns and wavers at each step that sympathy which some would set up as the supreme arbiter of the good. Benevolence does not vary less. We have souls naturally more or less affectionate, more or less animated. And, then, like sympathy, benevolence receives the counter-stroke of different passions that are mingled with it. Friendship, for example, often renders us, in spite of ourselves, more benevolent than justice would wish.

Is it not a rule of prudence not to listen to, without always disdaining them, the inspirations—often capricious—of the heart? Governed by reason, sentiment becomes to it an admirable support. But, delivered up to itself, in a little while it degenerates into passion, and passion is fantastic, excessive, unjust; it gives to the soul spring and energy, but generally troubles and perverts it. It is even not very far from egoism, and it usually terminates in that, wholly generous as it is or seems to be in the beginning. Unless we always keep in sight the good and the inflexible obligation that is attached to it, unless we always keep in sight this fixed and immutable point, the soul knows not where to betake itself on that moving ground that is called sensibility; it floats from sentiment to passion, from generosity to selfishness, ascending one day to the pitch of enthusiasm, and the next day descending to all the miseries of personality.

Thus the ethics of sentiment, although superior to those of interest, are not less insufficient: 1st. They give as the foundation of the idea of the good what is founded on this same idea; 2d. The rule that they propose is too mobile to be universally obligatory.[205]

---

[205] We do not grow weary of citing M. Royer-Collard. He has marked the defects of the ethics of sentiment in a lively and powerful passage, from which we borrow some traits. Œuvres de Reid, vol. iii., p. 410, 411: "The perception of the moral qualities of human actions is accompanied by an emotion of the soul that is called sentiment. Sentiment is a support of nature that invites us to good by the attraction of the noblest joys of which man is capable, and turns us from evil by the contempt, the aversion, the horror with which it inspires us. It is a fact that by the contemplation of a beautiful action or a noble character, at the same time that we perceive these qualities of the action and the character (perception, which is a judgment), we feel for the person a love mingled with respect, and sometimes an admiration that is full of tenderness. A bad action, a

There is another system of which I will also say, as of the preceding, that it is not false, but incomplete and insufficient.

The partisans of the ethics of utility and happiness have tried to save their principle by generalizing it. According to them, the good can be nothing but happiness; but egoism is wrong in understanding by that the happiness of the individual; we must understand by it the general happiness.

Let us establish, in the first place, that the new principle is entirely opposed to that of personal interest, for, according to circumstances, it may demand, not only a passing sacrifice, but an irreparable sacrifice, that of life. Now, the wisest calculations of personal interest cannot go thus far.

And, notwithstanding, this principle is far from containing true ethics and the whole of ethics.

The principle of general interest leans towards disinterestedness, and this is certainly much; but disinterestedness is the condition of virtue, not virtue itself. We may commit an injustice with the most entire disinterestedness. From the fact that an action does not profit him who does it, it does not follow that it may not be in itself very unjust, in seeking general interest before all, we escape, it is true, that vice of soul which is called selfishness, but we may fall into a thousand iniquities. Or, indeed, it must be felt, that general interest is always conformed to justice. But these two ideas are not adequate to each other. If they very often go together, they are sometimes also separated.

---

loose and perfidious character, excite a contrary perception and sentiment. The internal approbation of conscience and remorse are sentiments attached to the perception of the moral qualities of our own actions.... I do not weaken the part of sentiment; yet it is not true that ethics are wholly in sentiment; if we maintain this, we annihilate moral distinctions.... Let ethics be wholly in sentiment, and nothing is in itself good, nothing is in itself evil; good and evil are relative; the qualities of human actions are precisely such as each one feels them to be. Change sentiment, and you change every thing; the same action is at once good, indifferent, and bad, according to the affection of the spectator. Silence sentiment, and actions are only physical phenomena; obligation is resolved into inclinations, virtue into pleasure, honesty into utility. Such are the ethics of Epicurus: Dii meliora piis!"

Themistocles proposed to the Athenians to burn the fleet of the allies that was in the port of Athens, and thus to secure to themselves the supremacy. The project is useful, says Aristides, but it is unjust, and on account of this simple speech, the Athenians renounce an advantage that must be purchased by an injustice. Observe that Themistocles had no particular interest in that; he thought only of the interest of his country. But, had he hazarded or given his life in order to engage the Athenians in such an act, he would only have been consecrating—what has often been seen—an admirable devotion to a course in itself immoral.

To this it is replied, that if, in the example cited, justice and interest exclude each other, it is because the interest was not sufficiently general; and the celebrated maxim is arrived at, that one must sacrifice himself to his family, his family to the city, the city to country, country to humanity, that, in fine, the good is the interest of the greatest number.[206]

When you have gone thus far, you have not yet attained even the idea of justice. The interest of humanity, like that of the individual, may accord in fact with justice, for in that there is certainly no incompatibility, but the two things are none the more identical, so that we cannot say with exactness that the interest of humanity is the foundation of justice. A single case, even a single hypothesis, in which the interest of humanity should not accord with the good, is sufficient to enable us to conclude that one is not essentially the other.

We go farther: if it is the interest of humanity that constitutes and measures justice, that only is unjust which this interest declares to be so. But you are not able to affirm absolutely, that, in any circumstance, the interest of humanity will not demand such or such an action; and if it demands it, by virtue of your principle, it will be necessary to do it, whatever it may be, and to do it inasmuch as it is just.

You order me to sacrifice particular interest to general interest. But in the name of what do you order me to do this? Is it

---

[206] In this formula is recognized the system of Bentham, who, for some time, had numerous partisans in England, and even in France.

in the name of interest? If interest, as such, must touch me, evidently my interest must also touch me, and I do not see why I should sacrifice it to that of others.

The supreme end of human life, you say, is happiness. I hence conclude very reasonably, that the supreme end of my life is my happiness.

In order to ask of me the sacrifice of my happiness, it must be called for by some other principle than happiness itself.

Consider to what perplexity this famous principle of the greatest good of the greatest number condemns me. I have already much difficulty in discerning my true interest in the obscurity of the future; by substituting for the infallible voice of justice the uncertain calculations of personal interest, you have not rendered action easy for me;[207] but it becomes impossible, if it is necessary to seek, before acting, what is the interest not only of myself, but of my family, not only of my family, but of my country, not only of my country, but of humanity. What! must I embrace the entire world in my foresight? What! is such the price of virtue? You impose upon me a knowledge that God alone possesses. Am I in his counsels so as to adjust my actions according to his decrees? The philosophy of history and the wisest diplomacy are not, then, sufficient for conducting ourselves well. Imagine, therefore, that there is no mathematical science of human life. Chance and liberty confound the profoundest calculations, overturn the best-established fortunes, relieve the most desperate miseries, mingle good fortune and bad, confound all foresight.

And would you establish ethics on a foundation so mobile? How much place you leave for sophism in that complaisant and enigmatical law of general interest![208] It will not be very difficult

---

[207] See lecture 12.

[208] 1st Series, vol. iv., p. 174: "If the good is that alone which must be the most useful to the greatest number, where can the good be found, and who can discern it? In order to know whether such an action, which I propose to myself to do, is good or bad, I must be sure, in spite of its visible and direct utility in the present moment, that it will not become injurious in a future that I do not yet know. I must seek whether, useful to mine and those that surround me, it

always to find some remote reason of general interest, which will excuse us from being faithful in the present moment to our friends, when they shall be in misfortune. A man in adversity addresses himself to my generosity. But could I not employ my money in a way more useful to humanity? Will not the country have need of it to-morrow? Let us virtuously keep it for the

will not have counter-strokes disastrous to the human race, of which I must think before all. It is important that I should know whether the money that I am tempted to give this unfortunate who needs it, could not be otherwise more usefully employed, in fact, the rule is here the greatest good of the greatest number. In order to follow it, what calculations are imposed on me? In the obscurity of the future, in the uncertainty of the somewhat remote consequences of every action, the surest way is to do nothing that is not related to myself, and the last result of a prudence so refined is indifference and egoism. Supposing you have received a deposit from an opulent neighbor, who is old and sick, a sum of which he has no need, and without which your numerous family runs the risk of dying with famine. He calls on you for this sum,—what will you do? The greatest number is on your side, and the greatest utility also; for this sum is insignificant for your rich neighbor, whilst it will save your family from misery, and perhaps from death. Father of a family, I should like much to know in the name of what principle you would hesitate to retain the sum which is necessary to you? Intrepid reasoner, placed in the alternative of killing this sick old man, or of letting your wife and children die of hunger, in all honesty of conscience you ought to kill him. You have the right, it is even your duty to sacrifice the less advantage of a single person to much the greater advantage of a greater number; and since this principle is the expression of true justice, you are only its minister in doing what you do. A vanquishing enemy or a furious people threaten destruction to a whole city, if there be not delivered up to them the head of such a man, who is, nevertheless, innocent. In the name of the greatest good of the greatest number, this man will be immolated without scruple. It might even be maintained that innocent to the last, he has ceased to be so, since he is an obstacle to the public good. It having once been declared that justice is the interest of the greatest number, the only question is to know where this interest is. Now, here, doubt is impossible, therefore, it is perfectly just to offer innocence as a holocaust to public safety. This consequence must be accepted, or the principle rejected."

country then. Moreover, even where the interest of all seems evident, there still remains some chance of error; it is, therefore, better to withhold. It will always be wisdom to withhold. Yes, when it is necessary, in order to do well, to be sure of serving the greatest interest of the greatest number, none but the rash and senseless will dare to act. The principle of general interest will produce, I admit, great devotedness, but it will also produce great crimes. Is it not in the name of this principle that fanatics of every kind, fanatics in religion, fanatics in liberty, fanatics in philosophy, taking it upon themselves to understand the eternal interest of humanity, have engaged in abominable acts, mingled often with a sublime disinterestedness?

Another error of this system is that it confounds the good itself with one of its applications. If the good is the greatest interest of the greatest number, the consequence is clear, that there are only public and social ethics, and no private ethics; there is only a single class of duties, duties towards others, and there are no duties towards ourselves. But this is retrenching precisely those of our duties that most surely guarantee the exercise of all the rest.[209] The most constant relations that I sustain are with that being which is myself. I am my own most habitual society. I bear in myself, as Plato[210] has well said, a whole world of ideas, sentiments, desires, passions, emotions, which claim a legislation. This necessary legislation is suppressed.

Let us also say a word on a system that, under sublime appearances, conceals a vicious principle.

There are persons who believe that they are magnifying God, by placing in his will alone the foundation of the moral law, and the sovereign motive of humanity in the punishments and rewards that it has pleased him to attach to the respect and violation of his will.

Let us understand what we are about in a matter of such delicacy.

---

[209] See lecture 15, Private and Public Ethics.
[210] Plato, Republic, vol. ix. and x. of our translation.

It is certain, and we shall establish it for the good,[211] as we have done for the true and the beautiful,[212] it is certain that, from explanations to explanations, we come to be convinced that God is definitively the supreme principle of ethics, so that it may be very truly said, that the good is the expression of his will, since his will is itself the expression of the eternal and absolute justice that resides in him. God wills, without doubt, that we should act according to the law of justice that he has put in our understanding and our heart; but it is not at all necessary to conclude that he has arbitrarily instituted this law. Far from that, justice is in the will of God only because it has its roots in his intelligence and wisdom, that is to say, in his most intimate nature and essence.

While making, then, every reservation in regard to what is true in the system that founds ethics on the will of God, we must show what there is in this system, as it is presented to us, false, arbitrary, and incompatible with ethics themselves.[213]

In the first place, it does not pertain to the will, whatever it may be, to institute the good, any more than it belongs to it to institute the true and the beautiful. I have no idea of the will of God except by my own, to be sure with the differences that separate what is finite from what is infinite. Now, I cannot by my will found the least truth. Is it because my will is limited? No; were it armed with infinite power, it would, in this respect, be

---

[211] Lecture 16.

[212] Lectures 4 and 7.

[213] This polemic is not new. The school of St. Thomas engaged in it early against the theory of Occam, which was quite similar to that which we combat. See our Sketch of a General History of Philosophy, 2d Series, vol. ii., lect. 9, On Scholasticism. Here are two decisive passages from St. Thomas, 1st book of the Summation against the Gentiles, chap. lxxxvii: "Per prædicta autem excluditur error dicentiam omnia procedere a Deo secundum simplicem voluntatem, ut de nullo oporteat rationem reddere, nisi quia Deus vult. Quod etiam divinæ Scripturæ contrariatur, quæ Deum perhibet secundum ordinem sapientiæ suæ omnia fecisse, secundum illud Psalm ciii.: omnia in sapientia fecisti." Ibid., book ii., chap. xxiv.: "Per hoc autem excluditur quorundam error qui dicebant omnia ex simplica divina voluntate dependere aliqua ratione."

equally impotent. Such is the nature of my will that, in doing a thing, it is conscious of the power to do the opposite; and that is not an accidental character of the will, it is its fundamental character; if, then, it is supposed that truth, or that first part of it which is called justice, has been established as it is by an act of volition, human or Divine, it must be acknowledged that another act might have established it otherwise, and made what is now just unjust, and what is unjust just. But such mobility is contrary to the nature of justice and truth. In fact, moral truths are as absolute as metaphysical truths. God cannot make effects exist without a cause, phenomena without a substance; neither can he make it evil to respect his word, to love truth, to repress one's passions. The principles of ethics are immutable axioms like those of geometry. Of moral laws especially must be said what Montesquieu said of all laws in general,—they are necessary relations that are derived from the nature of things.

Let us suppose that the good and the just are derived from the divine will; on the divine will obligation will also rest. But can any will whatever be the foundation of obligation? The divine will is the will of an omnipotent being, and I am a feeble being. This relation of a feeble being to an omnipotent being, does not contain in itself any moral idea. One may be forced to obey the stronger, but he is not obligated to do it. The sovereign orders of the will of God, if his will could for a moment be separated from his other attributes, would not contain the least ray of justice; and, consequently, there would not descend into my soul the least shade of obligation.

One will exclaim,—It is not the arbitrary will of God that makes the foundation of obligation and justice; it is his just will. Very well. Every thing changes then. It is not the pure will of God that obligates us, it is the motive itself that determines his will, that is to say, the justice passed into his will. The distinction between the just and the unjust is not then the work of his will.

One of two things. Either we found ethics on the will of God alone, and then the distinction between good and evil, just and unjust, is gratuitous, and moral obligation does not exist; or you give authority to the will of God by justice, which, in your hypothesis, must have received from the will of God its authority, which is a *petitio principii*.

Another *petitio principii* still more evident. In the first place, you are compelled, in order legitimately to draw justice from the will of God, to suppose that this will is just, or I defy any one to show that this will alone can ever form the basis of justice. Moreover, evidently you cannot comprehend what a just will of God is, if you do not already possess the idea of justice. This idea, then, does not come from that of the will of God.

On the one hand, you may have, and you do have, the idea of justice, without understanding the will of God; on the other, you cannot conceive the justice of the divine will, without having conceived justice elsewhere.

Are not these reasons sufficient, I pray you, to conclude that the sole will of God is not for us the principle of the idea of the good?

And now, behold the natural consummation of the ethical system that we are examining:—the just and the unjust are what it has pleased God to declare such, by attaching to them the rewards and punishments of another life. The divine will manifests itself here only by an arbitrary order; it adds to this order promises and threats.

But to what human faculty are addressed the promise and threat of the chastisements and the rewards of another life? To the same one that in this life fears pain and seeks pleasure, shuns unhappiness and desires happiness, that is to say, to sensibility animated by imagination, that is to say, again, to what is most changing in each of us and most different in the human species. The joys and sufferings of another life excite in us the two most vivid but most mobile passions, hope and fear. Every thing influences our fears and hopes,—aye, health, the passing cloud, a ray of the sun, a cup of coffee, a thousand causes of this kind. I have known men, even philosophers, who on certain days hoped more, and other days less. And such a basis some would give to ethics! Then it is doing nothing else than proposing for human conduct an interested motive. The calculation which I obey is purer, if you will; the happiness that one makes me hope for is greater; but I see in that no justice that obligates me, no virtue and no vice in me, who know or do not know how to make this calculation, not having a head as strong as that of Pascal,[214] who yield to or resist those fears and hopes according to the deposition of my sensibility and my imagination, over which I have no power. Finally, the pains and pleasures of the future life are instituted on the ground of punishments and rewards. Now, none but actions in themselves good or bad can be rewarded and punished. If already there is in itself no good, no law that in conscience we are obligated to follow, there is neither merit nor demerit; recompense is not then recompense, nor penalty penalty, since they are such only on the condition of being the complement and the sanction of the idea of the good. Where this idea does not pre-exist, there remain, instead of recompense and penalty, only the attraction of pleasure and the fear of suffering, added to a prescription deprived in itself of morality. In that we come back to the punishments of earth invented for the purpose of frightening popular imagination, and supported solely on the decrees of legislators, on an abstraction of good and evil, of justice and injustice, of merit and demerit. It is the worst human justice that is found thus transported into heaven. We shall see that the human soul has foundation somewhat solider.[215]

These different systems, false or incomplete, having been rejected, we arrive at the doctrine that is to our eyes perfect truth, because it admits only certain facts, neglects none, and maintains for all of them their character and rank.

---

[214] See the famous calculus applied to the immortality of the soul, Des Pensées de Pascal, vol. i. of the 4th Series, p. 229-235 and p. 289-296.
[215] Lecture 16.

LECTURE XIV.

TRUE PRINCIPLES OF ETHICS.

Description of the different facts that compose the moral phenomena.—Analysis of each of these facts.—1st, Judgment and idea of the good. That this judgment is absolute. Relation between the true and the good.—2d, Obligation. Refutation of the doctrine of Kant that draws the idea of the good from obligation instead of founding obligation on the idea of the good.—3d, Liberty, and the moral notions attached to the notion of liberty.—4th, Principle of merit and demerit. Punishments and rewards.—5th, Moral sentiments.—Harmony of all these facts in nature and science.

Philosophic criticism is not confined to discerning the errors of systems; it especially consists in recognizing and disengaging the truths mixed with these errors. The truths scattered in different systems compose the whole truth which each of these almost always expresses on a single side. So, the systems that we have just run over and refuted deliver up to us, in some sort, divided and opposed to each other, all the essential elements of human morality. The only question is to collect them, in order to restore the entire moral phenomenon. The history of philosophy, thus understood, prepares the way for or confirms psychological analysis, as psychological analysis receives from the history of philosophy its light. Let us, then, interrogate ourselves in presence of human actions, and faithfully collect, without altering them by any preconceived system, the ideas and the sentiments of every kind that the spectacle of these actions produce in us.

There are actions that are agreeable or disagreeable to us, that procure us advantages or injure us, in a word, that are, in one way or another, directly or indirectly, addressed to our interest. We are rejoiced with actions that are useful to us, and shun those that may injure us. We seek earnestly and with the greatest effort what seems to us our interest.

This is an incontestable fact. Here is another fact that is not less incontestable.

There are actions that have no relation to us, that, consequently, we cannot estimate and judge on the ground of our interest, that we nevertheless qualify as good or bad.

Suppose that before your eyes a man, strong and armed, falls upon another man, feeble and disarmed, whom he maltreats and kills, in order to take away his purse. Such an action does not reach you in any way, and, notwithstanding, it fills you with indignation.[216] You do every thing in your power that this murderer may be arrested and delivered up to justice; you demand that he shall be punished, and if he is punished in one way or another, you think that it is just; your indignation is appeased only after a chastisement proportioned to the crime committed has been inflicted on the culprit. I repeat that in this you neither hope nor fear any thing for yourself. Were you placed in an inaccessible fortress, from the top of which you might witness this scene of murder, you would feel these sentiments none the less.

This is only a rude picture of what takes place in you at the sight of a crime. Apply now a little reflection and analysis to the different traits of which this picture is composed, without destroying their nature, and you will have a complete philosophic theory.

What is it that first strikes you in what you have experienced? It is doubtless the indignation, the instinctive horror that you have felt. There is, then, in the soul a power of raising indignation that is foreign to all personal interests! There are, then, in us sentiments of which we are not the end! There is an antipathy, an aversion, a horror, that are not related to what injures us, but to acts whose remotest influence cannot reach us, that we detest for the sole reason that we judge them to be bad!

Yes, we judge them to be bad. A judgment is enveloped under the sentiments that we have just mentioned. In fact, in the

---

[216] On indignation, see lecture II.

midst of the indignation that transports you, let one tell you that all this generous anger pertains to your particular organization, and that, after all, the action that takes place is indifferent,—you revolt against such an explanation, you exclaim that the action is bad in itself; you not only express a sentiment, you pronounce a judgment. The next day after the action, when the feelings that agitated your soul have been quieted, you none the less still judge that the action was bad; you judge thus six months after, you judge thus always and everywhere; and it is because you judge that this action is in itself bad, that you bear this other judgment, that it should not have been done.

This double judgment is at the foundation of sentiment; otherwise sentiment would be without reason. If the action is not bad in itself, if he who has done it was not obligated not to do it, the indignation that we experience is only a physical emotion, an excitement of the senses, of the imagination, of the heart,—a phenomenon destitute of every moral character, like the trouble that visits us before some frightful scene of nature. You cannot rationally feel indignation for the author of an indifferent action. Every sentiment of disinterested anger against the author of an action supposes in him who feels it, this double conviction:—1st, That the action is in itself bad; 2d, That it should not have been done.

This sentiment also supposes that the author of this action has himself a consciousness of the evil that he has done, and of the obligation that he has violated; for without this he would have acted like a brutal and blind force, not like an intelligent and moral force, and we should have felt towards him no more indignation than towards a rock that falls on our head, towards a torrent that sweeps us away into an abyss.

Indignation equally supposes in him who is the object of it an other character still, to wit, that he is free,—that he could do or not do what he has done. It is evident that the agent must be free in order to be responsible.

You desire that the murderer may be arrested and delivered up to justice, you desire that he may be punished; when he has been arrested, delivered up to justice, and punished, you are satisfied. What does that mean? Is it a capricious movement of the imagination and heart? No. Calm or indignant, at the moment of the crime or a long time after, without any spirit of personal vengeance, since you are not the least interested in this affair, you none the less declare that the murderer ought to be punished. If, instead of receiving a punishment, the culpable man makes his crime a stepping-stone to fortune, you still declare that, far from deserving prosperity, he deserves to suffer in reparation of his fault; you protest against lot, and appeal to a superior justice. This judgment philosophers have called the judgment of merit and demerit. I suppose, in the mind of man, the idea of a supreme law that attaches happiness to virtue, unhappiness to crime. Omit the idea of this law, and the judgment of merit and demerit is without foundation. Omit this judgment, and indignation against prosperous crime and the neglect of virtue is an unintelligible, even an impossible sentiment, and never, at the sight of crime, would you think of demanding the chastisement of a criminal.

All the parts of the moral phenomenon are connected together; all are equally certain parts,—destroy one, and you completely overturn the whole phenomenon. The most common observation bears witness to all these facts, and the least subtle logic easily discovers their connection. It is necessary to renounce even sentiment, or it must be avowed that sentiment covers a judgment, the judgment of the essential distinction between good and evil, that this distinction involves an obligation, that this obligation is applied to an intelligent and free agent; in fine, it must be observed that the distinction between merit and demerit, that corresponds to the distinction between good and evil, contains the principle of the natural harmony between virtue and happiness.

What have we done thus far? We have done as the physicist or chemist does, who submits a composite body to analysis and reduces it to its simple elements. The only difference here is that the phenomenon to which our analysis is applied is in us, instead of being out of us. Besides, the processes employed are exactly the same; there is in them neither system nor hypothesis; there are only experience and the most immediate induction.

In order to render experience more certain, we may vary it. Instead of examining what takes place in us when we are spectators of bad or good actions in another, let us interrogate our own consciousness when we are doing well or ill. In this case, the different elements of the moral phenomenon are still more striking, and their order appears more distinctly.

Suppose that a dying friend has confided to me a more or less important deposit, charging me to remit it after his death to a person whom he has designated to me alone, and who himself knows not what has been done in his favor. He who confided to me the deposit dies, and carries with him his secret; he for whom the deposit has been made to me has no knowledge of it; if, then, I wish to appropriate this deposit to myself, no one will ever be able to suspect me. In this case what should I do? It is difficult to imagine circumstances more favorable for crime. If I consult only interest, I ought not to hesitate to return the deposit. If I hesitate, in the system of interest, I am senseless, and I revolt against the law of my nature. Doubt alone, in the impunity that is assured me, would betray in me a principle different from interest.

But naturally I do not doubt, I believe with the most entire certainty, that the deposit confided to me does not belong to me, that it has been confided to me to be remitted to another, and that to this other it belongs. Take away interest, and I should not even think of returning this deposit,—it is interest alone that tempts me. It tempts me, it does not bear me away without resistance. Hence the struggle between interest and duty,—a struggle filled with troubles, opposite resolutions, by turns taken and abandoned; it energetically attests the presence of a principle of action different from interest and quite as powerful.

Duty succumbs, interest triumphs over it. I retain the deposit that has been confided to me, and apply it to my own wants, and to the wants of my family; it makes me rich, and in appearance happy; but I internally suffer with that bitter and secret suffering that is called remorse.[217] The fact is certain; it has been a thousand times described; all languages contain the word, and there is no one who, in some degree, has not experienced the thing, that sharp gnawing at the heart which is caused by every fault, great or small, as long as it has not been expiated. This painful recollection follows me in the midst of pleasures and prosperity. The applauses of the crowd are not able to silence this inexorable witness. Only a long habit of sin and crime, an accumulation of oft-repeated faults, can compass this sentiment, at once avenging and expiatory. When it is stifled, every resource is lost, and an end is made of the soul's life; as long as it endures, the sacred fire is not wholly extinguished.

Remorse is a suffering of a particular character. In remorse I do not suffer on account of such an impression made upon my senses, nor on account of the thwarting of my natural passions, nor on account of the injury done or threatened to my interest, nor by the disquietude of my hopes and the agony of my fears: no, I suffer without any external cause, yet I suffer in the most cruel manner. I suffer for the sole reason that I have a consciousness of having committed a bad action which I knew I was obligated not to commit, which I was able not to commit, which leaves behind it a chastisement that I know to be deserved. No exact analysis can take away from remorse, without destroying it, a single one of these elements. Remorse contains the idea of good and evil, of an obligatory law, of liberty, of merit and demerit. All these ideas were already in the struggle between good and evil; they reappear in remorse. In vain interest counselled me to appropriate the deposit that had been confided to me; something said to me, and still says to me, that to appropriate it is to do evil, is to commit an injustice; I judged, and judge, thus, not such a day, but always, not under such a circumstance, but under all circumstances. In vain I say to myself that the person to whom I ought to remit this deposit has no need of it, and that it is necessary to me; I judge that a deposit must be respected without

---

[217] On remorse, see lecture II.

regard to persons, and the obligation that is imposed on me appears inviolable and absolute. Having taken upon myself this obligation, I believe by this fact alone that I have the power to fulfil it: this is not all; I am directly conscious of this power, I know with the most certain knowledge that I am able to keep this deposit or to remit it to the lawful owner; and it is precisely because I am conscious of this power that I judge that I have deserved punishment for not having made the use of it for which it was given me. It is, in fine, because I have a lively consciousness of all that, that I experience this sentiment of indignation against myself, this suffering of remorse which expresses in itself the moral phenomenon entire.

According to the rules of the experimental method, let us take an opposite course; let us suppose that, in spite of the suggestions of interest, in spite of the pressing goad of misery, in order to be faithful to pledged faith, I send the deposit to the person that had been designated to me; instead of the painful scene that just now passed in consciousness, there passes another quite as real, but very different. I know that I have done well; I know that I have not obeyed a chimera, an artificial and mendacious law, but a law true, universal, obligatory upon all intelligent and free beings. I know that I have made a good use of my liberty; I have of this liberty, by the very use that I have made of it, a sentiment more distinct, more energetic, and, in some sort, triumphant. Every opinion would accuse me in vain, I appeal from it to a better justice, and this justice is already declared in me by sentiments that press upon each other in my soul. I respect myself, esteem myself, and believe that I have a right to the esteem of others; I have the sentiment of my dignity; I feel for myself only sentiments of affection opposed to that species of horror for myself with which I was just now inspired. Instead of remorse, I feel an incomparable joy that no one can deprive me of, that, were every thing else wanting to me, would console and support me. This sentiment of pleasure is as penetrating, as profound as was the remorse. It expresses the satisfaction of all the generous principles of human nature, as remorse represented their revolt. It testifies by the internal happiness that it gives me to the sublime accord between happiness and virtue, whilst remorse is the first link in that fatal chain, that chain of iron and adamant, which, according to Plato,[218] binds pain to transgression, trouble to passion, misery to faithlessness, vice, and crime.

Moral sentiment is the echo of all the moral judgments and entire moral life. It is so striking that it has been regarded by a somewhat superficial philosophy as sufficient to found entire ethics; and, nevertheless, we have just seen that this admirable sentiment would not exist without the different judgments that we have just enumerated; it is their consequence, but not their principle; it supplies, but does not constitute them; it does not take their place, but sums them up.

Now that we are in possession of all the elements of human morality, we proceed to take these elements one by one, and submit them to a detailed analysis.

That which is most apparent in the complex phenomenon that we are studying is sentiment; but its foundation is judgment.

The judgment of good and evil is the principle of all that follows it; but this judgment rests only on the constitution itself of human nature, like the judgment of the true and the judgment of the beautiful. As well as these two judgments,[219] that of the good is a simple, primitive, indecomposable judgment.

Like them, again, it is not arbitrary. We cannot but fear this judgment in presence of certain acts; and, in fearing it, we know that it does not make good or evil, but declares it. The reality of moral distinctions is revealed by this judgment, but it is independent of it, as beauty is independent of the eye that perceives it, as universal and necessary truths are independent of the reason that discovers them.[220]

Good and evil are real characters of human actions, although these characters might not be seen with our eyes nor touched with our hands. The moral qualities of an action are none the less real

---

[218] See the Gorgias, with the Argument, vol. iii. of our translation.
[219] Lectures I and 6.
[220] Lectures 2, 3, and 6.

for not being confounded with the material qualities of this action. This is the reason why actions materially identical may be morally very different. A homicide is always a homicide; nevertheless, it is often a crime, it is also often a legitimate action, for example, when it is not done for the sake of vengeance, nor for the sake of interest, in a strict case of self-defence.

It is not the spilling of blood that makes the crime, it is the spilling of innocent blood. Innocence and crime, good and evil, do not reside in such or such an external circumstance determined one for all. Reason recognizes them with certainty under the most different appearances, in circumstances sometimes the same and sometimes dissimilar.

Good and evil almost always appear to us connected with particular actions; but it is not on account of what is particular in them that these actions are good or bad. So when I declare that the death of Socrates is unjust, and that the devotion of Leonidas is admirable, it is the unjust death of a wise man that I condemn, and the devotion of a hero that I admire. It is not important whether this hero be called Leonidas or d'Assas, whether the immolated sage be called Socrates or Bailly.

The judgment of the good is at first applied to particular actions, and it gives birth to general principles which in course serve us as rules for judging all actions of the same kind. As after having judged that such a particular phenomenon has such a particular cause, we elevate ourselves to the general principle that every phenomenon has its cause;[221] so we erect into a general rule the moral judgment that we have borne in regard to a particular fact. Thus, at first we admire the death of Leonidas, thence we elevate ourselves to the principle that it is good to die for one's country. We already possess the principle in its first application to Leonidas; otherwise, this particular application would not have been legitimate, it would not have been even possible; but we possess it implicitly; as soon as it is disengaged, it appears to us

---

[221] 1st part, lecture 2.

under its universal and pure form, and we apply it to all analogous cases.

Ethics have their axioms like other sciences; and these axioms are rightly called in all languages moral truths.

It is good not to violate one's oath, and in this is also involved a truth. In fact, an oath is founded in the truth of things,—its good is only derived. Moral truths considered in themselves have no less certainty than mathematical truths. The idea of a deposit being given, I ask whether the idea of faithfully keeping it is not necessarily attached to it, as to the idea of a triangle is attached the idea that its three angles are equal to two right angles. You may withhold a deposit; but, in withholding it, do not believe that you change the nature of things, nor that you make it possible for a deposit ever to become property. These two ideas exclude each other. You have only a false semblance of property; and all the efforts of passion, all the sophisms of interest will not reverse the essential differences. This is the reason why moral truth is so troublesome,—it is because, like all truth, it is what it is, and does not bend to any caprice. Always the same and always present, in spite of all our efforts, it inexorably condemns, with a voice always heard, but not always listened to, the sensible and the culpable will which thinks to hinder it from being by denying it, or rather by pretending to deny it.

Moral truths are distinguished from other truths by the singular character that, as soon as we perceive them, they appear to us as the rule of our conduct. If it is true that a deposit is made to be remitted to its legitimate possessor, it is necessary to remit it to him. To the necessity of believing is here added the necessity of practising.

The necessity of practising is obligation. Moral truths, in the eyes of reason necessary, are to the will obligatory.

Moral obligation, like the moral truth that is its foundation, is absolute. As necessary truths are not more or less necessary,[222]

---

[222] Lecture 2.

so obligation is not more or less obligatory. There are degrees of importance between different obligations; but there are no degrees in the same obligation. We are not somewhat obligated, almost obligated; we are either wholly obligated, or not at all.

If obligation is absolute, it is immutable and universal. For, if the obligation of to-day were not the obligation of to-morrow, if what is obligatory for me were not so for you, obligation would differ from itself, would be relative and contingent.

This fact of absolute, immutable, universal obligation is so certain and so manifest, in spite of all the efforts of the doctrine of interest to obscure it, that one of the profoundest moralists of modern philosophy, particularly struck with this fact, has regarded it as the principle of the whole of ethics. By separating duty from interest which ruins it, and from sentiment which enervates it, Kant restored to ethics their true character. He elevated himself very high in the century of Helvetius, in elevating himself to the holy law of duty; but he still did not ascend high enough, he did not reach the reason itself of duty.

The good for Kant is what is obligatory. But logically, whence comes the obligation of performing an action, if not from the intrinsic goodness of this act? Is it not because that, in the order of reason, it is absolutely impossible to regard a deposit as a property, that we cannot appropriate it to ourselves without a crime? If one action must be performed, and another action must not, it is because there is apparently an essential difference between these two acts. To found the good on obligation, instead of founding obligation on the good, is, therefore, to take the effect for the cause, is to draw the principle from the consequence.

If I ask an honest man who, in spite of the suggestions of misery, has respected the deposit that was intrusted to him, why he respected it, he will answer me,—because it was my duty. If I persist, and ask why it was his duty, he will very rightly answer,— because it was just, because it was good. That point having been reached, all answers are stopped; but questions also are stopped. No one allows a duty to be imposed upon him without rendering to himself a reason for it; but as soon as it is recognized that this duty is imposed upon us because it is just, the mind is satisfied; for it reaches a principle beyond which it has nothing more to seek, justice being its own principle. First truths carry with them their reason for being. Now, justice, the essential distinction between good and evil in the relations of men among themselves, is the primary truth of ethics.

Justice is not a consequence, since we cannot ascend to another more elevated principle; and duty is not, rigorously speaking, a principle, since it supposes a principle above it, that explains and authorizes it, to wit, justice.

Moral truth no more becomes relative and subjective, to take for a moment the language of Kant, in appearing to us obligatory, than truth becomes relative and subjective in appearing to us necessary; for in the very nature of truth and the good must be sought the reason of necessity and obligation. But if we stop at obligation and necessity, as Kant did, in ethics as well as in metaphysics, without knowing it, and even against our intention, we destroy, or at least weaken truth and the good.[223]

Obligation has its foundation in the necessary distinction between good and evil; and is itself the foundation of liberty. If man has duties, he must possess the faculty of fulfilling them, of resisting desire, passion, and interest, in order to obey law. He ought to be free, therefore he is free, or human nature is in contradiction with itself. The direct certainty of obligation implies the corresponding certainty of liberty.

This proof of liberty is doubtless good; but Kant is deceived in supposing it the only legitimate proof. It is very strange that he should have preferred the authority of reasoning to that of consciousness, as if the former had no need of being confirmed by the latter; as if, after all, my liberty ought not to be a fact for me.[224] Empiricism must be greatly feared to distrust the testimony of consciousness; and, after such a distrust, one must be very credulous to have a boundless faith in reasoning. We do not

---

[223] Ist part, lecture 3. See also vol. v. of the Ist Series, lecture 8.
[224] Ist Series, vol. v., lecture 7.

believe in our liberty as we believe in the movement of the earth. The profoundest persuasion that we have of it comes from the continual experience that we carry with ourselves.

Is it true that in presence of an act to be done I am able to will or not to will to do it? In that lies the whole question of liberty.

Let us clearly distinguish between the power of doing and the power of willing. The will has, without doubt, in its service and under its empire, the most of our faculties; but that empire, which is real, is very limited. I will to move my arm, and I am often able to do it,—in that resides, as it were, the physical power of will; but I am not always able to move my arm, if the muscles are paralyzed, if the obstacle to be overcome is too strong, &c.; the execution does not always depend on me; but what always depends on me is the resolution itself. The external effects may be hindered, my resolution itself can never be hindered. In its own domain, will is sovereign.

And I am conscious of this sovereign power of the will. I feel in myself, before its determination, the force that can determine itself in such a manner or in such another. At the same time that I will this or that, I am equally conscious of the power to will the opposite; I am conscious of being master of my resolution, of the ability to arrest it, continue it, repress it. When the voluntary act ceases, the consciousness of the power does not cease,—it remains with the power itself, which is superior to all its manifestations. Liberty is therefore the essential and always-subsisting attribute of will.[225]

The will, we have seen,[226] is neither desire nor passion,—it is exactly the opposite. Liberty of will is not, then, the license of desires and passions. Man is a slave in desire and passion, he is free only in will. That they may not elsewhere be confounded,

---

[225] See, for the entire development of the theory of liberty, 1st Series, vol. iii., lecture 1, Locke, p. 71; lecture 3, Condillac, p. 116, 149, etc.; vol. iv., lecture 23, Reid, p. 541-574; 2d Series, vol. iii., Examination of the System of Locke, lecture 25.

[226] Lecture 12.

liberty and anarchy must not be confounded in psychology. Passions abandoning themselves to their caprices, is anarchy. Passions concentrated upon a dominant passion, is tyranny. Liberty consists in the struggle of will against this tyranny and this anarchy. But this combat must have an aim, and this aim is the duty of obeying reason, which is our true sovereign, and justice, which reason reveals to us and prescribes for us. The duty of obeying reason is the law of will, and will is never more itself than when it submits to its law. We do not possess ourselves, as long as to the domination of desire, of passion, of interest, reason does not oppose the counterpoise of justice. Reason and justice free us from the yoke of passions, without imposing upon us another yoke. For, once more, to obey them, is not to abdicate liberty, but to save it, to apply it to its legitimate use.

It is in liberty, and in the agreement of liberty with reason and justice, that man belongs to himself, to speak properly. He is a person only because he is a free being enlightened by reason.

What distinguishes a person from a simple thing, is especially the difference between liberty and its opposite. A thing is that which is not free, consequently that which does not belong to itself, that which has no self, which has only a numerical individuality, a perfect effigy of true individuality, which is that of person.

A thing, not belonging to itself, belongs to the first person that takes possession of it and puts his mark on it.

A thing is not responsible for the movements which it has not willed, of which it is even ignorant. Person alone is responsible, for it is intelligent and free; and it is responsible for the use of its intelligence and freedom.

A thing has no dignity; dignity is only attached to person.

A thing has no value by itself; it has only that which person confers on it. It is purely an instrument whose whole value consists in the use that the person using it derives from it.[227]

---

[227] See Ist Series, vol. iv., Lecture on Smith and on the true principle of political economy, p. 278-302.

Obligation implies liberty; where liberty is not, duty is wanting, and with duty right is wanting also.

It is because there is in me a being worthy of respect, that I have the duty of respecting it, and the right to make it respected by you. My duty is the exact measure of my right. The one is in direct ratio with the other. If I had no sacred duty to respect what makes my person, that is to say, my intelligence and my liberty, I should not have the right to defend it against your injuries. But as my person is inviolable and sacred in itself, it follows that, considered in relation to me, it imposes on me a duty, and, considered in relation to you, it confers on me a right.

I am not myself permitted to degrade the person that I am by abandoning myself to passion, to vice and crime, and I am not permitted to let it be degraded by you.

The person is inviolable; and it alone is inviolable.

It is inviolable not only in the intimate sanctuary of consciousness, but in all its legitimate manifestations, in its acts, in the product of its acts, even in the instruments that it makes its own by using them.

Therein is the foundation of the sanctity of property. The first property is the person. All other properties are derived from that. Think of it well. It is not property in itself that has rights, it is the proprietor, it is the person that stamps upon it, with its own character, its right and its title.

The person cannot cease to belong to itself, without degrading itself,—it is to itself inalienable. The person has no right over itself; it cannot treat itself as a thing, cannot sell itself, cannot destroy itself, cannot in any way abolish its free will and its liberty, which are its constituent elements.

Why has the child already some rights? Because it will be a free being. Why have the old man, returned to infancy, and the insane man still some rights? Because they have been free beings. We even respect liberty in its first glimmerings or its last vestiges. Why, on the other hand, have the insane man and the imbecile old man no longer all their rights? Because they have lost liberty. Why do we enchain the furious madman? Because he has lost knowledge and liberty. Why is slavery an abominable institution? Because it is an outrage upon what constitutes humanity. This is the reason why, in fine, certain extreme devotions are sometimes sublime faults, and no one is permitted to offer them, much less to demand them. There is no legitimate devotion against the very essence of right, against liberty, against justice, against the dignity of the human person.

We have not been able to speak of liberty, without indicating a certain number of moral notions of the highest importance which it contains and explains; but we could not pursue this development without encroaching upon the domain of private and public ethics and anticipating the following lecture.

We arrive, then, at the last element of the moral phenomenon, the judgment of merit and demerit.

At the same time that we judge that a man has done a good or bad action, we bear this other judgment quite as necessary as the former, to wit, that if this man has acted well he has merited a reward, and if he has acted ill, he has merited a punishment. It is exactly the same with this judgment as with that of the good. It may be outwardly expressed in a more or less lively manner, according as it is mingled with more or less energetic feelings. Sometimes it will be only a benevolent disposition towards the virtuous agent, and an unfavorable disposition towards the culpable agent; sometimes it will be enthusiasm or indignation. In some cases one will make himself the executor of the judgment that he bears, he will crown the hero and load the criminal with chains. But when all your feelings are calmed, when enthusiasm has cooled as well as indignation, when time and separation have rendered an action almost indifferent to you, you none the less persist in judging that the author of this action merits a reward or a punishment, according to the quality of the action. You decide that you were right in the sentiments that you felt, and, although they are extinguished, you declare them legitimate.

The judgment of merit and demerit is essentially tied to the judgment of good and evil. In fact, he who does an action without knowing whether it is good or bad, has neither merit nor demerit in doing it. It is with him the same as with those physical agents that accomplish the most beneficent or the most destructive works, to which we never think of attributing knowledge and will, consequently accountability. Why are there no penalties attached to involuntary crimes? Because for that very reason they are not regarded as crimes. Hence it comes that the question of premeditation is so grave in all criminal processes. Why is the child, up to a certain age, subject to none but light punishments? Because where the idea of the good and liberty are wanting, merit and demerit are also wanting, which alone authorize reward and punishment. The author of an injurious but involuntary action is condemned to an indemnity corresponding to the damage done; he is not condemned to a punishment properly so called.

Such are the conditions of merit and demerit. When these conditions are fulfilled, merit and demerit manifest themselves, and involve reward and punishment.

Merit is the natural right we have to be rewarded; demerit the natural right that others have to punish us, and, if we may thus speak, the right that we have to be punished. This expression may seem paradoxical, nevertheless it is true. A culpable man, who, opening his eyes to the light of the good, should comprehend the necessity of expiation, not only by internal repentance, without which all the rest is in vain, but also by a real and effective suffering, such a culpable man would have the right to claim the punishment that alone can reconcile him with order. And such reclamations are not so rare. Do we not every day see criminals denouncing themselves and offering themselves up to avenge the public? Others prefer to satisfy justice, and do not have recourse to the pardon that law places in the hands of the monarch in order to represent in the state charity and mercy, as tribunals represent in it justice. This is a manifest proof of the natural and profound roots of the idea of punishment and reward.

Merit and demerit imperatively claim, like a lawful debt, punishment and reward; but reward must not be confounded with merit, nor punishment with demerit; this would be confounding cause and effect, principle and consequence. Even were reward and punishment not to take place, merit and demerit would subsist. Punishment and reward satisfy merit and demerit, but do not constitute them. Suppress all reward and all punishment and you do not thereby suppress merit and demerit; on the contrary, suppress merit and demerit, and there are no longer true punishments and true rewards. Unmerited goods and honors are only material advantages; reward is essentially moral, and its value is independent of its form. One of those crowns of oak that the early Romans decreed to heroism is worth more than all the riches in the world, when it is the sign of the recognition and the admiration of a people. To reward is to give in return. He who is rewarded must have first given something in order to deserve to be rewarded. Reward accorded to merit is a debt; reward without merit is a charity or a theft. It is the same with punishment. It is the relation of pain to a fault,—in this relation, and not in the pain alone, is the truth as well as the shame of chastisement.

'Tis crime and not the scaffold makes the shame.[228]

There are two things that must be unceasingly repeated, because they are equally true,—the first is, that the good is good in itself, and ought to be pursued whatever may be the consequences; the second is, that the consequences of the good cannot fail to be fortunate. Happiness, separated from the good, is only a fact to which is attached no moral idea; but, as an effect of the good, it enters into the moral order and completes it.

Virtue without happiness, and crime without unhappiness, are a contradiction, a disorder. If virtue supposes sacrifice, that is to say, suffering, it is of eternal justice that the sacrifice, generously accepted and courageously borne, have for a reward the very happiness that has been sacrificed. So, it is of eternal justice that crime be punished by the unhappiness of the culpable happiness which it has tried to obtain by stealth.

Now, when and how is the law fulfilled that attaches pleasure and pain to good and evil? Most of the time even here below. For order rules in this world, since the world endures. If

---

[228] Le crime fait la honte et non pas l'échafaud.

order is sometimes disturbed, and happiness and unhappiness are not always distributed in right proportion to crime and virtue, still the absolute judgment of the good, the absolute judgment of obligation, the absolute judgment of merit and demerit, subsist inviolable and imprescriptible,—we remain convinced that he who has put in us the sentiment and the idea of order cannot in that fail himself, and that sooner or later he will re-establish the sacred harmony between virtue and happiness by the means that to him belong. But the time has not come to sound these mysterious prospects.[229] It is sufficient for us, but it was necessary to mark them, in order to show the nature and the end of moral truth.

We terminate this analysis of the different parts of the complex phenomenon of morality by recalling that one which is the most apparent of all, which, however, is only the accompaniment, and, thus to speak, the echo of all the others—sentiment. Sentiment has for its object to render sensible to the soul the tie between virtue and happiness. It is the direct and vital application of the law of merit and demerit. It precedes and authorizes the punishments and rewards that society institutes. It is the internal model according to which the imagination, guided by faith, represents to itself the punishments and rewards of the divine city. The world that we place beyond this is, in great part, our own heart transported into heaven. Since it comes thence, it is just that it should return thither.

We will not dwell upon the different phenomena of sentiment; we have sufficiently explained them in the last lecture. A few words will replace them under your eyes.

We cannot witness a good action, whoever may be its author, another or ourselves, without experiencing a particular pleasure, analogous to that which is attached to the perception of the beautiful; and we cannot witness a bad action without feeling a contrary sentiment, also analogous to that which the sight of an

---

[229] See lecture 16, God, the Principle of the Idea of the Good.

ugly and deformed object excites in us. This sentiment is profoundly different from agreeable or disagreeable sensation.

Are we the authors of the good action? We feel a satisfaction that we do not confound with any other. It is not the triumph of interest nor that of pride,—it is the pleasure of modest honesty or dignified virtue that renders justice to itself. Are we the authors of the bad action? We feel offended conscience groaning within us. Sometimes it is only an importunate reclamation, sometimes it is a bitter agony. Remorse is a suffering the more poignant on account of our feeling that it is deserved.

The spectacle of a good action done by another also has something delicious to the soul. Sympathy is an echo in us that responds to whatever is noble and good in others. When interest does not lead us astray, we naturally put ourselves in the place of him who has done well. We feel in a certain measure the sentiments that animate him. We elevate ourselves to the mood of his spirit. Is it not already for the good man an exquisite reward to make the noble sentiments that animate him thus pass into the hearts of his fellow-men? The spectacle of a bad action, instead of sympathy, excites an involuntary antipathy, a painful and sad sentiment. Without doubt, this sentiment is never acute like remorse. There is in innocence something serene and placid that tempers even the sentiment of injustice, even when this injustice falls on us. We then experience a sort of shame for humanity, we mourn over human weakness, and, by a melancholy return upon ourselves, we are less moved to anger than to pity. Sometimes also pity is overcome by a generous anger, by a disinterested indignation. If, as we have said, it is a sweet reward to excite a noble sympathy, an enthusiasm almost always fertile in good actions, it is a cruel punishment to stir up around us pity, indignation, aversion, and contempt.

Sympathy for a good action is accompanied by benevolence for its author. He inspires us with an affectionate disposition. Even without knowing it, we would love to do good to him; we desire that he may be happy, because we judge that he deserves to be. Antipathy also passes from the action to the person, and engenders against him a sort of bad will, for which we do not blame ourselves, because we feel it to be disinterested and find it legitimate.

Moral satisfaction and remorse, sympathy, benevolence, and their opposites are sentiments and not judgments; but they are sentiments that accompany judgments, the judgment of the good, especially that of merit and demerit. These sentiments have been given us by the sovereign Author of our moral constitution to aid us in doing good. In their diversity and mobility, they cannot be the foundations of absolute obligation which must be equal for all, but they are to it happy auxiliaries, sure and beneficent witnesses of the harmony between virtue and happiness.

These are the facts as presented by a faithful description, as brought to light by a detailed analysis.

Without facts all is chimera; without a severe distinction of facts, all is confusion; but, also, without the knowledge of their relations, instead of a single vast doctrine, like the total phenomenon that we have undertaken to embrace, there can be only different systems like the different parts of this phenomenon, consequently imperfect systems, systems always at war with each other.

We set out from common sense; for the object of true science is not to contradict common sense, but to explain it, and for this end we must commence by recognizing it. We have at first painted in its simplicity, even in the gross, the phenomenon of morality. Then we have separated its elements, and carefully marked the characteristic traits of each of them. It only remains for us to re-collect them all, to seize their relations, and thus to find again, but more precise and more clear, the primitive unity that served us as a point of departure.

Beneath all facts analysis has shown us a primitive fact, which vests only on itself,—the judgment of the good. We do not sacrifice other facts to that, but we must establish that it is the first both in date and in importance.

By its close resemblance to the judgment of the true and the beautiful, the judgment of the good has shown us the affinities of ethics, metaphysics, and æsthetics.

The good, so essentially united to the true, is distinguished from it in that it is practical truth. The good is obligatory. These two ideas are inseparable, but not identical. For obligation rests on the good,—in this intimate alliance, from the good obligation borrows its universal and absolute character.

The obligatory good is the moral law. Therein is for us the foundation of all ethics. Thereby it is that we separate ourselves from the ethics of interest and the ethics of sentiment. We admit all the facts, but we do not admit them in the same rank.

To the moral law in the reason of man corresponds liberty in action. Liberty is deduced from obligation, and moreover it is a fact of an irresistible evidence.

Man as a being free and subject to obligation, is a moral person. The idea of person contains several moral notions, among others that of right. Person alone can have rights.

To all these ideas is added that of merit and demerit, which serves as their sanction.

Merit and demerit suppose the distinction between good and evil, obligation and liberty, and give birth to the idea of reward and punishment.

It is on the condition that the good may be an object of reason, that ethics can have an immovable basis. We have therefore insisted on the rational character of the idea of the good, but without misconceiving the part of sentiment.

We have distinguished that particular sensibility, which is stirred in us in the train of reason itself, from physical sensibility, which needs an impression made upon the organs in order to enter into exercise.

All our moral judgments are accompanied by sentiments that respond to them. The sight of an action which we judge to be good gives us pleasure,—the consciousness of having performed an obligatory act, and of having performed it freely, is also a pleasure; the judgment of merit and demerit makes our hearts beat by taking the form of sympathy and benevolence.

It must be avowed that the law of duty, although it ought to be fulfilled for its own sake, would be an ideal almost inaccessible to human weakness, if to its austere prescriptions were not added some inspiration of the heart. Sentiment is in some sort a natural grace that has been given us, either to supply the light of reason that is sometimes uncertain, or to succor the will wavering in the presence of an obscure or painful duty. In order to resist the violence of culpable passions, the aid of generous passions is needed; and when the moral law exacts the sacrifice of natural sentiments, of the sweetest and most lively instincts, it is fortunate that it can support itself on other sentiments, or other instincts which also have their charm and their force. Truth enlightens the mind; sentiment warms the soul and leads to action. It is not cold reason that determines a Codrus to devote himself for his countrymen, a d'Assas to utter, beneath the steel of the enemy, the generous cry that brings him death and saves the army. Let us guard ourselves, then, from weakening the authority of sentiment; let us honor and sustain enthusiasm; it is the source whence spring great and heroic actions.

And shall interest be entirely banished from our system? No; we recognize in the human soul a desire for happiness which is the work of God himself. This desire is a fact,—it must then have its place in a system founded upon experience. Happiness is one of the ends of human nature; only it is neither its sole end nor its principal end.

Admirable economy of the moral constitution of man! Its supreme end is the good, its law is virtue, which often imposes on it suffering, and thereby it is the most excellent of all things that we know. But this law is very hard and in contradiction with the instinct of happiness. Fear nothing,—the beneficent author of our being has placed in our souls, by the side of the severe law of duty, the sweet and amiable force of sentiment,—he has, in general, attached happiness to virtue; and, for the exceptions, for there are exceptions, at the end of the course he has placed hope.[230]

Our doctrine is now known. Its only pretension is to express faithfully each fact, to express them all, and to make appear at once their differences and their harmony.

Beyond that there is nothing new to attempt in ethics. To admit only a single fact and to sacrifice to that all the rest,—such is the beaten way. Of all the facts that we have just analyzed, there is not one that has not in its turn played the part of sole principle. All the great schools of moral philosophy have each seen only one side of truth,—fortunate when they have not chosen among the different phases of the moral phenomenon, in order to found upon them their entire system, precisely those that are least adapted to that end!

Who could now return to Epicurus, and, against the most manifest facts, against common sense, against the very idea of all ethics, found duty, virtue, the good, on the desire of happiness alone? It would be proof of great blindness and great barrenness. On the other hand, shall we immolate the need of happiness, the hope of all reward, human or divine, to the abstract idea of the good? The Stoics have done it,—we know with what apparent grandeur, with what real impotence. Shall we confine with Kant the whole of ethics to obligation? That is straitening still more a system that is already very narrow. Moreover, one may hope to surpass Kant in extent of views, by a completer knowledge and more faithful representation of facts; one cannot hope to be more profound in the point of view that he has chosen. Or, in another order of ideas, shall we refer to the will of God alone the obligation of virtue, and found ethics on religion, instead of giving religion to ethics as their necessary perfection? We still invent nothing new, we only renew the ethics of the theologians of the Middle Age, or rather of a particular school which has had for its adversaries the most illustrious doctors. Finally, shall we reduce all morality to sentiment, to sympathy, to benevolence? It

---

[230] See lecture 16.

only remains to follow the footsteps of Hutcheson and Smith, abandoned by Reid himself, or the footsteps of a celebrated adversary of Kant, Jacobi.[231]

The time of exclusive theories has gone by; to renew them is to perpetuate war in philosophy. Each of them, being founded upon a real fact, rightly refuses the sacrifice of this fact; and it meets in hostile theories an equal right and an equal resistance. Hence the perpetual return of the same systems, always at war with each other, and by turns vanquished and victorious. This strife can cease only by means of a doctrine that conciliates all systems by comprising all the facts that give them authority.

It is not the preconceived design of conciliating systems in history that suggests to us the idea of conciliating facts in reality. It is, on the contrary, the full possession of all the facts, analogous and different, that forces us to absolve and condemn all systems on account of the truth that is in each of them, and on account of the errors that are mixed with the truth.

It is important to repeat continually, that nothing is so easy as to arrange a system, by suppressing or altering the facts that embarrass it. But is it, then, the object of philosophy to produce at any cost a system, instead of seeking to understand the truth and express it as it is?

It is objected that such a doctrine has not sufficient character. But is it not sporting with philosophy to demand of it any other character than that of truth? Do men complain that modern chemistry has not sufficient character, because it limits itself to studying facts in their relations, and also in their differences, and because it does not end at a single substance? The only true philosophy that is proper for a century returned from all exaggerations, is a picture of human nature whose first merit is fidelity, which must offer all the traits of the original in their right proportion and real harmony. The unity of the doctrine that we profess is in that of the human soul, whence we have drawn it. Is it not one and the same being that perceives the good, that

---

[231] On Jacobi, see Tennemann's Manual of the History of Philosophy, vol. iii., p. 318, etc.

knows that he is obligated to fulfil it, that knows that he is free in fulfilling it, that loves the good, and judges that the fulfilment or violation of the good justly brings after it reward or punishment, happiness or misery? We draw, then, a true unity from the intimate relation between all the facts that, as we have seen, imply and sustain each other. But by what right is the unity of a doctrine placed in allowing in it only a single principle? Such a unity is possible only in those regions of mathematical abstraction, where one is not disturbed by what is, where one retrenches at will from the object that he is studying, in order to simplify it continually, where every thing is reduced to pure notions. In the reality all is determined, and consequently, all is complex. A science of facts is not a series of equations. In it must be found again the life that is in things, life with its harmony doubtless, but also with its richness and diversity.[232]

---

[232] On this important question of method, see lecture 12.

LECTURE XV.

PRIVATE AND PUBLIC ETHICS.

Application of the preceding principles.—General formula of interest,—to obey reason.—Rule for judging whether an action is or is not conformed to reason,—to elevate the motive of this action into a maxim of universal legislation.—Individual ethics. It is not towards the individual, but towards the moral person that one is obligated. Principle of all individual duties,—to respect and develop the moral person.—Social ethics,—duties of justice and duties of charity.—Civil society. Government. Law. The right to punish.

We know that there is moral good and that there is moral evil: we know that this distinction between good and evil engenders an obligation, a law, duty; but we do not yet know what our duties are. The general principle of ethics is laid down; it must be followed at least into its most important applications.

If duty is only truth become obligatory, and if truth is known only by reason, to obey the law of duty, is to obey reason.

But to obey reason is a precept very vague and very abstract:—how can we be sure that our action is conformed or is not conformed to reason?

The character of reason being, as we have said, its universality, action, in order to be conformed to reason, must possess something universal; and as it is the motive itself of the action that gives it its morality, it is also the motive that must, if the action is good, reflect the character of reason. By what sign, then, do you recognize that an action is conformed to reason, that it is good? By the sign that the motive of this action being generalized, appears to you a maxim of universal legislation, which reason imposes upon all intelligent and free beings. If you are not able thus to generalize the motive of an action, and if it is the opposite motive that appears to you a universal maxim, your action, being opposed to this maxim, is thereby proved to be contrary to reason and duty,—it is bad. If neither the motive of your action nor the motive of the opposite action can be erected into a universal law, the action is neither good nor bad, it is indifferent. Such is the ingenious measure that Kant has applied to the morality of actions. It makes known with the last degree of clearness where duty is and where it is not, as the severe and naked form of syllogism, being applied to reasoning, brings out in the precisest manner its error or its truth.

To obey reason,—such is duty in itself, the duty superior to all other duties, giving to all others their foundation, and being itself founded only on the essential relation between liberty and reason.

It may be said that there is only a single duty, that of obeying reason. But man having different relations, this single and general duty is determined by these different relations, and divided into a corresponding number of particular duties.

Of all the beings that we know, there is not one with whom we are more constantly in relation than with ourselves. The actions of which man is at once the author and the object, have rules as well as other actions. Hence that first class of duties which are called the duties of man towards himself.

At first sight, it is strange that man should have duties towards himself. Man, being free, belongs to himself. What is most to me is myself:—this is the first property and the foundation of all other properties. Now, is it not the essence of property to be at the free disposition of the proprietor, and consequently, am I not able to do with myself what I please?

No; from the fact that man is free, from the fact that he belongs only to himself, it must not be concluded that he has over himself all power. On the contrary, indeed, from the fact alone that he is endowed with liberty, as well as intelligence, I conclude that he can no more degrade his liberty than his intelligence, without transgressing. It is a culpable use of liberty to abdicate it. We have said that liberty is not only sacred to others, but is so to itself. To subject it to the yoke of passion, instead of increasing it under the liberal discipline of duty, is to abase in us what deserves our respect as much as the respect of others. Man is not a thing; it has not, then, been permitted him to treat himself as a thing.

If I have duties towards myself, it is not towards myself as an individual, it is towards the liberty and intelligence that make me a free moral person. It is necessary to distinguish closely in us what is peculiar to us from what pertains to humanity. Each one of us contains in himself human nature with all its essential elements; and, in addition, all these elements are in him in a certain manner that is not the same in two different men. These particularities make the individual, but not the person; and the person alone in us is to be respected and held as sacred, because it alone represents humanity. Every thing that does not concern the moral person is indifferent. In these limits I may consult my tastes, even my fancies to a certain extent, because in them there is nothing absolute, because in them good and evil are in no way involved. But as soon as an act touches the moral person, my liberty is subjected to its law, to reason, which does not allow liberty to be turned against itself. For example, if through caprice, or melancholy, or any other motive, I condemn myself to an abstinence too prolonged, if I impose on myself vigils protracted and beyond my strength; if I absolutely renounce all pleasure, and, by these excessive privations, endanger my health, my life, my reason, these are no longer indifferent actions. Sickness, death, madness, may become crimes, if we voluntarily bring them upon ourselves.

I have not established this obligation of self-respect imposed on the moral person, therefore I cannot destroy it. Is self-respect founded on one of those arbitrary conventions that cease to exist when the two contracting parties freely renounce them? Are the two contracting parties here *me* and myself? By no means; one of the contracting parties is not *me*, to wit, humanity, the moral person. And there is here neither convention nor contract. By the fact alone that the moral person is in us, we are obligated towards it, without convention of any sort, without contract that can be cancelled, and by the very nature of things. Hence it comes that obligation is absolute.

Respect of the moral person in us is the general principle whence are derived all individual duties. We will cite some of them.

The most important, that which governs all others, is the duty of remaining master of one's self. One may lose possession of himself in two ways, either by allowing himself to be carried away, or by allowing himself to be overcome, by yielding to enervating passions or to overwhelming passions, to anger or to melancholy. On either hand there is equal weakness. And I do not speak of the consequences of those vices for society and ourselves,—certainly they are very injurious; but they are much worse than that, they are already bad in themselves, because in themselves they give a blow to moral dignity, because they diminish liberty and disturb intelligence.

Prudence is an eminent virtue. I speak of that noble prudence that is the moderation in all things, the foresight, the fitness, that preserve at once from negligence and that rashness which adorns itself with the name of heroism, as cowardice and selfishness sometimes usurp the name of prudence. Heroism, without being premeditated, ought always to be rational. One may be a hero at intervals; but, in every-day life, it is sufficient to be a wise man. We must ourselves hold the reins of our life, and not prepare difficulties for ourselves by carelessness or bravado, nor create for ourselves useless perils. Doubtless we must know how to dare, but still prudence is, if not the principle, at least the rule of courage; for true courage is not a blind transport, it is before all coolness and self possession in danger. Prudence also teaches temperance; it keeps the soul in that state of moderation without which man is incapable of recognizing and practising justice. This is the reason why the ancients said that prudence is the mother and guardian of all the virtues. Prudence is the government of liberty by reason, as imprudence is liberty escaped from reason:—on the one side, order, the legitimate subordination of our faculties to each other; on the other, anarchy and revolt.[233]

Veracity is also a great virtue. Falsehood, by breaking the natural alliance between man and truth, deprives him of that which makes his dignity. This is the reason why there is no graver insult than giving the lie, and why the most honored virtues are sincerity and frankness.

One may degrade the moral person by wounding it in its instruments. For this reason the body is to man the object of imperative duties. The body may become an obstacle or a means. If you refuse it what sustains and strengthens it, or if you demand too much from it by exciting it beyond measure, you exhaust it, and by abusing it, deprive yourself of it. It is worse still if you pamper it, if you grant every thing to its unbridled desires, if you make yourself its slave. It is being unfaithful to the soul to enfeeble its servant; it is being much more unfaithful to it still, to enslave it to its servant.

But it is not enough to respect the moral person, it is necessary to perfect it; it is necessary to labor to return the soul to God better than we received it; and it can become so only by a constant and courageous exercise. Everywhere in nature, all things are spontaneously developed, without willing it, and without knowing it. With man, if the will slumbers, the other faculties degenerate into languor and inertion; or, carried away by the blind impulse of passion, they are precipitated and go astray. It is by the government and education of himself that man is great.

Man must, before every thing else, occupy himself with his intelligence. It is in fact our intelligence that alone can give us a clear sight of the true and the good, that guides liberty by showing it the legitimate object of its efforts. No one can give himself another mind than the one that he has received, but he may train and strengthen it as well as the body, by putting it to a task of some kind, by rousing it when it is drowsy, by restraining it when it is carried away, by continually proposing to it new

---

[233] See the Republic, book iv., vol. ix., of our translation.

objects,—for it is only by continually enriching it that it does not grow poor. Sloth benumbs and enervates the mind; regular work excites and strengthens it, and work is always in our power.

There is an education of liberty as well as our other faculties. It is sometimes in subduing the body, sometimes in governing our intelligence, especially in resisting our passions, that we learn to be free. We encounter opposition at each step,—the only question is not to shun it. In this constant struggle liberty is formed and augmented, until it becomes a habit.

Finally, there is a culture of sensibility itself. Fortunate are those who have received from nature the sacred fire of enthusiasm! They ought religiously to preserve it. But there is no soul that does not conceal some fortunate vein of it. It is necessary to watch it and pursue, to avoid what restrains it, to seek what favors it, and, by an assiduous culture, draw from it, little by little, some treasures. If we cannot give ourselves sensibility, we can at least develop what we have. We can do this by giving ourselves up to it, by seizing all the occasions of giving ourselves up to it, by calling to its aid intelligence itself; for, the more we know of the beautiful and the good, the more we love it. Sentiment thereby only borrows from intelligence what it returns with usury. Intelligence in its turn finds, in the heart, a rampart against sophism. Noble, sentiments, nourished and developed, preserve from those sad systems that please certain spirits so much only because their hearts are so small.

Man would still have duties, should he cease to be in relation with other men.[234] As long as he preserves any intelligence and any

---

[234] On our principal duties towards ourselves, and on that error, too much accredited in the eighteenth century, of reducing ethics to our duties towards others, see 1st Series, vol. iii., lectures on the ethics of Helvetius and Saint-Lambert, lecture vi., p. 235: "To define virtue an habitual disposition to contribute to the happiness of others, is to concentrate virtue into a single one of its applications, is to suppress its general and essential character. Therein is the fundamental vice of the ethics of the eighteenth century. Those ethics are an exaggerated reaction against the somewhat mystical ethics of the preceding age, which, rightly occupied with perfecting the internal man, often fell into

liberty, the idea of the good dwells in him, and with it duty. Were we cast upon a desert island, duty would follow us thither. It would be beyond belief strange that it should be in the power of certain external circumstances to affranchise an intelligent and free being from all obligation towards his liberty and his

---

asceticism, which is not only useless to others, but is contrary to well-ordered human life. Through fear of asceticism, the philosophy of the eighteenth century forgot the care of internal perfection, and only considered the virtues useful to society. That was retrenching many virtues, and the best ones. I take, for example, dominion over self. How make a virtue of it, when virtue is defined a disposition to contribute to the happiness of others? Will it be said that dominion over self is useful to others? But that is not always true; often this dominion is exercised in the solitude of the soul over internal and wholly personal movements; and there it is most painful and most sublime. Were we in a desert, it would still be for us a duty to resist our passions, to command ourselves, and to govern our life as it becomes a rational and free being. Beneficence is an adorable virtue, but it is neither the whole of virtue, nor its most difficult employment. What auxiliaries we have when the question is to do good to our fellow-creatures,—pity, sympathy, natural benevolence! But to resist pride and envy, to combat in the depths of the soul a natural desire legitimate in itself, often culpable in its excesses, to suffer and struggle in silence, is the hardest task of a virtuous man. I add that the virtues useful to others have their surest guaranty in those personal virtues that the eighteenth century misconceived. What are goodness, generosity, and beneficence without dominion over self, without the form of soul attached to the religious observance of duty? They are, perhaps, only the emotions of a beautiful nature placed in fortunate circumstances. Take away these circumstances, and, perhaps, the effects will disappear or be diminished. But when a man, who knows himself to be a rational and free being, comprehends that it is his duty to remain faithful to liberty and reason, when he applies himself to govern himself, and pursue, without cessation, the perfection of his nature through all circumstances, you may rely upon that man; he will know how, in case of need, to be useful to others, because there is no true perfection for him without justice and charity. From the care of internal perfection you may draw all the useful virtues, but the reciprocal is not always true. One may be beneficent without being virtuous; one is not virtuous without being beneficent."

intelligence. In the deepest solitude he is always and consciously under the empire of a law attached to the person itself, which, by obligating him to keep continual watch over himself, makes at once his torment and his grandeur.

If the moral person is sacred to me, it is not because it is in me, it is because it is the moral person; it is in itself respectable; it will be so, then, wherever we meet it.

It is in you as in me, and for the same reason. In relation to me it imposes on me a duty; in you it becomes the foundation of a right, and thereby imposes on me a new duty in relation to you.

I owe to you truth as I owe it to myself; for truth is the law of your reason as of mine. Without doubt there ought to be measure in the communication of truth,—all are not capable of it at the same moment and in the same degree; it is necessary to portion it out to them in order that they may be able to receive it; but, in fine, the truth is the proper good of the intelligence; and it is for me a strict duty to respect the development of your mind, not to arrest, and even to favor its progress towards truth.

I ought also to respect your liberty. I have not even always the right to hinder you from committing a fault. Liberty is so sacred that, even when it goes astray, it still deserves, up to a certain point, to be managed. We are often wrong in wishing to prevent too much the evil that God himself permits. Souls may be corrupted by an attempt to purify them.

I ought to respect you in your affections, which make part of yourself; and of all the affections there are none more holy than those of the family. There is in us a need of expanding ourselves beyond ourselves, yet without dispelling ourselves, of establishing ourselves in some souls by a regular and consecrated affection,— to this need the family responds. The love of men is something of the general good. The family is still almost the individual, and not merely the individual,—it only requires us to love as much as ourselves what is almost ourselves. It attaches one to the other, by the sweetest and strongest of all ties—father, mother, child; it gives to this sure succor in the love of its parents—to these hope, joy, new life, in their child. To violate the conjugal or paternal right, is to violate the person in what is perhaps its most sacred possession.

I ought to respect your body, inasmuch as it belongs to you, inasmuch as it is the necessary instrument of your person. I have neither the right to kill you, nor to wound you, unless I am attacked and threatened; then my violated liberty is armed with a new right, the right of defence and even constraint.

I owe respect to your goods, for they are the product of your labor; I owe respect to your labor, which is your liberty itself in exercise; and, if your goods come from an inheritance, I still owe respect to the free will that has transmitted them to you.[235]

Respect for the rights of others is called justice; every violation of a right is an injustice.

Every injustice is an encroachment upon our person,—to retrench the least of our rights, is to diminish our moral person, is, at least, so far as that retrenchment goes, to abase us to the condition of a thing.

The greatest of all injustices, because it comprises all others, is slavery. Slavery is the subjecting of all the faculties of one man to the profit of another man. The slave develops his intelligence a little only in the interest of another,—it is not for the purpose of enlightening him, but to render him more useful, that some exercise of mind is allowed him. The slave has not the liberty of his movements; he is attached to the soil, is sold with it, or he is chained to the person of a master. The slave should have no affection, he has no family, no wife, no children,—he has a female and little ones. His activity does not belong to him, for the product of his labor is another's. But, that nothing may be wanting to slavery, it is necessary to go farther,—in the slave must be destroyed the inborn sentiment of liberty, in him must be extinguished all idea of right; for, as long as this idea subsists, slavery is uncertain, and to an odious power may respond the

---

[235] On the true foundation of property see the preceding lecture.

terrible right of insurrection, that last resort of the oppressed against the abuse of force.[236]

Justice, respect for the person in every thing that constitutes the person, is the first duty of man towards his fellow-man. Is this duty the only one?

When we have respected the person of others, when we have neither restrained their liberty, nor smothered their intelligence, nor maltreated their body, nor outraged their family, nor injured their goods, are we able to say that we have fulfilled the whole law in regard to them? One who is unfortunate is suffering before us. Is our conscience satisfied, if we are able to bear witness to ourselves that we have not contributed to his sufferings? No; something tells that it is still good to give him bread, succor, consolation.

There is here an important distinction to be made. If you have remained hard and insensible at the sight of another's misery, conscience cries out against you; and yet this man who is suffering, who, perhaps, is ready to die, has not the least right over the least part of your fortune, were it immense; and, if he used violence for the purpose of wresting from you a single penny, he would commit a crime. We here meet a new order of duties that do not correspond to rights. Man may resort to force

---

[236] Voluntary servitude is little better than servitude imposed by force. See 1st Series, vol. iii., lecture 4, p. 240: "Had another the desire to serve us as a slave, without conditions and without limits, to be for us a thing for our use, a pure instrument, a staff, a vase, and had we also the desire to make use of him in this manner, and to let him serve us in the same way, this reciprocity of desires would authorize for neither of us this absolute sacrifice, because desire can never be the title of a right, because there is something in us that is above all desires, participated or not participated, to wit, duty and right,—justice. To justice it belongs to be the rule of our desires, and not to our desires to be the rule of justice. Should entire humanity forget its dignity, should it consent to its own degradation, should it extend the hand to slavery, tyranny would be none the more legitimate; eternal justice would protest against a contract, which, were it supported by desires, reciprocal desires most authentically expressed and converted into solemn laws, is none the less void of all right, because, as Bossuet very truly said, there is no right against right, no contracts, no conventions, no human laws against the law of laws, against natural law."

in order to make his rights respected; he cannot impose on another any sacrifice whatever. Justice respects or restores; charity gives, and gives freely.

Charity takes from us something in order to give it to our fellow-men. If it goes so far as to inspire us to renounce our dearest interests, it is called devotedness.

It certainly cannot be said that to be charitable is not obligatory. But this obligation must not be regarded as precise, as inflexible as the obligation to be just. Charity is a sacrifice; and who can find the rule of sacrifice, the formula of self-renunciation? For justice, the formula is clear,—to respect the rights of another. But charity knows neither rule nor limit. It transcends all obligation. Its beauty is precisely in its liberty.

But it must be acknowledged that charity also has its dangers. It tends to substitute its own action for the action of him whom it wishes to help; it somewhat effaces his personality, and makes itself in some sort his providence,—a formidable part for a mortal! In order to be useful to others, one imposes himself on them, and runs the risk of violating their natural rights. Love, in giving itself, enslaves. Doubtless it is not interdicted us to act upon another. We can always do it through petition and exhortation. We can also do it by threatening, when we see one of our fellows engaged in a criminal or senseless action. We have even the right to employ force when passion carries away liberty and makes the person disappear. So we may, we even ought to prevent by force the suicide of one of our fellow-men. The legitimate power of charity is measured by the more or less liberty and reason possessed by him to whom it is applied. What delicacy, then, is necessary in the exercise of this perilous virtue! How can we estimate with sufficient certainty the degree of liberty still possessed by one of our fellow-men to know how far we may substitute ourselves for him in the guiding of his destiny? And when, in order to assist a feeble soul, we take possession of it, who is sufficiently sure of himself not to go farther, not to pass from the person governed to the love of domination itself? Charity is often the commencement and the excuse, and always the pretext of usurpation. In order to have the right of abandoning one's self to the emotions of charity, it is necessary to be fortified against one's self by a long exercise of justice.

To respect the rights of others and do good to men, to be at once just and charitable,—such are social ethics in the two elements that constitute them.

We speak of social ethics, and we do not yet know what society is. Let us look around us:—everywhere society exists, and where it is not, man is not man. Society is a universal fact which must have universal foundations.

Let us avoid at first the question of the origin of society.[237] The philosophy of the last century delighted in such questions

---

[237] On the danger of seeking at first the origin of human knowledge, see 1st Series, vol. iii., lecture on Hobbes, p. 261: "Hobbes is not the only one who took the question of the origin of societies as the starting-point of political science. Nearly all the publicists of the eighteenth century, Montesquieu excepted, proceed in the same manner. Rousseau imagines at first a primitive state in which man being no longer savage without being yet civilized, lived happy and free under the dominion of the laws of nature. This golden age of humanity disappearing carries with it all the rights of the individual, who enters naked and disarmed into what we call the social state. But order cannot reign in a state without laws, and since natural laws perished in the shipwreck of primitive manners, new ones must be created. Society is formed by aid of a contract whose principle is the abandonment by each and all of their individual force and rights to the profit of the community, of the state, the instrument of all forces, the depository of all rights. The state, for Hobbes, will be a man, a monarch, a king; for Rousseau, the state is the collection itself of citizens, who by turns are considered as subjects and governors, so that instead of the despotism of one over all, we have the despotism of all over each. Law is not the more or less happy, more or less faithful expression of natural justice; it is the expression of the general will. This general will is alone free; particular wills are not free. The general will has all rights, and particular wills have only the rights that it confers on them, or rather lends them. Force, in The Citizen is the foundation of society, of order, of laws, of the rights and duties which laws alone institute. In the Contrat Social, the general will plays the same part, fulfils the same function. Moreover, the general will scarcely differs in itself

too much. How can we demand light from the regions of darkness, and the explanation of reality from an hypothesis? Why go back to a pretended primitive state in order to account for a present state which may be studied in itself in its unquestionable characters? Why seek what may have been in the germ that which may be perceived, that which it is the question to understand, completed and perfect? Moreover, there is great peril in starting with the question of the origin of society. Has such or such an origin been found? Actual society is arranged according to the type of the primitive society that has been dreamed of, and political society is delivered up to the mercy of historical romances. This one imagines that the primitive state is violence, and he sets out from that in order to authorize the right of the strongest, and to consecrate despotism. That one thinks that he has found in the family the first form of society, and he compares government to the father of a family, and subjects to children; society in his eyes is a minor that must be held in tutelage in the hands of the paternal power, which in the origin is absolute, and consequently, must remain so. Or has one thrown himself to the extreme of the opposite opinion, and into the hypothesis of an agreement, of a contract that expresses the will of all or of the greatest number? He delivers up to the mobile will of the crowd the eternal laws of justice and the inalienable rights of the person.

---

from force. In fact, the general will is number, that is to say, force still. Thus, on both sides, tyranny under different forms. One may here observe the power of method. If Hobbes, if Rousseau especially had at first studied the idea of right in itself, with the certain characters without which we are not able to conceive it, they would have infallibly recognized that if there are rights derived from positive laws, and particularly from conventions and contracts, there are rights derived from no contract, since contracts take them for principles and rules; from no convention, since they serve as the foundation to all conventions in order that these conventions may be reputed just;—rights that society consecrates and develops, but does not make,—rights not subject to the caprices of general or particular will, belonging essentially to human nature, and like it, inviolable and sacred."

Finally, are powerful religious institutions found in the cradle of society? It is hence concluded, that power belongs of right to priesthoods, which have the secret of the designs of God, and represent his sovereign authority. Thus a vicious method in philosophy leads to a deplorable political system,—the commencement is made in hypothesis, and the termination is in anarchy or tyranny.

True politics do not depend on more or less well directed historical researches into the profound night of a past forever vanished, and of which no vestige subsists: they rest on the knowledge of human nature.

Wherever society is, wherever it was, it has for its foundations:—1st, The need that we have of our fellow-creatures, and the social instincts that man bears in himself; 2d, The permanent and indestructible idea and sentiment of justice and right.

Man, feeble and powerless when he is alone, profoundly feels the need that he has of the succor of his fellow-creatures in order to develop his faculties, to embellish his life, and even to preserve it.[238] Without reflection, without convention, he claims the hand,

---

[238] 1st Series, vol. iii., p. 265: "What!" somewhere says Montesquieu, "man is everywhere in society, and it is asked whether man was born for society! What is this fact that is reproduced in all the vicissitudes of the life of humanity, except a law of humanity? The universal and permanent fact of society attests the principle of sociability. This principle shines forth in all our inclinations, in our sentiments, in our beliefs. It is true that we love society for the advantages that it brings; but it is none the less true, that we also love it for its own sake, that we seek it independently of all calculation. Solitude saddens us; it is not less deadly to the life of the moral being, than a perfect vacuum is to the life of the physical being. Without society what would become of sympathy, which is one of the most powerful principles of our soul, which establishes between men a community of sentiments, by which each lives in all and all live in each? Who would be blind enough not to see in that an energetic call of human nature for society? And the attraction of the sexes, their union, the love of parents for children,—do they not found a sort of natural society, that is increased and developed by the power of the same causes which produced it?

the experience, the love of those whom he sees made like himself. The instinct of society is in the first cry of the child that calls for the mother's help without knowing that it has a mother, and in the eagerness of the mother to respond to the cries of the child. It is in the feelings for others that nature has put in us—pity, sympathy, benevolence. It is in the attraction of the sexes, in their union, in the love of parents for their children, and in the ties of every kind that these first ties engender. If Providence has attached so much sadness to solitude, so much charm to society, it is because society is indispensable for the preservation of man and for his happiness, for his intellect and moral development.

But if need and instinct begin society, it is justice that completes it.

In the presence of another man, without any external law, without any compact,[239] it is sufficient that I know that he is a

---

Divided by interest, united by sentiment, men respect each other in the name of justice. Let us add that they love each other in virtue of natural charity. In the sight of justice, equal in right, charity inspires us to consider ourselves as brethren, and to give each other succor and consolation. Wonderful thing! God has not left to our wisdom, nor even to experience, the care of forming and preserving society,—he has willed that sociability should be a law of our nature, and a law so imperative that no tendency to isolation, no egoism, no distaste even, can prevail against it. All the power of the spirit of system was necessary in order to make Hobbes say that society is an accident, as an incredible degree of melancholy to wring from Rousseau the extravagant expression that society is an evil."

[239] 1st Series, vol. iii., p. 283: "We do not hold from a compact our quality as man, and the dignity and rights attached to it; or, rather, there is an immortal compact which is nowhere written, which makes itself felt by every uncorrupted conscience, that compact which binds together all beings intelligent, free, and subject to misfortune, by the sacred ties of a common respect and a common charity.... Laws promulgate duties, but do not give birth to them; they could not violate duties without being unjust, and ceasing to merit the beautiful name of laws—that is to say, decisions of the public authority worthy of appearing obligatory to the conscience of all. Nevertheless, although laws have no other virtue than that of declaring what exists before

man, that is to say, that he is intelligent and free, in order to know that he has rights, and to know that I ought to respect his rights as he ought to respect mine. As he is no freer than I am, nor I than he, we recognize towards each other equal rights and equal duties. If he abuses his force to violate the equality of our rights, I know that I have the right to defend myself and make myself respected; and if a third party is found between us, without any personal interest in the quarrel, he knows that it is his right and his duty to use force in order to protect the feeble, and even to make the oppressor expiate his injustice by a chastisement. Therein is already seen entire society with its essential principles,—justice, liberty, equality, government, and punishment.

Justice is the guaranty of liberty. True liberty does not consist in doing what we will, but in doing what we have a right to do. Liberty of passion and caprice would have for its consequence the enslavement of the weakest to the strongest, and the enslavement of the strongest themselves to their unbridled desires. Man is truly free in the interior of his consciousness only in resisting passion and obeying justice; therein also is the type of true social liberty. Nothing is falser than the opinion that society diminishes our mutual liberty; far from that, it secures it, develops it: what it suppresses is not liberty; it is its opposite, passion. Society no more injures liberty than justice, for society is nothing else than the very idea of justice realized.

---

them, we often found on them right and justice, to the great detriment of justice itself, and the sentiment of right. Time and habit despoil reason of its natural rights in order to transfer it to law. What then happens? We either obey it, even when it is unjust, which is not a very great evil, but we do not think of reforming it little by little, having no superior principle that enables us to judge it,—or we continually change it, in an invincible impotence of founding any thing, by not knowing the immutable basis on which written law must rest. In either case, all progress is impossible, because the laws are not related to their true principle, which is reason, conscience, sovereign and absolute justice."

In securing liberty, justice secures equality also. If men are unequal in physical force and intelligence, they are equal in so far as they are free beings, and consequently equally worthy of respect. All men, when they bear the sacred character of the moral person, are to be respected, by the same title, and in the same degree.[240]

The limit of liberty is in liberty itself; the limit of right is in duty. Liberty is to be respected, but provided it injure not the liberty of an other. I ought to let you do what you please, but on the condition that nothing which you do will injure my liberty. For then, in virtue of my right of liberty, I should regard myself as obligated to repress the aberrations of your will, in order to protect my own and that of others. Society guaranties the liberty of each one, and if one citizen attacks that of another, he is arrested in the name of liberty. For example, religious liberty is sacred; you may, in the secret of consciousness, invent for yourself the most extravagant superstition; but if you wish publicly to inculcate an immoral worship, you threaten the liberty and reason of your citizens: such preaching is interdicted.

From the necessity of repressing springs the necessity of a constituted repressive force.

Rigorously, this force is in us; for if I am unjustly attacked, I have the right to defend myself. But, in the first place, I may not be the strongest; in the second place, no one is an impartial judge in his own cause, and what I regard or give out as an act of legitimate defence may be an act of violence and oppression.

So the protection of the rights of each one demands an impartial and disinterested force, that may be superior to all particular forces.

This disinterested party, armed with the power necessary to secure and defend the liberty of all, is called government.

The right of government expresses the rights of all and each. It is the right of personal defence transferred to a public force, to the profit of common liberty.

---

[240] Lecture 12.

Government is not, then, a power distinct from and independent of society; it draws from society its whole force. It is not what it has seemed to two opposite schools of publicists,—to those who sacrifice society to government,—to those who consider government as the enemy of society. If government did not represent society, it would be only a material, illegitimate, and soon powerless force; and without government, society would be a war of all against all. Society makes the moral power of government, as government makes the security of society. Pascal is wrong[241] when he says, that not being able to make what is just powerful, men have made what is powerful just. Government, in principle at least, is precisely what Pascal desired,—justice armed with force.

It is a sad and false political system that places society and government, authority and liberty, in opposition to each other, by making them come from two different sources, by presenting them as two contrary principles. I often hear the principle of authority spoken of as a principle apart, independent, deriving from itself its force and legitimacy, and consequently made to rule. No error is deeper and more dangerous. Thereby it is thought to confirm the principle of authority; far from that, from it is taken away its solidest foundation. Authority—that is to say, legitimate and moral authority—is nothing else than justice, and justice is nothing else than the respect of liberty; so that there is not therein two different and contrary opinions, but one and the same principle, of equal certainty and equal grandeur, under all its forms and in all its applications.

Authority, it is said, comes from God: doubtless; but whence comes liberty, whence comes humanity? To God must be referred every thing that is excellent on the earth; and nothing is more excellent than liberty. Reason, which in man commands liberty, commands it according to its nature; and the first law that reason imposes on liberty is that of self-respect.

---

[241] See 4th Series, vol. i., p. 40.

Authority is so much the stronger as its true title is better understood; and obedience is the easiest when, instead of degrading, it honors; when, instead of resembling servitude, it is at once the condition and guaranty of liberty.

The mission, the end of government, is to make justice, the protector of the common liberty, reign. Whence it follows, that as long as the liberty of one citizen does not injure the liberty of another, it escapes all repression. So government cannot be severe against falsehood, intemperance, imprudence, levity, avarice, egoism, except when these vices become prejudicial to others. Moreover, it is not necessary to confine government within too narrow limits. Government, which represents society, is also a moral person; it has a heart like the individual; it has generosity, goodness, charity. There are legitimate, and even universally admired facts, that are not explained, if the function of government is reduced to the protection of rights alone.[242] Government owes to the citizens, in a certain measure, to guard their well-being, to develop their intelligence, to fortify their morality, for the interest of society, and even for the interest of humanity. Hence sometimes for government the formidable right of using force in order to do good to men. But we are here touching upon that delicate point where charity inclines to despotism. Too much intelligence and wisdom, therefore, cannot be demanded in the employment of a power perhaps necessary, but dangerous.

Now, on what condition is government exercised? Is an act of its own will sufficient for it in order to employ to its own liking under all circumstances, as it shall understand them, the power that has been confided to it? Government must have been thus exercised in early society, and in the infancy of the art of governing. But the power, exercised by men, may go astray in different ways, either through weakness or through excess of

---

[242] See our pamphlet entitled Justice and Charity, composed in 1848, in the midst of the excesses of socialism, in order to remind of the dignity of liberty, the character, bearing, and the impassable limits of true charity, private and civil.

force. It must, then, have a rule superior to itself, a public and known rule, that may be a lesson for the citizens, and for the government a rein and support: that rule is called law.

Universal and absolute law is natural justice, which cannot be written, but speaks to the reason and heart of all. Written laws are the formulas wherein it is sought to express, with the least possible imperfection, what natural justice requires in such or such determined circumstances.

If laws propose to express in each thing natural justice, which is universal and absolute justice, one of the necessary conditions of a good law is the universality of its character. It is necessary to examine in an abstract and general manner what is required by justice in such or such a case, to the end that this case being presented may be judged according to the rule laid down, without regard to circumstances, place, time, or person.

The collection of those rules or laws that govern the social relations of individuals is called positive right. Positive right rests wholly on natural right, which at once serves as its foundation, measure, and limit. The supreme law of every positive law is that it be not opposed to natural law: no law can impose on us a false duty, nor deprive us of a true right.

The sanction of law is punishment. We have already seen that the right to punish springs from the idea of demerit.[243] In the

---

[243] See on the theory of penalty, the Gorgias, vol. iii. of the translation of Plato, and our argument, p. 367: "The first law of order is to be faithful to virtue, and to that part of virtue which is related to society, to wit, justice; but if one is wanting in that, the second law of order is to expiate one's fault, and it is expiated by punishment. Publicists are still seeking the foundation of penalty. Some, who think themselves great politicians, find it in the utility of the punishment for those who witness it, and are turned aside from crime by fear of its menace, by its preventive virtue. And that it is true, is one of the effects of penalty, but it is not its foundation; for punishment falling upon the innocent, would produce as much, and still more terror, and would be quite as preventive. Others, in their pretensions to humanity, do not wish to see the legitimacy of punishment except in its utility for him who undergoes it, in its corrective virtue,—and that, too, is one of the possible effects of punishment,

universal order, to God alone it belongs to apply a punishment to all faults, whatever they may be. In the social order, government is invested with the right to punish only for the purpose of protecting liberty by imposing a just reparation on those who violate it. Every fault that is not contrary to justice, and does not strike at liberty, escapes, then, social retribution. Neither is the right to punish the right of avenging one's self. To render evil for evil, to demand an eye for an eye, a tooth for a tooth, is the barbarous form of a justice without light; for the evil that I do you will not take away the evil that you have done me. It is not the pain felt by the victim that demands a corresponding pain; it is violated justice that imposes on the culpable man the expiation of suffering. Such is the morality of penalty. The principle of penalty is not the reparation of damage caused. If I have caused you damage without intending it, I pay you an indemnity; that is

---

but not its foundation; for that punishment may be corrective, it must be accepted as just. It is, then, always necessary to recur to justice. Justice is the true foundation of punishment,—personal and social utility are only consequences. It is an incontestable fact, that after every unjust act, man thinks, and cannot but think that he has incurred demerit, that is to say, has merited a punishment. In intelligence, to the idea of injustice corresponds that of penalty; and when injustice has taken place in the social sphere, merited punishment ought to be inflicted by society. Society can inflict it only because it ought. Right here has no other source than duty, the strictest, most evident, and most sacred duty, without which this pretended right would be only that of force, that is to say, an atrocious injustice, should it even result in the moral profit of him who undergoes it, and in a salutary spectacle for the people,—what it would not then be; for then the punishment would find no sympathy, no echo, either in the public conscience or in that of the condemned. The punishment is not just, because it is preventively or correctively useful; but it is in both ways useful, because it is just." This theory of penalty, in demonstrating the falsity, the incomplete and exclusive character of two theories that divide publicists, completes and explains them, and gives them both a legitimate centre and base. It is doubtless only indicated in Plato, but is met in several passages, briefly but positively expressed, and on it rests the sublime theory of expiation.

not a penalty, for I am not culpable; whilst if I have committed a crime, in spite of the material indemnity for the evil that I have done, I owe a reparation to justice by a proper suffering, and in that truly consists the penalty.

What is the exact proportion of chastisements and crimes? This question cannot receive an absolute solution. What is here immutable, is that the act opposed to justice merits a punishment, and that the more unjust the act is, the severer ought to be the punishment. But by the side of the right to punish is the duty of correcting. To the culprit must be left the possibility of repairing his crime. The culpable man is still a man; he is not a thing of which we ought to rid ourselves as soon as it becomes injurious, a stone that falls on our heads, that we throw into a gulf that it may wound no more. Man is a rational being, capable of comprehending good and evil, of repenting, and of being one day reconciled with order. These truths have given birth to works that honor the close of the eighteenth century and the beginning of the nineteenth. The conception of houses of correction reminds one of those early times of Christianity when punishment consisted in an expiation that permitted the culprit to return through repentance to the ranks of the just. Here intervenes, as we have just indicated, the principle of charity, which is very different from the principle of justice. To punish is just, to ameliorate is charitable. In what measure ought those two principles to be united? Nothing is more delicate, more difficult to determine. It is certain that justice ought to govern. In undertaking the amendment of the culprit, government usurps, with a very generous usurpation, the rights of religion; but it ought not to go so far as to forget its proper function and its rigorous duty.

Let us pause on the threshold of politics, properly so called. Nothing in them but these principles is fixed and invariable; all else is relative. The constitutions of states have something absolute by their relation to the inviolable rights which they ought to guarantee; but they also have a relative side by the variable forms with which they are clothed, according to times, places, manners, history. The supreme rule of which philosophy reminds politics, is that politics ought, in consulting all circumstances, to seek always those social forms and institutions that best realize those eternal principles. Yes, they are eternal; because they are drawn from no arbitrary hypothesis, because they rest on the immutable nature of man, on the all-powerful instincts of the heart, on the indestructible notion of justice, and the sublime idea of charity, on the consciousness of person, liberty, and equality, on duty and right, on merit and demerit. Such are the foundations of all true society, worthy of the beautiful name of human society, that is to say, formed of free and rational beings; and such are the maxims that ought to direct every government worthy of its mission, which knows that it is not dealing with beasts but with men, which respects them and loves them.

Thank God, French society has always marched by the light of this immortal idea, and the dynasty that has been at its head for some centuries has always guided it in these generous ways. It was Louis le Gros, who, in the Middle Age, emancipated the communes; it was Philippe le Bel who instituted parliaments—an independent and gratuitous justice; it was Henri IV. who began religious liberty; it was Louis XIII. and Louis XIV. who, while they undertook to give to France her natural frontiers, and almost succeeded in it, labored to unite more and more all parts of the nation, to put a regular administration in the place of feudal anarchy, and to reduce the great vassals to a simple aristocracy, from day to day deprived of every privilege but that of serving the common country in the first rank. It was a king of France who, comprehending the new wants, and associating himself with the progress of the times, attempted to substitute for that very real, but confused and formless representative government, that was called the assemblies of the nobility, the clergy, and the *tiers état*, the true representative government that is proper for great civilized nations,—a glorious and unfortunate attempt that, if royalty had then been served by a Richelieu, a Mazarin, or a Colbert, might have terminated in a necessary reform, that, through the fault of every one, ended in a revolution full of excess, violence, and crime, redeemed and covered by an incomparable courage, a sincere patriotism, and the most brilliant triumphs. Finally, it was the brother of Louis XVI. who, enlightened and not discouraged by the misfortunes of his family, spontaneously gave to France that liberal and wise constitution of which our fathers had dreamed, about which Montesquieu had written, which, loyally adhered to, and necessarily developed, is admirably fitted for the present time, and sufficient for a long future. We are fortunate in finding in the Charter the principles that we have just explained, that contain our views and our hopes for France and humanity.[244]

---

[244] As it is perceived, we have confined ourselves to the most general principles. The following year, in 1819, in our lectures on Hobbes, 1st Series, vol. iii., we gave a more extended theory of rights, and the civil and political guaranties which they demand; we even touched the question of the different forms of government, and established the truth and beauty of the constitutional monarchy. In 1828, 2d Series, vol. i., lecture 13, we explained and defended the Charter in its fundamental parts. Under the government of July, the part of defender of both liberty and royalty was easy. We continued it in 1848; and when, at the unexpected inundation of democracy, soon followed by a passionate reaction in favor of an absolute authority, many minds, and the best, asked themselves whether the young American republic was not called to serve as a model for old Europe, we did not hesitate to maintain the principle of the monarchy in the interest of liberty; we believe that we demonstrated that the development of the principles of 1789, and in particular the progress of the lower classes, so necessary, can be obtained only by the aid of the constitutional monarchy,—6th Series, Political Discourses, with an introduction on the principles of the French Revolution and representative government.

LECTURE XVI.

GOD THE PRINCIPLE OF THE IDEA OF THE GOOD.

Principle on which true theodicea rests. God the last foundation of moral truth, of the good, and of the moral person.—Liberty of God.—The divine justice and charity.—God the sanction of the moral law. Immortality of the soul; argument from merit and demerit; argument from the simplicity of the soul; argument from final causes.—Religious sentiment.—Adoration.—Worship.—Moral beauty of Christianity.

The moral order has been confirmed,—we are in possession of moral truth, of the idea of the good, and the obligation that is attached to it. Now, the same principle that has not permitted us to stop at absolute truth,[245] and has forced us to seek its supreme reason in a real and substantial being, forces us here again to refer the idea of the good to the being who is its first and last foundation.

Moral truth, like every other universal and necessary truth, cannot remain in a state of abstraction. In us it is only conceived. There must somewhere be a being who not only conceives it, but constituted it.

As all beautiful things and all true things are related—these to a unity that is absolute truth, and those to another unity that is absolute beauty, so all moral principles participate in the same principle, which is the good. We thus elevate ourselves to the conception of the good in itself, of absolute good, superior to all particular duties, and determined in these duties. Now, can the absolute good be any thing else than an attribute of him who, properly speaking, is alone absolute being?

Would it be possible that there might be several absolute beings, and that the being in whom are realized absolute truth and

---

[245] Lectures 4 and 7.

absolute beauty might not also be the one who is the principle of absolute good? The very idea of the absolute implies absolute unity. The true, the beautiful, and the good, are not three distinct essences; they are one and the same essence considered in its fundamental attributes. Our mind distinguishes them, because it can comprehend them only by division; but, in the being in whom they reside, they are indivisibly united; and this being at once triple and one, who sums up in himself perfect beauty, perfect truth, and the supreme good, is nothing else than God.

So God is necessarily the principle of moral truth and the good. He is also the type of the moral person that we carry in us.

Man is a moral person, that is to say, he is endowed with reason and liberty. He is capable of virtue, and virtue has in him two principal forms, respect of others, and love of others, justice and charity.

Can there be among the attributes possessed by the creature something essential not possessed by the Creator? Whence does the effect draw its reality and its being, except from its cause? What it possesses, it borrows and receives. The cause at least contains all that is essential in the effect. What particularly belongs to the effect, is inferiority, is a lack, is imperfection: from the fact alone that it is dependent and derived, it bears in itself the signs and the conditions of dependence. If, then, we cannot legitimately conclude from the imperfection of the effect in that of the cause, we can and must conclude from the excellence of the effect in the perfection of the cause, otherwise there would be something prominent in the effect which would be without cause.

Such is the principle of our theodicea. It is neither new nor subtle; but it has not yet been thoroughly disengaged and elucidated, and it is, to our eyes, firm against every test. It is by the aid of this principle that we can, up to a certain point, penetrate into the true nature of God.

God is not a being of logic, whose nature can be explained by way of deduction, and by means of algebraic equations. When, setting out from a first attribute, we have deduced the attributes of God from each other, after the manner of geometricians and the schoolmen, what do we possess,[246] I pray you, but abstractions? It is necessary to leave these vain dialectics in order to arrive at a real and living God.

The first notion that we have of God, to wit, the notion of an infinite being, is itself given to us independently of all experience. It is the consciousness of ourselves, as being at once, and as being limited, that elevates us directly to the conception of a being who is the principle of our being, and is himself without bounds. This solid and single argument, which is at bottom that of Descartes,[247] opens to us a way that must be followed, in which Descartes too quickly stopped. If the being that we possess forces us to recur to a cause which possesses being in an infinite degree, all that we have of being, that is to say, of substantial attributes, equally requires an infinite cause. Then, God will no longer be merely the infinite, abstract, or at least indeterminate being in which reason and the heart know not where to betake themselves,[248] he will be a real and determined being, a moral

---

[246] Such is the common vice of nearly all theodiceas, without excepting the best—that of Leibnitz, that of Clarke; even the most popular of all, the Profession de Foi du Vicaire Savoyard. See our small work entitled Philosophie Populaire, 3d edition, p. 82.

[247] On the Cartesian argument, see above, part 1st, lecture 4; see also 1st Series, vol. iv., lecture 12, and especially vol. v., lecture 6.

[248] Fragments de Philosophie Cartésienne, p. 24: "The infinite being, inasmuch as infinite, is not a mover, a cause; neither is he, inasmuch as infinite, an intelligence; neither is he a will; neither is he a principle of justice, nor much less a principle of love. We have no right to impute to him all these attributes in virtue of the single argument that every contingent being supposes a being that is not so, that every finite supposes an infinite. The God given by this argument is the God of Spinoza, is rigorously so; but he is almost as though he were not, at least for us who with difficulty perceive him in the inaccessible heights of an eternity and existence that are absolute, void of thought, of liberty, of love, similar to nonentity itself, and a thousand times inferior, in his infinity and eternity, to an hour of our finite and perishable existence, if during this fleeting hour we know what we are, if we think, if we love something else than ourselves, if we feel capable of freely sacrificing to an idea the few minutes that have been accorded to us."

person like ours and psychology conducts us without hypothesis to a theodicea at once sublime and related to us.[249]

Before all, if man is free, can it be that God is not free? No one contends that he who is cause of all causes, who has no cause but himself, can be dependent on any thing whatever. But in freeing God from all external constraint, Spinoza subjects him to an internal and mathematical necessity, wherein he finds the perfection of being. Yes, of being which is not a person; but the essential character of personal being is precisely liberty. If, then, God were not free, God would be beneath man. Would it not be strange that the creature should have the marvellous power of disposing of himself, and of freely willing, and that the being who has made him should be subjected to a necessary development, whose cause is only in himself, without doubt, but, in fine, is a sort of abstract power, mechanical or metaphysical, but very inferior to the personal and voluntary cause that we are, and of which we have the clearest consciousness? God is therefore free, since we are free. But he is not free as we are free; for God is at once all that we are, and nothing that we are. He possesses the same attributes that we possess, but elevated to infinity. He possesses an infinite liberty, joined to an infinite intelligence; and, as his intelligence is infallible, excepted from the uncertainties of

---

[249] This theodicea is here in résumé, and in the 4th and 5th lectures of part first, as well as in the lecture that follows. The most important of our different writings, on this point, will be found collected and elucidated by each other, in the Appendix to the 5th lecture of the first volume of the 1st Series.—See our translation of this entire Series of M. Cousin's works, under the title of the History of Modern Philosophy.

deliberation, and perceiving at a glance where the good is, so his liberty spontaneously, and without effort, fulfils it.[250]

---

[250] 3d Series, vol. iv., advertisement to the 3d edition: "Without vain subtilty, there is a real distinction between free will and spontaneous liberty. Arbitrary freedom is volition with the appearance of deliberation between different objects, and under this supreme condition, that when, as a consequence of deliberation, we resolve to do this or that, we have the immediate consciousness of having been able, and of being able still, to will the contrary. It is in volition, and in the retinue of phenomena which surround it, that liberty more energetically appears, but it is not thereby exhausted. It is at rare and sublime moments in which liberty is as much greater as it appears less to the eyes of a superficial observation. I have often cited the example of d'Assas. D'Assas did not deliberate; and for all that, was d'Assas less free, did he not act with entire liberty? Has the saint who, after a long and painful exercise of virtue, has come to practise, as it were by nature, the acts of self-renunciation which are repugnant to human weakness; has the saint, in order to have gone out from the contradictions and the anguish of this form of liberty which we called volition, fallen below it instead of being elevated above it; and is he nothing more than a blind and passive instrument of grace, as Luther and Calvin have inappropriately wished to call it, by an excessive interpretation of the Augustinian doctrine? No, freedom still remains; and far from being annihilated, its liberty, in being purified, is elevated and ennobled; from the human form of volition it has passed to the almost divine form of spontaneity. Spontaneity is essentially free, although it may be accompanied with no deliberation, and although often, in the rapid motion of its inspired action, it escapes its own observation, and leaves scarcely a trace in the depths of consciousness. Let us transfer this exact psychology to theodicea, and we may recognize without hypothesis, that spontaneity is also especially the form of God's liberty. Yes, certainly, God is free; for, among other proofs, it would be absurd that there should be less freedom in the first cause than in one of its effects, humanity; God is free, but not with that liberty which is related to our double nature, and made to contend against passion and error, and painfully to engender virtue and our imperfect knowledge; he is free, with a liberty that is related to his own divine nature, that is a liberty unlimited, infinite, recognizing no obstacle. Between justice and injustice, between good and evil, between reason and its contrary, God cannot deliberate, and, consequently, cannot will after our manner. Can one conceive, in fact, that he could take what we call the

In the same manner as we transfer to God the liberty that is the foundation of our being, we also transfer to him justice and charity. In man, justice and charity are virtues; in God, they are attributes. What is in us the laborious conquest of liberty, is in him his very nature. If respect of rights is in us the very essence of justice and the sign of the dignity of our being, it is impossible that the perfect being should not know and respect the rights of the lowest beings, since it is he, moreover, who has imparted to them those rights. In God resides a sovereign justice, which renders to each one his due, not according to deceptive appearances, but according to the truth of things. Finally, if man, that limited being, has the power of going out of himself, of forgetting his person, of loving another than himself, of devoting himself to another's happiness, or, what is better, to the perfecting of another, should not the perfect being have, in an infinite degree, this disinterested tenderness, this charity, the supreme virtue of the human person? Yes, there is in God an infinite tenderness for his creatures: he at first manifested it in giving us the being that he might have withheld, and at all times it appears in the innumerable signs of his divine providence. Plato knew this love of God well, and expressed it in those great words, "Let us say that the cause which led the supreme ordainer to produce and compose this universe is, that he was good; and he who is good has no species of envy. Exempt from envy, he willed that all things should be, as much as possible, like himself."[251] Christianity went farther: according to the divine doctrine, God so loved men that he gave them his only Son. God is inexhaustible in his charity, as he is inexhaustible in his essence. It

---

bad part? This very supposition is impious. It is necessary to admit that when he has taken the contrary part, he has acted freely without doubt, but not arbitrarily, and with the consciousness of having been able to choose the other part. His nature, all-powerful, all-just, all-wise, is developed with that spontaneity which contains entire liberty, and excludes at once the efforts and the miseries of volition, and the mechanical operation of necessity. Such is the principle and the true character of the divine action."

[251] Timæus, p. 119, vol. xii. of our translation.

is impossible to give more to the creature; he gives him every thing that he can receive without ceasing to be a creature; he gives him every thing, even himself, so far as the creature is in him and he in the creature. At the same time nothing can be lost; for being absolute being, he eternally expands and gives himself without being diminished. Infinite in power, infinite in charity, he bestows his love in exhaustless abundance upon the world, to teach us that the more we give the more we possess. It is egoism, whose root is at the bottom of every heart, even by the side of the sincerest charity, that inculcates in us the error that we lose by self-devotion: it is egoism that makes us call devotion a sacrifice.

If God is wholly just and wholly good, he can will nothing but what is good and just; and, as he is all-powerful, every thing that he wills he can do, and consequently does do. The world is the work of God; it is therefore perfectly made, perfectly adapted to its end.

And nevertheless, there is in the world a disorder that seems to accuse the justice and goodness of God.

A principle that is attached to the very idea of the good, says to us that every moral agent deserves a reward when he does good, and a punishment when he does evil. This principle is universal and necessary: it is absolute. If this principle has not its application in this world, it must either be a lie, or this world is ordered ill.

Now, it is a fact that the good is not always followed by happiness, nor evil always by unhappiness.

Let us, in the first place, remark that if the fact exists, it is rare enough, and seems to present the character of an exception.

Virtue is a struggle against passion; this struggle, full of dignity, is also full of pain; but, on one side, crime is condemned to much harder pains; on the other, those of virtue are of short duration; they are a necessary and almost always beneficent trial.

Virtue has its pains, but the greatest happiness is still with it, as the greatest unhappiness is with crime; and such is the case in small and great, in the secret of the soul, and on the theatre of life, in the obscurest conditions and in the most conspicuous situations.

Good and bad health are, after all, the greatest part of happiness or unhappiness. In this regard, compare temperance and its opposite, order and disorder, virtue and vice; I mean a temperance truly temperate, and not an atrabilarious asceticism, a rational virtue, and not a fierce virtue.

The great physician Hufeland[252] remarks that the benevolent sentiments are favorable to health, and that the malevolent sentiments are opposed to it. Violent and sinful passions irritate, inflame, and carry trouble into the organization as well as the soul; the benevolent affections preserve the measured and harmonious play of all the functions.

Hufeland again remarks that the greatest longevities pertain to wise and well-regulated lives.

Thus, for health, strength, and life, virtue is better than vice: it is already much, it seems to me.

I surely mean to speak of conscience only after health; but, in fine, with the body, our most constant host is conscience. Peace or trouble of conscience decides internal happiness or unhappiness. At this point of view, compare again order and disorder, virtue and vice.

And without us, in society, to whom come esteem and contempt, consideration and infamy? Certainly opinion has its mistakes, but they are not long. In general, if charlatans, intriguers, impostors of every kind, for some time surreptitiously get suffrages, it must be that a sustained honesty is the surest and the almost infallible means of reaching a good renown.

I regret that upon this point time does not allow of any development. It would have afforded me delight, after having distinguished virtue from happiness, to show them to you almost always united by the admirable law of merit and demerit. I should have been pleased to show you this beneficent law already governing human destiny, and called to preside over it more

---

[252] De l'Art de prolonger sa Vie, etc.

exactly from day to day by the ever-increasing progress of lights in governments and peoples, by the perfecting of civil and judicial institutions. It would have been my wish to make pass into your minds and hearts the consoling conviction that, after all, justice is already in this world, and that the surest road to happiness is still that of virtue.

This was the opinion of Socrates and Plato; and it is also that of Franklin, and I gather it from my personal experience and an attentive examination of human life. But I admit that there are exceptions; and were there but one exception, it would be necessary to explain it.

Suppose a man, young, beautiful, rich, amiable, and loved, who, placed between the scaffold and the betrayal of a sacred cause, voluntarily mounts the scaffold at twenty years of age. What do you make of this noble victim? The law of merit and demerit seems here suspended. Do you dare blame virtue, or how in this world do you accord to it the recompense that it has not sought, but is its due?

By careful search you will find more than one case analogous to that.

The laws of this world are general; they turn aside to suit no one: they pursue their course without regard to the merit or demerit of any. If a man is born with a bad temperament, it is in virtue of certain obscure but undeviating physical laws, to which he is subject, like the animal and the plant, and he suffers during his whole life, although personally innocent. He is brought up in the midst of flames, epidemics, calamities that strike at hazard the good as well as the bad.

Human justice condemns many that are innocent, it is true, but it absolves, in fault of proof, more than one who is culpable. Besides, it knows only certain derelictions. What faults, what basenesses occur in the dark, which do not receive merited chastisement! In like manner, what obscure devotions of which God is the sole witness and judge! Without doubt nothing escapes the eye of conscience, and the culpable soul cannot escape remorse. But remorse is not always in exact relation with the fault committed; its vivacity may depend on a nature more or less delicate, on education and habit. In a word, if it is in general very true that the law of merit and demerit is fulfilled in this world, it is not fulfilled with mathematical rigor.

What must we conclude from this? That the world is ill-made? No. That cannot be, and is not. That cannot be, for incontestably the world has a just and good author; that is not, for, in fact, we see order reigning in the world; and it would be absurd to misconceive the manifest order that almost everywhere shines forth on account of a few phenomena that we cannot refer to order. The universe endures, therefore it is well made. The pessimism of Voltaire is still more opposed to the aggregate of facts than an absolute optimism. Between these two systematic extremes which facts deny, the human race places the hope of another life. It has found it very irrational to reject a necessary law on account of some infractions; it has, therefore, maintained the law; and from infractions it has only concluded that they ought to be referred to the law, that there will be a reparation. Either this conclusion must be admitted, or the two great principles previously admitted, that God is just, and that the law of merit and demerit is an absolute law, must be rejected.

Now, to reject these two principles is to totally overthrow all human belief.

To maintain them, is implicitly to admit that actual life must be, elsewhere terminated or continued.

But is this continuation of the person possible? After the dissolution of the body, can any thing of us remain?

In truth, the moral person, which acts well or ill, which awaits the reward or punishment of its good or bad actions, is united to a body,—it lives with the body, makes use of it, and, in a certain measure, depends on it, but is not it.[253] The body is composed of parts, may decrease or increase; is divisible,

---

[253] On the spirituality of the soul, see all our writings. We will limit ourselves to two citations. 2d Series, vol. iii., lecture 25, p. 859: "It is impossible to know any phenomenon of consciousness, the phenomena of sensation, or volition, or of intelligence, without instantly referring them to a subject one and identical, which is the me; so we cannot know the external phenomena of resistance, of solidity, of impenetrability, of figure, of color, of smell, of taste, etc., without judging that these are not phenomena in appearance, but phenomena which belong to something real, which is solid, impenetrable, figured, colored, odorous, savory, etc. On the other hand, if you did not know any of the phenomena of consciousness, you would never have the least idea of the subject of these phenomena; if you did not know any of the external phenomena of resistance, of solidity, of impenetrability, of figure, of color, etc., you would not have any idea of the subject of these phenomena: therefore the characters, whether of the phenomena of consciousness, or of exterior phenomena, are for you the only signs of the nature of the subjects of these phenomena. In examining the phenomena which fall under the senses, we find between them grave differences upon which it is useless here to insist, and which establish the distinction of primary qualities and of secondary qualities. In the first rank among the primary qualities is solidity, which is given to you in the sensation of resistance, and inevitably accompanied by form, etc. On the contrary, when you examine the phenomena of consciousness, you do not therein find this character of resistance, of solidity, of form, etc.; you do not find that the phenomena of your consciousness have a figure, solidity, impenetrability, resistance; without speaking of secondary qualities which are equally foreign to them, color, savor, sound, smell, etc. Now, as the subject is for us only the collection of the phenomena which reveal it to us, together with its own existence in so far as the subject of the inherence of these phenomena, it follows that, under phenomena marked with dissimilar characters and entirely foreign to each other, the human mind conceives dissimilar and foreign subjects. Thus as solidity and figure have nothing in common with sensation, will, and thought, as every solid is extended for us, and as we place it necessarily in space, while our thoughts, our volitions, our sensations, are for us unextended, and while we cannot conceive them and place them in space, but only in time, the human mind concludes with perfect strictness that the subject of the exterior phenomena has the character of the latter, and that the subject

of the phenomena of consciousness has the character of the former; that the one is solid and extended, and that the other is neither solid nor extended. Finally, as that which is solid and extended is divisible, and as that which is neither solid nor extended is indivisible, hence divisibility is attributed to the solid and extended subject, and indivisibility attributed to the subject which is neither extended nor solid. Who of us, in fact, does not believe himself an indivisible being, one and identical, the same yesterday, to-day, and to-morrow? Well, the word body, the word matter, signifies nothing else than the subject of external phenomena, the most eminent of which are form, impenetrability, solidity, extension, divisibility. The word mind, the word soul, signifies nothing else than the subject of the phenomena of consciousness, thought, will, sensation, phenomena simple, unextended, not solid, etc. Behold the whole idea of spirit, and the whole idea of matter! See, therefore, all that must be done in order to bring back matter to spirit, and spirit to matter: it is necessary to pretend that sensation, volition, thought, are reducible in the last analysis to solidity, extension, figure, divisibility, etc., or that solidity, extension, figure, etc., are reducible to thought, volition, sensation." 1st Series, vol. iii., lecture I, Locke. "Locke pretends that we cannot be certain by the contemplation of our own ideas, that matter cannot think; on the contrary, it is in the contemplation itself of our ideas that we clearly perceive that matter and thought are incompatible. What is thinking? Is it not uniting a certain number of ideas under a certain unity? The simplest judgment supposes several terms united in a subject, one and identical, which is me. This identical me is implied in every real act of knowledge. It has been demonstrated to satiety that comparison exacts an indivisible centre that comprises the different terms of the comparison. Do you take memory? There is no memory possible without the continuation of the same subject that refers to self the different modifications by which it has been successively affected. Finally, consciousness, that indispensable condition of intelligence,—is it not the sentiment of a single being? This is the reason why each man cannot think without saying me, without affirming that he is himself the identical and one subject of his thoughts. I am me and always me, as you are always yourself in the most different acts of your life. You are not more yourself to-day than you were yesterday, and you are not less yourself to-day than you were yesterday. This identity and this indivisible unity of the me inseparable from the least thought, is what is called its spirituality, in opposition to the evident and necessary characters of matter. By what, in fact, do you know matter? It is especially by essentially divisible, and even infinitely divisible. But that something that has consciousness of itself, that says, *I, me*, that feels itself to be free and responsible, does it not also feel that there is in it no division, even no possible division, that it is a being one and simple? Is the *me* more or less *me*? Is there a half of *me*, a quarter of *me*? I cannot divide my person. It remains identical to itself under the diversity of the phenomena that manifest it. This identity, this indivisibility of the person, is its spirituality. Spirituality is, therefore, the very essence of the person. Belief in the spirituality of the soul is involved in the belief of this identity of the *me*, which no rational being has ever called in question. Accordingly, there is not the least hypothesis for affirming that the soul does not essentially differ from the body. Add that when we say the soul, we mean to say, and do say the person, which is not separated from the consciousness of the attributes that constitute it, thought and will. The being without consciousness is not a person. It is the person that is identical, one, simple. Its attributes, in developing it, do not divide it. Indivisible, it is indissoluble, and may be immortal. If, then, divine justice, in order to be exercised in regard to us, demands an

---

form, by extension, by something solid that stops you, that resists you in different points of space. But is not a solid essentially divisible? Take the most subtile fluids,—can you help conceiving them as more or less susceptible of division? All thought has its different elements like matter, but in addition it has its unity in the thinking subject, and the subject being taken away, which is one, the total phenomenon no longer exists. Far from that, the unknown subject to which we attach material phenomena is divisible, and divisible ad infinitum; it cannot cease to be divisible without ceasing to exist. Such are the ideas that we have, on the one side, of mind, on the other, of matter. Thought supposes a subject essentially one; matter is infinitely divisible. What is the need of going farther? If any conclusion is legitimate, it is that which distinguishes thought from matter. God can indeed make them exist together, and their co-existence is a certain fact, but he cannot confound them. God can unite thought and matter, he cannot make matter thought, nor what is extended simple."

immortal soul, it does not demand an impossible thing. The spirituality of the soul is the necessary foundation of immortality. The law of merit and demerit is the direct demonstration of this. The first proof is called the metaphysical proof, the second, the moral proof, which is the most celebrated, most popular, at once the most convincing and the most persuasive.

What powerful motives are added to these two proofs to fortify them in the heart! The following, for example, is a presumption of great value for any one that believes in the virtue of sentiment and instinct.

Every thing has its end. This principle is as absolute as that which refers every event to a cause.[254] Man has, therefore, an end. This end is revealed in all his thoughts, in all his ways, in all his sentiments, in all his life. Whatever he does, whatever he feels, whatever he thinks, he thinks upon the infinite, loves the infinite, tends to the infinite.[255] This need of the infinite is the mainspring of scientific curiosity, the principle of all discoveries. Love also stops and rests only there. On the route it may experience lively joys; but a secret bitterness that is mingled with them soon makes it feel their insufficiency and emptiness. Often, while ignorant of its true object, it asks whence comes that fatal disenchantment by which all its successes, all its pleasures are successively extinguished. If it knew how to read itself, it would recognize that if nothing here below satisfies it, it is because its object is more elevated, because the true bourne after which it aspires is infinite perfection. Finally, like thought and love, human activity is without limits. Who can say where it shall stop? Behold this earth almost known. Soon another world will be necessary for us. Man is journeying towards the infinite, which is always receding before him, which he always pursues. He conceives it, he feels it, he bears it, thus to speak, in himself,—how should his end be elsewhere? Hence that unconquerable instinct of immortality, that universal hope of another life to which all worships, all poesies, all traditions bear witness. We tend to the infinite with all our

---

[254] See 1st part, lecture I.
[255] See lecture 5, Mysticism.

powers; death comes to interrupt the destiny that seeks its goal, and overtakes it unfinished. It is, therefore, likely that there is something after death, since at death nothing in us is terminated. Look at the flower that to-morrow will not be. To-day, at least, it is entirely developed: we can conceive nothing more beautiful of its kind; it has attained its perfection. My perfection, my moral perfection, that of which I have the clearest idea and the most invincible need, for which I feel that I am born,—in vain I call for it, in vain I labor for it; it escapes me, and leaves me only hope. Shall this hope be deceived? All beings attain their end; should man alone not attain his? Should the greatest of creatures be the most ill-treated? But a being that should remain incomplete and unfinished, that should not attain the end which all his instincts proclaim for him, would be a monster in the eternal order,—a problem much more difficult to solve than the difficulties that have been raised against the immortality of the soul. In our opinion, this tendency of all the desires and all the powers of the soul towards the infinite, elucidated by the principle of final causes, is a serious and important confirmation of the moral proof and the metaphysical proof of another life.

When we have collected all the arguments that authorize belief in another life, and when we have thus arrived at a satisfying demonstration, there remains an obstacle to be overcome. Imagination cannot contemplate without fright that unknown which is called death. The greatest philosopher in the world, says Pascal, on a plank wider than it is necessary in order to go without danger from one side of an abyss to the other, cannot think without trembling on the abyss that is beneath him. It is not reason, it is imagination that frightens him; it is also imagination that in great part causes that remnant of doubt, that trouble, that secret anxiety which the firmest faith cannot always succeed in overcoming in the presence of death. The religious man experiences this terror, but he knows whence it comes, and he surmounts it by attaching himself to the solid hopes furnished him by reason and the heart. Imagination is a child that must be educated, by putting it under the discipline and government of better faculties; it must be accustomed to go to intelligence for aid instead of troubling intelligence with its phantoms. Let us acknowledge that there is a terrible step to be taken when we meet death. Nature trembles when face to face with the unknown eternity. It is wise to present ourselves there with all our forces united,—reason and the heart lending each other mutual support, the imagination being subdued or charmed. Let us continually repeat that, in death as in life, the soul is sure to find God, and that with God all is just, all is good.[256]

We now know what God truly is. We have already seen two of his adorable attributes,—truth and beauty. The most august attribute is revealed to us,—holiness. God is the holy of holies, as the author of the moral law and the good, as the principle of liberty, justice, and charity, as the dispenser of penalty and reward. Such a God is not an abstract God, but an intelligent and free person, who has made us in his own image, from whom we hold the law itself that presides over our destiny, whose judgments we await. It is his love that inspires us in our acts of charity; it is his justice that governs our justice, that of our societies and our laws. If we do not continually remind ourselves that he is infinite, we degrade his nature; but he would be for us as if he were not, if his infinite essence had no forms that pertain to us, the proper forms of our reason and our soul.

---

[256] 4th Series, vol. iii., Santa-Rosa: "After all, the existence of a divine Providence is, to my eyes, a truth clearer than all lights, more certain than all mathematics. Yes, there is a God, a God who is a true intelligence, who consequently has a consciousness of himself, who has made and ordered every thing with weight and measure, whose works are excellent, whose ends are adorable, even when they are veiled from our feeble eyes. This world has a perfect author, perfectly wise and good. Man is not an orphan; he has a father in heaven. What will this father do with his child when he returns to him? Nothing but what is good. Whatever happens, all will be well. Every thing that he has done has been done well; every thing that he shall do, I accept beforehand, and bless. Yes, such is my unalterable faith, and this faith is my support, my refuge, my consolation, my solace in this fearful moment."

By thinking upon such a being, man feels a sentiment that is *par excellence* the religious sentiment. All the beings with whom we are in relation awaken in us different sentiments, according to the qualities that we perceive in them; and should he who possesses all perfections excite in us no particular sentiment? When we think upon the infinite essence of God, when we are penetrated with his omnipotence, when we are reminded that the moral law expresses his will, that he attaches to the fulfilment and the violation of this law recompenses and penalties which he dispenses with an inflexible justice, we cannot guard ourselves against an emotion of respect and fear at the idea of such a grandeur. Then, if we come to consider that this all-powerful being has indeed wished to create us, us of whom he has no need, that in creating us he has loaded us with benefits, that he has given us this admirable universe for enjoying its ever-new beauties, society for ennobling our life in that of our fellow-men, reason for thinking, the heart for loving, liberty for acting; without disappearing, respect and fear are tinged with a sweeter sentiment, that of love. Love, when it is applied to feeble and limited beings, inspires us with a desire to do good to them; but in itself it proposes to itself no advantage from the person loved; we love a beautiful or good object, because it is beautiful or good, without at first regarding whether this love may be useful to its object and ourselves. For a still stronger reason, love, when it ascends to God, is a pure homage rendered to his perfections; it is the natural overflow of the soul towards a being infinitely lovable.

Respect and love compose adoration. True adoration does not exist without possessing both of these sentiments. If you consider only the all-powerful God, master of heaven and earth, author and avenger of justice, you crush man beneath the weight of the grandeur of God and his own feebleness, you condemn him to a continual trembling in the uncertainty of God's judgments, you make him hate the world, life, and himself, for every thing is full of misery. Towards this extreme, Port-Royal inclines. Read the *Pensées de Pascal*.[257] In his great humility, Pascal forgets two things,—the dignity of man and the love of God. On the other hand, if you see only the good God and the indulgent father, you incline to a chimerical mysticism. By substituting love for fear, little by little with fear, we run the risk of losing respect. God is no more a master, he is no more even a father; for the idea of a father still to a certain point involves that of a respectful fear; he is no more any thing but a friend, sometimes even a lover. True adoration does not separate love and respect; it is respect animated by love.

Adoration is a universal sentiment. It differs in degrees according to different natures; it takes the most different forms; it is often even ignorant of itself; sometimes it is revealed by an exclamation springing from the heart, in the midst of the great scenes of nature and life, sometimes it silently rises in the mute and penetrated soul; it may err in its expressions, even in its object; but at bottom it is always the same. It is a spontaneous, irresistible emotion of the soul; and when reason is applied to it, it is declared just and legitimate. What, in fact, is more just than to fear the judgments of him who is holiness itself, who knows our actions and our intentions, and will judge them according to the highest justice? What, too, is more just than to love perfect goodness and the source of all love? Adoration is at first a natural sentiment; reason makes it a duty.

Adoration confined to the sanctuary of the soul is what is called internal worship—the necessary principle of all public worships.

Public worship is no more an arbitrary institution than society and government, language and arts. All these things have their roots in human nature. Adoration abandoned to itself, would easily degenerate into dreams and ecstasy, or would be dissipated in the rush of affairs and the necessities of every day. The more energetic it is, the more it tends to express itself outwardly in acts that realize it, to take a sensible, precise, and

---

[257] See our discussion on the Pensées de Pascal, vol. i. of the 4th Series.

regular form, which, by a proper reaction on the sentiment that produced it, awakens it when it slumbers, sustains it when it languishes, and also protects it against extravagances of every kind to which it might give birth in so many feeble or unbridled imaginations. Philosophy, then, lays the natural foundation of public worship in the internal worship of adoration. Having arrived at that point, it stops, equally careful not to betray its rights and not to go beyond them, to run over, in its whole extent and to its farthest limit, the domain of natural reason, as well as not to usurp a foreign domain.

But philosophy does not think of trespassing on the ground of theology; it wishes to remain faithful to itself, and also to follow its true mission, which is to love and favor every thing that tends to elevate man, since it heartily applauds the awakening of religious and Christian sentiment in all noble souls, after the ravages that have been made on every hand, for more than a century, by a false and sad philosophy. What, in fact, would not have been the joy of a Socrates and a Plato if they had found the human race in the arms of Christianity! How happy would Plato—who was so evidently embarrassed between his beautiful doctrines and the religion of his times, who managed so carefully with that religion even when he avoided it, who was forced to take from it the best possible part, in order to aid a favorable interpretation of his doctrine—have been, if he had had to do with a religion which presents to man, as at once its author and its model, the sublime and mild Crucified, of whom he had an extraordinary presentiment, whom he almost described in the person of a just man dying on the cross;[258] a religion which came to announce, or at least to consecrate and expand the idea of the unity of God and that of the unity of the human race; which proclaims the equality of all souls before the divine law, which thereby has prepared and maintains civil equality; which prescribes charity still more than justice, which teaches man that he does not live by bread alone, that he is not wholly contained in

---

[258] See the end of the first book of the Republic, vol. ix. of our translation.

his senses and his body, that he has a soul, a free soul, whose value is infinite, above the value of all worlds, that life is a trial, that its true object is not pleasure, fortune, rank, none of those things that do not pertain to our real destiny, and are often more dangerous than useful, but is that alone which is always in our power, in all situations and all conditions, from end to end of the earth, to wit, the improvement of the soul by itself, in the holy hope of becoming from day to day less unworthy of the regard of the Father of men, of the examples given by him, and of his promises. If the greatest moralist that ever lived could have seen these admirable teachings, which in germ were already at the foundation of his spirit, of which more than one trait can be found in his works, if he had seen them consecrated, maintained, continually recalled to the heart and imagination of man by sublime and touching institutions, what would have been his tender and grateful sympathy for such a religion! If he had come in our own times, in that age given up to revolutions, in which the best souls were early infected by the breath of skepticism, in default of the faith of an Augustine, of an Anselm, of a Thomas, of a Bossuet, he would have had, we doubt not, the sentiments at least of a Montesquieu,[259] of a Turgot,[260] of a Franklin,[261] and very far from putting the Christian religion and a good philosophy at war with each other, he would have been forced to unite them, to elucidate and fortify them by each other. That great mind and that great heart, which dictated to him the *Phedon*, the *Gorgias*, the *Republic*, would also have taught him that such books are made for a few sages, that there is needed for the human race a philosophy at once similar and different, that this philosophy is a

---

[259] Esprit des Lois, passim.
[260] Works of Turgot, vol. ii., Discours en Sorbonne sur les Avantages que l'établissement du Christianisma procurés au Genre Humain, etc.
[261] In the Correspondence, the letter to Dr. Stiles, March 9, 1790, written by Franklin a few months before his death: "I am convinced that the moral and religious system which Jesus Christ has transmitted to us is the best that the world has seen or can see."—We here re-translate, not having the works of Franklin immediately at hand.

religion, and that this desirable and necessary religion is the Gospel. We do not hesitate to say that, without religion, philosophy, reduced to what it can laboriously draw from perfected natural reason, addresses itself to a very small number, and runs the risk of remaining without much influence on manners and life; and that, without philosophy, the purest religion is no security against many superstitions, which little by little bring all the rest, and for that reason it may see the best minds escaping its influence, as was the case in the eighteenth century. The alliance between true religion and true philosophy is, then, at once natural and necessary; natural by the common basis of the truths which they acknowledge; necessary for the better service of humanity. Philosophy and religion differ only in the forms that distinguish, without separating them. Another auditory, other forms, and another language. When St. Augustine speaks to all the faithful in the church of Hippone, do not seek in him the subtile and profound metaphysician who combated the Academicians with their own arms, who supports himself on the Platonic theory of ideas, in order to explain the creation. Bossuet, in the treatise *De la Connaissance de Dieu et Soi-même*, is no longer, and at the same time he is always, the author of the *Sermons*, of the *Elévations*, and the incomparable *Catéchisme de Meaux*. To separate religion and philosophy has always been, on one side or the other, the pretension of small, exclusive, and fanatical minds; the duty, more imperative now than ever, of whomsoever has for either a serious and enlightened love, is to bring together and unite, instead of dividing and wasting the powers of the mind and the soul, in the interest of the common cause and the great object which the Christian religion and philosophy pursue, each in its own way,—I mean the moral grandeur of humanity.[262]

---

[262] We have not ceased to claim, to earnestly call for, the alliance between Christianity and philosophy, as well as the alliance between the monarchy and liberty. See particularly 3d Series, vol. iv., Philosophie Contemporaine, preface of the second edition; 4th Series, vol. i., Pascal, 1st and 2d preface, passim; 5th Series, vol. ii., Discours à la Chambre des Paris pour le Defence de l'Université

et de la Philosophie. We everywhere profess the most tender veneration for Christianity,—we have only repelled the servitude of philosophy, with Descartes, and the most illustrious doctors of ancient and modern times, from St. Augustine and St. Thomas, to the Cardinal de la Lucerne and the Bishop of Hermopolis. Moreover, we love to think that those quarrels, originating in other times from the deplorable strife between the clergy and the University, have not survived it, and that now all sincere friends of religion and philosophy will give each other the hand, and will work in concert to encourage desponding souls and lift up burdened characters.

LECTURE XVII.

RÉSUMÉ OF DOCTRINE.

Review of the doctrine contained in these lectures, and the three orders of facts on which this doctrine rests, with the relation of each one of them to the modern school that has recognized and developed it, but almost always exaggerated it.—Experience and empiricism.—Reason and idealism.—Sentiment and mysticism.—Theodicea. Defects of different known systems.—The process that conducts to true theodicea, and the character of certainty and reality that this process gives to it.

Having arrived at the limit of this course, we have a final task to perform,—it is necessary to recall its general spirit and most important results.

From the first lecture, I have signalized to you the spirit that should animate this instruction,—a spirit of free inquiry, recognizing with joy the truth wherever found, profiting by all the systems that the eighteenth century has bequeathed to our times, but confining itself to none of them.

The eighteenth century has left to us as an inheritance three great schools which still endure—the English and French school, whose chief is Locke, among whose most accredited representatives are Condillac, Helvetius, and Saint-Lambert; the Scotch school, with so many celebrated names, Hutcheson, Smith, Reid, Beattie, Ferguson, and Dugald Stewart;[263] the German school, or rather school of Kant, for, of all the philosophers beyond the Rhine, the philosopher of Kœnigsberg is almost the only one who belongs to history. Kant died at the beginning of the nineteenth century;[264] the ashes of his most illustrious disciple,

---

[263] Still living in 1818, died in 1828.
[264] In 1804.

Fichte,[265] are scarcely cold. The other renowned philosophers of Germany still live,[266] and escape our valuation.

But this is only an ethnographical enumeration of the schools of the eighteenth century. It is above all necessary to consider them in their characters, analogous or opposite. The Anglo-French school particularly represents empiricism and sensualism, that is to say, an almost exclusive importance attributed in all parts of human knowledge to experience in general, and especially to sensible experience. The Scotch school and the German school represent a more or less developed spiritualism. Finally, there are philosophers, for example, Hutcheson, Smith, and others, who, mistrusting the senses and reason, give the supremacy to sentiment.

Such are the philosophic schools in the presence of which the nineteenth century is placed.

We are compelled to avow, that none of these, to our eyes, contains the entire truth. It has been demonstrated that a considerable part of knowledge escapes sensation, and we think that sentiment is a basis neither sufficiently firm, nor sufficiently broad, to support all human science. We are, therefore, rather the adversary than the partisan of the school of Locke and Condillac, and of that of Hutcheson and Smith. Are we on that account the disciple of Reid and Kant? Yes, certainly, we declare our preference for the direction impressed upon philosophy by these two great men. We regard Reid as common sense itself, and we believe that we thus eulogize him in a manner that would touch him most. Common sense is to us the only legitimate point of departure, and the constant and inviolable rule of science. Reid never errs; his method is true, his general principles are incontestable, but we will willingly say to this irreproachable genius,—*Sapere aude*. Kant is far from being as sure a guide as Reid. Both excel in analysis; but Reid stops there, and Kant builds

---

[265] Died, 1814.
[266] This was said in 1818. Since then, Jacobi, Hegel, and Schleiermacher, with so many others, have disappeared. Schelling alone survives the ruins of the German philosophy.

upon analysis a system irreconcilable with it. He elevates reason above sensation and sentiment; he shows with great skill how reason produces by itself, and by the laws attached to its exercise, nearly all human knowledge; there is only one misfortune, which is that all this fine edifice is destitute of reality. Dogmatical in analysis, Kant is skeptical in his conclusions. His skepticism is the most learned, most moral, that ever existed; but, in fine, it is always skepticism. This is saying plainly enough that we are far from belonging to the school of the philosopher of Kœnigsberg.

In general, in the history of philosophy, we are in favor of systems that are themselves in favor of reason. Accordingly, in antiquity, we side with Plato against his adversaries; among the moderns, with Descartes against Locke, with Reid against Hume, with Kant against both Condillac and Smith. But while we acknowledge reason as a power superior to sensation and sentiment, as being, *par excellence*, the faculty of every kind of knowledge, the faculty of the true, the faculty of the beautiful, the faculty of the good, we are persuaded that reason cannot be developed without conditions that are foreign to it, cannot suffice for the government of man without the aid of another power: that power which is not reason, which reason cannot do without, is sentiment; those conditions, without which reason cannot be developed, are the senses. It is seen what for us is the importance of sensation and sentiment: how, consequently, it is impossible for us absolutely to condemn either the philosophy of sensation, or, much more, that of sentiment.

Such are the very simple foundations of our eclecticism. It is not in us the fruit of a desire for innovation, and for making ourself a place apart among the historians of philosophy; no, it is philosophy itself that imposes on us our historical views. It is not our fault if God has made the human soul larger than all systems, and we also aver that we are also much rejoiced that all systems are not absurd. Without giving the lie to the most certain facts signalized and established by ourself, it was indeed necessary, on finding them scattered in the history of philosophy, to recognize and respect them, and if the history of philosophy, thus considered, no longer appeared a mass of senseless systems, a chaos, without light, and without issue; if, on the contrary, it became, in some sort, a living philosophy, that was, it should seem, a progress on which one might felicitate himself, one of the most fortunate conquests of the nineteenth century, the very triumphing of the philosophic spirit.

We have, therefore, no doubt in regard to the excellence of the enterprise; the whole question for us is in the execution. Let us see, let us compare what we have done with what we have wished to do.

Let us ask, in the first place, whether we have been just towards that great philosophy represented in antiquity by Aristotle, whose best model among the moderns is the wise author of the Essay on the *Human Understanding*.

There is in the philosophy of sensation what is true and what is false. The false is the pretension of explaining all human knowledge by the acquisitions of the senses; this pretension is the system itself; we reject it, and the system with it. The true is that sensibility, considered in its external and visible organs, and in its internal organs, the invisible seats of the vital functions, is the indispensable condition of the development of all our faculties, not only of the faculties that evidently pertain to sensibility, but of those that seem to be most remote from it. This true side of sensualism we have everywhere recognized and elucidated in metaphysics, æsthetics, ethics, and theodicea.

For us, theodicea, ethics, æsthetics, metaphysics, rest on psychology, and the first principle of our psychology is that the condition of all exercise of mind and soul is an impression made on our organs, and a movement of the vital functions.

Man is not a pure spirit; he has a body which is for the spirit sometimes an obstacle, sometimes a means, always an inseparable companion. The senses are not, as Plato and Malebranche have too often said, a prison for the soul, but much rather windows looking out upon nature, through which the soul communicates with the universe. There is an entire part of Locke's polemic against the theories of innate ideas that is to our eyes perfectly true. We are the first to invoke experience in philosophy. Experience saves philosophy from hypothesis, from abstraction, from the exclusively deductive method, that is to say, from the geometrical method. It is on account of having abandoned the solid ground of experience, that Spinoza, attaching himself to certain sides of Cartesianism,[267] and closing his eyes to all the others, forgetting its method, its essential character, and its most certain principles, reared a hypothetical system, or made from an arbitrary definition spring with the last degree of rigor a whole series of deductions, which have nothing to do with reality. It is also on account of having exchanged experience for a systematic analysis, that Condillac, an unfaithful disciple of Locke, undertook to draw from a single fact, and from an ill-observed fact, all knowledge, by the aid of a series of verbal transformations, whose last result is a nominalism, like that of the later scholastics. Experience does not contain all science, but it furnishes the conditions of all science. Space is nothing for us without visible and tangible bodies that occupy it, time is nothing without the succession of events, cause without its effects, substance without its modes, law without the phenomena that it rules.[268] Reason would reveal to us no universal and necessary truth, if consciousness and the senses did not suggest to us particular and contingent notions. In æsthetics, while severely distinguishing between the beautiful and the agreeable, we have shown that the agreeable is the constant accompaniment of the beautiful,[269] and that if art has for its supreme law the expression of the ideal, it must express it under an animated and living form which puts it in relation with our senses, with our imagination, above all, with our heart. In ethics, if we have placed Kant and stoicism far above epicureanism and Helvetius, we have guarded ourselves against an insensibility and an asceticism which are contrary to human nature. We have given to reason neither the

---

[267] Fragments de Philosophie Cartésienne, p. 429: Des Rapports du Cartésienisme et du Spinozisme.
[268] Part 1st, lectures 1 and 2.
[269] Part 2d.

duty nor the right to smother the natural passions, but to rule them; we have not wished to wrest from the soul the instinct of happiness, without which life would not be supportable for a day, nor society for an hour; we have proposed to enlighten this instinct, to show it the concealed but real harmony which it sustains with virtue, and to open to it infinite prospects.[270]

With these empirical elements, idealism is guarded from that mystical infatuation which, little by little, gains and seizes it when it is wholly alone, and brings it into discredit with sound and severe minds. In our works—and why should we not say it?—we have often presented the thought of Locke, whom we regard as one of the best and most sensible men that ever lived. He is among those secret and illustrious advisers with whom we support our weakness. More than one happy thought we owe to him; and we often ask ourself whether investigations directed with the circumspect method which we try to carry into ours, would not have been accepted by his sincerity and wisdom. Locke is for us the true representative, the most original, and altogether the most temperate of the empirical school. Tied to a system, he still preserves a rare spirit of liberty,—under the name of reflection he admits another source of knowledge than sensation; and this concession to common sense is very important. Condillac, by rejecting this concession, carried to extremes and spoiled the doctrine of Locke, and made of it a narrow, exclusive, entirely false system,—sensualism, to speak properly. Condillac works upon chimeras reduced to signs, with which he sports at his ease. We seek in vain in his writings, especially in the last, some trace of human nature. One truly believes himself to be in the realm of shades, *per inania regna*.[271] The *Essay on the Human Understanding* produces the opposite impression. Locke is a disciple of Descartes, whom the excesses of Malebranche have thrown to an opposite excess: he is one of the founders of psychology, he is one of the finest and most profound

---

[270] Part 3d.
[271] On Condillac, 1st Series, vol. i., passim, and particularly vol. iii., lectures 2 and 3.

connoisseurs of human nature, and his doctrine, somewhat unsteady but always moderate, is worthy of having a place in a true eclecticism.[272]

By the side of the philosophy of Locke, there is one much greater, which it is important to preserve from all exaggeration, in order to maintain it in all its height. Founded in antiquity by Socrates, constituted by Plato, renewed by Descartes, idealism embraces, among the moderns, men of the highest renown. It speaks to man in the name of what is noblest in man. It demands the rights of reason; it establishes in science, in art, and in ethics fixed and invariable principles, and from this imperfect existence it elevates us towards another world, the world of the eternal, of the infinite, of the absolute.

This great philosophy has all our preferences, and we shall not be accused of having given it too little place in these lectures. In the eighteenth century it was especially represented in different degrees by Reid and Kant. We wholly accept Reid, with the exception of his historical views, which are too insufficient, and often mixed with error.[273] There are two parts in Kant,—the analytical part, and the dialectical part, as he calls them.[274] We admit the one and reject the other. In this whole course we have borrowed much from the *Critique of Speculative Reason*, the *Critique of Judgment*, and the *Critique of Practical Reason*. These three works are, in our eyes, admirable monuments of philosophic genius,—they are filled with treasures of observation and analysis.[275]

---

[272] We have never spoken of Locke except with sincere respect, even while combating him. See 1st Series, vol. i., course of 1817, Discours d'Ouverture, vol. ii., lecture I, and especially 2d Series, vol. iii., passim.

[273] See 1st Series, vol. iv., lectures on Reid.

[274] Ibid., vol. v.

[275] For more than twenty years we have thought of translating and publishing the three Critiques, joining to them a selection from the smaller productions of Kant. Time has been wanting to us for the completion of our design; but a young and skilful professor of philosophy, a graduate of the Normal School, has been willing to supply our place, and to undertake to give to the French public a faithful and intelligent version of the greatest thinker of the eighteenth

With Reid and Kant, we recognize reason as the faculty of the true, the beautiful, and the good. It is to its proper virtue that we directly refer knowledge in its humblest and in its most elevated part. All the systematic pretensions of sensualism are broken against the manifest reality of universal and necessary truths which are incontestably in our mind. At each instant, whether we know it or not, we bear universal and necessary judgments. In the simplest propositions is enveloped the principle of substance and being. We cannot take a step in life without concluding from an event in the existence of its cause. These principles are absolutely true, they are true everywhere and always. Now, experience apprises us of what happens here and there, to-day or yesterday; but of what happens everywhere and always, especially of what cannot but happen, how can it apprise us, since it is itself always limited to time and space? There are, then, in man principles superior to experience.

Such principles can alone give a firm basis to science. Phenomena are the objects of science only so far as they reveal something superior to themselves, that is to say, laws. Natural history does not study such or such an individual, but the generic type that every individual bears in itself, that alone remains unchangeable, when the individuals pass away and vanish. If there is in us no other faculty of knowing than sensation, we never know aught but what is passing in things, and that, too, we know only with the most uncertain knowledge, since sensibility will be its only measure, which is so variable in itself and so different in different individuals. Each of us will have his own science, a science contradictory and fragile, which one moment produces and another destroys, false as well as true, since what is true for me is false for you, and will even be false for me in a little while. Such are science and truth in the doctrine of sensation. On the contrary, necessary and immutable principles found a science necessary and immutable as themselves,—the truth which they

---

century. M. Barni has worthily commenced the useful and difficult enterprise which we have remitted to his zeal, and pursues it with courage and talent.

gave as is neither mine nor yours, neither the truth of to-day, nor that of to-morrow, but truth in itself.

The same spirit transferred to æsthetics has enabled us to seize the beautiful by the side of the agreeable, and, above different and imperfect beauties which nature offers to us, to seize an ideal beauty, one and perfect, without a model in nature, and the only model worthy of genius.

In ethics we have shown that there is an essential distinction between good and evil; that the idea of the good is an idea just as absolute as the idea of the beautiful and that of the true; that the good is a universal and necessary truth, marked with the particular character that it ought to be practised. By the side of interest, which is the law of sensibility, reason has made us recognize the law of duty, which a free being can alone fulfil. From these ethics has sprung a generous political doctrine, giving to right a sure foundation in the respect due to the person, establishing true liberty, and true equality, and calling for institutions, protective of both, which do not rest on the mobile and arbitrary will of the legislator, whether people or monarch, but on the nature of things, on truth and justice.

From empiricism we have retained the maxim which gives empiricism its whole force—that the conditions of science, of art, of ethics, are in experience, and often in sensible experience. But we profess at the same time this other maxim, that the foundation of science is absolute truth, that the direct foundation of art is absolute beauty, that the direct foundation of ethics and politics is the good, is duty, is right, and that what reveals to us these absolute ideas of the true, the beautiful, and the good, is reason. The foundation of our doctrine is, therefore, idealism rightly tempered by empiricism.

But what would be the use of having restored to reason the power of elevating itself to absolute principles, placed above experience, although experience furnishes their external conditions, if, to adopt the language of Kant,[276] these principles

---

[276] Part 1st, Lecture 3.

have no objective value? What good could result from having determined with a precision until then unknown the respective domains of experience and reason, if, wholly superior as it is to the senses and experience, reason is captive in their inclosure, and we know nothing beyond with certainty? Thereby, then, we return by a *detour* to skepticism to which sensualism conducts us directly, and at less expense. To say that there is no principle of causality, or to say that this principle has no force out of the subject that possesses it,—is it not saying the same thing? Kant avows that man has no right to affirm that there are out of him real causes, time, or space, or that he himself has a spiritual and free soul. This acknowledgment would perfectly satisfy Hume; it would be of very little importance to him that the reason of man, according to Kant, might conceive, and even could not but conceive, the ideas of cause, time, space, liberty, spirit, provided these ideas are applied to nothing real. I see therein, at most, only a torment for human reason, at once so poor and so rich, so full and so void.

A third doctrine, finding sensation insufficient, and also discontented with reason, which it confounds with reasoning, thinks to approach common sense by making science, art, and ethics rest on sentiment. It would have us confide ourselves to the instinct of the heart, to that instinct, nobler than sensation, and more subtle than reasoning. Is it not the heart, in fact, that feels the beautiful and the good? Is it not the heart that, in all the great circumstances of life, when passion and sophism obscure to our eyes the holy idea of duty and virtue, makes it shine forth with an irresistible light, and, at the same time, warms us, animates us, and gives us the courage to practise it?

We also have recognized that admirable phenomenon which is called sentiment; we even believe that here will be found a more precise and more complete analysis of it than in the writings where sentiment reigns alone. Yes, there is an exquisite pleasure attached to the contemplation of the truth, to the reproduction of the beautiful, to the practice of the good; there is in us an innate love for all these things; and when great rigor is not aimed at, it may very well be said that it is the heart which discerns truth, that the heart is and ought to be the light and guide of our life.

To the eyes of an unpractised analysis, reason in its natural and spontaneous exercise is confounded with sentiment by a multitude of resemblances.[277] Sentiment is intimately attached to reason; it is its sensible form. At the foundation of sentiment is reason, which communicates to it its authority, whilst sentiment lends to reason its charm and power. Is not the widest spread and the most touching proof of the existence of God that spontaneous impulse of the heart which, in the consciousness of our miseries, and at the sight of the imperfections of our race which press upon our attention, irresistibly suggests to us the confused idea of an infinite and perfect being, fills us, at this idea, with an inexpressible emotion, moistens our eyes with tears, or even prostrates us on our knees before him whom the heart reveals to us, even when the reason refuses to believe in him? But look more closely, and you will see that this incredulous reason is reasoning supported by principles whose bearing is insufficient; you will see that what reveals the infinite and perfect being is precisely reason itself;[278] and that, in turn, it is this revelation of the infinite by reason, which, passing into sentiment, produces the emotion and the inspiration that we have mentioned. May heaven grant that we shall never reject the aid of sentiment! On the contrary, we invoke it both for others and ourself. Here we are with the people, or rather we are the people. It is to the light of the heart, which is borrowed from that of reason, but reflects it more vividly in the depths of the soul, that we confide ourselves, in order to preserve all great truths in the soul of the ignorant, and even to save them in the mind of the philosopher from the aberrations or refinements of an ambitious philosophy.

We think, with Quintilian and Vauvenargues, that the nobility of sentiment makes the nobility of thought. Enthusiasm is the principle of great works as well as of great actions. Without

---

[277] Lecture 5, Mysticism.
[278] This pretended proof of sentiment is in fact, the Cartesian proof itself. See lectures 4 and 16.

the love of the beautiful, the artist will produce only works that are perhaps regular but frigid, that will possibly please the geometrician, but not the man of taste. In order to communicate life to the canvas, to the marble, to speech, it must be born in one's self. It is the heart mingled with logic that makes true eloquence; it is the heart mingled with imagination that makes great poetry. Think of Homer, of Corneille, of Bossuet,—their most characteristic trait is pathos, and pathos is a cry of the soul. But it is especially in ethics that sentiment shines forth. Sentiment, as we have already said, is as it were a divine grace that aids us in the fulfilment of the serious and austere law of duty. How often does it happen that in delicate, complicated, difficult situations, we know not how to ascertain wherein is the true, wherein is the good! Sentiment comes to the aid of reasoning which wavers; it speaks, and all uncertainties are dissipated. In listening to its inspirations, we may act imprudently, but we rarely act ill: the voice of the heart is the voice of God.

We, therefore, give a prominent place to this noble element of human nature. We believe that man is quite as great by heart as by reason. We have a high regard for the generous writers who, in the looseness of principles and manners in the eighteenth century, opposed the baseness of calculation and interest with the beauty of sentiment. We are with Hutcheson against Hobbes, with Rousseau against Helvetius, with the author of Woldemar[279] against the ethics of egoism or those of the schools. We borrow from them what truth they have, we leave their useless or dangerous exaggerations. Sentiment must be joined to reason; but reason must not be replaced by sentiment. In the first place, it is contrary to facts to take reason for reasoning, and to envelop them in the same criticism. And then, after all, reasoning is the legitimate instrument of reason; its value is determined by that of the principles on which it rests. In the next place, reason, and especially spontaneous reason, is, like sentiment, immediate and direct; it goes straight to its object, without passing through

---

[279] M. Jacobi. See the Manual of the History of Philosophy, by Tennemann, vol. ii., p. 318.

analysis, abstraction, and deduction, excellent operations without doubt, but they suppose a primary operation, the pure and simple apperception of the truth.[280] It is wrong to attribute this apperception to sentiment. Sentiment is an emotion, not a judgment; it enjoys or suffers, it loves or hates, it does not know. It is not universal like reason; and as it still pertains on some side to organization, it even borrows from the organization something of its inconstancy. In fine, sentiment follows reason, and does not precede it. Therefore, in suppressing reason, we suppress the sentiment which emanates from it, and science, art, and ethics lack firm and solid bases.

Psychology, æsthetics, and ethics, have conducted us to an order of investigations more difficult and more elevated, which are mingled with all the others, and crown them—theodicea.

We know that theodicea is the rock of philosophy. We might shun it, and stop in the regions—already very high—of the universal and necessary principles of the true, the beautiful, and the good, without going farther, without ascending to the principles of these principles, to the reason of reason, to the source of truth. But such a prudence is, at bottom, only a disguised skepticism. Either philosophy is not, or it is the last explanation of all things. Is it, then, true that God is to us an inexplicable enigma,—he without whom the most certain of all things that thus far we have discovered would be for us an insupportable enigma? If philosophy is incapable of arriving at the knowledge of God, it is powerless; for if it does not possess God, it possesses nothing. But we are convinced that the need of knowing has not been given us in vain, and that the desire of knowing the principle of our being bears witness to the right and power of knowing which we have. Accordingly, after having discoursed to you about the true, the beautiful, and the good, we have not feared to speak to you of God.

More than one road may lead us to God. We do not pretend to close any of them; but it was necessary for us to follow the one

---

[280] On spontaneous reason and reflective reason, see 1st part, lect. 2 and 3.

that was open to us, that which the nature and subject of our instruction opened to us.

Universal and necessary truths are not general ideas which our mind draws by way of reasoning from particular things; for particular things are relative and contingent, and cannot contain the universal and necessary. On the other hand, these truths do not subsist by themselves; they would thus be only pure abstractions, suspended in vacuity and without relation to any thing. Truth, beauty, and goodness are attributes and not entities. Now there are no attributes without a subject. And as here the question is concerning absolute truth, beauty and goodness, their substance can be nothing else than absolute being. It is thus that we arrive at God. Once more, there are many other means of arriving at him; but we hold fast to this legitimate and sure way.

For us, as for Plato, whom we have defended against a too narrow interpretation,[281] absolute truth is in God,—it is God himself under one of his phases. Since Plato, the greatest minds, Saint Augustine, Descartes, Bossuet, Leibnitz, agree in putting in God, as in their source, the principles of knowledge as well as existence. From him things derive at once their intelligibility and their being. It is by the participation of the divine reason that our reason possesses something absolute. Every judgment of reason envelops a necessary truth, and every necessary truth supposes necessary being.

If all perfection belongs to the perfect being, God will possess beauty in its plenitude. The father of the world, of its laws, of its ravishing harmonies, the author of forms, colors, and sounds, he is the principle of beauty in nature. It is he whom we adore, without knowing it, under the name of the ideal, when our imagination, borne on from beauties to beauties, calls for a final beauty in which it may find repose. It is to him that the artist, discontented with the imperfect beauties of nature and those that he creates himself, comes to ask for higher inspirations. It is in him that are summed up the main forms of every kind of beauty,

---

[281] Lectures 4 and 5.

the beautiful and the sublime, since he satisfies all our faculties by his perfections, and overwhelms them with his infinitude.

God is the principle of moral truths, as well as of all other truths. All our duties are comprised in justice and charity. These two great precepts have not been made by us; they have been imposed on us; from whom, then, can they come, except from a legislator essentially just and good? Therein, in our opinion, is an invincible demonstration of the divine justice and charity:—this demonstration elucidates and sustains all others. In this immense universe, of which we catch a glimpse of a comparatively insignificant portion, every thing, in spite of more than one obscurity, seems ordered in view of general good, and this plan attests a Providence. To the physical order which one in good faith can scarcely deny, add the certainty, the evidence of the moral order that we bear in ourselves. This order supposes the harmony of virtue and goodness; it therefore requires it. Without doubt this harmony already appears in the visible world, in the natural consequences of good and bad actions, in society which punishes and rewards, in public esteem and contempt, especially in the troubles and joys of conscience. Although this necessary law of order is not always exactly fulfilled, it nevertheless ought to be, or the moral order is not satisfied, and the intimate nature of things, their moral nature, remains violated, troubled, perverted. There must, then, be a being who takes it upon himself to fulfil, in a time that he has reserved to himself, and in a manner that will be proper, the order of which he has put in us the inviolable need; and this being is again, God.

Thus, on all sides, on that of metaphysics, on that of æsthetics, especially on that of ethics, we elevate ourselves to the same principle, the common centre, the last foundation, of all truth, all beauty, all goodness. The true, the beautiful, and the good, are only different revelations of the same being. Human intelligence, interrogated in regard to all these ideas which are incontestably in it, always makes us the same response; it sends us back to the same explanation,—at the foundation of all, above all, God, always God.

We have arrived, then, from degree to degree, at religion. We are in fellowship with the great philosophies which all proclaim a God, and, at the same time, with the religions that cover the earth, with the Christian religion, incomparably the most perfect and the most holy. As long as philosophy has not reached natural religion,—and by this we mean, not the religion at which man arrives in that hypothetical state that is called the state of nature, but the religion which is revealed to us by the natural light accorded to all men,—it remains beneath all worship, even the most imperfect, which at least gives to man a father, a witness, a consoler, a judge. A true theodicea borrows in some sort from all religious beliefs their common principle, and returns it to them surrounded with light, elevated above all uncertainty, guarded against all attack. Philosophy may present itself in its turn to mankind; it also has a right to man's confidence, for it speaks to him of God in the name of all his needs and all his faculties, in the name of reason and sentiment.

Observe that we have arrived at these high conclusions without any hypothesis, by the aid of processes at once very simple and perfectly rigorous. Truths of different orders being given, truths which have not been made by us, and are not sufficient for themselves, we have ascended from these truths to their author, as one goes from the effect to the cause, from the sign to the thing signified, from phenomenon to being, from quality to subject. These two principles—that every effect supposes a cause, and every quality a subject—are universal and necessary principles. They have been put by us in their full light, and demonstrated in the manner in which principles undemonstrable, because they are primitive, can be demonstrated. Moreover, to what are these necessary principles applied? To metaphysical and moral truths, which are also necessary. It was therefore necessary to conclude in the existence of a cause and a necessary being, or, indeed, it was necessary to deny either the necessity of the principle of cause and the principle of substance, or the necessity of the truths to which we applied them, that is to say, to renounce all notions of common sense; for these very principles and these truths, with their character of universality and necessity, compose common sense.

Not only is it certain that every effect supposes a cause, and every quality a being, but it is equally certain that an effect of such a nature supposes a cause of the same nature, and that a quality or an attribute marked with such or such essential characters supposes a being in which these same characters are again found in an eminent degree. Whence it follows, that we have very legitimately concluded from truth in an intelligent cause and substance, from beauty in a being supremely beautiful, and from a moral law composed at once of justice and charity in a legislator supremely just and supremely good.

And we have not made a geometrical and algebraical theodicea, after the example of many philosophers, and the most illustrious. We have not deduced the attributes of God from each other, as the different terms of an equation are converted, or as from one property of a triangle the other properties are deduced, thus ending at a God wholly abstract, good perhaps for the schools, but not sufficient for the human race. We have given to theodicea a surer foundation—psychology. Our God is doubtless also the author of the world, but he is especially the father of humanity; his intelligence is ours, with the necessity of essence and infinite power added. So our justice and our charity, related to their immortal exemplar, give us an idea of the divine justice and charity. Therein we see a real God, with whom we can sustain a relation also real, whom we can comprehend and feel, and who in his turn can comprehend and feel our efforts, our sufferings, our virtues, our miseries. Made in his image, conducted to him by a ray of his own being, there is between him and us a living and sacred tie.

Our theodicea is therefore free at once from hypothesis and abstraction. By preserving ourselves from the one, we have preserved ourselves from the other. Consenting to recognize God only in his signs visible to the eyes and intelligible to the mind, it is on infallible evidence that we have elevated ourselves to God. By a necessary consequence, setting out from real effects and real attributes, we have arrived at a real cause and a real substance, at a cause having in power all its essential effects, at a substance rich in attributes. I wonder at the folly of those who, in order to know God better, consider him, they say, in his pure and absolute essence, disengaged from all limitative determination. I believe that I have forever removed the root of such an extravagance.[282] No; it is not true that the diversity of determinations, and, consequently, of qualities and attributes, destroys the absolute unity of a being; the infallible proof of it is that my unity is not the least in the world altered by the diversity of my faculties. It is not true that unity excludes multiplicity, and multiplicity unity; for unity and multiplicity are united in me. Why then should they not be in God? Moreover, far from altering unity in me, multiplicity develops it and makes its productiveness appear. So the richness of the determinations and the attributes of God is exactly the sign of the plenitude of his being. To neglect his attributes, is therefore to impoverish him; we do not say enough, it is to annihilate him,—for a being without attributes exists not; and the abstraction of being, human or divine, finite or infinite, relative or absolute, is nonentity.

Theodicea has two rocks,—one, which we have just signalized to you, is abstraction, the abuse of dialectics; it is the vice of the schools and metaphysics. If we are forced to shun this rock, we run the risk of being dashed against the opposite rock, I mean that fear of reasoning that extends to reason, that excessive predominance of sentiment, which developing in us the loving and affectionate faculties at the expense of all the others, throws us into anthropomorphism without criticism, and makes us institute with God an intimate and familiar intercourse in which we are somewhat too forgetful of the august and fearful majesty of the divine being. The tender and contemplative soul can neither love nor contemplate in God the necessity, the eternity, the infinity, that do not come within the sphere of imagination and the heart, that are only conceived. It therefore neglects them.

---

[282] See particularly lecture 5.

Neither does it study God in truth of every kind, in physics, metaphysics, and ethics, which manifest him; it considers in him particularly the characters to which affection is attached. In adoration, Fenelon retrenches all fear that nothing but love may subsist, and Mme. Guyon ends by loving God as a lover.

We escape these opposite excesses of a refined sentimentality and a chimerical abstraction, by always keeping in mind both the nature of God, by which he escapes all relation with us,—necessity, eternity, infinity, and at the same time those of his attributes which are our own attributes transferred to him, for the very simple reason that they came from him.

I am able to conceive God only in his manifestations and by the signs which he gives of his existence, as I am able to conceive any being only by the attributes of that being, a cause only by its effects, as I am able to conceive myself only by the exercise of my faculties. Take away my faculties and the consciousness that attests them to me, and I am not for myself. It is the same with God,—take away nature and the soul, and every sign of God disappears. It is therefore in nature and the soul that he must be sought and found.

The universe, which comprises nature and man, manifests God. Is this saying that it exhausts God? By no means. Let us always consult psychology. I know myself only by my acts; that is certain; and what is not less certain is, that all my acts do not exhaust, do not equal my power and my substance; for my power, at least that of my will, can always add an act to all those which it has already produced, and it has the consciousness, at the same time that it is exercised, of containing in itself something to be exercised still. Of God and the world must be said two things in appearance contrary,—we know God only by the world, and God is essentially distinct and different from the world. The first cause, like all secondary causes, manifests itself only by its effects; it can even be conceived only by them, and it surpasses them by all of the difference between the Creator and the created, the perfect and the imperfect. The world is indefinite; it is not infinite; for, whatever may be its quantity, thought can always add to it. To the myriads of worlds that compose the totality of the world, may be added new worlds. But God is infinite, absolutely infinite in his essence, and an indefinite series cannot equal the infinite; for the indefinite is nothing else than the finite more or less multiplied and capable of continuous multiplication. The world is a whole which has its harmony; for a God could make only a complete and harmonious work. The harmony of the world corresponds to the unity of God, as indefinite quantity is a defective sign of the infinity of God. To say that the world is God, is to admit only the world and deny God. Give to this whatever name you please, it is at bottom atheism. On the one hand, to suppose that the world is void of God, and that God is separate from the world, is an insupportable and almost impossible abstraction. To distinguish is not to separate. I distinguish myself, but do not separate myself from my qualities and my acts. So God is not the world, although he is in it everywhere present in spirit and in truth.[283]

---

[283] We place here this analogous passage on the true measure in which it may be said that God is at once comprehensible and incomprehensible, 1st Series, vol. iv., lecture 12, p. 12: "We say in the first place that God is not absolutely incomprehensible, for this manifest reason, that, being the cause of this universe, he passes into it, and is reflected in it, as the cause in the effect; therefore we recognize him. 'The heavens declare his glory.' and 'the invisible things of him from the creation of the world are clearly seen, being understood by the things that are made;' his power, in the thousands of worlds sown in the boundless regions of space; his intelligence in their harmonious laws; finally, that which there is in him most august, in the sentiments of virtue, of holiness, and of love, which the heart of man contains. It must be that God is not incomprehensible to us, for all nations have petitioned him, since the first day of the intellectual life of humanity. God, then, as the cause of the universe, reveals himself to us; but God is not only the cause of the universe, he is also the perfect and infinite cause, possessing in himself, not a relative perfection, which is only a degree of imperfection, but an absolute perfection, an infinity which is not only the finite multiplied by itself in those proportions which the human mind is able always to enumerate, but a true infinity, that is, the absolute negation of all limits, in all the powers of his being. Moreover, it is

Such is our theodicea: it rejects the excesses of all systems, and contains, we believe at least, all that is good in them. From

not true that an indefinite effect adequately expresses an infinite cause; hence it is not true that we are able absolutely to comprehend God by the world and by man, for all of God is not in them. In order absolutely to comprehend the infinite, it is necessary to have an infinite power of comprehension, and that is not granted to us. God, in manifesting himself, retains something in himself which nothing finite can absolutely manifest; consequently, it is not permitted us to comprehend absolutely. There remains, then, in God, beyond the universe and man, something unknown, impenetrable, incomprehensible. Hence in the immeasurable spaces of the universe, and beneath all the profundities of the human soul, God escapes us in that inexhaustible infinitude, whence he is able to draw without limit new worlds, new beings, new manifestations. God is to us, therefore, incomprehensible; but even of this incomprehensibility we have a clear and precise idea; for we have the most precise idea of infinity. And this idea is not in us a metaphysical refinement, it is a simple and primitive conception which enlightens us from our entrance into this world, both luminous and obscure, explaining everything, and being explained by nothing, because it carries us at first, to the summit and the limit of all explanation. There is something inexplicable for thought,—behold then whither thought tends; there is infinite being,—behold then the necessary principle of all relative and finite beings. Reason explains not the inexplicable, it conceives it. It is not able to comprehend infinity in an absolute manner, but it comprehends it in some degree in its indefinite manifestations, which reveal it, and which veil it; and, further, as it has been said, it comprehend it so far as incomprehensible. It is, therefore, an equal error to call God absolutely comprehensible, and absolutely incomprehensible. He is both invisible and present, revealed and withdrawn in himself, in the world and out of the world, so familiar and intimate with his creatures, that we see him by opening our eyes, that we feel him in feeling our hearts beat, and at the same time inaccessible in his impenetrable majesty, mingled with every thing, and separated from every thing, manifesting himself in universal life, and causing scarcely an ephemeral shadow of his eternal essence to appear there, communicating himself without cessation, and remaining incommunicable, at once the living God, and the God concealed, 'Deus vivus et Deus absconditus.'"

sentiment it borrows a personal God as we ourselves are a person, and from reason a necessary, eternal, infinite God. In the presence of two opposite systems,—one of which, in order to see and feel God in the world, absorbs him in it; the other of which, in order not to confound God with the world, separates him from it and relegates him to an inaccessible solitude,—it gives to both just satisfaction by offering to them a God who is in fact in the world, since the world is his work, but without his essence being exhausted in it, a God who is both absolute unity and unity multiplied, infinite and living, immutable and the principle of movement, supreme intelligence and supreme truth, sovereign justice and sovereign goodness, before whom the world and man are like nonentity, who, nevertheless, is pleased with the world and man, substance eternal, and cause inexhaustible, impenetrable, and everywhere perceptible, who must by turns be sought in truth, admired in beauty, imitated, even at an infinite distance, in goodness and justice, venerated and loved, continually studied with an indefatigable zeal, and in silence adored.

Let us sum up this *résumé*. Setting out from the observation of ourselves in order to preserve ourselves from hypothesis, we have found in consciousness three orders of facts. We have left to each of them its character, its rank, its bearing, and its limits. Sensation has appeared to us the indispensable condition, but not the foundation of knowledge. Reason is the faculty itself of knowing; it has furnished us with absolute principles, and these absolute principles have conducted us to absolute truths. Sentiment, which pertains at once to sensation and reason, has found a place between both. Setting out from consciousness, but always guided by it, we have penetrated into the region of being; we have gone quite naturally from knowledge to its objects by the road that the human race pursues, that Kant sought in vain, or rather misconceived at pleasure, to wit, that reason which must be admitted entire or rejected entire, which reveals to us existences as well as truths. Therefore, after having recalled all the great metaphysical, æsthetical, and moral truths, we have referred them to their principle; with the human race we have pronounced the name of God, who explains all things, because he has made all things, whom all our faculties require,—reason, the heart, the senses, since he is the author of all our faculties.

This doctrine is so simple, is to such an extent in all our powers, is so conformed to all our instincts, that it scarcely appears a philosophic doctrine, and, at the same time, if you examine it more closely, if you compare it with all celebrated doctrines, you will find that it is related to them and differs from them, that it is none of them and embraces them all, that it expresses precisely the side of them that has made them live and sustains them in history. But that is only the scientific character of the doctrine which we present to you; it has still another character which distinguishes it and recommends it to you much more. The spirit that animates it is that which of old inspired Socrates, Plato, and Marcus Aurelius, which makes your hearts beat when you are reading Corneille and Bossuet, which dictated to Vauvenargues the few pages that have immortalized his name, which you feel especially in Reid, sustained by an admirable good sense, and even in Kant, in the midst of, and superior to the embarrassments of his metaphysics, to wit, the taste of the beautiful and the good in all things, the passionate love of honesty, the ardent desire of the moral grandeur of humanity. Yes, we do not fear to repeat that we tend thither by all our views; it is the end to which are related all the parts of our instruction; it is the thought which serves as their connection, and is, thus to speak, their soul. May this thought be always present to you, and accompany you as a faithful and generous friend, wherever fortune shall lead you, under the tent of the soldier, in the office of the lawyer, of the physician, of the savant, in the study of the literary man, as well as in the studio of the artist! Finally, may it sometimes remind you of him who has been to you its very sincere but too feeble interpreter!

APPENDIX.

"What a destiny was that of Eustache Lesueur!"

It is perceived that we have followed, as regards his death, the tradition, or rather the prejudices current at the present day, and which have misled the best judges before us. But there have appeared in a recent and interesting publication, called *Archives de l'Art français*, vol. iii., certain incontrovertible documents, never before published, on the life and works of the painter of St. Bruno, which compel us to withdraw certain assertions agreeable to general opinion, but contrary to truth. The notice of Lesueur's death, extracted for the first time from the *Register of Deaths of the parish church of Saint-Louis in the isle of Notre-Dame*, preserved amongst the archives of the Hotel de Ville at Paris, clearly prove that he did not die at the Chartreux, but in the isle of Notre-Dame, where he dwelt, in the parish of St. Louis, and that he was buried in the church of Saint-Etienne du Mont, the resting-place of Pascal and Racine. It appears also that Lesueur died before his wife, Geneviève Goussé, since the *Register of Births* of the parish of Saint-Louis, contains under the date 18th February, 1655, a notice of the baptism of a fourth child of Lesueur. Now, Geneviève Goussé must have deceased almost immediately after her confinement, supposing her to have died before her husband's decease, which occurred on the 1st of the following May. If this were the case, we should have found a notice of her death in the *Register of Deaths* for the year 1655, as we do that of her husband. Such a notice, however, which could alone disprove the probability, and authenticate the vulgar opinion, is nowhere to be found amongst the archives of the Hotel de Ville, at least the author of the *Nouvelles Recherches* has nowhere been able to meet with it.

In the other particulars our rapid sketch of Lesueur's history remains untouched. He never was in Italy; and according to the account of Guillet de Saint-Georges, which has so long remained in manuscript, he never desired to go there. He was poor, discreet, and pious, tenderly loved his wife, and lived in the closest union with his three brothers and brother-in-law, who were all pupils and fellow-laborers of his. It appears to be a refinement of criticism which denies the current belief of an acquaintance between Lesueur and Poussin. If no document authenticates it, at all events it is not contradicted by any, and appears to us to be highly probable.

Every one admits that Lesueur studied and admired Poussin. It would certainly be strange if he did not seek his acquaintance, which he could have obtained without difficulty, since Poussin was staying at Paris from 1640 to 1642. It would be difficult for them not to have met. After Vouet's death in 1641, Lesueur acquired more and more a peculiar style; and in 1642, at the age of twenty-five, entirely unshackled, and with a taste ripe for the antique and Raphael, he must frequently have been at the Louvre, where Poussin resided. Thus it is natural to suppose that they frequently saw each other and became acquainted, and with their sympathies of character and talent, acquaintance must have resulted in esteem and love. If Poussin's letters do not mention Lesueur, we would remark that neither do they mention Champagne, whose connection with Poussin is not disputed. The argument built on the silence of Guillet de Saint-Georges' account is far from convincing; inasmuch as being intended to be read before a Sitting of the Academy, it could only contain a notice of the great artist's career, without those biographical details in which his friendships would be mentioned. Lastly, it is impossible to deny Poussin's influence upon Lesueur, which it seems to us at least probable was as much due to his counsels as to his example.

"But the marvel of the picture is the figure of St. Paul."

We have recently seen, at Hampton Court, the seven cartoons of Raphael, which should not be looked at, still less criticised, but on bended knee. Behold Raphael arrived at the summit of his art, and in the last years of life! And these were but drawings for tapestry! These drawings alone would reward the journey to England, even were the figures from the friezes of the Parthenon not at the *British Museum*. One never tires of contemplating these grand performances even in the obscurity of that ill-lighted room. Nothing could be more noble, more magnificent, more imposing, more majestic. What draperies, what attitudes, what forms! Notwithstanding the absence of color, the effect is immense; the mind is struck, at once charmed and transported; but the soul, we can speak for ourselves, remains well-nigh insensible. We request any one to compare carefully the sixth cartoon, clearly one of the finest, representing the Preaching of St. Paul at Ephesus, with the painting we have described of Lesueur's. One, immediately and at the first sight, transports you into the regions of the ideal; the other is less striking at first, but stay, consider it well, study it in detail, then take in the whole: by degrees you are overcome by an ever-increasing emotion. Above all, examine in both the principal character, St. Paul. Here, you behold the fine long folds of a superb robe which at once envelops and sets off his height, whilst the figure is in shade, and the little you see of it has nothing striking. There he confronts you, inspired, terrible, majestic. Now say which side lays claim to moral effect.

"The great works of Lesueur, Poussin, and so many others scattered over Europe."

Of all the paintings of Lesueur which are in England, that which we regret most not having seen is *Alexander and his Physician*, painted for M. de Nouveau, director-general of the *Postes*, which passed from the Hotel Nouveau to the Place Royale in the Orleans Gallery, from thence into England, where it was bought by Lady Lucas at the great London sale in 1800. The sale catalogue, with the prices and names of the purchasers, will be found at the end of vol. i. of M. Waagen's excellent work, *Œuvres d'Art et Artistes en Angleterre*, 2 vols., Berlin, 1837 and 1838.

We were both consoled and agreeably surprised on our return, to meet, in the valuable gallery of M. le Comte d'Houdetot, an ancient peer of France, and free member of the Academy of Fine Arts, with another Alexander and his physician Philip, in which the hand of Lesueur cannot be mistaken. The composition of the entire piece is perfect. The drawing is exquisite. The amplitude and nobleness of the draperies recall those of Raphael. The form of Alexander fine and languid; the person of Philip the physician grave and imposing. The coloring, though not powerful, is finely blended in tone. Now, where is the true original, is it with M. Houdetot or in England? The painting sold in London in 1800 certainly came from the Orleans' gallery, which would seem most likely to have possessed the original. On the other hand, it is impossible M. Houdetot's picture is a copy. They must, therefore, both be equally the work of Lesueur, who has in this instance treated the same subject twice over, as he has likewise done the Preaching of St. Paul; of which there is another, smaller than that at the Louvre, but equally admirable, at the Place Royale, belonging to M. Girou de Buzariengues, corresponding member of the Academy of Sciences.[284]

We borrow M. Waagen's description of the works of Lesueur, found by that eminent critic in the English collections: *The Queen of Sheba before Solomon*, the property of the Duke of Devonshire, vol. i., p. 245. *Christ at the foot of the Cross supported by his Family*, belonging to the Earl of Shrewsbury, vol. ii., p. 463, "the sentiment deep and truthful," remarks M. Waagen. *The Magdalen pouring the ointment on the feet of Jesus*, the property of Lord Exeter, vol. ii., p. 485, "a picture full of the purest sentiment;" lastly, in the possession of M. Miles, a *Death of Germanicus*, "a rich and noble composition, completely in Poussin's style," remarks M. Waagen, vol. ii., p. 356. Let us add that this last work is not met with in any catalogue, ancient or modern. We ask ourselves whether this may not be a copy of the Germanicus of Poussin attributed to Lesueur.

---

[284] This is the sketch which Félibien so justly praises, part v., p. 37, of the 1st edition, in 4to.

The author of *Musées d'Allemagne et du Russie* (Paris, 1844) mentions at Berlin a *Saint Bruno adoring the Cross in his Cell, opening upon a landscape*, and pretends that this picture is as pathetic as the best Saint Brunos in the Museum at Paris. It is probably a sketch, like the one we have, or one of the wanting panels; for as for the pictures themselves, there were never more than twenty-two at the Chartreux, and these are at the Louvre. Perhaps, however, it may be the picture which Lesueur made for M. Bernard de Rozé, see Florent Lecomte, vol. iii., p. 98, which represented a Carthusian in a cell. At St. Petersburg, the catalogue of the Hermitage mentions seven pictures of Lesueur, one of which, *The infant Moses exposed on the Nile*, is admitted by the author cited to be authentic. Can this be one of two *Moses* which were painted by Lesueur for M. de Nouveau, as we learn from Guillet de Saint-Georges? Unless M. Viardot is deceived, and mistakes a copy for an original, we must regret that a real Lesueur should Lave been suffered to stray to St. Petersburg, with many of Poussin's most beautiful Claudes (see p. 474), Mignards, Sebastian Bourdons, Gaspars, Stellas, and Valentins.

Some years ago, at the sale of Cardinal Fesch's gallery, we might have acquired one of Lesueur's finest pieces, executed for the church of Saint-Germain-l'Auxerrois, which had got, by some chance, into the possession of Chancellor Pontchartrain, afterwards into that of the Emperor's uncle. This celebrated picture, *Christ with Martha and Mary*, formed at Saint-Germain-l'Auxerrois, a pendent to the *Martyrdom of St. Lawrence*. Will it be believed that the French Government lost the opportunity, and permitted this little *chef-d'œuvre* to pass into the hands of the King of Bavaria? A good copy at Marseilles was thought, doubtless, sufficient, and the original was left to find its way to the gallery at Munich, and meet again the *St. Louis on his knees at Mass*, which the catalogue of that gallery attributes to Lesueur, on what ground we are not aware. In conclusion, we may mention that there is in the Museum at Brussels, a charming little Lesueur, *The Saviour giving his Blessing*, and in the Museums of Grenoble and Montpelier several fragments of the *History of Tobias*, painted for M. de Fieubet.

> "Those master-pieces of art that honor the nation depart without authorization from the national territory! There has not been found a government which has undertaken at least to repurchase those that we have lost, to get back again the great works of Poussin, Lesueur, and so many others, scattered in Europe, instead of squandering millions to acquire the baboons of Holland, as Louis XIV. said, or Spanish canvases, in truth of an admirable color, but without nobleness and moral expression."

Shall we give a recent instance of the small value we appear to set on Poussin? We blush to think that in 1848 we should have permitted the noble collection of M. de Montcalm to pass into England. One picture escaped: it was put up to sale in Paris on the 5th of March, 1850. It was a charming Poussin, undoubtedly authentic, from the Orleans gallery, and described at length in the catalogue of Dubois de Saint-Gelais. It represented the *Birth of Bacchus*, and by its variety of scenes and multitude of ideas, showed it belonged to Poussin's best period. We must do Normandy, rather the city of Rouen, the justice to say, that it made an effort to acquire it, but it was unsupported by Government; and this composition, wholly French, was sold at Paris for the sum of 17,000 francs, to a foreigner, Mr. Hope.

Miserable contrast! while five or six hundred thousand francs have been given for a *Virgin* by Murillo, which is now turning the heads of all who behold it. I confess that mine has entirely resisted. I admire the freshness, the sweetness, the harmony of color; but every other superior quality which one looks to find in such a subject is wanting, or at least escaped me. Ecstasy never transfigured that face, which is neither noble nor great. The lovely infant before me does not seem sensible of the profound mystery accomplished in her. What, then, can there be in this vaunted Virgin which so catches the multitude? She is supported by beautiful angels, in a fine dress, of a charming color, the effect of all which is doubtless highly pleasant.

> **"We endeavor to console ourselves for having lost the Seven Sacraments, and for not having known how to keep from England and Germany so many productions of Poussin, now buried in foreign collections," etc.**

After having expressed our regret that we were unacquainted with the *Seven Sacraments* save from the engravings of Pesne, we made a journey to London, to see with our own eyes, and judge for ourselves these famous pictures, with many others of our great countryman, now fallen into the possession of England, through our culpable indifference, and which have been brought under our notice by M Waagen.

In the few days we were able to dedicate to this little journey, we had to examine four galleries: the National Gallery, answering to our Museum, those of Lord Ellesmere and the Marquis of Westminster, and, at some miles from London, the collection at Dulwich College, celebrated in England, though but little known on the continent.

We likewise visited another collection, resulting from an institution which might easily be introduced into France, to the decided advantage of art and taste. A society has been formed in England, called the British Institution for promoting the Fine Arts in the United Kingdom. Every year it has, in London, an exhibition of ancient paintings, to which individual galleries send their choice pieces, so that in a certain number of years all the most remarkable pictures in England pass under the public eye. But for this exhibition, what riches would remain buried in the mansions of the aristocracy or unknown cabinets of provincial amateurs! The society, having at its head the greatest names of England, enjoys a certain authority, and all ranks respond eagerly to its appeal.

We ourselves saw the list of persons who this year contributed to the exhibition; there were her Majesty the Queen, the Dukes of Bedford, Devonshire, Newcastle, Northumberland, Sutherland, the Earls of Derby and Suffolk, and numerous other great men, besides bankers, merchants, *savants*, and artists. The exhibition is public, but not free, as you must pay both for admission and the printed catalogue. The money thus acquired is appropriated to defray the expenses of the exhibition; whatever remains is employed in the purchase of pictures, which are then presented to the National Gallery.

At this year's exhibition we saw three of Claude Lorrain's, which well sustained the name of that master. *Apollo watching the herds of Admetus*, a *Sea-port*, both belonging to the Earl of Leicester, and *Psyche and Amor*, the property of Mr. Perkins; a pretended Lesueur, the *Death of the Virgin*, from the Earl of Suffolk; seven Sebastian Bourdons, the *Seven Works of Mercy*,[285] lent by the Earl of Yarborough; a landscape by Gaspar Poussin, but not one *morceau* of his illustrious brother-in-law's.

We were more fortunate in the National Gallery.

There, to begin, what admirable Claudes! We counted as many as ten, some of them of the highest value. We will confine ourselves to the recapitulation of three, the Embarkation of St. Ursula, a large landscape, and the Embarkation of the Queen of Sheba.

1st. *The Embarkation of St. Ursula*, which was painted for the Barberini, and adorned their palace at Rome until the year 1760, when an English amateur purchased it from the Princess Barberini, with other works of the first class. This picture is 3 feet 8 inches high, 4 feet 11 inches wide.

2d. The large landscape is 4 feet 11 inches high, 6 feet 7 inches wide. Rebecca is seen, with her relatives and servants,

---

[285] This great work has been long in England, as remarked by Mariette, see the Abecedario, just published, article S. Bourdon, vol. i., p. 171. It appears to have been a favorite work of Bourdon, he having himself engraved it, see de Piles, Abrégé de la Vie des Peintres, 2d edition, p. 494, and the Peintre graveur français, of M. Robert Dumesnil, vol. i., p. 131, etc. The copperplates of the Seven Works of Mercy are at the Louvre.

waiting the arrival of Isaac, who comes from afar to celebrate their marriage.

3d. *The Embarkation of the Queen of Sheba*, going to visit Solomon, formed a pendent to the preceding figure, which it resembles in its dimensions. It is both a sea and landscape drawing, M. Waagen declares it to be the most beautiful *morceau* of the kind he is acquainted with, and asserts that Lorrain has here attained perfection, vol. i., p. 211. This masterpiece was executed by Claude for his protector, the Duke de Bouillon. It is signed "Claude GE. I. V., faict pour son Altesse le Duc de Bouillon, anno 1648." Doubtless the great Duke de Bouillon, eldest brother of Turenne. This French work, destined, too, for France, she has now forever lost, as well as the famous Book of Truth, *Libro di Verità*, in which Claude collected the drawings of all his paintings, drawings which may be themselves regarded as finished pictures. This invaluable treasure was, like the *Embarkation of the Queen of Sheba*, for a long time in the hands of a French broker, who would willingly have relinquished it to the Government, but failing to find purchasers in Paris in the last century, ultimately sold it for a mere nothing into Holland, whence it has passed into England.[286] The author of the *Musées d'Allemagne et de Russie*, mentions that in the gallery of the Hermitage at St. Petersburg, amongst a large number of Claudes, whose authenticity he appears to admit, there are four *morceaux*, which he does not hesitate to declare equal to the most celebrated *chefs-d'œuvre* of that master, in Paris or London, called the *Morning*, the *Noon*, the *Evening*, and the *Night*. They are from Malmaison. Thus the sale of the gallery of an empress has in our own time enriched Russia, as, twenty-five years before, the sale of the Orleans gallery enriched England.

In the National Gallery, along with the serene and quiet landscapes of Lorrain, are five of Caspar's, depicting nature under an opposite aspect—rugged and wild localities, and tempests.

---

[286] The Libro di Verità is now the property of the Duke of Devonshire. M. Léon de Laborde has given a detailed account of it in the Archives de l'Art français, tom. i., p. 435, et seq.

One of the most remarkable represents Eneas and Dido seeking shelter in a grotto from the violence of a storm. The figures are from the pencil of Albano, and for a length of time remained in the palace Falconieri. Two other landscapes are from the palace Corsini, and two from the palace Colonna.

But to return to our real subject, which is Poussin. There are eight paintings by his hand in the National Gallery, all worthy of mention. M. Waagen has merely spoken of them in general terms, but we shall proceed to give a description in detail.

Of these eight paintings, only one, representing the plague of Ashdod, is taken from sacred history. This is described in the printed catalogue as No. 105. The Israelites having been vanquished by the Philistines, the ark was taken by the victors and placed in the temple of Dagon at Ashdod. The idol falls before the ark, and the Philistines are smitten with the pestilence. This canvas is 4 feet 3 inches high, and 6 feet 8 inches, wide. A sketch or copy of the *Plague of the Philistines* is in the Museum of the Louvre, and has been engraved by Picard. Poussin was, in fact, fond of repeating a subject; there are two sets of the *Seven Sacraments*, two *Arcadias*,[287] two or three *Moses striking the Rock*, &c. The science of painting is here employed to portray the scene in all its terrors, and display every horror of the pestilence, and it would seem that Poussin had here endeavored to contend with Michael Angelo, even at the expense of beauty. It is said the commission for this work was given by Cardinal Barberini. It comes from the palace of Colonna. The subjects of the remaining seven pictures in the National Gallery are mythological, and may be nearly all referred to the early epoch of Poussin's career, when he paid tribute to the genius of the 16th century, and yielded to the influence of Marini.

No. 39. The *Education of Bacchus*, a subject chosen by Poussin more than once. On a small canvas 2 feet 3 inches high, and 3 feet 1 inch wide.

---

[287] The first composition of Arcadia, truly precious could it have been placed in the Louvre beside the second and better production, is in England, the property of the Duke of Devonshire.

No. 40. Another small picture 1 foot 6 inches high, and 3 feet 4 inches broad: *Phocion washing his Feet at a Public Fountain*, a touching emblem of the purity and simplicity of his life. To heighten this rustic scene, and impart its meaning, the painter shows us the trophies of the noble warrior hung on the trunk of a tree at a little distance. The whole composition is striking and full of animation. We believe that it has never been engraved. It forms a happy addition to the two other compositions consecrated by Poussin to Phocion, and which have been so admirably engraved by Baudet, *Phocion carried out of the City of Athens*, and the *Tomb of Phocion*.

No. 42. Here is one of the three bacchanals painted by Poussin for the Duke de Montmorency. The two others are said to be in the collection of Lord Ashburnham. This bacchanal is 4 feet 8 inches high, and 3 feet 1 inch wide. In a warm landscape Bacchus is sleeping surrounded by nymphs, satyrs, and centaurs, whilst Silenus appears under an arbor attended by sylvan figures.

No. 62. Another bacchanal, which may be considered one of Poussin's masterpieces. According to M. Waagen, it belonged to the Colonna collection, but the catalogue, published *by authority*, states that it was originally the property of the Comte de Vaudreueili, that it afterwards came into the hands of M. de Calonne, whence it passed into England, and ultimately found its way into the hands of Mr. Hamlet, from whom it was purchased by Parliament, and placed in the National Gallery. It is 3 feet 8 inches high, and 4 feet 8 inches wide. Its subject is a dance of fauns and bacchantes, which is interrupted by a satyr, who attempts to take liberties with a nymph. Besides the main subject, there are numerous spirited and graceful episodes, particularly two infants endeavoring to catch in a cup the juice of a bunch of grapes supported in air, and pressed by a bacchante of slim and fine form. The composition is full of fire, energy, and spirit. There is not a single group, not a figure, which will not repay an attentive study. M. Waagen does not hesitate to pronounce it one of Poussin's finest. He admires the truth and variety of heads, the freshness of color, and the transparent tone (*die Färbung von seltenster Frische, Helle und Klarheit in allen Theilen*). It has been engraved by Huart, and accurately copied by Landon, under the title of *Danse de Fauns et de Bacchantes*.

No. 65. *Cephalus and Aurora*. Aurora, captivated by the beauty of Cephalus, endeavors to separate him from his wife Procris. Being unsuccessful, in a fit of jealousy she gives to Cephalus the dart which causes the death of his adored spouse. 3 feet 2 inches high, 4 feet 2 inches wide.

No. 83. A large painting, 5 feet 6 inches high, and 8 feet wide, representing *Phineas and his Companions changed into Stones by looking on the Gorgon*. Perseus, having rescued Andromeda from the sea monster, obtains her hand from her father Cepheus, who celebrates their nuptials with a magnificent feast. Phineas, to whom Andromeda had been betrothed, rushes in upon the festivity at the head of a troop of armed men. A combat ensues, in which Perseus, being nearly overcome, opposes to his enemies the head of Medusa, by which they are instantly changed to stone. This composition is full of vigor, with brilliant coloring, although somewhat crude. It is nowhere mentioned, and we are not aware of its having been engraved.

No. 91. A charming little drawing, 2 feet 2 inches high, 1 foot 8 inches wide: *A sleeping Nymph, surprised by Lore and Satyrs*, engraved by Daullé, also in Landon's work.

Passing from the National Gallery to that of Bridgewater, we come upon another phase of Poussin's genius, and encounter not the disciple of Mariai but the disciple of the gospel, the graces of mythology giving way to the austerity and sublimity of Christianity. Such is the account of what we came to see; we looked for much, and found more than we expected.

The Bridgewater Gallery is so named after its founder, the Duke of Bridgewater, by whom it was formed about the middle of the eighteenth century. He bequeathed it to his brother, the Marquis of Stafford, on the condition of his leaving it to his second son, Lord Francis Egerton, now Lord Ellesmere. The best part of this collection was engraved during the life of the Marquis of Stafford, by Ottley, under the title of the Stafford Gallery, in 4 vols. folio.

It occupies the first place in England amongst private collections, on account of the number of masterpieces of the Italian, and Dutch, and French schools. A large number of paintings were added to it from the Orleans Gallery, and we could not repress a feeling of regret to meet at Cleveland Square with so many masterpieces formerly belonging to France, and which have been engraved in the two celebrated works: 1. *La Galerie du duc d'Orléans au Palais-Royal*, 2 volumes in folio; 2. *Recueil d'estampes d'après les plus beaux tableaux et dessins qui sont en France dans le cabinet du roi et celui de Monseigneur le duc d'Orléans*, 1729, 2 volumes in folio; a most valuable collection known also under the name of the *Cabinet of Crozat*. This admirable collection is deposited in a building worthy of it, in a veritable palace, and consists of nearly 300 paintings. The French school is here well represented. The *Musical Party*, from the Orleans Gallery, and engraved in the *Galerie du Palais-Royal*, three Bourguignons, four Gaspars, four fine Claudes, described by M. Waagen, vol. i., p. 331, the two former described in the catalogue as Nos. 11 and 41 were painted in 1664 for M. de Bourlemont, a gentleman of Lorraine; the former, *Demosthenes by the Sea-side*, offers a fine contrast between majestic ruins and nature eternally young and fresh; the second, *Moses at the Burning Bush*, a third, No. 103, of the year 1657, was likewise painted for a Frenchman, M. de Lagarde, and represents the *Metamorphosis of Apuleius into a Shepherd*; lastly, there is a fourth, No. 97, the freshest idyll that ever was, a *View of the Cascatelles of Tivoli*.

The memory of these charming compositions, however, soon fades before the view of the eight grand pictures of Poussin, marked in the catalogue Nos. 62-69, the *Seven Sacraments*, and *Moses striking the Rock with his Rod*.

It would be difficult to describe the religious sensations which took possession of us whilst contemplating the *Seven Sacraments*. Whatever M. Waagen may please to assert, there is certainly nothing theatrical about them. The beauty of ancient statuary is here animated and enlivened by the spirit of Christianity, and the genius of the painter. The moral expression is of the most exalted character, and is left to be noticed less in the details than in the general composition. In fact, it is in composition that Poussin excels, and, in this respect, we do not think he has any superior, not even of the Florentine and Roman school. As each *Sacrament* is a vast scene in which the smallest details go to enhance the effect of the whole, so the *Seven Sacraments* form a harmonious entirety, a single work, representing the development of the Christian life by means of its most august ceremonies, in the same way as the twenty-two *St. Brunos* of Lesueur express the whole monastic life, the intention of the variety being to give a truer conception of its unity. Can any one, in sincerity, say as much as this for the *Stanze* of the Vatican? Have they a common sentiment? Is the sentiment profound, and, indeed, Christian? No doubt Raphael elevates the soul, whatever is beautiful cannot fail to do that; but he touches only the surface, *circum præcordia ludit*; he penetrates not deep; moves not the inner fibres of our being: for why? he himself was not so moved. He snatches us from earth, and transports us into the serene atmosphere of eternal beauty; but the mournful side of life, the sublime emotions of the heart, magnanimity, heroism, in a word, moral grandeur, this he does not express; and why was this? because he did not possess it in himself, because it was not to be met with around him in the Italy of the 16th century, in a society semi-pagan, superstitious, and impious, given up to every vice and disorder, which Luther could not even catch a glimpse of without raging with horror, and meditating a revolution. From this corrupt basis, thinly hidden by a fictitious politeness, two great figures, Michael Angelo and Vittoria Colonna, show themselves. But the noble widow of the Marquis of Pescaria was not of the company of the Fornarina; and what common ground could the chaste lover of the second Beatrice, the Dante of painting and of sculpture, the intrepid engineer who defended Florence, the melancholy author of *the Last Judgment* and of

Lorenzo di Medici, have with such men as Perugino boldly professing atheism, at the same time that he painted, at the highest price possible, the most delicate Madonnas; and his worthy friend Aretino, atheist, and moreover hypocrite, writing with the same hand his infamous sonnets and the life of the Holy Virgin; and Giulio Romano, who lent his pencil to the wildest debaucheries, and Marc' Antonio, who engraved them? Such is the world in which Raphael lived, and which early taught him to worship material beauty, the purest taste in design, if not the strongest, fine drawing, sweet contours, of light, of color, but which always hides from him the highest beauty, that is, moral beauty. Poussin belongs to a very different world. Thanks to God, he had learned to know in France others besides artists without faith or morals, elegant amateurs, rich prelates, and compliant beauties. He had seen with his eyes heroes, saints, and statesmen. He must have met, at the court of Louis XIII., between 1640 and 1642, the young Condé and the voting Turenne, St. Vincent de Paul, Mademoiselle de Vigean, and Mademoiselle de Lafayette; had shaken hands with Richelieu, with Lesueur, with Champagne, and no doubt also with Corneille. Like the last, he is grave and masculine; he has the sentiment of the great, and strives to reach it. If, above every thing, he is an artist, if his long career is an assiduous and indefatigable study of beauty, it is pre-eminently moral beauty that strikes him: and when he represents historic or Christian scenes, one feels he is there, like the author of the Cid, of Cinna, and of Polyeuete, in his natural element. He shows, assuredly, much spirit and grace in his mythologies, and like Corneille in several of his elegies and in the Declaration of Love to Psyche: but also like him, it is in the thoughtful and noble style that Poussin excels: it is on the moral ground that he has a place exalted and apart in the history of art.

It is not our intention to describe the *Seven Sacraments*, which has been done by others more competent to the task than ourselves. We will only inquire whether Bossuet himself, in speaking of the sacrament of the *Ordination*, could have employed more gravity and majesty than Poussin has done in the noble painting, so well preserved, in the gallery of Lord Ellesmere. It is worthy of remark, in this as in the other paintings of Poussin's best period, how admirably the landscape accords with the historic portion. Whilst the foreground is occupied with the great scene in which Christ transmits his power to St. Peter before the assembled apostles,[288] in the distance, and above the heights, are descried edifices rising and in decay. Doubtless, the *Extreme Unction* is the most pathetic; affects and attracts us most by its various qualities, particularly by a certain austere grace shed around the images of death;[289] but, unhappily, this striking

---

[288] In the first set of the Seven Sacraments, executed for the Chevalier del Pozzo, now in England, the property of the Duke of Rutland, and with which we are acquainted only through engravings, Christ is placed on the left hand; it is less masterly and imposing, and the centre has a vacant appearance. In the second set, painted five or six years after the former for M. de Chanteloup, Christ is placed in the centre: this new disposition changes the entire effect of the piece. Poussin never repeated himself in treating the same subject a second time, but improved on it, aiming ever at perfection. And the memorable answer which he once made to one who inquired of him by what means he had attained to so great perfection, "I never neglected any thing," should be always present to the mind of every artist, painter, sculptor, poet, or composer.

[289] Poussin writes to M. de Chanteloup, April 25, 1644 (Lettres de Poussin, Paris, 1824), "I am working briskly at the Extreme Unction, which is indeed a subject worthy of Apelles, who was very fond of representing the dying." He adds, with a vivacity which seems to indicate that he took a particular fancy to this painting, "I do not intend to quit it whilst I feel thus well-disposed, until I have put it in fair train for a sketch. It is to contain seventeen figures of men, women, and children, young and old, one part of whom are drowned in tears, whilst the others pray for the dying. I will not describe it to you more in detail. In this, my clumsy pen is quite unfit, it requires a gilded and well-set pencil. The principal figures are two feet high; the painting will be about the size of your Manne, but of better proportion." Félibien, a friend and confidant of Poussin, likewise remarks (Entretiens, etc., part iv., p. 293), that the Extreme Unction was one of the paintings which pleased him most. We learn at length, from Poussin's letters, that he finished it and sent it into France in this same year, 1644. Fénoien informs us that in 1646 he completed the Confirmation,

composition has almost totally disappeared under the black tint, which has little by little gained on the other colors, and obscured the whole painting, so that we are well-nigh reduced to the engraving of Pesne, and the beautiful drawing preserved in the museum of the Louvre.[290]

Most unhappily a technical error, into which even the most inconsiderable painter would not now fall, has deprived posterity of one half of Poussin's labors. He was in the habit of covering his canvas with a preparation of red, which has been changed by the effect of time into black, and thus absorbed the other colors, destroying the effect of the etherial perspective. As every one knows, this does not occur with a white preparation, which, instead of destroying the colors, preserves them for a length of time in their original state. This last process Poussin appears to have adopted in the *Moses striking the Rock with his Staff*, incomparably the finest of all the *Strikings of the Rock* which proceeded from his pencil. This masterpiece is well known, from the engraving by Baudet, and has passed, with the *Seven Sacraments*, from the Orleans gallery into the collection at Bridgewater. What unity is in this vast composition, and yet what variety in the action, the pose, the features of the figures! It consists of twenty different pictures, and yet is but one; and not even one of the episodes could be taken away without considerable injury to the *ensemble* of the piece. At the same time, what fine coloring! The impastation is both solid and light, and the colors are combined in the happiest manner. No doubt they might possess greater brilliancy; but the severity of the

---

in 1647 the Baptism, the Penance, the Ordination and the Eucharist, and that he sent the last sacrament, that of Marriage, at the commencement of the year 1648. Bellori (le Vite de Pittori, etc., Rome, 1672) gives a full and detailed description of the Extreme Unction; and, as he lived with Poussin, it seems credible that his explanations are for the most part those he had himself received from the great artist.

[290] The drawing of the Extreme Unction is at the Louvre; the drawings of the five other sacraments are in the rich cabinet of M. de la Salle, that of the seventh is the property of the well-known print seller, M. Deter.

subject agrees well with a moderate tone. It is important to remember this. In the first place, every subject demands its proper color: in the second, grave subjects require a certain amount of coloring, which, however, must not be exceeded. Although the highest art does not consist in coloring, it would nevertheless be folly to regard it as of small importance: for, in that case, drawing would be every thing, and color might be altogether dispensed with. In attempting too far to please the eye, the risk is incurred of not going beyond and penetrating to the soul. On the other hand, want of color, or what is perhaps still worse, a disagreeable, crude, and improper coloring, while it offends the eye, likewise impairs the moral effect, and deprives even beauty of its charm. Color is to painting what harmony is to poetry and prose. There is equal defect whether in the case of too much or too little harmony, while one same harmony continued must be looked upon as a serious fault. Is Corneille happily inspired? His harmony, like his words, are true, beautiful, admirable in their variety. The tones differ with his different characters, but are always consistent with the conditions of harmony imposed by poesy. Is he negligent? his style then becomes rude, unpolished, at times intolerable. The harmony of Racine is slightly monotonous, his men talk like women, and his lyre was but one tone, that of a natural and refined elegance. There is but one man amongst us who speaks in every tone and in all languages, who has colors and accents for every subject, *naïve* and sublime, vividly correct yet unaffectedly simple. Sweet as Racine in his lament of Madame, masculine and vigorous as Corneille or Tacitus when he comes to describe Retz or Cromwell, clear as the battle trumpet when his strain is Roeroy or Condé, suggestive of the equal and varied flow of a mighty river in the majestic harmony of his Discourse on Universal History, a History which, in the grandeur and extent of its composition, in its vanquished difficulties, its depth of art, where art even ceases to appear as such, in its perfect unity, and, at the same time, almost infinite variety of tone and style, is perhaps the most finished work which has ever come from the hand of man.

To return to Poussin. At Hampton Court, where, by the side of the seven cartoons of Raphael, the nine magnificent Montegnas representing the triumph of Cæsar, and the fine portraits of Albert Durer and Holbein, French art makes so small a figure, there is a Poussin[291] of particularly fine color, *Satyrs finding a Nymph*. The transparent and lustrous body of the nymph forms the entire picture. It is a study of design and color, evidently of the period when Poussin, to perfect himself in every branch of his art, made copies from Titian.

Time fails us to give the least idea of the rich gallery of the Marquess of Westminster, in Grosvenor-street. We refer for this to what M. Waagen has said, vol. ii., p. 113-130. The Flemish and Dutch schools preponderate in this gallery. One sees there in all their glory the three great masters of that school, Rubens, Van Dyck, and Rembrandt, accompanied by a numerous suite of inferior masters, at present much in vogue, Hobbéma, Cuyp, Both, Potter, and others, who, to our idea, fade completely before some half-dozen by Claude of all sizes, of every variety of subject, and nearly all of the best time of the great landscape-painter, between 1651 and 1661. Of these paintings, the greatest and most important is perhaps the *Sermon on the Mount*. Poussin appears worthily by the side of Lorrain in the gallery at Grosvenor-street. M. Waagen admires particularly *Calisto changed into a Bear, and placed by Jupiter among the Constellations*, and still more a *Virgin with the infant Jesus surrounded by Angels*. He extols in this *morceau* the surpassing clearness of coloring, the noble and melancholy sentiment of nature, together with a warm and powerful tone. M. Waagen places this painting amongst the masterpieces of the French painter (*gehört zu dem vortrefflichsten was ich von ihm kenne*). Whilst fully concurring in this judgment, we beg leave to point

---

[291] There is here likewise a charming Francis II., wholly from the hand of Clouet, and the portrait of Fénelon by Rigaud, which may be the original or at all events is not inferior to the painting in the gallery at Versailles.

out in the same gallery two other canvases of Poussin, two delicious pieces from the easel, first a touching episode in *Moses striking the Rock*, in the gallery of Lord Ellesmere, of a mother who, heedless of herself, hastens to give her children drink, whilst their father bends in thanksgiving to God; the other, *Children at play*. Never did a more delightful scene come from the pencil of Albano. Two children look, laughing, at each other; another to the right holds a butterfly on his finger; a fourth endeavors to catch a butterfly which is flying from him; a fifth, stooping, takes fruit from a basket.

But we must quit the London galleries to betake ourselves to that which forms the ornament of the college situated in the charming village of Dulwich.

Stanislas, king of Poland, charged a London amateur, M. Noël Desenfans, to form him a collection of pictures. The misfortunes of Stanislas, and the dismemberment of Poland left on M. Desenfans' hands all he had collected; these he made a present of to a friend of his, M. Bourgeois, a painter, who still further enriched this fine collection, and bequeathed it, at his death, to Dulwich College, where it now is in a very commodious and well-lighted building. It consists of nearly 350 paintings. M. Waagen, who visited it, pronounces judgment with some severity. The catalogue is ill-compiled, it is true, but in this it does not differ from numerous other catalogues. Mediocrity is frequently placed side by side with excellence, and copies given as originals; this is the case with more than one gallery. This one, however, has to us the merit of containing a considerable number of French paintings, to some of which even M. Waagen cannot refuse his admiration.

We will, first of all, mention without describing them, a Lenain, two Bourguignons, three portraits by Rigaud, or after Rigaud, a Louis XIV., a Boileau, and another personage unknown to us, two Lebruns, the *Massacre of the Innocents*, and *Horatius Cocles defending the Bridge*, in which M. Waagen discovers happy imitations of Poussin, three or four Gaspars and seven Claude Lorrains, the beauty of most of which is a sufficient guarantee of their authenticity; together with a very fine *Fête champêtre* by Watteau, and a *View near Rome*, by Joseph Vernet. Of Poussin, the catalogue points out eighteen, of which the following is a list:

No. 115. *The Education of Bacchus*; 142, *a Landscape*; 249, *a Holy Family*; 253, *the Apparition of the Angels to Abraham*; 260, *a Landscape*; 269, *the Destruction of Niobe*; 279, *a Landscape*; 291, *the Adoration of the Magi*; 292, *a Landscape*; 295, *the Inspiration of the Poet*; 300, *the Education of Jupiter*; 305, *the Triumph of David*; 310, *the Flight into Egypt*; 315, *Renald and Armida*; 316, *Venus and Mercury*; 325, *Jupiter and Antiope*; 336, *the Assumption of the Virgin*; 352, *Children*.

Of these eighteen pictures, M. Waagen singles out five, which he thus characterizes:

The Assumption of the Virgin, No. 336. In a landscape of powerful poesy, the Virgin is carried off to heaven in clouds of gold: a small picture, of which the sentiment is noble and pure, the coloring strong and transparent (*in der Farbe kraftiges und klaares Bild*). *Children*, No. 352. Replete with loveliness and charm. *The Triumph of David*, No. 305. A rich picture, but theatrical.

Jupiter suckled by the goat Amalthea, No. 300. A charming composition, transparent tone. *A Landscape*, No. 260. A well-drawn landscape, breathing a profound sentiment of nature; but which has become rather blackened.

We are unable to recognize in the *Triumph of David* the theatrical character which shocked M. Waagen. On the contrary, we perceive a bold and almost wild expression, a great deal of passion finely subdued.

A triumph must always contain some formality; here, however, there is the least possible, and that with which we are struck is its vigor and truth to nature. The giant's head stuck on the pike has the grandest effect: and we believe that the able German critic has, in this instance, likewise yielded to the prejudices of his country, which, in its passion for what it styles reality, fancies it perceives the theatrical in whatever is noble. We admit that at the close of the seventeenth century, under Louis XIV. and Lebrun, the noble was merged in the theatrical and academic; but under Louis XIII. and the Regency, in the time of Corneille and Poussin, the academic and theatrical style was wholly unknown. We entreat the sagacious critic not to forget this distinction between the divisions of the seventeenth century, nor to confound the master with his disciples, who, although they were still great, had slightly degenerated, and who were oppressed by the taste of the age of Louis XIV.

But our gravest reproach against M. Waagen is, that he did not notice at Dulwich numerous *morceaux* of Poussin, which well merited his attention; amongst others, the *Adoration of the Magi*, far superior, for its coloring, to that in the Museum at Paris; and, above all, a picture which seems to us a masterpiece in the difficult art of conveying a philosophic idea under the living form of a myth and an allegory.

In this art, Poussin excelled: he is pre-eminently a philosophical artist, a thinker assisted by all the resources of the science of design. He has ever an idea which guides his hand, and which is his main object. Let us not tire to reiterate this: it is moral beauty which he everywhere seeks, both in nature and humanity. As we have stated in relation to the sacrament of *Ordination*, the landscapes of Poussin are almost always designed to set off and heighten human life, whilst Claude is essentially a landscape painter, with whom both history and humanity are made subservient to nature. Subjects derived from Christianity were exactly suited to Poussin, inasmuch as they afforded the sublimest types of that moral grandeur in which he delighted, although we do not see in him the exquisite piety of Lesueur and Champagne; and if Christian greatness speaks to his soul, it appears to do so with no authority beyond that of Phocion, of Scipio, or of Germanicus. Sometimes neither sacred nor profane history suffices him: he invents, he imagines, he has recourse to moral and philosophic allegory. It is here, perhaps, that he is most original, and that his imagination displays itself in its greatest freedom and elevation. *Arcadia* is a lesson of high philosophy under the form of an idyll. *The Testament of Eudamidas* portrays the sublime confidence of friendship. *Time Rescuing Truth from the assaults of Envy and Discord, the Ballet of Human Life*, are celebrated models of this style. We have had the good fortune to meet at Dulwich with a work of Poussin's almost unknown, and of whose existence we had not even an idea, sparkling at the same time with the style we have been describing, and with the most eminent qualities of the chief of the French school.

This work, entirely new to us, is a picture of very small size, marked No. 295, and described in the catalogue as *The Inspiration of the Poet*, a delightful subject, and treated in the most delightful manner. Fancy the freshest landscape, in the foreground a harmonious group of three personages. The poet, on bended knee, carries to his lips the sacred cup which Apollo, the god of poesy, has presented to him. Whilst he quaffs, inspiration seizes him, his face is transfigured, and the sacred intoxication becomes apparent in the motion of his hands and his whole body. Beside Apollo, the Muse prepares to collect the songs of the poet. Above this group, a genius, frolicking in air, weaves a chaplet, whilst other genii scatter flowers. In the background, the clearest horizon. Grace, spirit, depth—this enchanting composition unites the whole. Added to this, the color is well-grounded and of great brilliancy.

It is very singular that neither Bellori nor Félibien, who both lived on terms of intimacy with Poussin, and are still his best historians, say not a word of this work. It is not referred to in the catalogues of Florent Lecomte, of Gault de St. Germain, or of Castellan; nor does M. Waagen himself, who, having been at Dulwich, must have seen it there, make the least mention of it. We are, therefore, ignorant in what year, on what occasion, and for whom this delicious little painting was executed: but the hand of Poussin is seen throughout, in the drawing, in the composition, in the expression. Nothing theatrical or vulgar: truth combined with beauty. The whole scene conveys unmixed delight, and its impression is at once serene and profound. In our idea, *The*

Inspiration of the Poet may be ranked as almost equal with *The Arcadia*.

Notwithstanding this, *The Inspiration* has never been engraved, at least we have not met with it in any of the rich collections of engravings from Poussin we have been enabled to consult, those of M. de Baudicour, of M. Gatteaux, member of the Academy of Fine Arts, and lastly, the cabinet of prints in the *Bibliothèque Nationale*. We hope that these few words may suggest to some French engraver the idea of undertaking the very easy pilgrimage to Dulwich, and making known to the lovers of national art an ingenious and touching production of Poussin, strayed and lost, as it, were, in a foreign collection.

FINIS.

www.ingramcontent.com/pod-product-compliance
Lightning Source LLC
Chambersburg PA
CBHW051034160426
43193CB00010B/936